THE NEW BLACK GODS

RELIGION IN NORTH AMERICA
Catherine L. Albanese and Stephen J. Stein, editors

THE
NEW
BLACK
GODS

ARTHUR HUFF FAUSET
AND THE STUDY OF
AFRICAN AMERICAN
RELIGIONS

EDITED BY
EDWARD E. CURTIS IV AND
DANIELLE BRUNE SIGLER

INDIANA UNIVERSITY PRESS
Bloomington and Indianapolis

This book is a publication of

Indiana University Press
601 North Morton Street
Bloomington, IN 47404-3797 USA

http://iupress.indiana.edu

Telephone orders 800-842-6796
Fax orders   812-855-7931
Orders by e-mail iuporder@indiana.edu

The paper used in this publication meets the
minimum requirements of American National
Standard for Information Sciences—Permanence
of Paper for Printed Library Materials,
ANSI Z39.48-1984.

Manufactured in the United States of America

Library of Congress Cataloging-in-Publication Data
The new Black gods : Arthur Huff Fauset and the study
of African American religions / edited by Edward E.
Curtis IV and Danielle Brune Sigler.
        p. cm. — (Religion in North America)
    Includes bibliographical references and index.
    ISBN 978-0-253-35282-8 (cloth : alk. paper) —
    ISBN 978-0-253-22057-8 (pbk. : alk. paper) 1. African
Americans—Religion. I. Curtis, Edward E., [date]
II. Sigler, Danielle Brune.
    BL2525.N484 2009
    200.89'96073—dc22
                                    2008038720

1 2 3 4 5   14 13 12 11 10 09

To Cece Neef Brune
D.B.S.

To the School of Liberal Arts at IUPUI
E.C.

CONTENTS

FOREWORD

In 1986, we launched the Religion in North America series at Indiana University Press with the publication of William L. Andrews's edited collection *Sisters of the Spirit*. The book, with its careful introduction by Andrews, contained the nineteenth-century autobiographies of African Americans Jarena Lee, Zilpha Elaw, and Julia A. J. Foote. The Andrews *Sisters*, as we fondly dubbed the volume (and gave away our ages), signaled a series that wanted to attend to new material in new ways, that intended to put the overlooked and underexplored under the scrutiny of scholarly eyes and to help in the task of revising our understanding of American religiosity.

Over the years, the Religion in North America series has arguably done its share to address American religious diversity. However, not until now has the series succeeded in publishing another volume on African American religion. So it is with special pleasure that we, as series editors, welcome the addition of this new collection of essays to our list. In *The New Black Gods: Arthur Huff Fauset and the Study of African American Religions*, Edward E. Curtis IV and Danielle Brune Sigler have gathered a remarkably coherent group of pieces, for the most part by a group of younger scholars whose professional research and interests intersect in one way or another with African American religions. Their essays are the result of a collaborative research grant from the American Academy of Religion as well as additional help from Indiana

University–Purdue University Indianapolis. They support and cross-reference each other and generally think together on their problem area. The essays at once call our attention to the vital contribution of Arthur Huff Fauset to the study of black religion and use his groundbreaking work to launch explorations of their own, revisiting the religious worlds of his subjects and advancing a series of historiographical and interpretive themes regarding them and American black religions in general.

Black Gods of the Metropolis, originally published in 1944, was Fauset's dissertation produced at the University of Pennsylvania under the guidance of anthropologist Frank Speck (noted for his work on American Indian materials). The groups that Fauset studied were all situated in the city of Philadelphia, where he accomplished his fieldwork with easy access to the university. Indeed, there seems to have been little revision when the university's press produced the slim book that became a classic in the field. It was Fauset who first gave us Father Divine and Daddy Grace, along with Noble Drew Ali who began the trajectory that would lead to Elijah Muhammad's Nation of Islam. It was Fauset, too, who gave us Prophet F. S. Cherry with his Black Jews and Bishop Ida Robinson with her combinative holiness-Pentecostal-spiritual-healing Mt. Sinai Holy Church of America. And as the editors remark, Fauset's scholarship involved more than *Black Gods of the Metropolis.* He wrote about the Harlem Renaissance and about "Negro Folklore," and he was also active in the social and political life of the city of Philadelphia. With his radically democratic vision and with government suspicion that he had links to the Communist Party of the time, he even caught the attention of the FBI.

Introducing the 1971 paperback edition of *Black Gods* (University of Pennsylvania Press, xi), a later Fauset evoked Martin Luther King Jr. and Father Divine ("the Father Divine movement may properly lay claim to being a forerunner of the contemporary love-not-hate world movement") alongside "Black Muslims" and Black Panthers. He had, like King, been to the mountain, and he pointed to the significance of the so-called cults he had earlier studied. "Truly those who ponder the future of our own great nation would do well to recall the aphorism, 'Mighty oaks from tiny acorns grow.'"

The authors who have contributed essays to this volume clearly agree. Fauset took the groups he treated seriously as religious actors, runs their message. With anthropological sophistication, he did ethnography at a time when that kind of approach was basically untried for this sort of material. With historical insight, too, Fauset tracked blacks who came up from the South and settled in urban areas in the context of the Great Migration. He tackled superficial and religiously prejudiced judgments that dismissed the "cults" of poor urban blacks. Instead, he wanted to know why they appealed, how they could be distinguished, what contributions/ deficits they offered to their adherents, and how racial matters entered into the new religious equations. He countered fear and disdain for these groups and their leaders head on, and he succeeded in pointing to their appeal, their contributions to the lives of their adherents, and the relationship of these movements to American racialism. He noticed the powerful role of women in the groups, and he noticed as well the intellectual agenda that ran through the movements. Far from simple outlets for excess emotion, the groups emerged, under Fauset's anthropological eye and the consensus of these later scholars, as problem solvers for religious questions and dilemmas. With his attention to religious practice, too, Fauset moved from ideas to disciplines and showed the seamless connection.

The Curtis/Sigler volume, however, is more than a panegyric of praise. It is, instead, a work of multidisciplinary scholarship by authors from the fields of anthropology, folklore, American studies, history, and religious studies, who use Fauset as a springboard to address their present-day concerns in black religious studies scholarship. The essays return to the original groups that Fauset studied (plus one additional spiritualist group) and offer fresh and important insights about the material.

In this context, editors Curtis and Sigler set out to contextualize the life and work of Arthur Huff Fauset. They note, especially, the important task of their own reconnection with his view of black religion, a view that has been lost, in their judgment, by virtue of the sharp line drawn between the "Black Church" and black "cults." By avoiding the lens of Christian church history, Fauset provides an important methodological resource for present-day scholars who want to recover a black American religiosity that is best seen in more continuous terms than a church-sect framework. And with their revisionary embrace of religious forms, these groups, as Fauset presents them, challenge noncritical scholarship that sticks to textbook versions of religious traditions. The essays pursue, too, the "transnational consciousness" among black religious groups. They explore the diverse ethnic identities held by African Americans, as blacks identify with Islam, with Asia, with Middle Eastern Judaica (but not "textbook" versions) in a search for spiritual identity. They also exhibit a critical strain by faulting the common failure of those writing about black religion to take seriously, as Fauset did, its intellectual dimensions. The essays, thus, are representative of new trends in the larger historical field, including concerns about gender and ethnicity, postcolonial perspectives, ethnographic approaches, and cross-cultural comparisons.

Fauset's volume itself, of course, has been a staple in the field of American religious history for many decades, providing material for historians, sociologists, and religionists of various stripes. In fact, it would be difficult to overstate the central function that Fauset's book played for many academics who have attempted to address African American religious activity outside the bounds of established Christian denominations in the United States. It is fair to add, too, that Fauset's subjects have received considerable attention from another set of academics, those over the past several decades who have been part of the scholarly attention formerly directed to "sects and cults" and now to "new religious movements." But different from work that has simply used Fauset, what all of the chapters herein share is a measure of respect for the ways that Fauset set the stage for the study of African American religions and anticipated directions that need to be followed at the present. In fact, the theoretical suggestions offered in these chapters are a potential challenge to another generation of scholars. The challenge is to follow up on the work of Fauset, to expand the theoretical and methodological approaches employed, and to leave behind the assumptions that have often been disincentives to further study of African American religions.

So it is that beyond returning to the original groups (and the one other) that Fauset studied (a project that constitutes roughly the first half of the book), the chapters (in the second part of the book) quite explicitly criticize major directions in the present-day study of African American religions. They tease out questions already often present and even explored to some extent in the first half of the work, and they revisit the debate on African survivals. They probe church-sect distinctions as well as other, mainstream-marginal ones. And, even as in the first part of the work, they set the controversial issue of "Orientalism" into a black context that makes it appear ideologically in far different terms from the way that it does in white postcolonialist scholarship.

In sum, this is a volume that is fresh and original, highly unified, important for American black religious studies scholarship, *and* important for the general insights it raises for the religious studies field as a whole. We are pleased and proud to see it join the Andrews *Sisters of the Spirit* after all these years, and we hope it is not too long before other works on African American religion will also grace our series.

Catherine L. Albanese and Stephen J. Stein, Series Editors

ACKNOWLEDGMENTS

In creating this volume, contributors circulated their first drafts via e-mail, and then brought their comments and suggestions on each other's work to a weekend writers' meeting at Indiana University–Purdue University Indianapolis (IUPUI) in April 2007. Those present offered one another encouragement in addition to criticism, and for many of us, the weekend stands out as one of the most collegial gatherings of our careers. In addition to reading and commenting on each other's work, the writers attended a community forum of local religious leaders who shared their insights on the themes of Arthur Huff Fauset's *Black Gods of the Metropolis.* Thanks go to Dr. Thomas Brown, Ebenezer Missionary Baptist Church; Father Boniface Hardin, president of Martin University; Evangelist Kandy Morrell, Living Water Apostolic Church; and Imam Michael Saahir, Nur Allah Islamic Center, for their time and comments. IUPUI students of African American religions also read Fauset's book and voiced their questions and concerns at the forum, which was open to the general public.

Rebecca Vasko of IUPUI's Center for the Study of Religion and American Culture helped to organize these events, and the center's director, Philip Goff, provided sound advice and support in the planning stages.

Financial support for the weekend's events came largely from the American Academy of Religion, which awarded the project a collaborative research grant, and the School of Liberal Arts at IUPUI, whose generosity is truly appreciated. Additional support was provided by the Departments of History and Religious Studies, and the Center for the Study of Religion and American Culture at IUPUI.

This book also benefited from the support and constructive feedback of Indiana University Press senior sponsoring editor Dee Mortensen and series editors Catherine L. Albanese and Stephen J. Stein. Jeremy Rehwaldt-Alexander read every word of the manuscript, and his corrections and clarifications made it a much better book.

Edward Curtis dedicates this volume to the School of Liberal Arts at IUPUI, whose administrators, faculty, and staff members have turned IUPUI into a spectacular place for research and teaching in African American studies. Special thanks go to Dean Robert White, who led a dramatic expansion of student scholarship opportunities, curricular options, and faculty positions devoted to black studies.

Danielle Brune Sigler dedicates this book to Cece Neef Brune, who made her include a bibliography in her first-grade science fair project and has shown unflagging support for her research ever since.

THE NEW BLACK GODS

Introduction

EDWARD E. CURTIS IV AND DANIELLE BRUNE SIGLER

As much as W. E. B. Du Bois and Carter G. Woodson, Arthur Huff Fauset deserves a place in the pantheon of African American religious studies' founding figures, for more than any early scholar, Fauset inscribed a vision of the modern, cosmopolitan black religious subject. This collection of chapters is about much more than restoring a neglected scholar's image—it is about resurrecting his vision of African American religion in order to illuminate contemporary scholarship. The book questions the divide between the "Black Church" and black "cults," showing the dynamic movement of individuals and ideas between various African American religious groups during the Great Migration. In so doing, it also reveals a world of black religious activity where women mattered as much as men, the intellect played as large a role as emotion, and practitioners had as much power as leaders. This book, in short, restores Fauset's democratic view of black religion.

In order to understand why this relatively unknown figure is so important to the contemporary study of African American religions, we must briefly reintroduce him and retrace the steps that led Fauset to capture the "negro cults of the urban north." In 1899, Fauset was born in New Jersey to an AME minister father, Redmon Fauset, and Bella Huff Fauset, a child of Jewish parents who later converted to Christianity. Arthur Huff Fauset was the middle child of Bella and Redmon's three children and became part of a larger family comprised of children from both of his parents' previous marriages. Perhaps the most notable of these siblings—indeed a sibling who is better known than Arthur himself—was his half sister, Jessie Redmon Fauset.[1] Jessie is best known for penning the novel *Plum Bun* (1929) and for exerting tremendous influence on the Harlem Renaissance through her role as literary editor of the *Crisis*, the official magazine of the National Association for the Advancement of Colored People (NAACP).

While Arthur Huff Fauset contributed to a number of seminal works of the Harlem Renaissance, he is generally overlooked by scholars of the movement. He is usually known, when known at all, as the author of *Black Gods of the Metropolis*—the book that provides an important corrective for scholars of African American religion and forms the foundation of this anthology. He is also, however, a man who provided piano accompaniment for legendary singer Marian Anderson, who won awards for his short fiction, who wrote a biography of Sojourner Truth, who was briefly married to Crystal Bird Fauset—the first African American woman in the Pennsylvania state legislature—and a man who aspired to leadership on a scale he was never quite able to achieve.

One of Fauset's first major publications appeared in 1925, when he contributed an essay entitled "American Negro Folk Literature" and a corresponding bibliography to Alain Locke's landmark anthology, *The New Negro*. Years before, Fauset had been tapped by Frank Speck, his University of Pennsylvania advisor, to collect folklore for noted anthropologist Elsie Clews Parsons in Canada, the American South, and the West Indies. In his essay, Fauset wrote of this body of folklore: "It rivals in amount as well as in quality that of any people on the face of the globe, and is not confined to stories of Uncle Remus type, but includes a rich variety of story forms, legends, saga cycles, songs, proverbs and phantastic, almost mythical, material."[2] He argued eloquently for its preservation and systematic study: "There is strong need of a scientific collecting of Negro folk lore before the original sources of this material altogether lapse. Sentimental admiration and amateurish praise can never adequately preserve or interpret this precious material."[3] But Fauset himself turned elsewhere, while others preserved and explored the material that Fauset wanted to rescue from writers like Joel Chandler Harris, whose adaptations of "Uncle Remus" stories had dominated popular knowledge of the field. Fauset consistently railed against attitudes toward African American thought and culture that he found problematic—whether coming from outside or within.

Fauset remained engaged in the periodicals and discussions at the heart of the Renaissance. In June 1926, his short story "Symphonesque," based on his observation of an Alabama baptism during a folklore-gathering trip, was awarded *Opportunity Magazine*'s award for first prize. That same year, he helped fund and wrote an essay for the first, and only, issue of *Fire!!*, a revolutionary magazine that challenged the "art for racial uplift" ideology permeating much of the Renaissance. Alongside fiction and poetry by Zora Neale Hurston, Langston Hughes, and Wallace Thurman, and amid Aaron Douglas's illustrations, Fauset commented on the state of the so-called intelligentsia. A critical Fauset's disdain for pretenders to the title of "intelligentsia" drips from the page:

> One can admire truly intellectual types like Sinclair Lewis, H. L. M. and Shaw, men who are in every respect thinkers. What one cannot swallow is this carrion prostrated at the altar of Liberalism when as a matter of fact their lying hearts are as faint as they are insipid. Their pelts are as mangy as Main Streeters' and their sentiments as hypocritical as those of the most pious Kluxer in the Bible Belt. They are by far more to be despised than the "morons" whom they single out with such avidity; for the latter do at least make an attempt to earn their salt, and to express themselves honestly, while the intelligentsia steal all they can get away with and never do anything unless it be in the attitude of a dethroned prince who suddenly has to go to work.[4]

This essay provides a glimpse of a man who had a disdain for the artifice of "advanced society," who aspired not to a particular class or label, but to taking an active role in the social and political life of Philadelphia and the nation. It is the Fauset who wrote *For Freedom* (1927), "a biographical study of the American Negro," at the behest of the Philadelphia public schools, who reorganized the Philadelphia teachers' union, who began writing his own column called "I Write as I See" in the *Philadelphia Tribune* in the 1930s, and who joined the National Negro Congress (1936–1940).[5] It is also the Fauset who caught the attention of the FBI as America went to war in the 1940s and as he began the research for the work that ultimately became *Black Gods of the Metropolis.*[6]

Fauset examined Daddy Grace's House of Prayer, Father Divine's Peace Mission, Noble Drew Ali's Moorish Science Temple, Prophet Cherry's Church of God, and Bishop Ida Robinson's Mt. Sinai Holy Church of America, Incorporated. Each of these organizations had churches or temples in Philadelphia, the city in which he lived and conducted most of his fieldwork, and he found them representative of the range and popularity of cults in the urban North. It is little wonder that Arthur Huff Fauset completed most of his fieldwork for his dissertation in Philadelphia. He had moved to the city as a young boy; attended its public schools, later becoming a teacher and then principal in the same schools; and received his B.A., M.A., and Ph.D. from the University of Pennsylvania. The inspiration for the book, however, came from a trip to the West. In his unpublished autobiography, he wrote,

> While visiting San Francisco, I had noted within the black group a new sharp line dividing those older black residents from more recent arrivals. . . . The traditional

religious centers . . . were becoming huge social clubs. . . . [O]n my way east, I stopped over at Chicago and Detroit. There I noted little "storefront" churches had sprung up everywhere in the Black Belt. Formerly one had counted the numerous taverns in the ghettos; even more numerous now were those miniscule temples of religious devotion, with their sound of tambourines, drums, wind and stringed instruments.[7]

The storefront churches that captivated Fauset's attention had multiplied as hundreds of thousands of African Americans moved to the North amid the Great Migration. While some of these churches were affiliated with preexisting denominations, many were independent, established by migrants seeking to recreate forms of worship from their homes or by those dissatisfied members who had defected from other congregations. The resulting organizations drew on increasingly diverse strands of American religious thought in the United States, including Judaism, Islam, New Thought, and Christian Science. Some of them also incorporated African nationalism, a philosophy that embraced the connections between and emphasized the achievements of peoples of African descent throughout the world. Many united these traditions with Holiness beliefs and practices, emphasizing the necessity of a "second blessing" after conversion. The resulting combinations of religions that emerged were often labeled "black sects and cults" because, at least to outsiders, they defied classification as conventional faiths or denominations.

The organizations that intrigued Fauset alarmed leaders of traditional African American denominations as well as race leaders like W. E. B. Du Bois. Both factions were concerned that these religious organizations and their leaders did not provide the proper kind of influence for an up-and-coming race. They characterized the leaders as uneducated charlatans, preaching unsophisticated ideas and bilking followers out of their hard-earned money. In 1938, Rev. Adam Clayton Powell Jr., leader of the prestigious Abyssinian Baptist Church, dismissed "cult leaders" Father Divine and Daddy Grace and predicted their speedy demise: "Nothing to it. Just another of the long line of imposters who have each only lasted for a brief season."[8]

While Powell and Du Bois were busy urging an end to what they perceived as unsophisticated worship and imposter ministers, Fauset wanted to know why the storefronts were proving so enduring. He approached them with the perspective and methodology of an anthropologist. He attended services, sometimes covertly, interviewed members and ex-members, and spoke with leaders when they would oblige. He filled notebooks with his observations and complemented his fieldwork with readings in the secondary literature of African American religion, including E. Franklin Frazier, Melville Herskovits, and Carter G. Woodson. The result was *Black*

Gods of the Metropolis (1944), originating from his dissertation, and later published as a monograph (with little revision) on "Negro religious cults in the Urban North." His purpose, he explained, was "to probe beneath the merely superficial aspects . . . in order to arrive at a deeper understanding of what is and has been taking place for many years among these Negroes in the development of their religious concepts and practices . . . especially in our great northern cities."[9] By moving beyond the "superficial aspects," Fauset set himself apart from those who assumed all storefronts were not only exactly the same, but also entirely problematic. Fauset wanted to determine why the cults appealed to African Americans, what they did or did not contribute to the lives of their followers, and how they were reflective (if at all) of the limitations imposed by America's racial dichotomy.

The finished work had so impressed Fauset's dissertation advisor, Frank Speck, that he recommended it for publication by the University of Pennsylvania Press. During the review process, a professor in Penn's sociology department nearly stymied the entire effort by objecting to statistics Fauset quoted regarding the slave trade.[10] Despite the objection, the book went to press, retaining the original figure.

However, the book soon came under the critical eye of at least one of the leaders that Fauset had discussed, Bishop Ida Robinson, who threatened to file suit. She considered the book an "intrusion on the privacy" of her organization.[11] Fauset explained to Robinson that the press had no plans to publicize the work, Robinson was satisfied with his response, and the university remained blissfully unaware. The book made its debut to positive reviews in the *New York Times* and the *Journal of Negro History.*

Fauset, in spite of the positive response to his book, did not enter the world of academia, and he effectively faded from public view. In 1970, when Fauset was seventy-one, Canadian folklorist Carole H. Carpenter interviewed him. She described him as a "genteel, soft-spoken man of slight build and medium height" who "was as delighted to be discovered by the academy as [she] was to find him."[12] He was teaching English at the Spanish American Institute—and worried his real age would be discovered and he would be forced to retire. Fauset died in 1983 and portions of his papers have been preserved in the University of Pennsylvania's library where they remain today. Amid the drafts of *Black Gods of the Metropolis* are his notebooks filled with field observations, copies of *Grace Magazine,* and a Moorish Science Temple membership card. The work that he did to capture a particular moment in African American religion continues to bear fruit for scholars. This is certainly the case for the contributors of this volume who represent a variety of disciplines: anthropology, folklore, American studies, history, and religious studies.

Indeed, Fauset's work still has much to contribute to the field of African American religion, a field that has largely perpetuated the intelligentsia's approach of Du Bois and Powell in its dismissive treatment of faiths outside of the mainline denominations. Consider Milton Sernett's *African American Religious History: A Documentary Witness*. The table of contents divides documents into sections including "From the Great Migration to World War II," which focuses on the "black church," and "Twentieth Century Religious Alternatives" devoted to Garvey, Judaism, Islam, and the "cults." Though many of these documents were written at and represent the same moment in history, the "alternatives" are segregated from the mainline denominations, reinforcing both that they are something altogether different from Christian denominations and that they are by their very definition "alternative." This delineation is not entirely surprising given Sernett's explanation in his *Bound for the Promised Land: African American Religion and the Great Migration* that he "consciously highlight[s] the mainline African American denominations because of the inordinate attention that scholarly and popular accounts of the period between the two wars have given to what is commonly termed the rise of the cults and sects."[13] While Sernett may make a compelling case for the necessity of reexamining the "mainline denominations" during the Great Migration, in failing to note the fluidity, movement, and exchanges taking place among these denominations and the cults and sects he reductively terms "exotic," he perpetuates the artificial and dated church/cult dichotomy, and assumes Christianity as normative and all other traditions as foreign or "other."

On the surface, it appears that Anthony Pinn's *Varieties of African American Religious Experience* counters this trend by introducing readers to the diversity of African American religion. Indeed, Pinn argues that though "anthropologists, sociologists, historians of religion, and those in the arts" have examined a variety of African American traditions, theologians have not. Pinn sets about rectifying this, but does so with the explicit goal of understanding how Christian theology "address[es] traditions that fall outside the Christian context."[14] Though Pinn refrains from the use of "exotic," his classification is also reductive, undermining the very significance of these understudied organizations through his classification of religions as either Christian or non-Christian, as well as through his argument for the necessity of studying these faiths primarily as a means of broadening and enhancing the study of African American Christian theology. Insofar as Pinn is a Christian theologian, this approach is a reasonable one for him to take. However, his approach, and Sernett's for that matter, become problematic when a Christian-centered, church-history lens so dominates the field of African American religion that alternate voices become relegated to a secondary status and are studied only when deemed instructive in a comparative sense or are invoked only in support of a better understanding of Christian traditions. Fauset's *Black Gods of the Metropolis*, though not without its own flaws, provides a model that by and large accepts a variety of faiths on their own terms and seeks to understand what meaning these faiths have for their adherents.

That theoretical leap, made by Fauset in the 1930s, was truly innovative and truly courageous. Fauset imagined a black religious world in which African Americans themselves, not the "Black Church" or Christianity, were at the center of African American religious activity. Fauset displaced the romantic racialist view that cast blacks primarily as the worldly agents of Christ's redemption. He was able to conceptualize an African American universe of religious activity in which black bodies did more than perform emotional worship—black religion for Fauset was much more than a "jig and a song." In Fauset's view, Americans of African descent were modern and rational persons possessing as much human agency as anyone else. Democratic to the core, Fauset's vision also resisted the idea that black religion, especially "cult" religion, was a tragic, ultimately misguided, and ineffective political protest against social alienation and oppression. To the contrary, Fauset saw the seeds of effective social and political protest in the activism of cult members. The ideology underlying Fauset's work, his effort to listen to the voices of adherents, and his willingness to take those voices seriously established a new direction for the field.

Though Fauset is not generally credited by some scholars for pioneering this direction, others have called for changes in the field of African American religious studies that engender the spirit of his innovative approach. For example, in the introduction to their 2003 *African American Religious Thought: An Anthology*, Cornel West and Eddie S. Glaude Jr. note the strong, sometimes determining influence of black Christian theology within the field of African American religious studies. While arguing for theology's continued relevance, West and Glaude assert that black religious history and the sociology of black religion are "not reducible to theological claims." The sociology and history of black religions constitute categories worthy of exploration in their own right. In addition, West and Glaude advocate an approach among scholars of African American religion that is interdisciplinary, historicist, and self-critical.[15] In many ways, the chapters in this volume show how Fauset's ethnographic, democratic vision of black religion—updated for the new millennium —implements this scholarly agenda.

Part 1 of the volume revisits the religious groups that Fauset studied for his dissertation research, including Bishop Ida Robinson's Mt. Sinai Holy Church of

America, Bishop Charles Manuel "Daddy" Grace's United House of Prayer, Prophet F. S. Cherry's Church of God (Black Jews), the Moorish Science Temple, and Father Divine's Peace Mission Movement. In addition, part 1 includes a chapter about Father George Hurley's black Spiritualists, a group that did not originally appear in Fauset's volume. Part 2 then utilizes Fauset's legacy to identify and critique major themes and issues in the contemporary study of African American religions. All of the chapters in this volume do more than update Fauset's original account; they show how Fauset's insights provide models for understanding the modern, cosmopolitan nature of African American religions during and after the Great Migration. More specifically, these chapters emphasize (1) the flow of African American persons and ideas among various religious communities; (2) the ways in which the African American religionists created competing and complementary black ethnicities; and (3) the intellectual and ethical problems inherent in viewing African American religions during this era in terms of "church" and "cult," or mainstream and marginal.

The movement of modern African American religionists and their ideas from one religious community to another during this era was remarkable, and the authors of this volume see African Americans as people in motion as much as people standing still. Because ideas as well as people traveled so easily from one religious group to another, this book insists on seeing the so-called cults or new religious movements in relationship to the so-called Black Church. Many of the authors would simply like to jettison these terms, particularly when the Black Church is seen as a more authentic expression of black religion than the new religious movements. Offering an alternative view of African American religious life during and after the Great Migration, these chapters depict the contact, confrontation, and exchange among various religious groups, both marginal and mainstream.

For example, the lead chapter in the volume, Clarence E. Hardy's study of Bishop Ida Robinson's Mt. Sinai Church, reveals how Mt. Sinai members were part of an emerging Pentecostal religious culture in which southern female migrants in the North viewed themselves as deliberately transregional and transnational leaders. The Pentecostal religious culture that they created shared an important characteristic with black Muslims and other black nationalist groups: Their global vision refused to be confined by the boundaries of the American nation-state. Hardy sees Pentecostalism at the center of modern, cosmopolitan black religion—and as a bridge between new religious movements and other black Protestants.

The transnational consciousness that Hardy describes is hardly unique to black female Pentecostals. During and after the Great Migration, African American religious persons and institutions as a whole—whether Christian, Jewish, or Muslim—increasingly expressed their identity in transnational terms. This transnational sense of blackness constitutes an important and sometimes ignored element of African American identity—namely, the creation of black ethnicity, which is another powerful theme running through this book's chapters. As several authors point out, the absolute emphasis on the "racial" identity of blacks in some scholarship has robbed African Americans of their diverse and vibrant ethnic identities.

As the authors uncover the dynamic religious worlds that black Americans created in the era of the Great Migration, this volume thus reclaims the range of ethnic identities to which African Americans ascribed during and after this period. Nora L. Rubel's article on Prophet Cherry's black Jews, for example, highlights the differing ways in which African American Jews, Hebrews, and Israelites, during Prophet Cherry's life and after, appropriated and reinterpreted Jewish and Christian scriptures, the Hebrew language, and Jewish history in Africa and Asia in relocating their religious, historical, and linguistic roots. Other African American religionists sited their ethnic identity in oriental, Eastern, and Asian pasts. For example, Jacob S. Dorman's chapter, "A True Moslem Is a True Spiritualist," unveils the alliance of Father George Hurley, a leading black Spiritualist, with some early African American Muslims. Dorman argues that "black Orientalism" was a tradition embraced not only by African American Jewish and Muslim groups but also by a large array of African Americans fascinated by the mystic East. Dorman sees black Orientalism as a major but underappreciated component of African American ethnic identity-making in the first half of the twentieth century.

Many of the chapters in this volume forthrightly criticize the marginalization of the black religious subject within African American religious studies scholarship, arguing that too many black religions and black religionists have been labeled as heretical or just plain deluded. This volume insists that African American persons of faith, whether formally educated or not, were and are theologically minded actors just as invested in the intellectual components of faith as other human beings. For example, Danielle Brune Sigler's chapter on Charles Manuel "Daddy" Grace argues that even Fauset failed to understand the Christian theology that animated Daddy Grace's United House of Prayer for All People. Sigler traces the theological evolution of Daddy Grace's group, demonstrating that Grace did not claim to be a substitute for God, but instead saw himself as successor to Jesus. Edward E. Curtis's chapter on the Moorish Science Temple similarly tackles a new religious group generally seen as heretical within African American religious studies. Curtis asserts that some Americanists have applied a superficial "textbook Islam" in their understanding of the

Moorish Science Temple's Islamic identity, and he suggests the need for a more dynamic narrative of the movement's multiple and diverse influences.

The scholarly inscription of African American religionists as primitive and emotional is also critiqued in this volume. For instance, Kathryn Lofton's chapter about the perpetual primitive in African American religious historiography explores the preoccupation of the field of religious studies with racial primitivism, casting an especially critical eye toward the ways scholars have constructed the black religious body, particularly the bodies of black women such as the civil rights activist Fannie Lou Hamer. Though Fauset long ago proved that black religion is "more than a jig and a song," Lofton asserts, one is hard pressed to find portraits of Hamer that present the famous activist as an intellectually minded person of faith who does more than emote. In a similar vein, Sylvester A. Johnson advances a postcolonial critique of African American religious studies that indicts previous scholarship for its marginalization of black cult members. Reviewing the complicity of previous scholars and the state in systematically denying even the existence of non-mainstream religions in the accumulation and analysis of religious data, Johnson also shows how remarkable Fauset's ethnographic scholarship was for its time. He also suggests that too many students of African American religion have yet to adopt Fauset's democratic notion of what constitutes legitimate religion and outlines the implications of his critique for the future of the field.

Carolyn Rouse shows what it means to apply Johnson's and Lofton's concerns to a modern ethnography of Muslims in South Central Los Angeles. She argues that Fauset's anthropological functionalism is especially pertinent to understanding African American Muslim practice among males. But she also shows, in an engaging analysis of a conversation between a Muslim man and a Muslim woman, how in South Central L.A. at least some black Muslim women do not fit into Fauset's analytical scheme. She asserts that an "interpretivist" model of ethnography captures the experiences of Muslim women far more accurately. Also contributing an original ethnography to the volume, Leonard Norman Primiano revisits Father Divine's movement, comparing his experiences as an ethnographer of the Peace Mission with Fauset's. Primiano's reciprocal ethnography of the contemporary movement presents a new and original portrait of the group's innovative musical traditions.

Another ethnographically minded scholar, Kelly E. Hayes, provides a hemispheric perspective on Fauset's intellectual legacy by showing how the debate over African retentions in the study of Brazilian religions reverberated in North American scholarship. She explains how Melville J. Herskovits, who argued for the retention of African culture in African American religions, was influenced by Brazilian scholar Arthur Ramos. Ramos's view of African American religion did not acknowledge Fauset's belief in the culturally heterogeneous roots of African American religions, instead arguing that Brazilian candomblé was purely African in its origin. Then, in the volume's concluding chapter, the issue of African retentions is covered from a different angle by Stephen W. Angell, who brings to light Fauset's reactions to the debates among Robert Park, Melville Herskovits, and E. Franklin Frazier over the issue of African retentions and the innate religiosity of black people. Angell also reveals how Fauset's analysis in *Black Gods* reflected the scholar's political commitments. Fauset linked the new religious movements and African American religion more generally to democratic social change, anticipating the role that African American religious groups, of various religious stripes, would play in the era of civil rights and black power movements.

No matter what their particular arguments, the chapters in this volume show that Fauset's relatively slim book belies an important intellectual legacy needing to be reclaimed in African American religious studies. To be sure, Fauset was not a prolific academic. But his vision of the modern and cosmopolitan black religious subject still cries out for scholarly recognition. It is not simply that Fauset deserves to be celebrated, although he does—it is rather that Fauset established lines of inquiry still in need of exploration. The chapters in this volume begin that task by uncovering the dynamism of African American religion during and after the era of the Great Migration. Instead of foisting a hermeneutical wall between black churches and black new religious movements, this book looks for the connections among various African American religious groups. The complicated humanity of the "cult members" whom Fauset studied is thus celebrated as we attempt to view these human beings not only in the context of their own small groups, but as modern persons simultaneously part of local, regional, national, and international worlds of meaning and practice.

Notes

1. For the most comprehensive biographical treatment of Fauset to date, see Carole H. Carpenter, "Arthur Huff Fauset, Campaigner for Social Justice: A Symphony of Diversity," in *African-American Pioneers in Anthropology*, ed. Ira E. Harrison and Faye V. Harrison (Urbana: University of Illinois Press, 1999).

2. Arthur Huff Fauset, "American Negro Folk Literature," in *The New Negro*, ed. Alain Locke (1925; New York: Atheneum, 1970), 238.

3. Ibid., 241.

4. Arthur Huff Fauset, "Intelligentsia," *Fire!!* 1, no. 1 (1926): 45–46, 46.

5. Carpenter, "Arthur Huff Fauset," 234. See Fauset, *For Freedom* (Philadelphia: Franklin, 1927).

6. In the midst of Fauset's fieldwork, even before the publication of *Black Gods*, he had become the subject of an FBI investigation—one that would endure for decades. His FBI file is almost eighteen hundred pages long. On October 17, 1942, a letter to Special Agent in Charge instructed the Philadelphia office to create a five-by-eight white card "for filing in your Confidential Custodial Detention Card File." One month later, Fauset received a "B-2" "dangerousness classification" (A-1 being the most dangerous). In a June 6, 1942, report, the agent recorded, "In an article, the Philadelphia Tribune advised that Subject is the author of a manuscript on Negro Goals in the urban North which was recently accepted by the Philadelphia Anthropological Society of the University of Pennsylvania." The presumably accidental substitution of "goals" for "gods" suggested a potentially more revolutionary work. A report from J. Edgar Hoover to Major General George V. Strong of the War Department alerted the officer to the fact that Fauset was enlisting in the army. Fauset was sent to army officer training school in Grinnell, Iowa, but received an honorable discharge on the eve of receiving his commission. In a memorandum for the FBI, dated July 12, 1943, the War Department Military Intelligence Service explained, "He was discharged from the Army of the United States on 7 May 1943 for having Communist Party affiliations." Fauset later explained that he had never had any explicit relationship with the Communist Party.

7. Arthur Huff Fauset, unpublished autobiography in the Arthur Huff Fauset Collection, Special Collections Department, Van Pelt Library, University of Pennsylvania, Philadelphia.

8. "Denounce," *New York New Amsterdam News*, March 12, 1938, 1.

9. Arthur Huff Fauset, *Black Gods of the Metropolis: Negro Religious Cults of the Urban North* (1944; Philadelphia: University of Pennsylvania Press, 2002), 2.

10. Cited in Carpenter, "Arthur Huff Fauset," 238–239n9.

11. As quoted in ibid., 239n10.

12. Ibid., 216.

13. Milton Sernett, *African American Religious History: A Documentary Witness*, 2nd ed. (Durham, N.C.: Duke University Press, 1999); Milton Sernett, *Bound for the Promised Land: African American Religion and the Great Migration* (Durham, N.C.: Duke University Press, 1997), 7.

14. Anthony B. Pinn, *Varieties of African American Religious Experience* (Minneapolis: Fortress, 1998), 2.

15. Cornel West and Eddie S. Glaude Jr., eds., *African American Religious Thought: An Anthology* (Louisville, Ky.: Westminster John Knox, 2003), xi–xxv.

PART 1

New Religious Movement(s) of the Great Migration Era

ONE · Fauset's (Missing) Pentecostals: Church Mothers, Remaking Respectability, and Religious Modernism

CLARENCE E. HARDY III

In the final version of *Black Gods of the Metropolis*, Arthur Huff Fauset excluded the story of a "Mrs. W," a Pentecostal, "middle aged colored woman" who had moved to Philadelphia, like so many other African Americans, as part of the Great Migration. It is a telling exclusion since Mrs. W was likely more representative of fellow migrants than many of the African Americans Fauset chose to include. The rising popularity of urban Pentecostal churches such as the Church of God in Christ (COGIC), which had its beginnings in the rural Mississippi Delta but increasingly became an urban church through migration and focused city evangelism, demonstrates that Mrs. W's story must have been the story of many. In Virginia she had been a Baptist, but when confronted with one of the most notable vices the city made visible, she joined a local Pentecostal congregation for help and comfort. As Mrs. W explained: "I had come to Philadelphia from Virginia. I knew I needed something, but I didn't know just what. I looked outside my house one day and there were some men gambling on the doorstep. I never had seen anything like that before and I couldn't get over it. I said to myself, 'Oh, if only I had more power, I could keep men from gambling like that!'" After a dream in which a voice from heaven spoke to her and deepened her sense of restless anxiety, she went in search of divine power to a congregation where "some sanctified people" worshipped. Her faith, which had seemed adequate to her before, now was not. "When I walked in I felt the spirit," she remembered. "I said, 'I'm converted. I know I am. I'm leading a clean life in these times. But I need more power.'"[1] While modest numbers of migrants found religious alternatives beyond traditional Christianity in these early decades of the twentieth century, this period marks the emergence of a Pentecostalism that would become the dominant religious expression within black Protestantism and black America by century's end.

When Fauset recorded Mrs. W's memories before World War II, he knew that this increasingly intense wave of black migrants from the South had sparked an "adjustment of mental attitudes to new mores" and inaugurated a "transformation in the basic religious life" of black Americans.[2] Early in his classic text, Fauset approvingly notes sociologist Ira Reid's assessment that an "inordinate rise of religious cults and sects," including "Father Divine, Daddy Grace, Moslem sects, congregations of Black Jews and the Coptic Church," had come to define the black religious landscape. And Fauset's text served to present evocative portraits of these novel expressions of black religious life, which had adapted to the "sensationalism" of urban life and the "arduousness and bitter realities of race" even while established Baptist and Methodist churches with their "prayerful procrastinations," in Reid's estimation, had not.[3] In recent years, scholars have questioned the hold social scientists and particularly Chicago-trained sociologists have had on these initial interpretations of black religious culture during the interwar period.[4] In place of the "cults," historian Milton Sernett and others have emphasized the role Baptist and Methodist churches had as the principal institutional context for the religious expression of African Americans in those years.[5]

Rather than focus on the established churches or those at its outer margins among black Jews and Muslims, this chapter will explore instead those black Pentecostals that appear within or, like Mrs. W, hover just beyond the scope of Fauset's published text and consider how they helped remake the very contours of black religious life. In so doing, it recasts the history of black religious culture in the early decades of the twentieth century with Pentecostals at its center—bridging the proper forms of institutional religion with those new forms just emerging. While Judith Weisenfeld has argued that recent work on the interwar period has "tend[ed] to downplay or eradicate" the links new religious traditions had with established cultural forms, my focus on Fauset's (missing) Pentecostals represents one attempt to consider what she has called the unexamined "connection between the urban 'sects' and 'cults' and African American Protestant traditions."[6] By categorizing religious groups differently than most of his contemporaries, Fauset manages to suggest how these moments of religious innovation connect to more established forms of religion and to their larger cultural milieu. Barbara Savage in her recent introduction to *Black Gods* argued that Fauset rejected the "lead of other scholars"—principally prominent black social scientists and intellectuals of the era—when he excluded small Pentecostal churches from the charged category of "cults."[7] Fauset's study, however, did not precisely exclude Pentecostals from this category. Instead, by including the highly visible Pentecostal congregation of Bishop Ida Robinson, he suggested that the category was more complicated than others had presumed.

In 1924 Ida Robinson, a migrant born in Georgia and reared in Florida, founded a confederation of churches, in part to preserve women's right to ordination that she saw threatened within the United Holy Church, a Pentecostal denomination with origins in North Carolina that had originally ordained her to preach a few years before. By including a portrait of Robinson's Pentecostal group among the five in his study, Fauset offers no simple rule for determining the "cult" status of religious groups. What he offers, instead, is a broader map of the new religious terrain in which emerging groups can be measured by their "conformity" to "orthodox evangelical Christian denominations."[8] In Fauset's view, Pentecostal churches like those of Bishop Robinson became the first bridge from the established institutional expressions of Baptist and Methodist churches to the more heterodox. In the "comparative study" that comprises the seventh chapter of *Black Gods*, Mount Sinai and Daddy Grace's United House of Prayer are the groups that most conform to his imagined mainstream. For Fauset, both of these groups represent "doctrinal splits within the older established models," which later establish "developments" that would set the context for the "pronounced 'nationalistic' characteristics" of the other groups he describes.[9]

Whether we subscribe to the historical narrative Fauset offers, the excluded testimony of Mrs. W establishes an additional link between the mainstream and the esoteric. While he describes glossolalia and rhythmic music as important "deviations" from the "orthodox evangelical pattern," what really distinguishes Ida Robinson (and for that matter Daddy Grace) most decisively from the mainstream and from Mrs. W's own band of sanctified believers is the prime "importance" followers ascribe to their "leader."[10] For Fauset, charismatic leadership is most arresting in its expression among and through the women who lead and shape Mount Sinai. As he writes in his portrait of Robinson's Philadelphia congregation: "Mt. Sinai is distinctive among the cults considered here in the extent and degree of female participation. Many of the elders are women, as are also a larger number of the preachers."[11]

When Mrs. W's excluded story is viewed against Robinson's story, what is illuminated initially is the role black women assumed as increasingly visible religious leaders in the early decades of the twentieth century. Between these stories, both within the published work and without, Arthur Fauset provides a clear window into how black women grappled for the right to assert their own spiritual authority as black migrants and, unsatisfied with the choices immediately available, attached themselves to new religious communities. From this point of departure, this chapter will examine the connection between Mrs. W's fellowship and Mount Sinai's as a context for understanding the new contours of a black religious culture that remade old tropes of respectability and reconceived the very nature of (religious) community.

What truly differentiates Robinson from Mrs. W was that Robinson openly exercised spiritual power as a minister in the public square. Rooted in black Holiness and Pentecostal traditions, she was a "church mother" who represented, initiated, and participated in broad changes in black religious culture that embraced both the "cults" on the margins and the larger milieu of black Protestantism. In ways that both realized and extended far beyond Fauset's initial musings about the religious transformation then occurring, these "church mothers" shaped the ordinary religious lives and dreams of black people in the United States. While many studies in recent years have focused on black Pentecostal women as gospel singers and prominent church workers, planters, and builders, Fauset's work implicitly suggests that it is black women's emergence into the public square that best defines black Pentecostalism's flowering in those early years.[12] Just as the story of Pentecostals is at the center of the evolution of black religious culture in the interwar period, the story of black religious women's assertive entrance into the public arena is at the center of black Pentecostalism's emergence as an urban religion from its beginnings in the Mississippi Delta and border South.

The Dreams of Church Mothers

The same dream that had helped change Mrs. W into "an ardent worker in the Holiness group" established within her the right to speak for God against the vices made visible in the city. After witnessing men right outside her door gambling in open daylight, she had a dream that in the end would mark her entrance into a new religious community. Remembering how she became an apostolic Pentecostal, Mrs. W told Fauset:

> Then one day I had a dream I felt myself lifted on a high mountain. It was so high I could look and see over the world. When I looked behind me it seemed as if the sun was going down right at my back. It looked like it does in the country. Looks like if you

went to the end of the field you could touch it. Then a voice said to me, "This represents the son of God. It's almost down. You must warn men and women to be holy." I rushed down from the mountain crying. When I got down, there was a host of people waiting for me to listen to me. I talked to them. Then I woke up. Things went on so and so for two or three days. Then the same thing appeared in the kitchen while I was doing the dishes. I was wide awake. I clapped my hands. Then I went to a woman and asked her, "What shall I do?" She said, "Go down to one of these [sanctified] churches."[13]

The dreams she had—both waking and sleeping—captured memories of the rural life she had left behind. Established now in the city, she had visions of the fields and wide-open spaces of her life before. When she came down from the mountain she felt the sun on her back just "like it does in the country." But caught between worlds—North and South, urban and rural—Mrs. W's dream lent authority she did not apparently fully use in the waking world. On the mountain she had received a divine message of warning to be shared with others. Within the boundaries of dream, people were eager to hear her message. When she rushed down the mountain there "was a host of people waiting . . . to listen to me," she recalled. While we have no evidence that she would later embrace that authority as a preacher and evangelist, other women had done so before and would do so again. When popular evangelist and preacher Ida Robinson heard rumors in 1924 that the United Holy Church, the same Pentecostal denomination that had ordained her, would soon stop ordaining women (at least publicly), she received a divine vision after a ten-day fast that instructed her to "come out on Mount Sinai" and "loose the women."[14] Robinson's vision motivated her to establish Mount Sinai to provide institutional space for women to exercise clerical leadership.

The seeds for this move to Mount Sinai began many decades before. Shortly after Emancipation, black Baptist observers from the North believed that the power some black women exercised within rural religious communities in the South was an unfortunate heritage from the days of bondage and undoubtedly among the "vices and irregularities inseparably attendant upon the state of slavery." Though these "church mothers" or "gospel mothers" were, according to black missionary Charles Satchel in the late 1860s, "outside of the New Testament arrangement," these women nevertheless claimed "to be under the special influence of the Spirit" and began to "exercise an authority, greater in many cases, than that of ministers."[15] Whether this less formal expression of leadership actually had a more ancient pedigree stretched beyond slavery to Africa is unclear, but after many black women found their influence waning in congregational settings after Emancipation, black Holiness (and later

Pentecostal) networks represented a resurgence for some women in their power and influence over new congregations.[16]

This new power would take shape as women led Pentecostal bands into Northern cities under the jurisdiction of male-led denominations such as Charles Mason's COGIC or established themselves as bishops and central overseers over entire regional and multiregional church bodies they founded, led, and controlled. Within COGIC, church mothers "dug out," that is, planted and nurtured, new churches as they established a parallel power structure to that of male clergy. They exercised separate spiritual authority over the women in the congregation and they had profound influence over the entire congregation, often constraining the power of male pastors. Church mothers in the Women's Department of COGIC (est. 1911) "defined the content of their own roles" without interference from men. And male pastors who wanted to make significant changes in a congregation's worship practice often had to reckon with a church mother's informal power over the entire parish.[17]

Women such as Rosa Horn of Harlem, Lucy Smith of Chicago, Mary Magdalena Tate of Tennessee, and Ida Robinson of Philadelphia were often addressed as "Mother" as they built regional empires of faith, often with themselves at the center of power through active radio ministries. But even though they were addressed in a similar fashion as church mothers in COGIC, they exercised far greater authority. Whereas church mothers within COGIC wielded informal power within individual congregations, these women served as clerical leaders over multiregional networks of churches. In addition, since traditional church mothers were, as historian Wallace Best argues, "the most desexualized [category] in the black church tradition," reserved for older respected women, the "church mother" title "authenticated their calls to ministry" while "deflecting focus on her body or the nature of her personal relationships."[18] Defining their sacerdotal duties as mothering was a way women like Mrs. W could actually minister in a world where men limited opportunities for women to preach and lead congregations. In 1903, two decades before Robinson established her group, Mary Magdalena Tate, the first woman in the United States to head a predominantly black denomination as chief overseer and bishop, founded her own group, the Church of the Living God.[19] Though Tate concentrated in the mid-South, Georgia, and Florida, the movement spanned more than twenty states with churches spreading as far north as Connecticut and Pennsylvania by her death in 1930.[20] In her longest surviving letter, written around 1928, she begins with the salutation, "Now, loving children," and then includes a wide range of teachings from how to keep the Sabbath to how both men and women were capable of becoming "sons of God." With maternal love and longing, Tate ends her correspondence to her broader church much as she began: "Bye, bye, from your own Dear Mother."[21]

Church Mothers Embrace a Wider World

Around the same time Tate was active as a church builder up and down the eastern seaboard, Robinson had a vision that would establish the scope of her ministry before she became the leader of Mount Sinai. Robinson's vision anticipated the new cosmopolitan modern reality that mass migration would engender in black religious culture. In that vision, which set the stage for her career first as an evangelist and then as a preacher and denominational leader, she saw that "there was a great church being born in the city, with people coming from the North, South, East and West."[22] The diasporic moments of dispersal and unity Robinson imagined and preached about were like joints in the body—points of separation that were also points of linkage and connection—that provided the possibility for collective coordination and movement from a broader basis than before.[23] In coping with the effects of mass migration, women Pentecostal leaders like Robinson in the early decades of the twentieth century adopted a perspective that embraced a more expansive view of religious community. Black Holiness rhetoric had been baptized in the fire of the Pentecostal revivals at Azusa Street in Los Angeles in 1906 and then expanded as Pentecostal ministers and evangelists of both sexes spread this new faith into the Northeast and Midwest from the South and West over boundaries of territory and gender.[24]

Evangelism, of course, had provided an initial drive for much of this evolution, and women Pentecostal leaders in particular envisioned the entire world as their parish. Mother Rosa Horn of Harlem and Lucy Smith of Chicago found that radio evangelism not only made them more recognizable than Tate, but it also buttressed an imagined internationalism often unmoored from institutional demands and responsibilities. Horn, a South Carolina–born dressmaker turned preacher, founded the Mount Calvary Assembly Hall of the Pentecostal Faith Church for All Nations in 1926—a church of three thousand that fed thousands more during the Great Depression as the organization spread into five cities along the eastern seaboard by 1934. In her original building in Harlem, the windows bore the message "Jesus Saves" in English, French, and Spanish, demonstrating how a more globally inflected vision flowed from evangelism and stamped the Holiness ranks with a more internationalist orientation.[25] Through this "instrument of the devil" that was radio, these church mothers knit together religious community anew beyond the categories of denominations and institutional church bodies. As Horn told one newspaper reporter: "It is impossible to state accurately how many infidels have been converted and brought back to the church; how many healings have been wrought; how many estranged families have been reunited, and generally how much sunshine and cheer have been brought into the lives of many people. Even other ministers have told me that their lost members have returned to their churches."[26] Lucy Smith, who founded the influential All Nations Pentecostal Church at the same time that Horn founded her church, was a forerunner in live religious broadcasts in Chicago and built her congregation of the radio waves on her show, *The Glorious Church of the Air,* beginning in 1933, with a persona as a "mother to the drifting black masses." Like Horn, her universal church was unmoored from institutional fixtures. When one Chicago scholar mentioned to Smith that he had heard her broadcasts, Smith replied: "[M]y services are getting to be among all people, all over."[27]

The world in which church mothers evangelized as leaders of multiregional organizations and mothered their visible congregations and their invisible networks linked through radio was a more open world than the one fading away, where religious and cultural conformity reigned. These boundaries of conformity, which Pentecostal church mothers and others in the mass migration era violated, were established at the very formation of black Protestant institutions with national scope. Black Baptist leaders labored to forge larger regional organizations and then national ones in the decades immediately after the Civil War. They worked under the burdensome gaze of their white counterparts before an audience that haunted and shaped their institutional aspirations. As one prominent spokesman of an early black Baptist convention warned his colleagues in 1869: "Brethren, we are watched. We are not accepted as a body or denomination qualified to manage our own missionary and educational work, and many of those who most discredit our capacity . . . have set themselves up as our benefactors."[28]

Inspired by theorists Nancy Fraser and Jürgen Habermas, historian Evelyn Brooks Higginbotham demonstrates in her influential study, *Righteous Discontent,* how a language of respectability especially among black Baptist women became a "bridge discourse that mediated relations between black and white reformers" as African Americans built religious societies with a national presence.[29] In effect, the language of decorum, deportment, and restraint exemplified in the political and religious activity of black Baptist clubwomen tied together race and respectability— developing the language of respectability into the intimate face of the contested collective identity black people had forged during and after Reconstruction. "Respectability," Higginbotham writes, "demanded that every individual in the black community assume responsibility for behavioral self-regulation and self-improvement along moral, educational and economic lines."[30] This tension between black self-determination and American nationalism shaped black collective identity and defined a politics of respectability for a people navigating a Jim Crow America that would prefigure the emphasis on surveillance that animates the regulating procedures of the modern nation-state.[31]

While the politics of respectability pivoted on bodily awareness before unsympathetic "benefactors," participants in black Holiness culture practiced ritualized denials of self-awareness that differentiated them from established Baptist and Methodist churches as they developed new and different conceptions of religious community. Mrs. W's story illuminates, once again, how Pentecostals shaped black religion as a modern culture against a restrictive climate where racial uplift and group identity seemed to be emphasized more than individuality. As Pentecostals remade black religion, they reflected a broader cultural shift. Black Americans were remaking the language of respectability outside the gaze of white "benefactors" and beyond the cramped confines of U.S. societal expectations. In the past, joining a sanctified church was a risk Mrs. W would not take, but the city presented new problems and new opportunities for Philadelphia's newest arrivals. As she explained to Fauset: "[I]n Virginia we would have been ashamed to go to a Holiness church. The people in the little towns down there all know each other and this makes them afraid to be different. But we were in Philadelphia now, and in this big city we didn't have to worry about what our friends might think."[32] Years before Mrs. W had even left for Philadelphia, poet and writer Langston Hughes had announced, in a famous 1926 manifesto, the arrival of the shameless in black expressive culture with "the blare of Negro jazz bands and the bellowing voice of Bessie Smith." The logic of respectability and the fear of being seen as different that inhibited Mrs. W had in the poet's view long cramped the space for black creativity and were in desperate need of radical revision. With contempt and disdain Hughes rejected the public language of respectability at the very core of black collective advancement since the Civil War. Instead, he wanted to forge common cause with a new generation of black artists who would celebrate virtues other than prudence and restraint. "We younger Negro artists who create now," Hughes proclaimed, "intend to express ourselves without fear or shame."[33] In the past, sanctified worship with bodies uncontrolled in their movements or vocalizations would have embarrassed Mrs. W. But now, prompted by a dream and confronted with her own powerlessness, she was willing to be baptized again in a Pentecostal church—this time in "Jesus's name"—to claim a spiritual power that would address the powerlessness she felt. "When you get the power, the spirit of God gets all in your flesh," she explained to Fauset. "It's very great. Just like an electric shock."[34] For Mrs. W, the power of the Spirit ran through her "flesh" like electric current at the moment of sanctification. The anonymity of the city, coupled with how urban life made old temptations like gambling new, produced space for individuality and allowed for an embrace of a more globally inflected and expansive rhetoric of community.

Church Mothers and an Embryonic Transnationalism

The space that allowed for individuality and difference for Mrs. W had also helped church mothers like Horn, Robinson, and Tate generate notions of religious community less tied to the borders of the American nation-state. While evangelism in a newly variegated world certainly provided energy for these new communal conceptions, Tate, who did not have a radio ministry, demonstrates that it was mass migration itself that had provided not only the shield of anonymity to escape group expectations but also the basis for new expectations. Knowing that her parishioners were less tied to their former homes in the South, Mother Tate was the first woman as a religious leader to reconfigure the religious language of holiness to knit together a religious community that bridged sharp regional divisions with language made possible by mass migration. The migration forced Tate and her church to consider their ties to one another instead of their connections, formal and otherwise, to the possible outside observers before whom they would need to be respectable. Tate urged her followers never to allow any regional division within her church family. In an evocative section titled "Of United Universal Ones" that nearly concludes her central governing document, the *General Decree Book,* she wrote:

> There shall never be a Mason-Dixon Line, nor a middle wall of petition, nor any division or separation or difference of any description between the Saints and Churches herein named. North, South, East and West, home or foreign in the United States of America or in the Isles thereof or in any and all other lands and countries and Isles thereof. . . . There shall never be anticipated, or indulged or otherwise practice or in any way at all acts of state or sectional prejudices and differences among any of the members.

"Satan shall never seduce the true Saints into such confusions," Tate argued, because they would not allow "various manners of educations and of languages used" or the "dispositions of some sections and people's [*sic*] . . . to stop the love and unity and ones [i.e., oneness] of the true people and Saints of God."[35]

Even though her missionary activity beyond the United States was relatively minor, Tate's mention of languages, peoples, foreign lands, and islands demonstrates how an awareness of the world beyond U.S. borders bubbles up from conceptualizing cultural and political work in ways that span regional dimensions. Tate's refusal to accept the divisions created by her (white) countrymen not only established unity within her communion but also allowed migrating pilgrims to view themselves from outside national borders. Cultural and literary historian Michelle Stephens has reminded us how Frantz Fanon saw nationalism and transnationalism as coupled and emerging together as colonized peoples searched out the very possibilities of a national consciousness. As Fanon concluded his speech to the 1959 Second Congress of Black Artists and Writers in Rome: "It is at the heart of national consciousness that international consciousness lives and grows. And this two-fold emerging is ultimately only the source of all culture."[36] Tate's spiritual empire mirrors that imagined by figures like Marcus Garvey, who have generally been described simply as black nationalists and have been seen as quite different from Pentecostals, who often prided themselves on their ability to cross racial boundaries. Fauset identifies Black Jews and the Moorish Science Temple as both "Islamic" and "nationalistic." But what connects these groups with their Pentecostal counterparts is that they all frame their collective identity in far broader terms than U.S. society had allowed for those of African descent. As Stephens explained in reference to the Universal Negro Improvement Association (UNIA) founder, "Marcus Garvey held up an alternative model for the representation of a diasporic black political community, the notion of a worldwide black empire that would shadow the travels of the Western imperial powers." Garvey and other Caribbean colonials like Claude McKay and C. L. R. James "reimagined political identity, black specifically, in non-national and non-ethnocentric terms."[37]

Pentecostals' embryonic transnationalism evolved from different cultural networks and a different historical legacy than the transnationalism of Garvey or that of emergent Islamic alternatives. Black Pentecostals' globally inflected rhetoric was more tentative than its competitors among the Moors and the Garveyites. Caribbean migration to northern cities deepened the UNIA's dominant presence in Harlem and other northern neighborhoods and fostered the emergence of Garvey and the developing proto-Islamic movements. From Masonic underpinnings, the Moorish Science Temple and the Nation of Islam imagined an Asiatic black nation connecting all non-Europeans to a primordial past when ancient Egyptians reigned and black civilization was believed to emerge in Asia. In seeing people of African descent primarily as "Moorish" or as "Asiatic Black Men," these religionists argued implicitly that foreign lands were ultimately more significant than the United States in defining who black people were and to whom they belonged.[38] This message offered escape from the clutches of a land organized against black interests. As one early observer of the Moors argued, "Complete emancipation through a change of status from 'Negro' to 'Asiatic' promised an easy way to salvation."[39]

What Mother Tate (along with other Pentecostals) and the Moors (followed later by the Nation of Islam) represented were two, often competing, attempts to define themselves and their followers beyond their apparent links to the larger (white) society in the United States. When Moorish Science Temple founder Noble Drew Ali discussed what made the "Moorish Divine National Movement" significant and powerful, he explained that once followers were "incorporated in this government" of Moors, they could now become "recognized by all other nations of the world."[40] In their quest to escape (white) man-made divisions, black religionists reached for the world beyond the nation's borders. In the wake of the mass migrations after World War I, black activists and religionists reconceived the separatism that had animated the rise of black independent denominations in the decades immediately after slavery. Black organizational networks, religious and otherwise, spanned the old regional divisions, shaping how black people would define community to meet the demands of a new world. While black Holiness and Pentecostal leaders (of both sexes) asserted independence from (white) outsiders, onlookers, and benefactors, the Baptist churches and religious societies from which these religious leaders had emerged were immersed in the very muck of the American terrain and a necessary embrace of their white counterparts.

Father Divine, who held such a prominent place in Fauset's book, was the apotheosis of the nonracialist promise only ephemerally realized in the idealized memories of Azusa Street among the earliest Pentecostals. While Fauset linked Divine to "cults" defined by "faith healing" and "holiness" and not Pentecostalism, Divine's followers often practiced glossolalia, and Father Divine himself—when still called George Baker—had attended the 1906 revival at Azusa Street where he reportedly spoke in tongues as well.[41] Despite his stronger links to Charles Fillmore, Unity, and the New Thought movement of the prior century, Father Divine sought a new basis for religious community beyond U.S.-defined racial identity, as all of these northern cults did. With a stance that went far beyond simple "race neutrality" toward a perspective of determined nonracialism, Divine's ministry, which reached its height in Harlem during the thirties and then continued in Philadelphia in the forties, represented a radicalization of the sentiments for unity found in Tate's attempts to hold her church fellowship together. Nothing captured Divine's sentiments more than his simple refusal to describe people as white or black in an age obsessed with notions of racial purity. (He described people instead as "dark complected" and "light complected.")[42] His rejection of race paralleled his rejection of national identity. "I am none of your nationalities," Father Divine once said in reference to his divine identity. "You don't have to think I AM an American. . . . I AM none of them."[43]

But in truth few ministers were more committed than Robinson, Tate, Smith, and Horn to new conceptions of religious community that would overtake boundaries of region and even nation. And perhaps no one of these expressed this passion more bracingly than Robinson did directly in the teeth of an American nationalist sentiment unquestionably at its height. Not long after the Japanese attacked Pearl Harbor and the United States and Japan declared war on one another, an FBI report filed in 1942 alleged that Robinson was an agitator because she had stated publicly that she had "nothing against the Japanese."[44] For Robinson, sworn enemies of the United States were not the enemies of the people of God. And while many African Americans in this period did indeed feel kinship with the Japanese as an emerging nonwhite people and nation confronting the West, it was Mother Robinson's desire for converts that seemed to animate her reported views of the Japanese.[45] Robinson, Horn, and Tate would not achieve the actual global dimensions that their contemporary Father Divine did or their Pentecostal successors would in the postwar period. But black women leaders within Pentecostalism seem especially assertive in their embrace of expansive notions of religious community. They had already crossed the boundaries of gender and territory, and in their entrance to the public arena their very presence—more than any specific doctrine or practice—embodied the challenge black Pentecostalism represented to prior conceptions of respectability in the now more cosmopolitan world they inhabited.

Notes

1. Arthur Huff Fauset Collection, Special Collections Department, Van Pelt Library, University of Pennsylvania, Philadelphia, Box 5, Folder 96, unnumbered page.

2. Arthur Huff Fauset, *Black Gods of the Metropolis: Negro Religious Cults of the Urban North* (1944; Philadelphia: University of Pennsylvania Press, 2002), 7, 80.

3. Ira De A. Reid, *In a Minor Key: Negro Youth in Story and Fact* (Washington, D.C.: American Council on Education, 1940), 84–85, quoted in Fauset, *Black Gods*, 7.

4. See Barbara Dianne Savage, "Biblical and Historical Imperatives: Toward a History of Ideas about the Political Role of Black Churches," in *African Americans and the Bible: Sacred Texts and Social Textures*, ed. Vincent Wimbush (New York: Continuum, 2000), 367–88.

5. Milton Sernett, *Bound for the Promised Land: African American Religion and the Great Migration* (Durham, N.C.: Duke University Press, 1997), 7. See also Wallace D. Best, *Passionately Human, No Less Divine: Religion and Culture in Black Chicago, 1915–1952* (Princeton, N.J.: Princeton University Press, 2005), 2. Randall K. Burkett forcefully argues a similar case in "The Baptist Church in the Years of Crisis: J. C. Austin and Pilgrim Baptist Church, 1926–1950," in *African-American Christianity: Essays in History* (Berkeley: University of California Press, 1994), 135.

6. Judith Weisenfeld, "On Jordan's Stormy Banks: Margins, Center and Bridges in African American Religious History," in *New Directions in American Religious History*, ed. Harry S. Stout and D. G. Hart (New York: Oxford University Press, 1997), 433.

7. See Barbara Dianne Savage's foreword to the 2002 edition of Fauset's classic text, *Black Gods of the Metropolis* (Philadelphia: University of Pennsylvania Press), ix. There she writes: "Fauset did not follow the lead of other scholars at the time who designated as 'cults' most Christian holiness, Pentecostal, and storefront churches. He distinguished the latter institutions by referring to them not as cults but as 'orthodox evangelical churches.'"

8. Fauset, *Black Gods*, 68.

9. Ibid., 9.

10. Ibid., 69.

11. Ibid., 14.

12. See, for example, Jerma A. Jackson, *Singing in My Soul: Black Gospel Music in a Secular Age* (Chapel Hill: University of North Carolina Press, 2004) and Anthea D. Butler, *Women in the Church of God in Christ: Making a Sanctified World* (Chapel Hill: University of North Carolina Press, 2007).

13. Arthur Huff Fauset Collection, Special Collections Department, Van Pelt Library, University of Pennsylvania, Philadelphia, Box 5, Folder 96, unnumbered page.

14. For an account of Ida Robinson's visions, see Harold Dean Trulear, "Reshaping Black Pastoral Theology: The Vision of Bishop Ida B. Robinson," *Journal of Religious Thought* 46, no. 1 (Summer–Fall 1989): 21. For additional biographical information about her life, music, and sermons, see Harold Dean Trulear, "Ida B. Robinson: The Mother as Symbolic Presence," in *Portraits of a Generation: Early Pentecostal Leaders*, ed. James R. Goff Jr. and Grant Wacker (Fayetteville: University of Arkansas Press, 2002), 309–24, and Bettye Collier-Thomas, ed., *Daughters of Thunder: Black Women Preachers and Their Sermons, 1850–1979* (San Francisco: Jossey-Bass, 1998), 194–210.

15. *American Baptist*, June 26, 1868, as quoted in James Melvin Washington, *Frustrated Fellowship: The Black Baptist Quest for Social Power* (Macon, Ga.: Mercer University Press, 1986), 109.

16. For the African legacy evident in female leadership roles, see Cheryl Townsend Gilkes, "The Politics of 'Silence': Dual-Sex Political Systems and Women's Traditions of Conflict in African-American Religion," in *African American Christianity: Essays in History*, ed. Paul E. Johnson (Berkeley: University of California Press, 1997).

17. Cheryl Townsend Gilkes, "'Together and in Harness': Women's Traditions in the Sanctified Church," in *African American Religious Thought: An Anthology*, ed. Cornel West and Eddie S. Glaude Jr. (Louisville, Ky.: Westminster John Knox, 2003), 636, and see Anthea D. Butler, "Church Mothers and Migration in the Church of God in Christ," in *Religion in the*

American South: Protestants and Others in History and Culture, ed. Beth Barton Schweiger and Donald G. Mathews (Chapel Hill: University of North Carolina Press, 2004).

18. Wallace Best, " 'The Spirit of the Holy Ghost Is a Male Spirit': African American Preaching Women and the Paradoxes of Gender," in *Women and Religion in the African Diaspora: Knowledge, Power, and Performance,* ed. R. Marie Griffith and Barbara Dianne Savage (Baltimore, Md.: Johns Hopkins University Press, 2006), 117–18.

19. Kelly Willis Mendiola, "The Hand of a Woman: Four Holiness-Pentecostal Evangelists and American Culture, 1840–1930" (Ph.D. diss., University of Texas at Austin, 2002), 291–92.

20. Helen M. Lewis and Meharry H. Lewis, *Seventy-fifth Anniversary Yearbook of the Church of the Living God, Pillar and Ground of the Truth, 1903–1978* (Nashville, Tenn.: New and Living Way, 1978), 9–10.

21. Mary Magdalena Tate, "A Special Message from Mother to Her Children," in *Mary Lena Lewis Tate: Collected Letters and Manuscripts,* ed. Meharry H. Lewis (Nashville, Tenn.: New and Living Way, 2003), 36–41.

22. Quoted in Trulear, "Reshaping Black Pastoral Theology," 21.

23. I have adopted both the reading of Stuart Hall's ideas and the metaphor of joints from Brent Edwards, "The Uses of *Diaspora,*" *Social Text* 66 (Spring 2001): 64–66.

24. For an account of the complicated place the Azusa Street revival holds in Pentecostal origins, see Joe Creech, "Visions of Glory: The Place of the Azusa Street Revival in Pentecostal History," *Church History* 65 (1996): 405–24.

25. For a brief, biographical essay on Horn, along with a small selection of her sermons, see Collier-Thomas, *Daughters of Thunder,* 173–93. For Horn's place in the Harlem community and religious life, including descriptions of her church building, see Cheryl Lynn Greenberg, *Or Does It Explode? Black Harlem in the Great Depression* (New York: Oxford University Press, 1991), 59, and James Campbell, *Talking at the Gates: A Life of James Baldwin* (New York: Viking, 1991), 36.

26. "Church of All Faiths Now Favorite of Air Waves," *Amsterdam News,* October 31, 1936, Sherry Sherrod DuPree African-American Pentecostal and Holiness Collection, 1876–1989, Schomburg Center for Research in Black Culture, New York Public Library, New York, Box 10, Folder 17.

27. Best, *Passionately Human,* 115, 180; Best, "The Spirit of the Holy Ghost," 121.

28. Quoted in Paul Harvey, *Redeeming the South: Religious Cultures and Racial Identities among Southern Baptists, 1865–1925* (Chapel Hill: University of North Carolina Press, 1997), 63.

29. Evelyn Brooks Higginbotham, *Righteous Discontent: The Women's Movement in the Black Baptist Church, 1880–1920* (Cambridge, Mass.: Harvard University Press, 1993), 197; Nancy Fraser, *Unruly Practices: Power, Discourse, and Gender in Contemporary Social Theory* (Minneapolis: University of Minnesota Press, 1989), 174.

30. Higginbotham, *Righteous Discontent,* 196.

31. Linking together surveillance with state mechanisms of control, Michel Foucault argues: "The exercise of discipline presupposes a mechanism that coerces by means of observation." See his *Discipline and Punish: The Birth of the Prison,* trans. Alex Sheridan (New York: Vintage Books, 1977), 170.

32. Arthur Huff Fauset Collection, Special Collections Department, Van Pelt Library, University of Pennsylvania, Philadelphia, Box 5, Folder 96, unnumbered page.

33. Langston Hughes, "The Negro Artist and the Racial Mountain," in *The Norton Anthology of African American Literature*, ed. Henry Louis Gates Jr. and Nellie Y. McKay (New York: W. W. Norton, 1997), 1271.

34. Arthur Huff Fauset Collection, Special Collections Department, Van Pelt Library, University of Pennsylvania, Philadelphia, Box 5, Folder 96, unnumbered page. The reference to being baptized in Jesus's name suggests that Mrs. W was connected with Apostolic Oneness Pentecostalism—a minority expression within the Pentecostal movement that challenged traditional trinitarian doctrine.

35. Mary Magdalena Tate, *The Constitution Government and General Decree Book of the Church of the Living God, the Pillar and Ground of the Truth* (Chattanooga, Tenn.: New and Living Way, 1924), 58–59.

36. Michelle A. Stephens, "Black Transnationalism and the Politics of National Identity: West Indian Intellectuals in Harlem in the Age of War and Revolution," *American Quarterly* 50, no. 3 (September 1998): 592; Frantz Fanon, *The Wretched of the Earth*, trans. Constance Farrington (New York: Grove, 1963), 247–48.

37. Michelle Stephens, "Re-imagining the Shape and Borders of Black Political Space," *Radical History Review* 87 (Spring 1997): 173. See also Michelle Ann Stephens, *Black Empire: The Masculine Global Imaginary of Caribbean Intellectuals in the United States, 1914–1962* (Durham, N.C.: Duke University Press, 2005), especially chapter 3.

38. Nathaniel Deutsch, " 'The Asiatic Black Man': An African American Orientalism?" *Journal of Asian American Studies* 4, no. 3 (October 2001): 196–98.

39. Fauset, *Black Gods*, 42.

40. Noble Drew Ali, *Moorish Literature* (n.p., 1928), Moorish Science Temple of America Collection, 1926–1967, Schomburg Center for Research in Black Culture, New York Public Library, New York, Box 1, Folder 2, p. 6.

41. Jill Watts, *God, Harlem U.S.A.: The Father Divine Story* (Berkeley: University of California Press, 1992), 25. For more on Azusa Street's role as the mythical origin of the Pentecostal movement, see Creech, "Visions of Glory," 405–24.

42. See Robert Weisbrot, *Father Divine: The Utopian Evangelist of the Depression Era Who Became an American Legend* (Boston: Beacon, 1983), 100–102.

43. Quoted in Watts, *God, Harlem U.S.A.*, 88.

44. "Report on Foreign Inspired Agitation among American Negroes in Philadelphia Division," Federal Bureau of Investigation, File 100-135-37-2, August 9, 1942, as quoted in Trulear, "Ida B. Robinson," 317. See also Sherry Sherrod DuPree, *African-American Holiness Pentecostal Movement* (New York: Garland, 1996), 418.

45. For black kinship with Japanese nationalism before World War II, see Ernest Allen Jr., "When Japan Was 'Champion of the Darker Races': Satokata Takahashi and the Flowering of Black Messianic Nationalism," *Black Scholar* 24 (Winter 1994): 23–46, and Ernest Allen, "Waiting for Tojo: The Pro-Japan Vigil of Black Missourians, 1932–1943," *Gateway Heritage* 16 (Fall 1995): 38–55.

TWO · "Grace Has Given God a Vacation": The History and Development of the Theology of the United House of Prayer of All People

DANIELLE BRUNE SIGLER

In February 1942, in a nearly illegible hand, Arthur Huff Fauset scribbled in his notebook, recording his observations of Bishop Charles M. "Daddy" Grace's United House of Prayer for All People.

> If Bishop Grace himself is present, many worshipers will march or dance to the front and grasp his hand. Not infrequently the worshiper will place a bill of requisite denomination in his hand. Often the mere touch of the leader's hand is sufficient to induce terrific contortion of the body or to produce a state akin to catalepsy. The Bishop assures me there was nothing on his person (such as an electric battery) to account for this phenomenon. It is the action of the Holy Spirit he says.[1]

Fauset was interested in many of the aspects of the House of Prayer that he had captured in these notes: Grace's charismatic spiritual power, his followers' attitudes toward him, and the emphasis on money and fundraising during worship services. His notes also hinted at the skepticism with which Fauset and others outside of the church greeted Grace's claims. Could spiritual power really account for the ecstatic responses of his followers? Were Daddy Grace and the House of Prayer aberrations or were they similar to the other religious organizations that Fauset was observing?

In Fauset's final evaluation of the United House of Prayer, his dissertation and its published incarnation, *Black Gods of the Metropolis,* Fauset broadly categorized the church as a Holiness church with an interest in faith healing. He argued, however, that Daddy Grace's power and dominance had transformed the organization into something quite different. The church's beliefs, he wrote, "boil down to a worship of Daddy Grace. God appears to be all but forgotten."[2] He included a quote from Grace to make his point: "Never mind about God. Salvation is by Grace only. . . . Grace has given God a vacation, and since God is on His vacation, don't worry Him. . . . If you ask God to save you, He cannot save you. You must have Grace to be saved. Only I can save you."[3] According to Fauset, Grace had superseded God, a move that made the House of Prayer radically different from its Holiness forebears and from one of his other subjects, Bishop Ida Robinson's Mt. Sinai Holy Church.

When Fauset's book, *Black Gods of the Metropolis*, was published in May 1944, William H. Baldwin reviewed it in the *New York Times Book Review* under the headline "Negro Spellbinders." In spite of the fact that Fauset's book devoted more time to Father Divine, Baldwin devoted most of his review to extensive quotes from Fauset's discussion of Daddy Grace. He reprinted the quote that has come to dominate scholarship on Grace, "There is at least a spark of genius in this man, who assumes the name of 'Grace' . . . for the Bible is replete with references to one or another form of Grace. . . . [A]ccording to Dr. Fauset, he has been heard admonishing his worshippers, 'Grace has given God a vacation.' "[4] And so Baldwin inaugurated a trend that then continued among scholars working in the field of African American religion.[5]

These historians and scholars of religion have focused on the "Grace has given God a vacation" quote and have not paid attention to much else. E. Franklin Frazier quoted Fauset directly in *The Negro Church in America* (1964) and Joseph R. Washington recycled the excerpted quote in *Black Sects and Cults* (1972). Wilson Jeremiah Moses paraphrased Fauset's quote in *Black Messiahs and Uncle Toms* (1982), which he introduced with the explanation that "doctrine consisted of little more than a play on words." Even as recently as 1998, Benjamin Sevitch, in "When Black Gods Preached on Earth," similarly introduced Fauset's quote by adding, "[Grace's] theology became little more than a play on words."[6] By focusing almost exclusively on this excerpted quote, scholars have missed the complexity and richness of Grace and his ministry.

The full quotation from Grace, which appeared in Fauset's appendix, demonstrated the innovation of the House of Prayer's theology. Far from being a simple "play on words," the "vacation" statement revealed the compelling evolution of a Pentecostal-inspired theology. By examining this quote only in part, generations of scholars have missed the vital and fairly consistent theology at the heart of the House of Prayer and also underestimated Grace's ability to reconcile traditional Holiness/Pentecostal theology with innovations that centered on his background and personality.

It is important to recognize that by the time Fauset began his study of Grace and the House of Prayer, Grace had been preaching for twenty years. Fauset devoted only a few paragraphs to the "origin" of each organization that he studied. Fauset's goal was not to provide a comprehensive history of each organization, but to rely primarily on ethnography as a means of understanding each "cult." His approach was reasonable for an anthropologist seeking to understand "why the cults attract." Yet most subsequent historians and religious studies scholars who have utilized Fauset's work have focused on Fauset's analysis and neither made use of the testimonies and other materials he provided in the appendix nor examined the broader histories of these organizations.

The organization and theology that Fauset documented in 1939 had developed and changed as the House of Prayer grew and prospered. Over time, Grace had combined Pentecostal traditions with new ideas and practices borne of his unique personality and experience. Only by examining Daddy Grace's and the House of Prayer's growth and development can one continue Fauset's work of moving beyond the "merely superficial aspects" of the man and his ministry.

Apostolic Roots

The man who became famous as Daddy Grace arrived in New Bedford, Massachusetts, as Marcelino Manuel DeGraca at the turn of the twentieth century. He was an immigrant from the Cape Verde Islands, off the western coast of Africa. Fauset offered this brief assessment of his background: "The founder of this cult, Bishop Charles Emmanuel Grace, is a man of mixed parentage, said to be Negro and Portuguese. Bronze of color, and with flowing hair, he does not admit to being a Negro." Though Fauset clearly believed that Grace was a "Negro," Grace, like most Cape Verdean immigrants of his era, understood himself to be white and Portuguese. The disparity in his perception of his identity and most Americans' perceptions of his identity was a source of contention throughout his life.

Throughout southeastern Massachusetts, DeGraca, now known as Charles M. Grace, worked in the area's cranberry bogs, at a grocery store, and as a dishwasher in a hotel. Unlike another of Fauset's subjects, Father Divine, Grace had not chosen his last name in conjunction with his ministry. He had adopted the anglicized name "Grace" at least nine years before he founded his ministry. It is not entirely clear what ultimately prompted Grace to begin preaching the gospel. Unlike popular religious leaders like Billy Sunday and Aimee Semple McPherson, a conversion narrative was not part of Grace's preaching arsenal. In his later years, he seemed unwilling to acknowledge a past in which he might have been anything less than God's unique representative on earth. After frustration in southeastern Massachusetts and travel throughout the country, in 1919 Bishop Grace built his first House of Prayer himself, in a West Wareham, Massachusetts, field, and created the United House of Prayer for All People of the Church on the Rock of the Apostolic Faith.

The two components of the name of the church shed light on two major influences on Grace's ministry. The first, United House of Prayer for All People, emphasized the inclusiveness likely borne of Grace's own immigrant experience. Historian Timothy Smith has argued that American migrants and immigrants frequently have either turned to new faiths or reconfigured existing faiths that emphasized the "unity of all mankind."[7] Grace was no different. He had taken the name of his church from the Bible's book of Isaiah, a prophetic Old Testament book popular with and frequently quoted by Christians.[8] Isaiah's author, amid optimistic pronouncements of the future, explained that God's covenant extended to "the sons of the stranger, that join themselves to the LORD" and that God's vision was an inclusive one.[9] According to his prophecy in chapter 56, "Even [the sons of the stranger] will I bring to my holy mountain, and make them joyful in my house of prayer . . . for mine house shall be called an house of prayer for all people." Given its emphasis on inclusion, it is not surprising that Grace, the "son of a stranger" himself and a man so frequently excluded in his American life, turned to this verse. In creating the *United* House of Prayer for *All People*, Grace was like migrants before him, seeking to establish a faith that would address the "problems of unity and diversity" that had been attendant to a nation of immigrants. In doing so, he used his own personal history and national/ethnic identity that had previously been a liability to his advantage, in order to reach out to others who might feel alienated, to provide himself with a mysterious allure, and to create a missionary narrative supporting his ministry.

The second component of the House of Prayer's full name, one that Fauset, incidentally, did not include in *Black Gods of the Metropolis*, points to the influence of an Azusa-inspired Pentecostalism. Though he would offer conflicting accounts of his ordination (or lack of ordination) throughout his life, Grace once claimed that he had been "commissioned as an evangelist of the Church Founded on the Rock of the Apostolic Faith a number of years ago." Recently discovered photographic evidence provides the first documentation of Grace in Los Angeles and provides a likely location for his interaction with the theology of Azusa.[10] It is also possible that he experienced the teachings of emergent Pentecostalism through the thriving Holiness/Pentecostal community throughout southeastern Massachusetts. Though a connection with Azusa seems likely, there were a host of other ministries of the era that had incorporated "Apostolic" into their names, such as the Apostolic Faith Mission Church of God (est. 1906) and the Church of Christ of the Apostolic Faith (est. 1919). Like Grace, these organizations often chose "Apostolic" as a designation of their belief in "oneness," as opposed to trinitarian Pentecostal organizations. As a believer in oneness, Grace and House of Prayer members regarded "Father," "Son," and "Holy Spirit" as different "titles" of the same God, rather than different entities.[11] This did not mean that Jesus, the Holy Spirit, and God the Father were conflated; each continued to play a unique role and together they formed the core of the worship experience.

The theology that Grace initially offered his followers fit squarely within the Pentecostal tradition, something that was obvious to the New Bedford reporter who labeled Grace's church a "little pentecostal mission." Grace, his ministers, and House of Prayer members consistently expressed a preference for "Apostolic" as a designation of their faith, generally rejecting the term "Pentecostal." Nevertheless, Grace's earliest statements of doctrine exemplified the "'four-fold' gospel of Pentecostalism": a belief in "personal salvation, Holy Ghost Baptism, divine healing, and the Lord's soon return."[12] In 1921, in Grace's earliest recorded statement about the tenets of the House of Prayer's faith, he expounded this very fourfold gospel:

> We go back to the faith of the early Christians . . . and we literally interpret the Bible. We believe that these are the last days and that what the world needs is greater faith in God's word. People who come to our meetings get the baptism of the Holy Ghost. . . . As for receiving the gifts of unknown tongues that is promised in the Bible and the manifestations of this gift is only one of the many powers which is given to members of our church.[13]

Grace's statement is clearly based in a Pentecostal/apostolic faith with its emphasis on "baptism of the Holy Ghost," "the last days," and the "gifts" and "powers" congregants received. Indeed, Grace could recite verse after verse in support of his theology. A local reporter noted:

> Mr. Grace is especially familiar with those portions of the Scripture referring to the various "signs of Christ" upon which his faith depends. He can quote reference after reference. For instance, speaking of the gift of tongues, which comes with the Holy Ghost and which was exemplified once or twice by members of his following at the House of Prayer revival services, the bishop cited Mark 16:15–18, Joel 2:28, Acts 2:4, 39; I Cor. 14:2, Acts 10:44–47, and Acts 19:1–16 as Bible passages substantiating the speaking of unknown tongues.[14]

He turned to Psalm 149, Luke 15, and Jeremiah 31:13–15 to substantiate the dancing that took place in the House of Prayer.[15] Grace's comments made it clear that speaking in tongues as a sign of baptism in the Holy Spirit was a prominent part of House of Prayer worship. Pentecostals had located the foundation for their belief in (and had taken their name from) the description of speaking in tongues in the book of Acts, when the Holy Spirit bestowed "tongues of fire" upon the apostles on the day of Pentecost. In Pentecostal practice, as in Acts, most of these tongues were not known earthly languages. Though some sought to interpret these messages, for many, the experience itself was the focus, as the gift of tongues signified the presence of the Holy Spirit. However, some Pentecostals described not only speaking in "unknown tongues" but in actual human languages as well. This practice, sometimes referred to as "missionary tongues," was not altogether uncommon. There were, for instance, references to these occurrences at Azusa. The gift of missionary tongues had also been bestowed on Grace's followers. Grace explained, "People who have never spoken a word of any language other than English all their lives . . . have come to the mission and there, the inspiration has come upon them to speak in Chinese, Hindustan, Hebrew or some other language of which they have absolutely no knowledge."[16] This association between multilingual abilities and being spirit-filled may have worked to Grace's advantage, as he had at least three languages at his command. To be sure, for believers, there was a clear difference between the gift of missionary tongues and learned multilingual abilities. Nevertheless, it is possible that Grace's ability to speak several languages influenced and inspired his congregations as they sought related spiritual gifts.

Two other aspects of the fourfold gospel—the urgent need for personal salvation and the impending end times—became apparent to anyone who gave Grace's 1920s gospel car a cursory look. Bible verses painted on the vehicle instructed onlookers in the fundamental beliefs of the House of Prayer, and verses from the Book of Revelation encouraged salvation as the end of time neared. Across the running board, Grace cautioned sinners via Matthew 24:37 that "as the days of Noah were, so shall also the coming of the son of man be" and continued with Matthew 24:38 over the hub of the back left tire, "For as in the days that were before the flood they were eating and drinking, marrying and giving in marriage, until the day that Noah entered the ark." Grace cautioned that the end was near and that Jesus's return was imminent. Revelation 1:7 was painted across the top of the car: "Behold, he cometh with the clouds: and every eye shall see him." This emphasis on the prophecy of Matthew and Revelation not only placed Grace squarely within the context of Pentecostal theology but also proved, as it did for other ministers, to be a compelling motivation for people to attend House of Prayer meetings to seek salvation.

In the late 1930s he formalized the impending end and announced the opening of the Flood Gate, an action that unleashed "a great sword ordained to smite the earth with unimaginable death and destruction."[17] Accordingly, Grace "made a call for the people to come and get saved before 1940."[18] This meant the beginning of the end, and a rush to save souls and win converts ensued. By 1941, with the "great cloud of war hanging very low over all the earth" and it looking "as if the entire human race is doomed to death and destruction," salvation through Grace provided the only answer (according to Grace).[19] Fortunately, Grace intervened on man's behalf and God granted Grace's prayer for the delay of the destruction that was to occur in December 1940. All of his children were not yet saved and Grace, as a loving father, saw it his duty to delay the end. Yet into the late fifties, Grace continued to caution, "These are the last days before the advent of Jesus Christ. The wicked are soon destroyed."[20] Grace was increasingly emerging as an intermediary between humanity and God.

This relationship was also apparent through faith healing, another part of the "four-fold gospel of Pentecostalism" that was vitally important to the House of Prayer. The belief in the power to heal stemmed, in part, from the "Great Commission" in Mark 16:18: "[T]hey will lay their hands on the sick, and they will recover." Pentecostal faith healers usually invoked Jesus's name in the midst of healing. Grace did the same, laying on hands and saying, "In Christ's name be healed." According to Pentecostal believers, Jesus, and by extension God, could work through intermediaries like Grace to effect healing. This belief was apparent in one of the recorded sermons released by Paramount in 1926 entitled, "You May Be Healed By the Power of God." In this piece, Grace recounted the story from Luke 8 in which a woman touched the hem of Jesus's garment and was healed. As Grace concluded the story, he told listeners of "the wonderful powers of Christ to save the day." He added, "Therefore children let us believe. Let us be healed, for Jesus Christ is just the same today. Into this room, healing those who believe by faith and have been healed of all the manner of diseases. For Jesus Christ is our loving savior and healer too. Be glad for him. Amen." Jesus was at the heart of Grace's healing experience and healing was at the heart of his ministry.

As Fauset's transcriptions of House of Prayer testimonies demonstrated, faith healing proved to be a powerful draw for Grace and the many potential converts who came to his meetings seeking a healing experience.[21] It is somewhat surprising that very few subsequent scholars have devoted attention to Fauset's transcriptions of House of Prayer member testimonies. They provide answers not only about the appeal of the House of Prayer but also about the fundamental beliefs of its members. The emphasis on faith healing continued into the last decade of Grace's life. As Grace's ministry expanded, these "miracle converts" often became the foundation of the local Houses of Prayer.[22] They offered their testimony in meetings and helped spread the word of Grace and his healing powers. One House of Prayer member composed the following as a testimony to Grace's healing abilities and the beginnings of his ministry in a new city:

> He came to Augusta and pitched his tent,
> Began talking to his God,
> And every body that did believe
> is receiving their reward.

> They brought the cripples, they brought the lame,
> And some was even blind,
> And they all was healed that did believe,
> And even the sin sick mind.[23]

Outside of Pentecostal circles, the practice of faith healing remained controversial and it provided critics with the opportunity to challenge Grace's ministry. While Grace was traveling in 1926, opposing ministers tried to have him arrested for "treating human ailments without a license," and he was actually jailed for "preaching that the sick may recover by faith."[24] Grace seemed to suggest that this was a last-ditch effort after he had been "arrested and dismissed three times in court when specific charges were not brought against me."[25] Such a charge may not have been a common occurrence, but the practice of faith healing gave his critics grounds to challenge his right to preach. Grace spoke freely about such persecution, primarily because he had triumphed over it and because it placed him in the distinguished company of Jesus, the apostles, and early church fathers, connections he had begun to cultivate.

While the fourfold gospel remained at the core of House of Prayer theology (and does so to this day), it is important to recognize that as the ministry and Grace's status grew and changed, so too did the interpretation of traditional Christian ideas. Fauset was absolutely correct in assessing something highly unique in the House of Prayer traditions. He simply missed the depth of the change and its relationship to Grace's foreign birth. By asserting that the theology was little more than a "play on words," Fauset encouraged generations of scholars to discount the beliefs of House of Prayer members and to miss a truly intriguing alteration of conventional Christian theology. Contrary to Fauset's assertion, Grace had not displaced God the Father; Grace had usurped the role of Jesus. In doing so, he established his authority on his foreign birth and his spiritual gifts. The persecution he faced—something that was at the center of the "vacation quote"—also became a powerful indicator to himself and to his members that he and they were on the right path.

Evolution of the House of Prayer Theology

Throughout the early days of his ministry, Grace had been consistently vague about the land of his birth. He was pleased to be regarded as "foreign." Indeed, he likely accentuated his accent as a means of separating himself from American blacks. Such efforts were not uncommon among Cape Verdeans. Even decades later, Cape Verdean Belmira Nunes Lopes explained that when she traveled in the South, "I always acted as if I wasn't too well acquainted with the English language because I didn't want to be discriminated against. . . . I always put on a fake accent. . . . I didn't want anyone to think I was an American black because I am darker than most so-called white persons."[26] It was more advantageous to be identified as an immigrant or "foreigner" than it was an "American black." During his first trip to the American South, Grace labeled himself a "Portuguese Faith Healer," providing some connection with his actual past. That identity, however, soon gave way to a new one born of his 1923 pilgrimage to the Holy Land.

As countless pilgrims before him had done, when Grace recounted his travels he described walking in the path of biblical figures before him, including spending the "whole night in the manger at Bethlehem in Christmas of 1923 . . . and the next day . . . in the fields where the angels said to the shepherds 'Peace on earth.' "[27] Stories like these from the Holy Land took center stage as Grace told of his trip. Unlike most of his fellow pilgrims, Grace wanted not only to walk in the footsteps of Jesus but to do some of Jesus's work as well. By his own account, Grace had "worked hard, preaching, all the time I was away, and only rested on the voyage home. I preached every day, most of the time."[28]

The experience was so significant that even in the first days after he returned, Grace knew that his Holy Land trip would be integrated into his ministry. Grace had told reporters that he brought with him "costumes from Jerusalem" and that he "[expected] to wear the costumes when he gives talks to his congregation on his journey."[29] These robes gave Grace a visual connection with the Holy Land, a link that he also fostered with his new beard. He had grown the beard, he said, in deference to the customs of the land. Though initially he was unsure if he would, Grace kept the beard, thus offering followers another tangible connection between himself and the Holy Land. In adopting a Holy Land identity, Grace continued to challenge the designation "Negro" by further distancing himself from the connection with the Cape Verde Islands and their potential link to Africa.

The importance of his Holy Land connection became clear when Grace recorded two sermons on the Paramount record label in 1926. Though his appearance on the label placed him among African American performers including Blind Lemon Jefferson and Ma Rainey, Grace billed himself as "Bishop Grace from the Holy Land." From this point on, it was difficult to discern whether Grace had just visited or if the Holy Land was the mysterious land of his birth. The Paramount recordings also point to another aspect of Grace's ministry that may have helped to link him to the Holy Land: a clearly foreign but not easily identifiable accent. By adopting a Holy Land identity, not only had he severed potential connections to American "blackness," but he had laid the foundations for the missionary narrative that underscored his ministry. Grace pursued this tie to the Holy Land throughout his life. In 1934 he explained that his gospel "came not from men, neither from the institution of men, but from Jerusalem, where all of the prophets went to inquire of God."[30] According to this statement, even a visit to Jerusalem could substantiate his authority. Yet in a church publication from the 1950s, a large photo of Grace appeared accompanied by the caption "Bishop C. M. Grace, The Holy Prophet from Jerusalem," seeming to suggest that Jerusalem was Grace's homeland.[31]

Grace was insistent throughout his life that his foreign birth was fundamental to his claim to be a prophet, or a bringer of salvation. In a 1956 *Jet* magazine article, Grace made this abundantly clear when he cast aspersions on his then-rival Prophet Jones by asking, "How can an American be a Prophet? Where did he meet God to tell him to be a Prophet?"[32] Grace's questions demonstrated that from his perspective a prophet could not be American-born and proved just how vital his own foreign birth was to the authority of his ministry. Grace was, after all, "bringing them the word from Jerusalem."[33] Jones could make no such claims. After castigating Jones for claiming to be a prophet, Grace also connected his prophetic status with his practice of preaching "to all the people, black and white." Just as Isaiah had foretold in the chapters that Grace had taken for the name of the House of Prayer, the Lord would bring *everyone* together in his House of Prayer. Jones had failed that prophetic test as well. Grace, however, from the beginning had offered *all people* salvation via a Pentecostal-inspired gospel message.

Grace's foreign birth was obviously central to his claims of being a prophet of

God. He did, however, frequently describe himself as fulfilling a role more akin to savior. Indeed, as early as 1924, Grace placed himself in the tradition, if not the very position, of Jesus.[34] When Grace returned from the Holy Land, he carried not only robes and costumes, but also a photo of himself at the Sea of Galilee. In his right hand, he held a loaf of bread sliced into three pieces. In his left, a fish. The props ensured that an American audience could identify the location of the image. This photograph was a compelling visual indication of the shift Grace would make— increasingly aligning himself with Jesus.

In the early years of his ministry, even as Jesus remained at the heart of Grace's work as a healer and savior, Grace was the necessary channel through which the "power of God" could heal, and he was the man who helped people become a "friend" of Jesus. Grace began drawing parallels between Jesus's activities and his own. In his second recorded sermon, "The Power of God Can Raise His Friends from the Dead," Grace told the story of Jesus raising Lazarus from the dead from John 11. As he concluded, Grace told listeners, "We are also going to rise. Because we are the friend of Jesus and we have a hope to rise in the resurrection morning." This was a fairly conventional reading of John 11, but Grace may have had another reason for incorporating the story of Lazarus into his ministry. In 1925, Grace told followers that he had raised his own sister from the dead. That experience paralleled the story of Jesus and Lazarus. Grace's sister had been dead for several hours when he returned home. His family was weeping and mourning her loss. He prayed and prayed. Grace had told people that he could raise someone from the dead and now embraced the opportunity to prove it. After his prayers, his sister raised up and, according to Grace, "[was] alive again, singing the song of the resurrection."[35] In retelling his sister's story, Grace did not invoke Jesus's name specifically. He did, however, adopt the story and language of the gospels to describe his own actions, a fairly radical innovation.

Given this link early on in his ministry, it may be surprising to find that Grace did not immediately draw on his last name to substantiate his authority. Far from being "little more than a play on words," the theology that emerged had its roots in Pentecostalism and Grace's foreign, prophetic identity. Over time, Grace's connection to God would grow and change until it became a fully articulated theology that placed Grace in the context of biblical history. As this theology developed, references tying Grace's last name to the concept of biblical grace increased and became more central to the church's belief system. However, such connections are noticeably absent in the early years. Among the Bible verses written on one of Grace's early gospel cars was the following from Paul's Epistle to Titus 2:12, "teaching us that denying ungodliness and worldly lusts, we should live soberly, righteously, and godly, in the present world." It did not, however, include the preceding verse, "For the *grace* of God that bringeth salvation hath appeared to all men." As Grace's power grew, such references would become commonplace, but they were an outgrowth of his theology rather than the foundation of that theology.

Evidence for the conflation of Grace and Jesus can be found not only in the writings of House of Prayer members and Grace's sermons, but also in the visual traditions that emerged within the House of Prayer. In 1938 Grace posed before Harlem's best-known photographer, James VanDerZee.[36] In one of VanDerZee's photos, Grace sported robes that, if not the very ones he brought back from his Holy Land trip, would certainly evoke that voyage for his audience. Grace appeared as a shepherd, with a staff in one hand. Children gathered around him and he held one child in his arms. VanDerZee's vision became complete back in his studio as he inset a picture of Jesus similarly attired and surrounded by children in the upper left-hand corner of the print. The parallel was clear and compelling. The resulting photographs were incorporated into House of Prayer publications and were available to Grace's followers.[37] In later decades an even more overt image made its way into the House of Prayer. As G. Norman Eddy prepared his 1958–1959 article "Store-Front Religion," he noted, "In [Grace's] sanctuaries, he is pictured in the flowing robes associated with Christ. Upon the bishop's breast is depicted a bleeding sacred heart."[38] The September 1960 issue of *Grace Magazine,* appearing after Grace's death, featured a picture of Grace's head pasted onto the traditional body of a robed Jesus, with sacred heart and palms extended upward. Images, as they had throughout Grace's ministry, reinforced the theology of the House of Prayer and spoke to followers across Grace's religious empire.

Such images made the connection between Jesus and Grace quite clear, but essays in the House of Prayer's publication, *Grace Magazine,* clarified Grace's position. It was not as simple as graduate student Chancellor Williams had suggested when he conducted research for his dissertation in the 1940s. Williams noted, "The name of Jesus Christ was seldom mentioned. Daddy has taken His place."[39] His observation was accurate, but there was an interpretive structure that supported the tradition. Grace may have displaced Jesus in House of Prayer services, but in the sweep of biblical history, according to the House of Prayer, Grace could best be understood as being Jesus's successor.

Elder C. L. Jones, pastor of the Anacostia mission in Washington, D.C., contributed an article to *Grace Magazine,* entitled "One Man." Jones suspected that "some may think that I'm very partial in speaking of one man," but explained, "God has always in all ages had one man at a time who stood out above the others and held up the light of salvation to others."[40] Grace belonged to a lineage of men including Noah, Moses, David, John the Baptist, and Jesus before him. Sister Ruth Harris had explained, "When [Christ] had finished his work he chose another vessel to put his Grace in, and that chosen one would carry on the work of Grace."[41] Grace was a chosen and special man. Another House of Prayer member explained it this way: "God has always had a man to carry out His plan in behalf of the souls of men. That man is not God, but a servant of God." This concept of there being "one man" on earth throughout every era permeated the writing of Grace's followers and ministers. Even the name of his ministry supported such claims. Grace instructed his followers that "the House of Prayer is God's word therefore, the Blood of Jesus is in the word of God and God has only one man to carry the blood. How many men God will trust with the blood to save the world; to make one faith?"[42] Grace himself articulated his role. He explained, "There is one true religion, that of the House of Prayer. This was the faith of antiquity embraced by the great ones of old, including Jesus. . . . [I]t is being restored to the modern world by me."[43] Fauset himself picked up on this tradition. After noting "God was all but forgotten," Fauset wrote, "the followers concentrate their thoughts on His 'great man' Grace." Indeed, Fauset uses the language followers frequently adopted to talk about Grace as a "great man" or the "one man."[44] The rest of Fauset's analysis, however, seems to ignore what was clear to most of Grace's followers—that he was not a replacement for God but was instead a successor to Jesus.

As such, Grace's birth had come to take on a significant role. As he addressed the House of Prayer on the occasion of his birthday he said, "I suppose you all are happy and rejoicing highly because that one 25th day of January a boy child was born who is the cause of your joy here tonight."[45] A quick gloss of this statement might suggest an error. Clearly Grace meant December 25 and was referring to Jesus. The context of the article made it clear, however, that Grace had referred to himself and his own date of birth. The writer who quoted Grace continued: "On that night all of The Houses of Prayer throughout the world was born, all of the different auxiliaries were born. The different talented musicians of The House of Prayer were born. The stars that shone that night have never shone again. The wind that blew that night have never blown again, there has never been a night like that night since."[46] Grace had begun to reconfigure his life story in the image of Jesus.

In light of the connection to Jesus, Grace's persecution took on new life and took center stage within the ministry. Grace suggested that his own persecution was very much like Jesus's, that his cause was righteous and his suffering a sign of his

goodness. Unlike leaders including Marcus Garvey who also likened their persecution to Jesus but saw its roots in racism, Grace did not see race at the heart of his
persecution. It was religion, the true gospel that Grace offered, that had caused his
persecution. The parallel with Jesus was exact. Daddy Grace made this explicit as he
spoke to House of Prayer members in Charlotte months after his trial for violating
the federal Mann Act, which was generally used to prosecute interstate prostitution
and "acts of immorality": "All the men of God went to jail. Why shouldn't I? Going
to jail don't make me less, but greater. My congregation is now greater than ever. . . .
They spoke evil of Jesus and all of the prophets and you know that they will speak
evil of me. . . . I am standing for the people and you stand with me."[47]

Grace's frustration that people "will not hear his words" and that people were
speaking ill of him helps to explain his famous comment that he had given God a
vacation. Grace warned that "it is impossible to worship God acceptably and hate
His word." In other words, one could not worship God if he or she hated "His word"
as preached by Grace. He added that instead of coming to him, "people ignore Grace
and say all manner of evil against him and still pray to God." And it is as a caution to
those who would persecute him that Grace offered the following: "But remember, if
you sin against God, Grace can save you, but if you sin against Grace, God cannot
save you." God is not impotent in this scenario but cannot save someone who has
chosen to ignore or badmouth God's own messenger. By removing the discussion of
persecution that precedes the excerpted quote, Fauset made it read more like a threat
to God than the threat to potential persecutors and naysayers that Grace intended
it to be.[48]

With the understanding of Grace's role as God's "one man" on earth and Jesus's
successor, another dimension of the evolving House of Prayer theology became
apparent in the full text of Fauset's quote. "The great trouble with the world," Grace
explained, "is that people are worshipping God in heaven and still hate Grace and
will not hear his words. God and Grace are one. God is invisible and Grace is visible."
Grace had become an intermediary, a savior, working on behalf of God. He was the
seen while God remained unseen. In case the parallel with Jesus was not clear, Grace
continued: "God made His man and sent him to the people that they may follow
him." This is not simply a play on biblical references to "grace," nor is it a usurping of
God's position, but it is an assumption of the role conventionally performed by
Jesus. Not Jesus, but Grace, made and sent by God, had become the key to salvation.
Grace continued to use the language of salvation that was at the heart of the apostolic
faith, but with his followers' support he had inserted himself into the equation.
Indeed, if one rereads the "vacation quote" inserting "Jesus" where "Grace" appears,

it would look like this, "But remember, if you sin against God, Jesus can save you, but if you sin against Jesus, God cannot save you." The theological argument at work here provides a better, more accurate understanding of Grace's claims and the House of Prayer's theological understanding of his role. It is the savior (Jesus/Grace) that is at the heart of the message.[49]

The theology that emerged within the House of Prayer was revolutionary—and considered blasphemous by most other Christian traditions. Grace had assumed a remarkable role. It was, however, a traditional, familiar role supported by a pre-existing framework of apostolic theology. Understanding the broader beliefs of the House of Prayer, and Grace's location within that belief system, is vital to answering many of the questions that Fauset posed. Those beliefs shed light on the attraction to the House of Prayer, Grace's unique spiritual power, and his followers' devotion to him and the organization. They also begin to explain how an organization that purportedly was based on the worship of a single man survived and continued to grow after that man's death—a feat somewhat unique among the groups Fauset studied.

Grace died in 1960, but the House of Prayer lives on. A visit to God's White House, the House of Prayer on M Street NW in Washington, D.C., reveals services very much like those over which Grace and his contemporaries presided. Followers are filled with the Holy Spirit and rejoice in the gifts that Grace has bequeathed them. His portrait appears next to his two successors, Daddy McCollough and Daddy Madison. Though their portraits form a new kind of trinity, they can best be understood as a lineage, expanding the tradition of "one man" serving as God's representative on earth. Grace's spiritual gifts passed on to McCollough until his death and then on to Madison. They, like Grace before them, became the heart of the organization and continued to preach the rich gospel with its origins in Grace's own unique identity.

Notes

1. A slightly altered form of these notes made it into Fauset's final, published version. See Arthur Huff Fauset, *Black Gods of the Metropolis: Negro Religious Cults of the Urban North* (Philadelphia: University of Pennsylvania, 2002), 29–30. Some of Fauset's notebooks and research materials pertaining to *Black Gods* are included in the Arthur Huff Fauset Collection, Special Collections Department, Van Pelt Library, University of Pennsylvania, Philadelphia.

2. Fauset, *Black Gods*, 26.

3. The Arthur Huff Fauset Collection, Box 4, Folder 93, unnumbered page.

4. William H. Baldwin, "Negro Spellbinders," *New York Times Book Review*, May 7, 1944, section 7, page 8, column 4.

5. One notable exception is Albert N. Whiting, "The United House of Prayer for All People: A Case Study of a Charismatic Sect" (Ph.D. diss., American University, 1952). Whiting references Fauset but conducts his own fieldwork with the House of Prayer and adopts a similar perspective. Whiting's work, however, has not been widely available and thus has not exerted significant influence over subsequent scholars.

6. E. Franklin Frazier, *The Negro Church in America* (New York: Schocken Books, 1964); Joseph R. Washington, *Black Sects and Cults* (Lanham, Md.: University Press of America, 1972); Wilson Jeremiah Moses, *Black Messiahs and Uncle Toms* (University Park: Pennsylvania State University Press, 1982); and Benjamin Sevitch, "When Black Gods Preached on Earth," in *Black Religious Leadership from the Slave Community to the Million Man March*, ed. Felton O. Best (Lewiston, N.Y.: Edwin Mellen, 1998), 78.

7. Timothy L. Smith, "Religion and Ethnicity in America," *American Historical Review* 83 (1978): 1183.

8. Christians often read the prophecy in Isaiah 7:14 as referring to Jesus.

9. Quotations are from the King James or Authorized Version of the Bible, as this was the translation likely to have been most readily accessible to Grace and from which he frequently quoted.

10. Untitled photograph, c. 1915, from the Oakland Museum of California's Collection, # H95.71.1.

11. David Daniels, "African-American Pentecostalism in the 20th Century," in *The Century of the Holy Spirit*, ed. Vinson Synan (Nashville, Tenn.: Thomas Nelson, 2001), 278.

12. Grant Wacker, *Heaven Below: Early Pentecostals and American Culture* (Cambridge, Mass.: Harvard University Press, 2003), 1.

13. Charles M. Grace, "Call of God Brought Him," *New Bedford Standard Times*, January 8, 1922.

14. Incomplete draft of article, Grace, *New Bedford Standard Times*, clippings file, 2.

15. Incomplete draft of article, ibid.

16. Grace, "Call of God Brought Him."

17. *Grace Magazine* (a House of Prayer publication), December 1941, 5.

18. Ibid.

19. Ibid. It appears that this magazine went to press before Pearl Harbor. There are no explicit references to Pearl Harbor or the U.S. entrance into the war.

20. G. Norman Eddy, "Store-Front Religion," *Religion in Life*, Winter 1958–1959, 76.

21. See Whiting, "United House of Prayer"; and Chancellor Williams, "The Socio-Economic Significance of the Storefront Church Movement in the US since 1920" (Ph.D. diss., American University, 1949).

22. The term "miracle converts" appears in Whiting, "United House of Prayer," 151.

23. Andrew Woods, "The Footprints of Grace," as quoted in Whiting, "United House of Prayer," 70–71.

24. " 'Bishop Grace Finds South More Receptive to His Ideas," *New Bedford Standard Times*, clippings file, December 7, 1927.

25. Ibid.

26. As quoted in Marilyn Halter, *Between Race and Ethnicity: Cape Verdean Immigrants 1865–1960* (Urbana: University of Illinois Press, 1993), 163–64.

27. "Court Pulls Daddy Grace Back from Travelogues," *Chicago Defender,* January 10, 1952.

28. "Preaching—Converting—Healing Took Up His Time in Egypt," *Evening Standard* (New Bedford), June 18, 1921, 2.

29. Ibid.

30. Charles M. Grace, "A Message by Sweet Daddy Grace At the Charlotte Mission, D.C., April 16, 1934," in "Precious Memories," unnumbered page, from the private collection of the late Dr. Robert Washington.

31. Daddy Grace Collection, Manuscripts and Rare Books Library, Robert Woodruff Library, Emory University, Atlanta, Ga., Box 1, Item 5.

32. "Grace Says He's Only Man to Lead the People," *Jet,* May 18, 1956, 24.

33. Marc Crawford, "Daddy's Multi-Colored Castle," *Jet,* May 23, 1957, 49.

34. Images and their power to convey theological ideas became central to House of Prayer worship.

35. "Over 3,000 Negroes Meet 'Bishop' at Service Here," *New Bedford Standard Times,* clippings file, unnumbered.

36. VanDerZee had come to Harlem from Lenox, Massachusetts, establishing the Guarantee Photo Studio in 1917 at 109 West 135th Street after a series of starts and stops in photography. See Deborah Willis-Braithwaite, *VanDerZee Photographer 1886–1983* (New York: Harry N. Abrams, 1993), 42. He dramatized his work by not only retouching his photographs but also combining several negatives to create the final print. While the Great Depression, which had hit Harlem hard, caused VanDerZee's business to suffer, Daddy Grace's House of Prayer was thriving and he chose to document himself before the lens of the well-respected photographer.

37. See, for instance, the Daddy Grace Collection, Box 1, Item 4. Given the font of the accompanying caption and the materials out of which the card is made, the card featuring Grace in his Holy Land robes with an inset of Jesus appears to have been printed many years after Grace's 1938 session with VanDerZee.

38. Eddy, "Store-Front Religion," 68–85, 75.

39. Williams, "The Socio-Economic Significance," 123.

40. *Grace Magazine,* December 1941, 4.

41. *Grace Magazine,* December 1940, 3.

42. "Daddy Grace's Message—May 22, 1955 Norfolk, VA.," *Grace Magazine,* September 1960, 8.

43. As quoted by Eddy in "Store-Front Religion," 76.

44. See Marie Dallam, "By Daddy Grace Only: Bishop Grace and the Foundational Years of the United House of Prayer" (Ph.D. diss., Temple University, 2006), 45. Dallam makes a compelling argument linking this "one man" tradition with Catholic notions of apostolic succession.

45. "The Final Judgment . . . By Sweet Daddy Grace: January 12, 1933," reprinted in

Grace Magazine, December 1960, 10. The date in the title, 1933, does not match the date listed in the text of the article/sermon itself: January 27–28, 1942.

46. "The Final Judgment," 10.

47. "A Nation Must Respect God . . ." in *Grace Magazine,* December 1960, 8. Sermon originally delivered April 16, 1934.

48. Fauset, *Black Gods,* 112–13.

49. Ibid.

THREE · "Chased out of Palestine": Prophet Cherry's Church of God and Early Black Judaisms in the United States

NORA L. RUBEL

*[A]ll across Africa, America, the West Indies, there are tales
of the powers of Moses and great worship of him and his
powers. But it does not flow from the Ten Commandments.
It is his rod of power, the terror he showed before all Israel
and to Pharaoh, and THAT MIGHTY HAND.*

—ZORA NEALE HURSTON, *Moses, Man of the Mountain*

Against a backdrop of burgeoning black nationalism, black Jewish communities began appearing in major cities in the early twentieth century. Viewed by many as merely another peculiarity within the already diverse spectrum of African American religions, their emergence garnered little early attention from black or white media. The original expositors of a black Jewish identity were virtually indistinguishable from black Christians. Historically, black preachers tended to emphasize Old Testament stories of the enslavement and subsequent liberation of the Hebrews as an inspiration for fighting racial injustices in America. Similarly, research on slave songs reveals the most persistent imagery in that genre to be that of the "chosen people."[1] Like their African American Protestant peers, black Jews emphasized the

Exodus story, the dream of a Promised Land for the chosen people, and the dream of a messianic hero who would deliver African Americans from their social bondage.

Once these groups began to express a more overtly Judaic identity, scholars such as Arthur Fauset—along with members of the black and Jewish press—began to explore the unique contours of this religious curiosity, specifically Prophet Cherry's Church of God. Like other early black Jewish movements, the Church of God was identifiable by two primary characteristics: (1) a belief that black people were the original biblical Israelites and (2) a syncretic religious practice, including Jewish, Muslim, and Christian rituals. Alongside emergent voices of black nationalism, black Jews reconstructed black identity through the embrace of new Hebraic names, new languages (Hebrew and, in some cases, Yiddish), new spiritual homelands, and a new religious worldview. This chapter will revisit Cherry's Church of God in the context of more recent scholarship, seizing the opportunity to observe the overlap of other contemporaneous religio-political movements that provided an umbrella for the combining of Islamic history, Jewish practice, and Christian imagery in African American life during and in the wake of the Great Migration.

The story of black Judaism has been eclipsed by the later rise of black Islam, a far more successful spiritual movement among African Americans. However, black Judaism (or Hebrewism or Israelism) is significant despite its smaller numbers, for it is within these early groups that a clear counterreligious worldview emerges, one that seized and reinterpreted the biblical Exodus story as previously understood in America. Of course, African Americans were not the only group to appropriate the concept of the chosen people; most Judeo-Christian religious sects in the United States have done much the same. European settlers who believed that they were the chosen people brought this concept to America, and the Puritan experiment of the "city upon a hill" is testament to such a sentiment. New Englanders such as John Winthrop spoke of God's special destiny for the settlers of America. African Americans adopted this story, reversing the dominant perception of *who* was chosen. The uniqueness of the African American situation, however, is found within their identification with the *exiled* chosen people. Albert Raboteau explains, "Without doubt, the Exodus story was the most significant myth for American black identity, whether slave or free. White Americans had always thought of themselves as Israel, of course, but as Israelites in Canaan, the Promised Land. Black Americans were Israelites in Egypt."[2] The meaning and importance of the Exodus is very different within the African American context, and particularly in the black Jewish context, for there the identification with the Israelite children went a step beyond allegory or metaphor.

The Church of God's presence in the first half of the twentieth century was accompanied by a great variety of religio-nationalist movements. Included in this inventory were other black Israelites, Marcus Garvey's Universal Negro Improvement Association (UNIA), the Moorish Science Temple (MST), and the Nation of Islam, all of which radically redefined black identity, frequently in opposition to Christianity. These groups shared a cosmology, often advocating the concept of an original religion lost during slavery and broadening the location of black provenance to include North Africa and Palestine.[3] These movements also exhibited an awareness of both the "abhorrent racial practices within American Christianity" and the "intrinsically anti-black dimensions of the Christian Scripture and historical theology."[4] Finally, they also sought to reject, reverse, or reinterpret the biblical Hamitic myth of black inferiority, a story historically used to defend both slavery and racial hierarchies. This biblical tale, rooted in Genesis, features Noah's son Ham—the father of Canaan—who saw "the nakedness of his father." When Noah awoke from his drunken state, "he said, Cursed be Canaan; a servant of servants shall he be unto his brethren."[5] In further interpretations of this story, because Ham fails to cover Noah's nakedness (usually understood as an incestuous encounter), his descendants are damned to blackness and servitude. African American responses to white/European readings of the Hamitic destiny have been ambivalent, to say the least.[6] In the nineteenth century, African Americans introduced a redefinition of Hamitic significance. Ham becomes important precisely because of his place as the progenitor of the nations of Egypt (Mitzraim), Ethiopia (Cush), and Canaan. This lineage provides a justification for the Israelites being black and, subsequently, for Jesus being black.[7] In this way, what was once seen as a legacy of servitude could be reinterpreted as a destiny of greatness. Textual evidence for this destiny is found in the multiple biblical mentions of African nations, particularly Ethiopia.

The Church of God

F. S. Cherry—a former seaman and railroad worker—founded the Church of God in 1886.[8] Prophet Cherry began preaching in Chattanooga, Tennessee, and ultimately settled in Philadelphia, which became a hub of black Jewish activity between 1900 and 1920. Calling themselves "Black Jews," "Hebrew Israelites," or "Israelites," members of Cherry's congregation believed that blacks were the "true Jews"—descendants of Jacob—and the present white "so-called Jew" was both an "interloper and fraud."[9] The prophet alone could identify the true Israelites, descended from Jacob.[10] According to one congregant interviewed by Fauset, "We were chased out of Palestine by the Romans (Italian) into the west coast of Africa where we were captured and sold into this great U.S.A."[11] Cherry taught that (in addition to Jacob) God, Jesus, Adam, and Eve were black. Esau was red. White people were the descendants of a cursed servant, Gehazi (a reversal of the Hamitic myth).[12] Black people were the original inhabitants of the earth, and the rightful place of blacks was destined to be in "high places."[13] The "yellow" race was the result of Gehazi's mixing with black peoples.[14] This concern for genealogy and the creation of different races reflects a period where many peoples and movements were trying to make sense of racial diversity. Cherry's group offered a counterhistory to the dominant racial mythology of the era.

The Church of God also claimed to privilege alternative texts. In *Black Gods of the Metropolis,* Fauset writes: "One might state that the sacred text of the Church of God is the Christian Bible, but it would be more correct to say that it is the Talmud. The prophet always refers to the Hebrew Bible as his ultimate source."[15] At first glance, it seems quite probable that Fauset meant the Torah, as his further discussion of the Church of God repeatedly quotes the Hebrew Bible, not the Talmud or any other rabbinic source. Also, other contemporary Israelite groups are characterized by their rejection of the Talmud as a white, European creation. Therefore this description by Fauset regarding Talmudic centrality is questionable. Almost all subsequent work on the Church of God repeats the claim, citing *Black Gods* as their only source. However, this Talmud/Torah confusion was likely not the fault of Fauset, as James Landing, in his massive text *Black Judaism,* points out that Cherry himself referred to his sacred text as the Talmud, yet there is no indication that he used any Jewish source beyond the Hebrew Bible.[16]

The Ten Commandments were central to the prophet's teachings, particularly the prohibition against graven images. This observance can be seen in the ban on photographs; members did not possess pictures of people. This practice was also evident among the Commandment Keepers in Harlem. In Cherry's Israelite Bible Class, members learned Hebrew and studied the Bible.[17] Outsiders have interpreted this attention to the Hebrew language as evidence of the Jewish nature of the group. Male congregants wore skullcaps during worship at services held Sunday, Wednesday, Friday evenings, and all day Saturday, facing east toward Palestine. The prophet frequently engaged in profane language during his sermons, a rhetorical gift from God reserved for his use. Cherry prohibited use of the term "synagogue," preferring "House of Prayer" as detailed in the Torah. Israelites celebrated Friday night to Saturday at sundown as the Sabbath.[18] The observance of Passover replaced communion, again reflecting the importance of the Exodus story in the African American imagination.[19]

Congregants were forbidden to speak in tongues, eat pork, or divorce (except under certain circumstances). Unlike all other movements in Fauset's study, the consumption of alcohol was permitted and even encouraged (the Bible is quoted as a justification). Little attention was paid to death and funerals; burial was quick and private, as was the case with traditional Jewish funeral rites. Fauset and later observers pointed out the ritual's simplicity and noted it as a distinctive feature of this group.[20] For its practitioners, this worldview served as a counterpoint to African American traditions that emphasized long suffering and deliverance in heaven. In addition, this outlook on death was significant because, for the black Israelite, release and salvation could be achieved in *this* life. African Americans drawn to black Israelism or Islam saw the merits of receiving a more worldly deliverance from the burden of white supremacy.

Prophet Cherry died at the age of ninety-five, leaving his son Benjamin F. Cherry as his successor in 1963. According to later works on the Church of God, members denied that Cherry was actually dead, claiming instead that he lives on in an unidentified place. In order to maintain a connection with the prophet, a recording of one of Cherry's sermons was played every Sabbath.[21]

A Shared Universe

Fauset categorized the Church of God as "Islamic," "nationalistic," and "quasi-holiness."[22] These seemingly disparate categorizations actually reveal much about the movement, and we can see striking overlaps with other groups (particularly the Moorish Science Temple, which falls into the same categories). Hans A. Baer and Merrill Singer refer to these movements, characterized by overt racial distinctiveness and messianic emphasis, as messianic-nationalist sects.[23] These movements can take a Christian, Judaic, or Islamic bent, but ultimately they are more similar than they are different. Baer and Singer lay out five distinctive characteristics:

> (1) acceptance of a belief in a glorious Black history and subsequent "fall" from grace; (2) adoption of various rituals and symbols from established millenarian religious traditions; (3) messianic anticipation of divine retribution against the White oppressor; (4) assertion of Black sovereignty through the development of various nationalist symbols and interest in territorial separation or emigration; and (5) rejection of certain social patterns in the Black community, including family instability, female-headed households, and male marginality.[24]

The shared belief of an original religion and a soon-to-be-realized rise in power, as well as the belief in new spiritual homelands, placed the Church of God in a shared universe with a variety of nationalist-minded contemporaneous movements. Fauset noted that Cherry's Israelites emphasized communal identity. According to Cherry, "Without a national name, there can be no future for a people. Therefore you must not be called Negroes, colored, jigaboos, etc."[25] Fauset saw this emphasis on names as adding a political claim to the religious outlook, a claim also made by the Moorish Science Temple.

Various aspects of the Church of God resembled other religious movements increasingly popular among African Americans. For instance, the group's resistance to military service and refusal to salute the flag were shared by Jehovah's Witnesses and members of the Nation of Islam. Cherry's Israelites also believed that the United States was not their land (they were in it, but not of it). Pork was strictly forbidden, as it is in traditional Judaism and Islam, and these new dietary laws created markets for new businesses, such as grocery stores and restaurants. Prophet Cherry ran a vegetable store and butcher shop, and members of the group developed other businesses to cater to the needs of the community as well. The Nation of Islam similarly forbade pork, along with elements of the Southern African American slave diet such as corn bread and collard greens. This unorthodox ban on collards is similar to Cherry's proscription against hair straightening, a practice that could be seen as a denial of true blackness. This cosmetic prohibition is seen in all of Fauset's subjects with the exception of Daddy Grace's United House of Prayer.

Like the Moorish Science Temple, Cherry forbade congregants from using the term "Negro," allowing only for "Jew," "Hebrew," or "Israelite." Noble Drew Ali not only forbade "Negro" but "Ethiopian" as well, permitting only "Asiatic" or "Moorish American."[26] While Cherry's Israelism shared much with the Moorish Science Temple—and certainly among Fauset's subjects, these two had the most in common—the movements also differed on their attitude toward the United States. The members of the MST believed that they must obey the laws of the land, whereas the Church of God saw allegiance to the United States as idolatry.

Cherry also found fault with the MST's tribal origins. The members claimed to be descended from the ancient Moabites, close relations of the biblical Israelites. According to the MST's founder, Noble Drew Ali, the tribe migrated southward into Africa, ultimately becoming enslaved and arriving in America. Drawing a lineage from the biblical Moabite Ruth, an ancestor of both King David and Jesus, this identity puts the Moors in good company.[27] However, the book of Ruth is a notable exception as most biblical mentions of this tribe are negative. According to the Old Testament (Genesis 19:30–37), the Moabites were descendants of an incestuous union between Abraham's cousin Lot and his daughter. Cherry's derision toward the movement reputedly stemmed from his view of the MST as a bastard race.

The Church of God subscribed to a dispensationalist theology, popular among many evangelical Christian groups of the period. Cherry and his followers believed that history has been divided into two-thousand-year periods corresponding to God's covenants with humanity, as described in biblical texts. The first dispensation was the flood and God's covenant with Noah, the second was Jesus's birth, and the final, the millennium signaled by the Rapture and the Second Coming of Jesus. Cherry employed the commonly used millennial text of Revelation to describe the Battle of Armageddon in Palestine, a battle that precedes the Israelites' return to their land.[28] Cherry demanded patience until the reign of Gentiles (whites) ended. Later work on the group described a more specific Armageddon scenario of World War III being kicked off by conflict between Arabs and Israelis.[29]

According to Fauset, the prophet also frequently cited Amos 9 as central to this millennial theology. "'I will plant Israel in their own land, never again to be up-rooted from the land I have given them,' says the Lord your God" (Amos 9:15). This chapter describes Israel's destruction as well as its subsequent restoration, returning God's exiled people to their rightful land. This sort of millennialism, which was present in all of Fauset's groups, became popular in black religion in the late nine-teenth and early twentieth centuries, and is often referred to as Ethiopianism, due to the popularity of Psalm 68:31: "Princes shall come out of Egypt and Ethiopia shall stretch out her hands unto God."[30]

Despite its eschatological view drawn primarily from the New Testament, the Church of God exhibited an ambivalent attitude toward Christianity as well. Implicit in Cherry's theology was a harsh critique of black Christianity, and particularly of black ministers. The prophet frequently referred to Christian clergy as "damn fools" and "vultures."[31] This overt disdain for black preachers again has parallels in the Nation of Islam. Elijah Muhammad commonly expressed his disgust with black Christian ministers for their acceptance of a "white religion" and a "white god." Among African Americans—as seen in Garvey's African Orthodox Church, Father Divine's Peace Mission, and the Nation of Islam—this idea of a black man as God was a very powerful and seductive image at a time when blacks in America were facing rampant racism. Cherry notoriously offered money (of increasing sums) to anyone who could produce an accurate picture of Jesus, demonstrating the co-opting of Jesus by whites. It is important to note that the concepts of a black God and a black Jesus were not original to black Jews and Muslims. African Methodist Episcopal

Bishop Henry McNeal Turner famously claimed that there was no "hope for a race of people who do not believe that they look like God."[32] Turner asserted that Adam—and Jesus after him—was a black man.

The Church of God demanded baptism by immersion and used Christian hymns, yet it forbade members to observe Christian holidays such as Christmas and Easter (prohibitions also seen among Jehovah's Witnesses). The group also denounced white Jews for denying Jesus. The Church of God eschewed some Holiness traditions—such as speaking in tongues—yet embraced others—such as foot washing. Despite emphasis on the Old Testament (and lip service to the Talmud), the church still referred to the New Testament, as Fauset cited "Revelations [*sic*] 2:9, 3:90."[33] Cherry's syncretic theology, and the controversial tales of Gehazi, explained the black situation in America, as well as the potential for an earthly redemption.

Black Jews beyond *Black Gods*

In an essay on black sectarianism, Hans Baer and Merrill Singer cite a 1974 study from Chicago: "There are twenty Black groups [in Chicago] with titles such as 'Israelites . . . Jews, Hebrews, Canaanites, Essenes, Judaites, Rechabites, Falashas, and Abyssinians' (now generally defunct and replaced by the term Ethiopian). Although the terminology differs, all such groups perceive themselves as lineal descendants of the Hebrew Patriarchs."[34] These varied movements began to form in Washington, D.C., Chicago, New York, and Philadelphia in the early 1900s. It is in this black Jewish milieu that the Church of God became popular. In the 1940s, Fauset selected his movements for *Black Gods* (Church of God included) as being "the most important and best-known cults of their respective types, and hence among the most representative."[35] But as history has shown, the Church of God no longer remains the archetype of black Judaism.

Most of the historical information in this chapter relating to Prophet Cherry's Church of God stems from Fauset's original ethnography. Practically all scholarship on the subject cites Fauset or cites later scholars who have cited Fauset. *Black Gods* is the only in-depth work to have been undertaken during the prophet's lifetime. Two M.A. theses (published in 1968 and 1969) were written after the prophet's death in 1963.[36] Curiously, while the Church of God is the only black Jewish movement Fauset addresses, it is the group that has seen the least scholarly attention in recent studies of black Judaism.[37]

The absence of Church of God scholarship could be attributed to a variety of reasons: (1) numbers and continuity (it is doubtful that the movement is still in existence), (2) secrecy on the part of members, or (3) the lack of congruity between Cherry's movement and the black Jewish groups to follow, particularly on the issue of origins. Ultimately, this lack of attention to an otherwise attractive subject is significant, not for Fauset's foresight, but for the failure of the movement to sustain itself. One idea that sets Cherry's group apart from other black Jewish movements is his view that the black Jews were of Asiatic origins rather than African ones, a belief shared by Noble Drew Ali, leader of the Moorish Science Temple.

These movements incorporated several stereotypes of Africa as an uncivilized, savage place. Elijah Muhammad taught that black people were not "Negroes" but Asiatics from "East Asia" and Arabia. This early anti-African bias has been explored in contemporary scholarship on black Islamic—and Christian—movements, but scholarship on black Judaism is quiet on these debates over origins.[38] The issue of Africa as a place of origin within the Church of God is a tricky one. Cherry challenged the predominant Christianity of African Americans by claiming an innate Judaic heritage. At the same time, by asserting a quasi-Middle Eastern heritage, he denied and somewhat denigrated West African or Ethiopian origins. Adopting racist attitudes toward Africa, this theology demonstrates how ingrained racial categorization can become—especially among those attempting to eliminate feelings of racial inferiority. At the same time, it is important to add that most Israelites emphasized Africa or Ethiopia, not Palestine, as a point of origin or homeland. Followers of these other black Jewish factions criticized members of Islamic movements, including the Nation of Islam, for their denial of African roots, asserting that "they are just Negroes who don't want to admit that they're Negroes."[39]

Besides Cherry's Church of God, there were—and still are—many such black Jewish groups in the United States.[40] They include the Church of God and Saints of Christ, and the Commandment Keepers (both contemporaries of the Church of God), as well as the Original Hebrew Israelite Nation, which emerged later in the 1960s. These movements both popularized the Judaic theme within black religion and further diversified the forms of Jewish identity and practice among African Americans.

Most scholars agree that the first such Israelite congregation was William S. Crowdy's Church of God and Saints of Christ (CGSC). William Saunders Crowdy was a former slave who fought for the Union Army during the Civil War. After the war, he joined a Baptist church and spent a few years working as a hotel cook in Kansas City, Missouri. In 1893, Crowdy had a vision that resulted in the establishment of the Church of God and Saints of Christ. A subsequent revelation led to Crowdy's understanding of the "Stone of Truth" or the "Seven Keys" that became the foundation of his church. The "Seven Keys" are "(1) The Church of God and Saints of Christ, (2) Wine forbidden to be drank in the Church of God and Saints of Christ forever, (3) Unleavened bread and water for Christ's Body and blood, (4) Foot washing is a commandment, (5) The Disciple's prayer, (6) You must be breathed upon and saluted into the Church of God and Saints of Christ with a Holy Kiss, (7) The Ten Commandments."[41] He established his church in 1896 in Lawrence, Kansas. The movement spread quickly to the East Coast. He ultimately settled in Philadelphia, where the headquarters was established.

Crowdy taught that black Americans were the original Hebrews of the Bible. " 'Negroes' are Jews and descendants of the 'lost tribe of Israel'; and Jews were originally black."[42] Crowdy believed that his destiny was to return African Americans to their rightful place in the House of Israel.[43] He saw white Jews as the result of intermarriage. The church's tenets include adherence to the laws of both the Old and the New Testament and the acceptance of Jesus as Christ.[44] The CGSC was originally more Christian than Jewish in practice, retaining baptism and foot washing. Jewish practices included circumcision and the biblical practice of smearing animal blood over doorways in celebration of the Passover.

Rabbi Curtis Caldwell, a former leader of the Philadelphia chapter of the Church of God and Saints of Christ (now called First Tabernacle Zion), claims that this syncretism of Judaism and Christianity was part of Prophet Crowdy's long-range plan, since the reality was that most blacks were coming from a Christian context. "To move them [to Judaism] too swiftly away from [Christianity] would have resulted in no organization at all."[45] Today, the church adheres more closely to orthodox Jewish practice. The Church of God and Saints of Christ is hardly a Judaic-sounding title, but Christ does not refer only to Jesus. Jesus is important as a prophet, but not as a divine being. The Christ Spirit is "simply the 'anointed power' of God."[46] According to church teaching, Prophet Crowdy was a Christ, as were all of his successors. The Church of God and Saints of Christ still very much exists and currently has temples in the United States, South Africa, and Jamaica. The headquarters eventually moved to Belleville, Virginia. Today's communities within the Church of God and Saints of Christ focus on retaining social stability, parental values, and social welfare programs for their congregants.[47]

But the best documented, as well as largest, Israelite group was Wentworth Arthur Matthew's Commandment Keepers, Holy Church of the Living God in Harlem. This community grew out of Arnold Josiah Ford's 1923 Beth B'nai Abraham congregation. Born in Barbados, Ford was the son of an evangelist. He rejected Christianity after he moved to America, became a leader in Marcus Garvey's Universal Negro Improvement Association (UNIA), and attempted to convince Garvey to accept Judaism as the UNIA's official religion. Garvey did not accept this suggestion, but Ford remained active in the association until he founded Beth B'nai Abraham in New York. Perhaps in order to reinforce a connection to Africa, Ford insisted that his followers be called Ethiopian Hebrews rather than Jews. Ford's congregation opposed Christian ritual but embraced certain Islamic elements such as the fast of Ramadan.[48] From the beginning, this congregation had a large West Indian presence, one that was represented in other New York–area Israelite communities. Ford left New York in 1930 and moved to Ethiopia in order to form a black Jewish community.[49]

Ford's successor, Wentworth Matthew, has been described as "the most colorful, photogenic, inventive, and written about Black Rabbi on the Black Jewish pulpit."[50] Matthew taught that African Americans were American Falashas, as Ethiopian Jews were then known. In the early 1920s, more African Americans began to learn about the Falashas. "Falasha"—meaning outsider or stranger—is a term given to Jews in Ethiopia by their Christian neighbors. The Ethiopian Jews themselves prefer Beta Israel, or House of Israel.

The existence of a lost tribe of Jews in Ethiopia has been a source of romantic speculation for centuries. Various theories about how this community has evolved have been suggested, with equally varied degrees of acceptance. Some believe that the Beta Israel migrated to Ethiopia after the destruction of the First Temple in Jerusalem. Some suggest that Ethiopians were at one point all Jews and that Ethiopian Christianity was the result of conversion (thus explaining the distinctive Judaic elements of the Ethiopian Orthodox Church). Still others argue that the reverse is true, that Ethiopian Jews are a schismatic faction of Ethiopian Christianity and only became "Jews" through contact with outside observers. Popular folklore has it that the Beta Israel are descendants of Menelik, the son of King Solomon and the Queen of Sheba, although most Ethiopian rulers have claimed lineage from this son of Solomon. Despite speculation on origins, the Beta Israel practice a version of Judaism that predates the Talmud. Coincidentally, this lack of Talmudic adherence draws Israelite practice closer to that of the Beta Israel.

Publicity regarding this group of Jews in Ethiopia in the early twentieth century was influential among African Americans. Given the importance of the Exodus story in slave narratives—as well as the exalted position of Ethiopia in the Hebrew Bible—it makes sense that African Americans searching for a past that had been stolen from them would make the link between themselves and the black Jews of Ethiopia. It is important to note, however, that black Judaic sects did exist in America prior to popular knowledge of the Ethiopian Jews. Like Crowdy, Matthew's earlier teachings appeared more Christian than Judaic, but in the thirties he grew closer to orthodox Judaism. From the start, Matthew sought to rid his followers of typical African American religious behavior. Characteristics of ecstatic religion—what Matthew termed "niggeritions"—were prohibited.[51] Christian elements that remained were foot washing, healing, and the singing of gospel hymns. Matthew also practiced what he termed "Cabalistic" science, or numerology. In 1936, Matthew established the Royal Order of Ethiopian Hebrews, which ultimately developed branches reaching from the East Coast to the Midwest. He also created the Ethiopian Hebrew Rabbinical College, a seminary for black Jewish leaders and rabbis, and most New York–area black synagogues trace their roots to Rabbi Matthew's congregation. Essentially, Wentworth Matthew was the equivalent of the Hasidic "Rebbe" of black Judaism in New York.

Significantly, from the very beginning Matthew's Commandment Keepers was not a truly separatist congregation. White Jewish merchants from the area often attended worship services at Beth B'nai Abraham. In 1930, Matthew had 175 congregants. Six were white.[52] White visitors were always welcome to attend and ask questions. This contact with the white Jewish community of New York possibly contributed to the Commandment Keepers' move toward traditional Judaism. Today, this Israelite community is far closer to mainstream Judaism than other such congregations. When Matthew died in 1973, he had approximately three thousand followers in the New York area. His grandson, Rabbi David Dore, the second African American in history to graduate from the orthodox Yeshiva University, became his successor.[53]

While Matthew's community may be seen by some as the most recognizably "Jewish," the Original Hebrew Israelite Nation must be seen as the most challenging to categorize. This controversial sect pushed further the question of Jewish identification because its claim had legal repercussions. Founded in the 1960s by Ben Ami Carter and Shaleak Ben Yehuda, the Original Hebrew Israelite Nation grew out of the existing Abeta Hebrew Cultural Center in Chicago, an institution dedicated to African repatriation. Carter and Yehuda preached, like most of their predecessors, that the original Hebrews of the Bible were African. They explained that among the black people in America, some were Hebrew Israelites who did not remember their history. Like Cherry's movement, their narrative consists of a removal from Palestine: "In 70 CE the remnants of The African Hebrew Israelites were driven from Jerusalem by the Romans into different parts of the world, including Africa. Many Hebrew

Israelites migrated to West Africa where they, once again, were carried away captive —this time by Europeans on slave ships—to the Americas along with other African tribes people."[54] Established amid the racial turbulence of America in the sixties, Carter preached an apocalyptic view of America. The United States is a corrupt Babylon and has little time left, he claimed, further arguing that the Hebrew Israelites must return to the Holy Land. For the Hebrew Israelites, the Holy Land was Africa. Carter envisioned Liberia as the proper place to go, mainly because of its history as a colony for freed black slaves. One hundred sixty-two members left Chicago in 1965 to form a tent colony in Liberia.[55] For a variety of reasons, this stint in Africa was difficult and short-lived.

Many chose to go back home to the States, and others from America decided to go to Israel, also described as Northeast Africa, the Holy Land of the Bible. The Hebrews write that their brief sojourn in Liberia had gone according to plan because, like the ancient Hebrews of the Bible, they had to wander in the wilderness before reaching the Promised Land. According to Asiel Ben Israel:

> My nation moved through the wilderness, purging themselves of Negrotism in the wilds of Northern Africa, so that we could shake off the servitude we picked up after 400 years on the American continent. Going through this process on our way back to the Holy Land, we stopped in Liberia. . . . When we had completely removed the shackles of Negrotism from our minds and our bodies, that prepared us for our entry into the Holy Land.[56]

In 1968, twenty Hebrew Israelites arrived at Ben Gurion Airport in Tel Aviv and asked to be admitted under the Law of Return. Under Israeli law, the Law of Return holds special privileges for Jews who want to make *aliyah* (attain citizenship). Under *halakha* (Jewish law), a person is Jewish if her or his mother is Jewish, or if she or he undergoes a conversion process. While permanent status decisions about the Hebrew Israelites were pending, they were settled into southern Israel and given jobs.[57] More entered the country as visitors and joined them the following year.[58]

The years following the arrival of the Hebrew Israelites were fraught with tense relations with the Israeli government. The Israeli Supreme Court found the group to be "a separate sect, distinct from Judaism and remote from the Jewish world, its traditions and its culture and its heritage down the generations"; the group was therefore eligible for deportation. By the time of the ruling, the Israelites had more than two thousand members living in Dimona, Arad, and Mizpe Ramon. Carter responded to the court's ruling by warning the Israeli government that two million African Americans were going to arrive in Israel to take the land from the present Jewish inhabitants. He claimed that "the Lord personally ordered me to take possession of Israel."[59] These remarks turned public sympathy against the Hebrew Israelites.

Ultimately, both sides made attempts at reconciliation and in the last decade the Hebrew Israelites have achieved permanent residency status. Carter has recanted his exclusivist rhetoric and the government has embraced the community for its unique character in Israel. In addition to their vegan diet, the Hebrew Israelites wear only natural fabrics.[60] Like the Church of God, their diet and lifestyle have led them to establish their own businesses, including a successful chain of vegetarian restaurants around Israel and in the United States. Meanwhile, new generations of Hebrew Israelites have come of age and their presence has both influenced and been influenced by other Israelis. While they are not citizens—and therefore not eligible for the draft—the last few years have seen voluntary enlistment of the community's youth, demonstrating a feeling of security and belonging in the country.[61]

The Hebrew Israelites observe circumcision, marital purity laws, and the keeping of the Sabbath and biblical festivals. In addition, they observe several holidays of their own making, including the "New World Passover," which commemorates their exodus from America.[62] They uphold a strict vegan diet, which goes beyond the traditional Jewish dietary restrictions. One controversial biblical practice restored by Carter is polygamy. Among the Hebrew Israelite Nation, multiple wives are seen as a marker of social status; each man may have up to seven.

Like many other Israelite sects, the Hebrew Israelites do not view the Talmud as authoritative. Carter is referred to as the "Son of God or Prince of Peace."[63] Their religious leaders are not called rabbi, but nasi or prince. There are twelve princes (or *nesim*) below Ben Ami. These nesim represent the twelve apostles of Christ.[64] Found within this group are traces of Prophet Crowdy's theology (followers are called "saints"), and their religious practices include many elements from American black Christianity. The Israelites fast on the Sabbath and sing gospels during services.[65] Like Matthew's Commandment Keepers, they refrain from ecstatic religious behavior. Also like the Commandment Keepers, they now allow nonblack members, viewing the righteousness of one's character as the sole requisite for chosenness. The Hebrew Israelites' journey from separatism to inclusivity extends to their relations with African Americans and white American Jews in the United States. They—like the other two movements described—see themselves as a potential bridge between communities, groups frequently pitted against each other.

But Is It Jewish? (or Black?)

Scholars of religion are drawn to questions of practice as a way to describe religious peoples. The question of whether different practices are signs of, say, legitimately "authentic" Judaism or Islam is often inevitable. In the case of Cherry's Church of God—or black Judaisms in general—this question frequently arises in intergroup Jewish debates as the wider Jewish community questions the legitimacy of various black Jewish groups. The mainstream Jewish press has found black Jews as curious or exotic, while the black press has often accepted black Jews and rabbis, and, in some cases, has celebrated them as a source of black pride. In the 1960s, for example, the *Chicago Defender* developed a series of articles devoted to the question of black Jews.

Resistance to these black Jewish movements from the Euro-American Jewish establishment stems from concern over claims that black Jews are the only true Jews and that white Jews are usurpers—claims made by the Church of God and the Hebrew Israelite Nation in its early days. In response, the Jewish press has interrogated the nature of black Jewish practices. The need for black Jews to deliver a satisfactory response is indicative of what Walter Isaac correctly points out as "the black-Jewish differential," one that requires a litmus test in order to prove legitimacy.[66] Ironically, since World War II, most mainstream Jews deny that Jews are a race, yet the lack of observance by Jews who identify strongly as Jews make this litmus test somewhat irrelevant. Graenum Berger in his 1978 study asserted: "There can only be one test—halakha—for white and black."[67] This question of halakhicly determining who is a Jew is currently an issue among white Jews, due to the increase of intermarriage, so this method is not even useful here. Additionally, as many black Jewish groups reject Talmudic authority—a large source of *halakha*—this test is irrelevant in their self-understanding.

Regardless of this litmus test, Cherry's followers were popularly known as black Jews. In *Black Gods*, Fauset calls the Church of God a "modified Judaic form" or "modified Judaism" as well as a "nationalistic cult."[68] James Landing calls this movement "Christian Judaism,"[69] and Howard Brotz calls the adherents "Christians."[70] These terms are somewhat problematic, for they assume a normative Judaism, one that has emerged from the European experience. In response to such normative definitions of Judaism, Walter Isaac critiques anthropologist Ruth Landes for her statement that "[t]his [Afro-American] Judaism has never become significant in the Negro life of the United States or elsewhere; and it has been hardly more than a curiosity to American (white) Jews."[71] While Isaac is right to point out the hermeneutic of suspicion that black Jews seem to provoke from white Jews, notably seen in the title of Brotz's first article on the Commandment Keepers, "Negro 'Jews' in the United States," he fails to note the similar critiques (and strong dismissals) coming from black observers of black religion as well, such as Joseph Washington and E. Franklin Frazier, neither of whom favored these Israelite movements.

Washington, in his 1972 *Black Sects and Cults,* harshly criticizes the path taken by black Israelites who, like members of the Nation of Islam, attempt to create a nation within a nation: "To their credit, they have succeeded in creating cults which are impressive failures, for they further divide Black people and therefore forestall the one thing needed: a Black communal sense, a community of enriching differences."[72] He claims that the black Jews are "the antithesis of the Black *cult* and the Black ethos."[73] His reason for this isolation is due to the Israelites' denial of their West African roots.

Washington characterizes black Jews as a "small, varied, and desperate body of Blacks who in reaction to the extreme urban racism around 1915 accepted the rejection of Black worthfulness and took more seriously than Booker T. Washington intended his idea of imitating Jews."[74] Not only does such a dismissal characterize black Judaism as merely reactionary, but it also denies the legitimacy of a positive black Jewish identity. Attempts to exoticize such groups also serve to additionally marginalize these movements. Such critiques by both Jewish *and* black observers have led to a void in the vast, creative religious history of African Americans that is only now beginning to be filled.

The categories "black" and "Jewish" have been established with distinct rigidity by both scholarship and the media, yet these terms can alternatively refer to ethnic, racial, religious, and—as frequently seen in the discussion of black-Jewish relations— political loyalties.[75] While Jews are most often seen as an ethnic and cultural group, they are occasionally considered a racial group, "the seed of Abraham."[76] Not only have these categories consistently undergone adjustment, but the study of black Jews proves that they are also not mutually exclusive. By including the experiences of African American Jews (of whatever stripes) in religious studies (particularly American), we can seek to modify the ethnoracial, religious, and political categories used in regard to the often homogenous constructs of "black" and "Jew."

Arthur Fauset's *Black Gods* was groundbreaking for its ability to introduce new religious movements in a scholarly manner and to describe them in a way that situates them within the broader African American religious scene. Sixty years later, only a handful of scholars have done the same. In the past few decades, the field has expanded to address a slightly more diverse spectrum of religious practice. The centrality of the "Black [Protestant] Church" has been challenged in order to include Catholicism and Islam, and, most recently, Judaism. While Judaism among African Americans has not had the same cultural impact as Islam, it deserves attention, particularly for its contributions to early and mid-twentieth-century nationalist thought. By adding new dynamism and creativity to the study of African American religion, the study of black Judaism also offers a new perspective on American Jewry, adding yet another challenge to the definition of contemporary Jewish identity.[77]

Notes

The epigraph is from Zora Neale Hurston, *Moses, Man of the Mountain* (Philadelphia: J. B. Lippincott, 1939), xxiv.

1. Lawrence W. Levine, "Slave Songs and Slave Consciousness: An Exploration in Neglected Sources," in *African-American Religion: Interpretive Essays in History and Culture*, ed. Timothy E. Fulop and Albert J. Raboteau (New York: Routledge, 1997), 69.

2. Albert J. Raboteau, "The Black Experience in American Evangelicalism: The Meaning of Slavery," in Fulop and Raboteau, *African-American Religion*, 101.

3. For more on this shared universe, see Ernest Allen Jr., "Identity and Destiny: The Formative Views of the Moorish Science Temple and the Nation of Islam," in *Muslims on the Americanization Path?* ed. Yvonne Yazbeck Haddad and John L. Esposito (New York: Oxford University Press, 2000), 174.

4. R. Drew Smith, "Black Religious Nationalism and the Politics of Transcendence," *Journal of the American Academy of Religion* 66, no. 3 (1998): 539.

5. Genesis 9:22–25. For more on American interpretations of the Hamitic myth, see Paul Harvey, " 'A Servant of Servants Shall He Be': The Construction of Race in American Religious Mythologies," in *Religion and the Creation of Race and Ethnicity*, ed. Craig R. Prentiss (New York: New York University Press, 2003).

6. Allen, "Identity and Destiny," 169.

7. August Meir, "The Emergence of Negro Nationalism," *Midwest Journal* 4 (1952): 96.

8. Landing, *Black Judaism*, 340. The founding date of 1886 is according to Cherry's own account. Landing and others point out that this date is probably fabricated in order to usurp the Church of God and Saints of Christ's claims to be the first black Jewish group. The Church of God and Saints of Christ was established in 1896 in Kansas, but settled in Philadelphia and then Virginia. See Elly M. Wynia, *The Church of God and Saints of Christ: The Rise of Black Jews, Cults and Nonconventional Religious Groups* (New York: Garland, 1994).

9. Arthur Huff Fauset, *Black Gods of the Metropolis: Negro Religious Cults of the Urban North* (Philadelphia: University of Pennsylvania Press, 2002), 34. I will use the term "Israelite" to refer to members of any black Jewish group. This term is not meant to convey value or judgment, nor is it meant as a way to distinguish "real Jews" from "fake Jews." It is simply selected because of its prevalent use within Cherry's Church of God, as well as within

contemporary independent black Jewish communities, as a choice by their members and the leadership. This usage also attempts to avoid the confusion that emerges with the use of "white Jews" and "black Jews" or "Black Jews." Some scholars choose to use the term "Hebrew" or "Hebrew Israelite" as well in order to reflect the congregants' language. For a few examples, see James E. Landing, *Black Judaism: Story of an American Movement* (Durham, N.C.: Carolina Academic Press, 2001), 10; and Walter Isaac, "Locating Afro-American Judaism: A Critique of White Normativity," in *A Companion to African American Studies*, ed. Lewis R. Gordon and Jane Anna Gordon (Malden, Mass.: Blackwell, 2006), 538n1.

10. Landing, *Black Judaism*, 341.

11. Fauset, *Black Gods*, 115.

12. Ibid., 34–35.

13. Ibid., 35.

14. Like the Church of God's tale of Gehazi, the Nation of Islam also provided a creation myth which explained that the black race was the original race and that the white race was a race of devils maliciously created by a mad black scientist named Yakub. Steeped in the scientific language of the period from which the myth emerged, Fard Muhammad described the way that Yakub had grafted the color from some members of the Original Black Nation, the Original Tribe of Shabazz. Over a period of six hundred years, using the anachronistic philosophy and methods of (modern) eugenics, Yakub proceeded to create a lighter and lighter race of people. This painstaking process of hybridization resulted in the red and yellow peoples of the world, and, ultimately, the white race. See Claude Andrew Clegg, *An Original Man: The Life and Times of Elijah Muhammad* (New York: St. Martin's, 1997); and Edward E. Curtis, *Black Muslim Religion in the Nation of Islam, 1960–1975* (Chapel Hill: University of North Carolina Press, 2006).

15. Fauset, *Black Gods*, 34.

16. It is possible that this confusion with terminology stems from the rise of Talmud Torah schools in major cities at the turn of the century; these are elementary courses in Jewish education, particularly addressing the Torah. Roberta Gold notes that the Commandment Keepers of Harlem referred to their Hebrew school as Talmud Torah classes as well. Roberta S. Gold, "The Black Jews of Harlem: Representation, Identity, and Race, 1920–1939," *American Quarterly* 55, no. 2 (2003): 184.

17. Fauset, *Black Gods*, 36.

18. Ibid., 39.

19. It should be noted that forms of Passover observance have become more popular among evangelical Christian congregations, not just among Messianic Jews.

20. Frazier and Lincoln, *Negro Church in America* (New York: Schocken Books, 1964), 69.

21. Similar practices can be seen among some members of the Chabad-Lubavitch Hasidic movement (those who believe in the messianic status of the departed Rebbe Schneerson).

22. Fauset, *Black Gods*, 36.

23. Hans A. Baer and Merrill Singer, *African-American Religion in the Twentieth Century: Varieties of Protest and Accommodation* (Knoxville: University of Tennessee Press, 1992), 111.

24. Hans A. Baer and Merrill Singer, "Toward a Typology of Black Sectarianism as a Response to Racial Stratification," in Fulop and Raboteau, *African-American Religion*, 265.

25. Fauset, *Black Gods*, 99.

26. Ibid., 47.

27. Susan Nance, "Mystery of the Moorish Science Temple: Southern Blacks and American Alternative Spirituality in 1920s Chicago," *Religion and American Culture* 12, no. 2 (Summer 2002): 135.

28. Fauset, *Black Gods*, 115.

29. Landing, *Black Judaism*, 343.

30. Timothy Earl Fulop, " 'The Future Golden Day of the Race': Millennialism and Black Americans in the Nadir, 1877–1901," in Fulop and Raboteau, *African-American Religion*, 231.

31. Fauset, *Black Gods*, 32–33.

32. Larry Murphy, J. Gordon Melton, and Gary L. Ward, *Encyclopedia of African American Religions* (New York: Garland, 1993), 548.

33. Fauset, *Black Gods*, 35.

34. Baer and Singer, "Toward a Typology of Black Sectarianism," 266.

35. Fauset, *Black Gods*, 10.

36. D. Shapiro, "Double Damnation, Double Salvation: The Sources and Varieties of Black Judaism in the U.S." (M.A. thesis, Columbia University, 1969); and K. E. Simon, "A Grammar of the Mid-Week Service of the Church of the Living God" (M.A. thesis, Temple University, 1968).

37. There also appears to be confusion over the name of this congregation. While Fauset refers to it as the Church of God, other works may use the Church of the Living God or the Church of the Living God, The Pillar and Ground of Truth for All Nations. Other movements existed with the same name that may or may not be related in ideology.

38. Clegg, *An Original Man*. This anti-Africanism is also seen in black Christianity of the period. See James T. Campbell, *Songs of Zion: The African Methodist Episcopal Church in the United States and South Africa* (New York: Oxford University Press, 1998); and Charles I. Glicksberg, "Negro Americans and the American Dream," *Phylon* 8, no. 4 (1947).

39. Howard Brotz, *The Black Jews of Harlem: Negro Nationalism and the Dilemmas of Negro Leadership, Sourcebooks in Negro History* (New York: Schocken Books, 1970).

40. See further Yvonne Patricia Chireau and Nathaniel Deutsch, eds., *Black Zion: African American Religious Encounters with Judaism* (New York: Oxford University Press, 2000); Gold, "Black Jews of Harlem"; and Landing, *Black Judaism*.

41. Joseph R. Washington, *Black Sects and Cults* (Lanham, Md.: University Press of America, 1984), 132.

42. Ibid.

43. Graenum Berger, *Black Jews in America: A Documentary with Commentary* (New York: Commission on Synagogue Relations Federation of Jewish Philanthropies of New York, 1978), 68–69.

44. A South African branch of the Church of God and Saints of Christ underwent a split, which created a new sect called the Israelites. The Israelites rejected the New Testa-

ment altogether. See Gayraud S. Wilmore, *Black Religion and Black Radicalism: An Inter-pretation of the Religious History of Afro-American People*, 2nd ed. (Maryknoll, N.Y.: Orbis Books, 1983), 130.

45. Curtis Caldwell, personal interview, December 26, 1997. This gradual Judaization of the CGSC has parallels with the Islamicization of the Nation of Islam.

46. Hans A. Baer, "Black Spiritual Israelites in a Small Southern City: Elements of Protest and Accommodation in Belief and Oratory," *Southern Quarterly* 23 (1985): 110.

47. For further reading, see Wynia, *Church of God and Saints of Christ*.

48. Baer and Singer, *African-American Religion in the Twentieth Century*, 116.

49. Brotz, *Black Jews of Harlem*, 12.

50. Berger, *Black Jews in America*, 96.

51. Brotz, *Black Jews of Harlem*, 98.

52. Albert Ehrman, "The Commandment Keepers: A Negro Jewish Cult in America Today," *Judaism* 8 (Summer 1959): 267.

53. J. Gordon Melton, "Matthew, Wentworth Arthur," in *Biographical Dictionary of American Cult and Sect Leaders* (New York: Garland, 1986), 175.

54. *The African Hebrew Israelites of Jerusalem: Our Story*, www.kingdomofyah .com/our—story.htm, accessed May 1, 2007.

55. Berger, *Black Jews in America*, 195.

56. Ibid., 200.

57. Ibid., 196.

58. Israel J. Gerber, *The Heritage Seekers: American Blacks in Search of Jewish Identity* (Middle Village, N.Y.: Jonathan David, 1977), 124.

59. Bill Kurtis, "Strangers in the Holy Land," *New York Times*, March 22, 1981.

60. *The African Hebrew Israelites of Jerusalem* home page, http://village.ios.com/dckog/, accessed May 1, 2007.

61. See Merrill Singer and Ethan Michaeli's chapters in Chireau and Deutsch's *Black Zion*, 55–90.

62. Baer and Singer, *African-American Religion in the Twentieth Century*, 136.

63. Ibid., 117.

64. Ibid., 128.

65. Kurtis, "Strangers in the Holy Land."

66. Isaac, "Locating Afro-American Judaism," 515. The "Jesus litmus test" is also used in reference to "Messianic Jewish Congregations," which are primarily white.

67. Berger, *Black Jews in America*, 206.

68. Fauset, *Black Gods*, 69, 77, and 120. See Isaac, "Locating Afro-American Judaism," 512–42.

69. Landing, *Black Judaism*, 347.

70. Howard Brotz, "Negro 'Jews' in the United States," *Phylon* 13, no. 4 (1952).

71. Ruth Landes, "Negro Jews in Harlem," *Jewish Journal of Sociology* 9, no. 2 (December 1967): 176, as cited in Isaac, "Locating Afro-American Judaism," 515.

72. Washington, *Black Sects and Cults*, 134.

73. Ibid., 132.

74. Ibid., 155.

75. Anthropologist Karen Brodkin suggests the use of the term "ethnoracial" instead of marking a division between "ethnic" and "racial." Brodkin claims that the recent use of the term "ethnic" is in itself a racist affirmation, for it is used to refer mainly to differing peoples of European ancestry while "race" refers to everyone else's heritage. Karen Brodkin, *How Jews Became White Folks and What That Says About Race in America* (New Brunswick, N.J.: Rutgers University Press, 1998), 189n1. Ronald Takaki makes a similar point: "[R]ace . . . has been a social construction that has historically set apart racial minorities from European immigrants." Ronald T. Takaki, *A Different Mirror: A History of Multicultural America* (Boston: Little, Brown, 1993), 10.

76. Ethan Goffman, *Imagining Each Other: Blacks and Jews in Contemporary American Literature* (Albany: State University of New York Press, 2000), 228. This classification of Jews as a race is most often seen in anti-Semitic literature.

77. Racial diversity has recently begun to be analyzed within the Jewish community, albeit more within the understood "halakhic" categories. Diane Tobin, Gary A. Tobin, and Scott Rubin, *In Every Tongue: The Racial and Ethnic Diversity of the Jewish People* (San Francisco: Institute for Jewish & Community Research, 2005). For work on black converts to mainstream Judaism, see Nora L. Rubel, "Chicken Soup for the Souls of Black Folk: African American Converts to Judaism and the Negotiation of Identity," *Social Compass* 51, no. 3 (2004).

FOUR · Debating the Origins of the Moorish Science Temple: Toward a New Cultural History

EDWARD E. CURTIS IV

The fallen sons and daughters of the Asiatic Nation of North America need to learn to love instead of hate; and to know their higher self and lower self. This is the uniting of the Holy Koran of Mecca, for teaching and instructing all Moorish Americans, etc. The key of civilization was and is in the hands of the Asiatic nations. The Moorish, who were ancient Moabites, and the founders of the Holy City of Mecca. The Egyptians who were the Hamathites, and of a direct descendant of Mizraim, the Arabians, the seed of Hagar, Japanese and Chinese. The Hindoos of India, the descendants of the ancient Canaanites, Hittites, and Moabites of the land of Canaan. The Asiatic nations of North, South, and Central America; the Moorish Americans and Mexicans of North America, Brazilians, Argentinians and Chilians in South America. Columbians, Nicaraguans, and the natives of San Salvador in Central America, etc. All of these are Moslems. The Turks are the true descendants of Hagar, who are the chief protectors of the Islamic Creed of Mecca; beginning from Mohammed the First, the founder of the uniting of Islam, by the command of the great universal God-Allah.

—Holy Koran of the Moorish Science Temple 45:1–7

Established in 1925 by Timothy Drew, the Chicago-based Moorish Science Temple (MST) taught that African Americans were Moors from northwest Africa. Like all other Asiatic nonwhite peoples, argued their founder, their proper religion was Islam. Noble Drew Ali, as the prophet became known, insisted that this knowledge of black people's true national, religious, and racial origins would set them along a path of economic and political self-determination as well as moral renewal. In 1927, the prophet recorded his views for posterity in the *Holy Koran of the Moorish Science Temple*, and though he died in 1929, his movement spread to other northern U.S. cities and beyond.[1]

Arthur Huff Fauset's groundbreaking picture of the MST was among the first scholarly treatments of an African American Muslim community to appear in print. Though published in 1944, Fauset's short ten-page chapter on the movement stood for at least two decades as an authoritative source. When J. Milton Yinger published *Religion, Society, and the Individual: An Introduction to the Sociology of Religion* in 1957, he included Fauset's 1944 Moorish Science Temple chapter.[2] In the 1960s, the two most carefully researched books about Elijah Muhammad's Nation of Islam relied on Fauset as a main source on the MST, which was depicted as a precursor to the Nation of Islam.[3] Fauset's chapter had staying power. In fact, little new scholarship on the MST appeared until the 1990s and 2000s. This new scholarship was spurred by a renewed interest in the MST on the part of black studies scholars, as well as the development of African American Islam and Islam in America as subfields in religious studies.[4]

While much of this new scholarship surpassed Fauset's in its presentation of data, a vexing theoretical problem first encountered by Fauset continued to characterize the analysis of the MST. The problem emerged in attempting to answer questions about the origins of the group. Even though Fauset's chapter on the MST was full of rich ethnographic descriptions of the group, his *analysis* was concerned mainly with its psychological, political, and social benefits.[5] Avoiding cultural analysis of the movement was Fauset's answer to those scholars, like Melville J. Herskovits, who depicted black culture in heroic, but static and nearly atavistic terms.[6] Fauset's analysis of the contemporary contexts and functions of African American religious groups provided a useful antidote to Herskovits's ahistorical portrait of black religions in the United States. By stressing the larger contexts in which black persons lived, Fauset's alternative narrative of black religion showed that the "African's religious character" was neither monolithic nor unchanging.

But in devoting relatively little analysis to the historical origins of these new religious groups, Fauset ducked a question that would reappear with a vengeance in later African American studies scholarship. Herskovits's explorations of African retentions in African American culture were revived and reconstructed in the 1970s and 1980s.[7] Though old habits die hard, the field of black studies became increasingly diasporic in scope, at once reviving the importance of Africa to the study of black people in the United States while also insisting on a less static, more dynamic understanding of black cultures.[8] In the wake of this sea change, scholars writing about the MST brought back the question of origins as essential to understanding the movement. Was the MST influenced by African traditions? Was there continuity between the practices of West African Muslims and African American followers in the MST? If not from Africa, then from where did Noble Drew Ali get his ideas about the religious and national revival of black people?

In answering these questions, some old-fashioned, Herskovits-like Afrocentrists have insisted on direct continuity between black practices in Africa and those in America.[9] But most scholars of the African diaspora have seen the MST as the product of multiple influences, insisting, like Michael Gomez, that scholars examine the MST as a "convergence" of Islam, Freemasonry, New Thought, Rosicrucianism, black political thought, Garveyism, American Orientalism, Hoodoo, and Christian Science, among other traditions.[10] Contemporary scholars of the MST have debated the degree to which each of these traditions is expressed in the religious culture of the MST. Some accounts emphasize the cultural and social contexts of the Great Migration in the United States and claim that there are few African or Islamic influences on the movement.[11] Others, stressing a more transnational and diasporic view of the movement, see the MST not merely as a local or national phenomenon, but as the expression of modern black culture's global scope.[12] No matter what its particular bias, the best of this new scholarship utilizes dynamic notions of both black and Muslim identities to depict the human agency and creativity of those pioneering African Americans who called themselves "Moslems" in the 1920s. Utilizing this more recent scholarship, this chapter examines the multiple cultural influences on the origins of the MST while retaining Fauset's ethnographic sensitivity to the meaning of the movement for its participants. It suggests that a comprehensive cultural history of the MST has yet to be written and recommends lines of inquiry that must be pursued in creating a new account of the movement's origins.

Origins of the *Holy Koran of the Moorish Science Temple*

The sacred scripture Noble Drew Ali published in 1927 is a main source for existing scholarship on the MST. Also called the *Circle Seven Koran*, because of an encircled number "7" on its cover, this scripture argued that the national identity of Moors was tied inextricably to their racial heritage as Asiatics and their religious heritage as Muslims.[13] Noble Drew Ali refused to call himself Negro, black, or colored. "According to all true and divine records of the human race," he revealed, "there is no negro, black, or colored race attached to the human family, because all the inhabitants of Africa were and are of the human race" (47:9). He believed that all humans should separate themselves according to their respective national groups. Drew Ali's use of national and ethnic categories represented a reframing of the derogatory terms often associated with black people in the 1920s. For Drew Ali, a "nation" signified a common history, creed, and value system—in short, a whole culture. In this, his ideas were similar to those of many other Americans in the 1920s who saw culture as coterminous with race and religion.[14]

In place of this specifically "racial" understanding of black identity, Drew Ali offered a complex genealogy that viewed "Moors" in light of a glorious, but fallen past of historical achievements. According to the prologue of Drew Ali's *Holy Koran,* the "Moslems of northwest and southwest Africa are actually the Moabites, Hamathites, and Canaanites, all of whom were driven out of Canaan by Joshua. Having received permission from the Pharaohs to settle in Africa, these Muslims formed the modern-day kingdoms of Morocco, Algiers, Tunis, Tripoli, etc." Other Asiatic peoples, including the Egyptians, the Arabians, the Japanese and Chinese, the "Hindoos," the Turks, the South Americans, and even the "Mexicans in North America" settled the rest of the non-European world (45:1–7; 47:1–8). Synthesizing and rewriting various parts of ancient history, Noble Drew Ali explained that African Americans were the Moorish descendants of an ancient Asiatic race; their creed was Islam.[15]

For Drew Ali, it was not enough that blacks should be true to their nation; they should also be true to their particular creed. Specifically, he said, Moors should not "serve the gods of their [whites'] religion, because our forefathers are the true and divine founders of the first religious creed, for the redemption and salvation of mankind on earth" (48:6). Drew Ali, in other words, believed that being a good Moor meant keeping both foreign blood and foreign creeds out of the "nation." In constructing his Islamic tradition along lines of blood and geographic origins, Drew Ali also reinterpreted the meaning of Christ, arguing that Jesus was the Moors' genealogical ancestor: "Jesus himself was of the true blood of the ancient Cannanites and Moabites and the inhabitants of Africa" (46:2). Jesus had come to redeem "His people . . . from the pale skin nations of Europe" but "Rome crucified Him" (46:2–3). Drew Ali saw Jesus as a pan-Asiatic prophet whose teachings had been betrayed by the church. Christianity, founded by the Romans, had little to do with the message of Jesus, Drew Ali said. "The holy teaching of Jesus," he wrote, "was to the common people, to redeem them from under the great pressure of the hands of the unjust. That the rulers and the rich would not oppress the poor" (46:5). But Rome, according to Drew Ali, had essentially rejected these principles, which explained in part why white Christians had not acted in a Christian-like manner toward non-whites.[16]

The "pale skins" were not the only ones to blame for the degradation of the Moors, according to Noble Drew Ali. In fact, the prophet blamed the enslavement of blacks on moral and national decline among the Moors themselves. Because "they honored not the principles of their mother and father, and strayed after the gods of Europe," they had been stripped of their nationality and had been called "negro, black, and colored" (47:16–17). By not being true to their heritage and its obliga-tions, said Drew Ali, blacks had suffered the worst of fates: They did not know who they were and instead accepted the labels of their oppressors. "Through sin and disobedience," Drew Ali wrote, "every nation suffered slavery, due to the fact that they honored not the creed and principles of their forefathers" (47:17). Redemption, he taught, would come not from the acts of a single black messiah but through the collective actions of a whole nation—uplifting "fallen humanity," he insisted, must include linking oneself with the "families of nations" (48:11). Asiatics still held the "key to civilization," he continued, if they would only embrace their God Allah and seek national renewal. What this really meant for Drew Ali was not that blacks should return to Africa and establish nation-states, but that they should separate along racial lines from their oppressors. "Every nation shall and must worship under their own vine and fig tree, and return to their own and be one with their Father God-Allah" (48:3). Drew Ali desired a peaceful social separation from whites.

Like pan-African leader Marcus Garvey, Drew Ali denounced interracial rela-tionships, arguing implicitly that racial purity was necessary to black redemption: "We, as a clean and pure nation descended from the inhabitants of Africa, do not desire to amalgamate or marry into the families of the pale skin nations of Europe." Drew Ali also argued that only by returning to "their own kind" could humans hope to live in harmony: "All nations of the earth in these modern days are seeking peace, but there is but one true and divine way that peace may be obtained in these days and it is through Love, Truth, Peace, Freedom and Justice being taught universally to all nations, in all lands" (46:9). Peace among human beings would be possible, said Drew Ali, but only if every group would "learn of your forefathers' ancient and divine Creed. That you will learn to love instead of hate" (48:10). At the same time, Drew Ali seemed to support notions of Asiatic superiority and chosenness. The

Asiatics were of a "Divine origin," he said, failing to mention what he thought about the origins of whites. He also asserted that the church and Christianity might provide the Europeans with *earthly* salvation, but that Islam would grace Asiatics with earthly and *divine* salvation (48:7–8).

While chapters 45 through 48 of Noble Drew Ali's revelation focus on the religious, geographic, and national genealogy of African Americans, most other chapters were drawn from texts popular in the 1920s among various esoteric and metaphysical groups.[17] Chapters 1 through 19 of the *Holy Koran*, nearly half of the sixty-four-page text, are copied in exact form from the *Aquarian Gospel of Jesus the Christ*, a book written in 1908 by Levi H. Dowling (1844–1911). Dowling, a student of comparative religion and theosophy, wrote this alternative gospel of Jesus that, like other modern theosophical texts, incorporated beliefs in the universality of all religions, the mystical nature of the East, and the possibility of spiritual mastery of the "higher worlds." These themes, in addition to some information from the apocryphal Gospel of James, are apparent throughout Dowling's text. Dowling also borrowed from *La Vie Inconnue de Jesus Christ* (1894) by Nicolas Notovitch, who may have also influenced Ahmadiyya founder Ghulam Ahmad, author of *Jesus in India* (1899).[18]

Dowling himself explained the *Aquarian Gospel* as the product of his ability to "read" or sense the "Akashic Records," which existed in the highest realm of consciousness called the "Supreme Intelligence" or the "Universal Wisdom." According to Dowling, the Akashic Records were not physical things but a spiritual substance that reverberated throughout the universe. "When the mind of man," he wrote, "is in exact accord with the Universal Mind, man enters into a conscious recognition of these Akashic impressions, and may collect them and translate them into any language of the earth." His *Aquarian Gospel* posited that time was broken into dispensations determined by the rotation of the solar system around the center of the universe. Each age, he taught, was twenty-one hundred years long. As the world entered the twentieth century, a transition from the Piscean Age, or the Christian dispensation, to the Aquarian Age had begun. Dowling, reflecting theosophical influences, implicitly criticized the Christian age and the dominance of the church, claiming that the New Age, unlike the old, would be one of spirituality. Like other practitioners of metaphysical religion, Dowling believed in the possibility of mastering higher spiritual powers. In each human, he taught, there was a higher self, which was "human spirit clothed in soul," and a lower self, which was carnal and illusory. The soul, he said, was a divine thought planted in the human body, where it must undergo trials and tribulations before it could become pure soul again. These premises, the most fundamental in Dowling's creed, are highlighted in the first three chapters of the *Holy Koran*.[19]

Noble Drew Ali's text also includes Dowling's Christology. Christ, he taught, was no particular person, but a force, or logos, that might become manifest in any human. Like many theosophists, Dowling posited that belief in Christ's divinity must be understood symbolically rather than literally, lest humans mistake heaven as a reward for moral behavior. In Dowling's text, Jesus teaches that heaven is present to and abiding in the "conscious" soul. Drew Ali excerpted this lesson in chapters 11 and 12 of the *Holy Koran*. In addition, Dowling believed that Christ was a universal religious figure who had traveled throughout the entire ancient lettered world to spread his good news. During these travels, Dowling depicted Christ meeting with a representative of every world religion. Of these, Drew Ali selected for inclusion in the *Holy Koran* Jesus's meetings with a Buddhist priest, some Brahmins in India, and a Jewish scholar.[20] Finally, Drew Ali chose the stories of Elizabeth, John the Baptist, Jesus's Egyptian journeys, the crucifixion, the resurrection, and Jesus's "full materialization" (i.e., "transmutation of flesh into spirit-flesh") in different sites throughout the world to proclaim his resurrection.[21] In total, Drew Ali selected 19 of the 182 chapters and part of the introduction to Dowling's text for inclusion in his *Holy Koran*.

Chapters 20 through 44 of the *Holy Koran* were copied from either *Unto Thee I Grant* or *The Infinite Wisdom*. First published in Chicago in 1923 by the de Laurence Company, the latter work purported to be a translation of an ancient manuscript "found in the Grand Temple of Thibet" by a "Dr. Cao-Tsou, Prime Minister of China." The book's introductory sections included a letter supposedly written by the Chinese emperor to the Tibetan Grand Lama asking for permission on behalf of the prime minister to read and examine ancient Tibetan writings. Also included in these sections was a letter dated May 12, 1749, addressed to an anonymous English earl from the English translator of Cao-Tsou's Chinese translation of the original manuscript. This letter, which explained that the style of translation was intentionally biblical, also contained descriptions of Lhassa, the Potala, the Grand Lama, an account of Cao-Tsou's journey, and the text's Brahmin, Confuscian, and Taoist origins.[22]

In 1925, the Ancient and Mystical Order Rosae Crucis (AMORC), the largest Rosicrucian group in the United States, published a reprinted version of the text. These Rosicrucians were another modern esoteric group that traced their roots to early modern history, specifically to the Reformation and Counter-Reformation. Founded by the mythical Christian Rosencreutz, the Order of the Rose-Cross was as much an intellectual current as a real secret society. Rosicrucians believed that the heavenly realm of reality could be broached through the use of esoteric sciences. But their larger social goals by the 1900s were to use this knowledge in the reform of ethical behavior and education. In publishing *The Infinite Wisdom*, the order said that its first goal was to encourage "health, happiness, and peace in the earthly lives of men." Their second goal was "to enable men and women to live clean, normal, natural lives." In fact, the crux of the text espoused rather Victorian moral ideals that could have been mistaken for the basic civilizationist values of the mainline American Protestant denominations, both black and white.[23]

Noble Drew Ali selected a large portion of these for inclusion in the *Holy Koran*, including a number of passages regarding the duties of men, women, and children toward each other. Women were to be submissive, industrious, nurturing, and modest. Men were to select mates prudently and treat their wives with kindness. Children were to honor their parents. Masters were to be good to their servants, and servants were to be "patient" under the reproof of their master. All people, the text instructed, should be good citizens by avoiding envy, vanity, deception, oppression, inconstancy, weakness, and ignorance. Those who practiced the "infinite wisdom" would be thankful, sincere, truthful, consistent, and faithful. The pinnacle of wisdom, however, would be to accept life as it was, neither inherently good nor bad, but only what one makes of it. Only with work, the text urged, could humans avoid the miseries of life and lift themselves into a realm of pleasure and joy known only to the Universal Soul.[24]

All of these metaphysical texts offered the idea that human beings, through effort, might liberate themselves from their various forms of slavery, especially to a negative state of mind. Salvation was defined not as the otherworldly resting place of good souls, but as a this-worldly state of being. Drew Ali seemed to be saying that blacks could achieve true liberation in the here and now rather than in the afterlife. Noble Drew Ali's path to African American liberation can be summarized in the following way: Blacks must separate from whites, reclaim their original group identity, understand their divine origins, meditate upon the true spiritual nature of all being, and follow a strict moral code. Noble Drew Ali appropriated various strains of American and African American religious, political, and social thought to create his own understanding of what it meant to be a Moor. His religious identity was a hybrid; it was bricolage. But that did not make it any less authentic than any other religious identity.

Avoiding "Textbook Islam" in
Studying the Moorish Science Temple

The fact that the *Holy Koran of the Moorish Science Temple* contained no explicit references to or excerpts from the seventh-century Qur'an revealed to Muhammad of Arabia has often been seen as evidence that the group was, ultimately, fanciful and fake. Exploring the Islamic-ness of the MST has been a particularly daunting task for scholars, who have sometimes imposed a certain "textbook Islam" on the movement and, in so doing, come to doubt its authenticity as a Muslim group. This textbook Islam, created by Muslim and non-Muslim academics alike, too often adopts a modernist and reformist view of Islamic religiosity that will be familiar to most modern readers, since media pundits, Western policy makers, and some American Muslim missionaries constantly reproduce it.[25] Textbook Islam revolves around the Five Pillars of Islamic practice, a brief introduction to the Qur'an and Muhammad, an explanation of shari'a as "Islamic law," and the historical split between Sunni and Shi'a—with perhaps a sprinkling of Sufism or jihadism thrown in for good measure. For some students of the Moorish Science Temple and American religions more generally, this recipe seems to represent the total sum of their Islamic knowledge. On the one hand, the need for basic religious literacy among the general public makes such textbook knowledge a cultural imperative.[26] On the other hand, American studies scholars must be extremely cautious in foisting this rather simplistic model of Islamic religiosity upon Moorish American culture and practice. If scholars apply textbook Islam to the Moorish Science Temple, they may be tempted to conclude too hastily that the MST is not really Islamic and that Noble Drew was not a Muslim.[27] Textbook Islam generally ignores the contested and diverse meanings of being Muslim and often excludes folk Islam, antinomian Islam, and women's Islam.[28] It does not reflect the extent to which the so-called orthodox traditions of Islam have been connected in Islamic history to religious practices, like the veneration of the prophet Muhammad and his family, now out of favor among some modern Sunni Muslims.[29] If scholars are to reopen interpretive possibilities for understanding the cultural influences of Islamic tradition on the MST, they must become more familiar with such traditions.

One way to pursue the possibility of Islamic influence is to query the biography of MST founder Timothy Drew. Like the biographies of all prophets, his biography, as told by his followers, is a didactic and epic story, and it is difficult to separate historical fact from mythic truth. He was born January 8, 1886, in North Carolina to a Cherokee mother and "Moorish" father.[30] His North Carolinian provenance is evidence for at least one scholar that Timothy Drew may have been aware of Islamic practices or Muslim persons.[31] Certainly, there were practicing Muslims on the coasts of Georgia and the Carolinas, and one of the most well-known Muslim slaves in antebellum times, Omar ibn Sayyid, was discovered in North Carolina.[32] Of course, to what extent this presence of Islam and Muslims in the South influenced Noble Drew Ali's later appropriations of Islam is unclear, and it is hard to imagine the discovery of sources that will ever bear out such speculation. Scholars of the MST have not yet found any documents linking Timothy Drew to a particular time and place in the South, and in the absence of such sources, it is unclear how Drew Ali can be placed in a particular Muslim milieu there.

Furthermore, though more evidence of Islamic practice among North American slaves has emerged in the past two decades, scholars have not yet adequately theorized the problem of religious diversity among Muslim slaves. It is unlikely that all African American Muslims practiced the same forms of Islamic religiosity. With what type of Islamic expression might Noble Drew Ali have been familiar? The "Islam" of North American slaves was not monolithic or unchanging. Though urbane slaves like Omar ibn Sayyid were well versed in Qur'anic learning, Islamic *salat*, and Muslim saint worship, not all African Muslim slaves who were brought to the Americas would have had similar opportunities to study the Islamic sciences and visit the shrines of the saints in West Africa.[33] Furthermore, one must be sensitive to the possible diffusion of African Islamic practices into the African American religious culture often known as Conjure and the possibility that the meaning of such practices changed as they became part of a new cultural matrix. Persons who did not call themselves Muslims may have performed African Islamic practices whose Islamic meaning shifted or disappeared over time.[34]

Consider, for example, the Afro-Asian practice of using Qur'anic verses in the production of amulets.[35] It must be remembered that, despite the picture one may deduce from textbook Islam, for some Muslims, studying the exact claims of the Qur'an has not been central to their Muslim identity or spirituality. Indeed, there are examples of Muslims who barely talk about the Qur'an.[36] Certainly, until recently, many Muslims have not been able to read the Qur'an—they were illiterate. Even if they knew how to pronounce the letters, they may not have known what the words meant. Those verses that many Muslims know from the Qur'an have been memorized. Deep knowledge and analysis of the contents of the Qur'an and *tafsir*, or Qur'anic commentary, were generally left to religious specialists. Qur'anic literacy has increased in the modern world, but Muslims around the globe still enjoy reciting and listening to what is primarily an aural and oral text.[37] As in premodern times, the Qur'an also continues to be used not only as a theological and legal guide, but also as a source of healing and protection. If Noble Drew Ali was exposed to any part of African Islamic culture, he would have been far more likely to encounter amulets rather than a bound volume of the Qur'an. For many West African Muslims and even non-Muslims, verses of the Qur'an could be placed in an amulet to ward off evil or offer protection.[38] Often, a *shaykh,* or religious specialist, would instruct the layperson on how to use a particular amulet. Though there were many learned scholars of the Qur'an in West Africa and Arabic was an important lingua franca of the region, there were also Muslims and non-Muslims who had no idea how to read what was inside their amulets. What they knew was the text as talisman. Perhaps this was the Islam to which Noble Drew Ali was exposed, if he was exposed to Islam at all.

But Fauset's ethnographic coverage of the MST also reminds us that any search for the meaning of religious activity to African Americans must take account of the contemporary context in which that religion exists. Rather than locating the possible sources of Noble Drew Ali's Islam only in African retentions, one must also focus on the northern cities where Moorish Science was born. To place Noble Drew Ali's Islamic identity in the rich contexts of his time and place requires knowledge of the other forms of Islam that African Americans and others were practicing around Chicago, Detroit, and the other cities through which Noble Drew Ali moved. Michael Gomez helpfully speculates that the MST may have intentionally distanced itself from Sunni or "orthodox" Islam.[39] Prophet Noble Drew Ali, after all, offered revelation directly from God, investing himself with a divine authority that, for his followers, superseded the claims of other Muslims vying for the attention of black Americans in the 1920s. Rather than assuming that Noble Drew Ali was ignorant of other forms of Islam, this approach tries to understand what constructions of Islam he chose to include—and exclude—in his teachings.[40] The leader might have been exposed to numerous contemporaneous sources of Islamic knowledge, including Muslim immigrants from India and the Ottoman Empire, immigrant missionary tracts, African American veterans of the conflict with Muslims in the Philippines, Orientalist scholarship, the publications of the Universal Negro Improvement Association, the writings of Edward Blyden, and oral historical legends about Muslim ancestors in Africa.

The number of possible sources for Noble Drew Ali's Islam increases dramatically if one dates the establishment of the MST to 1925 rather than to 1913. A common mistake in the secondary and tertiary literature on the MST is to equate Noble Drew Ali's establishment of the *Canaanite* Temple in Newark, New Jersey, in 1913, with the establishment of the *Moorish Science* Temple in Chicago in 1925.[41] If the MST was established in Chicago, it is also likely that Noble Drew Ali knew about the success of the Ahmadiyya movement in converting African Americans to Islam. Even if Noble Drew Ali established the MST on the East Coast before 1920, he certainly would have learned later about the Ahmadiyya movement in Chicago. One way or another, Chicago, as Susan Nance has established, was a central place for the development, if not the birth of this movement. It was in Chicago, in the 1920s, where Noble Drew Ali published his *Holy Koran of the Moorish Science Temple*. And it was in Chicago, in 1928, where the Moorish Science Temple was officially incorporated and where the movement used Unity Hall, located on 3140 Indiana Avenue, as its headquarters.

Chicago was also an important center for the Ahmadiyya movement. Its Moslem Mosque and Mission House in Chicago was located by 1922 on 4448 Wabash Avenue, about two miles south of Unity Hall.[42] Originally established in 1889 in the Punjab by Ghulam Ahmad (d. 1908), the Ahmadiyya movement was a modern messianic group that sought the revival of Islam. Many of Ahmad's followers believed him to be a *mujaddid,* or a renewer of religion; the Islamic *mahdi,* an important figure in Islamic eschatology; and the Christian messiah. Though the group would face claims of heresy from other Muslims, Ahmadis were among the most successful Muslim missionaries in the first half of the 1900s.[43] In 1920, South Asian Ahmadi missionary Muhammad Sadiq arrived in the United States and quickly focused his evangelizing on African Americans. Sadiq promised black converts that they would experience true brotherhood and equality in Islam, claiming that "there is no question of color" in the East.[44] He also promoted Islam as the cultural and religious heritage of African Americans, stolen from them when the "Christian profiteers brought you out of your native lands of Africa and in Christianizing you made you forget the religion and language of your forefathers—which were Islam and Arabic."[45] The Ahmadi newspaper, the *Moslem Sunrise,* featured the stories of great black ancestors in Islam, persons like Bilal ibn Rabah, the first prayer-caller, and included pictures of black American Ahmadi leaders like P. Nathaniel Johnson or Sheik Ahmad Din.[46]

Speculating that Noble Drew Ali was at least familiar with this group by the time he revealed the *Holy Koran of the Moorish Science Temple,* one can conclude that Noble Drew Ali also knew the Ahmadi claim, repeated by African American converts, that Islam was part of their African heritage stolen from them during the Middle Passage. What is remarkable, continuing with this speculative line of reasoning, is how much of the Ahmadiyya he ignored. The Ahmadiyya missionaries were busy bringing translations of the Qur'an to African Americans in Chicago, but

Noble Drew Ali did not allude to any verses of the Qur'an in his own work. The Ahmadiyya taught their believers how to pray the *salat*, the prescribed Arabic prayers involving a series of prostrations toward the Ka'ba in Mecca. There is no evidence that the rituals of the MST included any aspects of these prayers. Ahmadi African American converts took on a variety of famous names from the history of Islam like Ahmad, Zeineb, Ayesha, and Abdul Basit; many of the Moors came to be known by the surname "Bey" or "El." There was, in sum, very little correspondence between the religious practice explicitly constituted as Islam in the MST and that in the Ahmadiyyah movement.

But there were other understandings of Islam available to Noble Drew Ali during this age, including the growing association of Islam with political protest and black resistance to colonialism and racism. Islam as a symbol of protest had been part of black English-speaking discourse at least since the era of the nineteenth-century leader Edward Wilmot Blyden, the African American Liberian professor and politician, whose English-language works, read in Britain, the Americas, and West Africa, praised Islam, the Qur'an, and West African Muslim society as effective vehicles of modern black manhood and nationalism.[47] Blyden's linkage of Islam and black nationalism was perpetuated in the English-speaking black world by the Universal Negro Improvement Association (UNIA). Arnold Ford, the musical director of the UNIA, included allusions to Allah in some of his movement songs, and the UNIA's *Negro World* supported pan-Islamic attempts to resist European imperialism. Marcus Garvey, the UNIA's founder, even compared himself to the prophet Muhammad, though he was careful to contrast his exclusively political aspirations with the religious goals of the Prophet.[48]

Noble Drew Ali's familiarity with Garveyism, and perhaps with the construction of Islam as political protest, is suggested most strongly by his explicit allusion to Garvey in the *Holy Koran:* "In these modern days there came a forerunner, who was divinely prepared by the great God-Allah and his name is Marcus Garvey, who did teach and warn the nations of the earth to prepare to meet the coming Prophet; who was to bring the true and divine Creed of Islam, and his name is Noble Drew Ali" (48:3). Noble Drew Ali hoped to assume the mantle of Garvey's leadership and to make the MST a successor to Garvey's UNIA. Unlike Garvey, however, Noble Drew Ali framed his mission in unmistakably religious terms. Whereas the Garvey movement supported the presence of religious diversity and the ecumenical African Orthodox Church, Noble Drew Ali condemned Christianity as a non-Asiatic religion. As one of the heirs competing for Garvey's legacy, Noble Drew Ali insisted that

Islam, not Christianity, was the proper religion of all Asiatics and that he was the prophet sent to bring the Moors back to their original religion.

Perhaps the greatest source of Noble Drew Ali's Islam was the culture of the Black Shriners, or the Ancient Egyptian Arabic Order of the Nobles of the Mystic Shrine, a Masonic group established at Chicago's World's Fair, or World's Columbian Exposition, in 1893. One indication of the Masonic influence on the MST, for example, is the way that Noble Drew Ali's hagiography was constructed as a classic Masonic tale: At age sixteen, Drew Ali traveled to Egypt as part of the merchant marine. In the land of the Pharaohs, he met the "last priest of an ancient cult of High Magic who took him to the Pyramid of Cheops, led him in blindfolded, and abandoned him." The priest offered Drew Ali initiation in the cult after making his way out. He became "Noble," a title used by Shriners. Noble Drew Ali's movement would come to incorporate many other Islamic symbols from the Shriners, including the star and crescent, the fez, and many Islamic names—the same names used in Shriner ceremony and architecture.[49]

In the past, scholars have asserted or at least implied that because Noble Drew Ali's understanding of Islam seems to be derived largely from the Shriners, his Islam was largely fake. For some, this Shriner's understanding of Islam reveals the chasm between Noble Drew Ali and "traditional Islam."[50] But why must one dismiss the Islamicness of the group just because their Islam came from the Shriners? Such criticisms construct a mythical authentic Islam against which the false Shriner's Islam of the MST can be measured. Taking a less imperious approach to Noble Drew Ali's Islam suggests another possibility—that the Shriners are no less an authentic source for Islam than any other. From the very beginning of Islam in the seventh century, Islamic ideas have drifted over the oceans and across the land through a variety of means, often being indigenized in the process.[51] Noble Drew Ali's appropriation of Islam, no matter what its source, need not be considered any less authentic just because its source is not listed in world religions textbooks.

To be sure, Noble Drew Ali's Islam bears little descriptive similarity to the orthodox Islam that is assumed to constitute the essence of real Islam in textbooks. But that point alone should not disqualify it as a form of Islam in the academic study of religion. If scholars have the right to make such judgments about the real Muslims versus the fake ones, they should be prepared to inform literally millions of Muslims around the world, from the Gayo to the Guyanese, that they are not real Muslims— since millions of Muslims do not practice many of the Islamic traditions supposedly essential to the religion of Islam.[52] Furthermore, scholars who exile certain Muslims to the margins of the academic study of religion blind themselves to the story of how so many human beings became Muslims. From the very beginning of Islamic history, Muslims reshaped the texts and traditions of Islam to reflect their local and regional identities and interests. Orthodox Islam itself is not a static entity, and understanding how "outsiders" shaped what today is considered mainstream Islam during the first several centuries of Islamic history is essential to understanding how Islamic law and ethics developed.[53] What Sunni and Shi'a Muslims established was not so much consensus about what their religion meant but rather networks of persons and institutions that debated the meaning of this religion over time and in space. "What people of faith share," Wilfred Cantwell Smith argued, "is not necessarily common definitions of what their religion means, but a common history." No person, said Smith, should be understood simply as a product of his or her tradition, but rather as a participant in that tradition.[54] The story of Islam must include all those persons who see themselves as part of that tradition, however construed. Once a scholar is thus freed from the limiting perspective of textbook Islam, one can take seriously Noble Drew Ali's mission as a Muslim messenger, and ask what he meant by calling himself a Muslim.

Religious Culture in the Moorish Science Temple

There are several essential questions about the meaning of being Muslim left to be answered. Following Susan Nance's lead, first one can learn more about the religious aspects of Freemasonry in the 1910s and 1920s. Noble Drew Ali's Islam may have been a familiar faith to those associated with American fraternal movements, particularly the Shriners. "Whether Masons, Shriners, Elks, or Pythians," writes Nance, "Ali and the initiates of other orders held in common rituals and philosophies, which some members perceived as only colorful remnants from a distant past, while those inclined to mysticism interpreted them as holding the key to spiritual transformation."[55] Like Masonic organizations, members of the MST learned secret knowledge and rituals meant to free them from the ignorance of the past and to permit them to serve others. In addition, like other African Americans touched in one way or another by American alternative religions, it is clear that the Moors' esoteric understanding of spiritual enlightenment and self-improvement was shaped by various metaphysical groups in the United States.[56]

There is a great deal of research yet to be done on the material culture and everyday activities of MST members. Little scholarship has been produced about the meaning and functions of their religious objects, ethical interactions, clothing styles, rituals, sacred space, and other forms of rank-and-file religious expression. For example, the Moors enjoyed not only religious services at their temple but grand displays and public rituals meant to expose others to Moorish wisdom and to build the group's popularity. Like many of black Chicago's other civic organizations, the Moors proudly participated in parades, donning turbans and waving American flags.[57] Did this pageantry have any religious importance? Or was it mere burlesque? Noble Drew Ali also performed public displays of his spiritual prowess, staging a "Moorish Drama" in which he promised to be hung with a rope like Jesus in the temple and to heal the sick. Other MST members performed songs and sold refreshments.[58] What religious meaning, if any, did this carnival have for those in attendance? In another event, reported the movement newspaper, the prophet performed a public exorcism. "Prophet's Spirit Routs Enemy from Hall," the *Moorish Guide* proclaimed.[59] Nance stresses the potential Masonic meanings of this act, but, given the context, it is worth asking whether members in the audience did not also see this as root work or Conjure.

There is other evidence to suggest that the material culture of the MST may have been more connected to African and African American folk practices than has been previously stated. Throughout many cities, the Moors became known for manufacturing and distributing various toiletries and herbal remedies. Their product line included Moorish Mineral and Healing Oil, and Moorish Body Builder and Blood Purifier, which was a tonic for "rheumatism, lung trouble, rundown constitutions, indigestion, and loss of manhood."[60] Nance interprets these products as evidence of Noble Drew Ali's Orientalism: "[I]n the early twentieth century, Americans would still have associated products like Moorish Mineral and Healing Oil, indeed Moorish-American identity itself, with magical transformation and Oriental abundance."[61] That may be so, but African Americans who had come north as part of the Great Migration may have equally associated the prophet's product with root work— the ancient wisdom of African or even Muslim ancestors.

There are other elements of Moorish religious culture mentioned by Fauset that remain largely unexplored in the literature. Even if we wish, like Fauset, to interpret the function of this religious expression in largely political and social terms, we still need to know much more about their meaning to the people who practiced them. For example, Fauset gives enticing descriptions of Moorish religious services, noting their quiet and contemplative nature, and the chanting, rather than the singing, of "Moslem's that Old Time Religion" to the tune of "Give Me that Old Time Religion."[62] At their Friday religious services, which began and ended on time, MST members quietly read the holy scripture of their prophet and were reminded of the importance of their name, their national origins, their religion, and their great Asiatic history in Canaan, Egypt, and Morocco. Followers extended their arms in a Masonic salute and prayed: "Allah, Father of the Universe, the father of Love, Truth, Peace, Freedom, and Justice. Allah is my protector, my Guide, and my Salvation by night and by day, through His Holy Prophet, Drew Ali. Amen." Just what theologies were being expressed as they prayed these words aloud? Fauset also noted that in Philadelphia, women and men were segregated in the temple, with the women sitting in front.[63] Was this an African American Victorian religious expression of "ladies first"? Fauset gives no interpretation, and there is precious little scholarship about women's religiosity in the MST more generally.[64]

Decades after it was published, it is remarkable that Fauset's account of the MST still provides leads for further exploration of the movement. In pursuing those leads, I have suggested, scholars must be weary of simplistic assumptions that limit the potential sources and meanings of Islam to members of the MST. Building on new scholarship about the MST, any comprehensive cultural history of the movement should also attempt to reveal more about the multiple meanings of the MST's religious culture to its participants, remembering that their imaginative worlds may have been shaped by their local circumstances, but were not limited by them. Understanding the meaning of Moorish religious culture can shed light on the question more generally of African American cultural formation during the Great Migration, revealing important insights about the role of religion in the material culture of the era. Exploring the cultural history of the MST might also explain better the relationship of African Americans to other Americans of color, especially immigrants from Muslim lands. Finally, it will provide scholars of the African diaspora with a better sense of how some African Americans were appropriating and constructing elements of the African heritage in their everyday life and practice.

Notes

1. See "The Moorish Science Temple of America," in Arthur Huff Fauset, *Black Gods of the Metropolis: Negro Religious Cults of the Urban North* (Philadelphia: University of Pennsylvania, 2002), 41–51.

2. See J. Milton Yinger, *Religion, Society, and the Individual: An Introduction to the Sociology of Religion* (New York: Macmillan, 1957), 498–507.

3. E. U. Essien-Udom, *Black Nationalism: A Search for an Identity in America* (Chicago: University of Chicago Press, 1962), 33–36, and C. Eric Lincoln, *The Black Muslims in America*, 3rd ed. (Grand Rapids, Mich.: William B. Eerdmans, 1994), 48–52.

4. See Susan Nance, "Respectability and Representation: The Moorish Science Tem-

ple, Morocco, and Black Public Culture in 1920s Chicago," *American Quarterly* 54, no. 4 (December 2002): 623–59; Susan Nance, "Mystery of the Moorish Science Temple: Southern Blacks and American Alternative Spirituality in 1920s Chicago," *Religion and American Culture* 12, no. 2 (Summer 2002): 123–66; Michael A. Gomez, *Black Crescent: The Experience and Legacy of African Muslims in the Americas* (Cambridge: Cambridge University Press, 2005), 203–75; Yvonne Y. Haddad and Jane I. Smith, *Mission to America: Five Islamic Sectarian Communities in North America* (Gainesville: University Press of Florida, 1993), 79–104; Ernest Allen Jr., "Identity and Destiny: The Formative Views of the Moorish Science Temple and the Nation of Islam," in *Muslims on the Americanization Path?*, ed. Yvonne Yazbeck Haddad and John L. Esposito (New York: Oxford University Press, 2000), 163–214; Richard Brent Turner, *Islam in the African American Experience,* 2nd ed. (Bloomington: Indiana University Press, 2003), 71–108; and Edward E. Curtis IV, *Islam in Black America: Identity, Liberation, and Difference in African-American Islamic Thought* (Albany: State University of New York Press, 2002), 45–62.

5. Fauset, *Black Gods,* 90–91.

6. Ibid., 3–4, 82n7, 101–104.

7. See, for example, Sterling Stuckey, *Slave Culture: Nationalist Theory and the Foundations of Black America* (New York: Oxford University Press, 1987).

8. See, for example, Paul Gilroy, *The Black Atlantic: Modernity and Double Consciousness* (Cambridge: Harvard University Press, 1993).

9. See Jose V. Pimienta-Bey, "Some Myths of the Moorish Science Temple: An Afrocentric Historical Analysis" (Ph.D. diss., Temple University, 1995).

10. Gomez, *Black Crescent,* 204.

11. See especially the work of Susan Nance, cited above.

12. For examples of more global approaches to the MST, see Turner, *Islam in the African American Experience,* and Gomez, *Black Crescent.*

13. My copy of the *Holy Koran,* now widely available in redacted forms through the internet, is from the MST's FBI file. See File 100–3095, 1/28/42, in HQ 62–25889, sec. 1 in *FBI File on the Moorish Science Temple of America* (Wilmington, Del.: Scholarly Resources, 1995).

14. See further Walter Benn Michaels, *Our America: Nativism, Modernism, and Pluralism* (Durham, N.C.: Duke University Press, 1995), 14–15, 30–32, 78, 84.

15. *Holy Koran of the MST,* 3, 56–59.

16. Ibid., 57–60.

17. See further Hans A. Baer, *The Black Spiritual Movement: A Religious Response to Racism* (Knoxville: University of Tennessee Press, 1984), 82–98.

18. Levi H. Dowling, *The Aquarian Gospel of Jesus the Christ,* 6th ed. (1908; London: L. N. Fowler, 1920), 13; and Edgar J. Goodspeed, *Modern Apocrypha* (Boston: Beacon, 1931), 15–17. Nicolas Notovitch's *La Vie Inconnue de Jesus Christ* was published by Paul Ollendorff (Paris) in 1894; Ghulam Ahmad, *Jesus in India* (1899; Rabwah, West Pakistan: Ahmadiyya Muslim Foreign Missions Dept., 1962).

19. Dowling, *Aquarian Gospel,* 5–12, 31–32.

20. Compare the *Holy Koran of the MST,* chapters 5, 6, 7, and 11, with Dowling, *Aquarian Gospel,* chapters 18, 21, 22, and 32 on pages 44, 47–49, and 60–62.

21. Compare *Holy Koran of the MST,* chapters 2, 4, and 13–19 with Dowling, *Aquarian Gospel,* chapters 1, 15, 47, 61, 65, 168, 178, 172, and 176 on pages 25, 40–41, 78–79, 93–94, 97–98, 239–40, 253–55, 244–46, and 250–51.

22. See the introduction to *The Infinite Wisdom* (Chicago: De Laurence, 1923). For a scholarly work on Tibetan Orientalism in the West, see Donald S. Lopez Jr., *Prisoners of Shangri-La: Tibetan Buddhism and the West* (Chicago: University of Chicago Press, 1998). *Unto Thee I Grant,* author unknown (San Francisco: Oriental Literature Syndicate, 1925).

23. See Sri Ramatherio, ed., *Unto Thee I Grant,* rev. ed. (San Jose, Calif.: Supreme Grand Lodge of the AMORC, 1953), 93–97; Stephen R. Prothero, "Rosicrucians," in Edward L. Queen et al., *The Encyclopedia of American Religious History* (New York: Facts on File, 1996), 575–76; Frances A. Yates, *The Rosicrucian Enlightenment* (London: Routledge and Kegan Paul, 1972), 220–23; and Harry Wells Fogarty, "Rosicrucians," in *The Encyclopedia of Religion,* ed. Mircea Eliade (New York: Macmillan, 1987), 12: 476–77.

24. Compare *Holy Koran of the MST,* 32–56, with *Infinite Wisdom,* 27–102, or its exact equivalent in the AMORC edition.

25. For examples, see Catherine L. Albanese, *America: Religions and Religion,* 3rd ed. (Belmont, Calif.: Wadsworth, 1999), 292–300; John Bowker, *World Religions* (New York: DK Publishing, 2006), 176–95; and Jamal J. Elias and Nancy D. Lewis, *The Pocket Idiot's Guide to Islam* (Indianapolis: Alpha, 2002). To clarify, these are effective textbook treatments, and I have taught each of them in my college classes. But their models of Islamic religion should not be applied in a normative fashion to all forms of Islamic religiosity.

26. See further Stephen Prothero, *Religious Literacy: What Every American Needs to Know—and Doesn't* (New York: HarperSanFrancisco, 2007).

27. Sylviane Diouf, for example, portrays Noble Drew Ali's claim to be a prophet "in total opposition to a crucial tenet of Islam." This pronouncement ignores the debates in Islamic tradition over the nature of prophecy and its status in the absence of Muhammad—and takes sides in an Islamic debate. See Sylviane A. Diouf, *Servants of Allah: African Muslims Enslaved in the Americas* (New York: New York University Press, 1998), 205–206.

28. For criticism of a "pamphlet Islam" that tends to present an overly simplistic vision of Islamic religion and excludes too many Muslim voices in favor of presenting a monolithic, modern, and reformist version of Islam to the public, see Omid Safi, ed., *Progressive Muslims: On Justice, Gender, and Pluralism* (Oxford: Oneworld, 2003), 22–23.

29. See further Carl W. Ernst, *Following Muhammad: Rethinking Islam in the Contemporary World* (Chapel Hill: University of North Carolina Press, 2004).

30. Peter Lamborn Wilson, *Sacred Drift: Essays on the Margins of Islam* (San Francisco: City Lights Books, 1993), 15.

31. Gomez, *Black Crescent,* 204.

32. See further Allan D. Austin, *African Muslims in Antebellum America: Transatlantic Stories and Spiritual Struggles* (New York: Routledge, 1997); Diouf, *Servants of Allah;* and Gomez, *Black Crescent,* 143–84.

33. For a reprint of Omar ibn Sayyid's 1831 autobiography in Arabic, see Edward E. Curtis IV, ed., *Columbia Sourcebook of Muslims in the United States* (New York: Columbia University Press, 2007).

34. Albert Raboteau makes a similar claim about the diffusion of Conjure and African religions more generally into African American Christianity. See *Slave Religion: The "Invisible Institution" in the Antebellum South*, updated ed. (New York: Oxford University Press, 2004), esp. 4–92.

35. For a sense of the importance of amulets, one cannot consult the typical textbook. Start with Kathleen Malone O'Connor, "Amulets," in *The Encyclopedia of the Qur'ān*, ed. Jane D. McAuliffe (Leiden: E. J. Brill, 2001), 77–79.

36. See, for example, James L. Peacock, *Purifying the Faith: The Muhamadijah Movement in Indonesian Islam* (Menlo Park, Calif.: Benjamin/Cummings, 1978).

37. For an introduction to the Qur'an as an aural and oral text, see Michael A. Sells, *Approaching the Qur'an: The Early Revelations* (Ashland, Ore.: White Cloud Press, 1999).

38. See further David Robinson, *Muslim Societies in African History* (Cambridge: Cambridge University Press, 2004), 44–45, 53.

39. Gomez, *Black Crescent*, 232.

40. Compare Nance, "Mystery of the Moorish Science Temple," 142. Nance asserts that African Americans would have known little about Islam other than the exotic images appearing in the *Chicago Defender*. Such an assumption ignores the fact that *some* African Americans knew a great deal more about Islam than that.

41. See, for example, Turner, *Islam in the African American Experience*, 92, and Jane I. Smith, *Islam in America* (New York: Columbia University Press, 1999), 79, 205.

42. *Moslem Sunrise* (Ahmadi newspaper), October 1922, 126.

43. See further Yohanan Friedman, *Prophecy Continuous: Aspects of Ahmadi Religious Thought and Its Medieval Background* (Berkeley: University of California Press, 1989).

44. *Moslem Sunrise*, October 1921, 41.

45. *Moslem Sunrise*, April and May 1923, 184. The similarity to Elijah Muhammad's later thought suggests that Elijah Muhammad was influenced by the Ahmadiyya.

46. See *Moslem Sunrise*, October 1932/January 1933, 31–33, and July 1922, 119.

47. See Edward Wilmot Blyden, *Christianity, Islam, and the Negro Race* (1887; Edinburgh: Edinburgh University Press, 1967); Hollis Lynch, *Edward Wilmot Blyden: Pan-Negro Patriot, 1832–1912* (London: Oxford University Press, 1967); Hollis Lynch, ed., *Selected Letters of Edward Wilmot Blyden* (Millwood, N.Y.: KTO Press, 1978); and Turner, *Islam in the African American Experience*, 47–59.

48. Randall K. Burkett, *Garveyism as a Religious Movement* (Metuchen, N.J.: Scarecrow, 1978), 178–81. Garvey's pan-Africanism was influenced partly by Dusé Mohammed Ali, publisher of the *African Times and Orient Review*. Garvey knew Ali from London, where he also read the works of Blyden in the British Library. See Turner, *Islam in the African American Experience*, 83–86; Gomez, *Black Crescent*, 259–60; and Ian Duffield, "Dusé Mohamed Ali and the Development of Pan-Africanism, 1866–1945" (Ph.D. diss., Edinburgh University, 1971).

49. Wilson, *Sacred Drift*, 6–7.

50. Susan Nance, for example, insists that Noble Drew Ali's "influences were not Muslim but rather distinctly American," creating a false dichotomy between Islam and America, and ignoring the fact that Islam had been an American tradition from the very

beginning of the Columbian Age. See Nance, "Mystery of the Moorish Science Temple," 125.

51. For various treatments of how Islam became indigenized in its growth and development, see Devin A. DeWeese, *Islamization and Native Religion in the Golden Horde: Baba Tükles and Conversion to Islam in Historical and Epic Tradition* (University Park: Pennsylvania State University Press, 1994); Richard M. Eaton, *Essays on Islam and Indian History* (New York: Oxford University Press, 2000); and Nehemia Levtzion, *Conversion to Islam* (New York: Holmes and Meier, 1979).

52. Compare David Robinson, "Western Views of Africa and Islam," in *Muslim Societies in African History*, 74–88.

53. Richard W. Bullet, *Islam: The View from the Edge* (New York: Columbia University Press, 1994).

54. See further Wilfred Cantwell Smith, *Toward a World Theology: Faith and Comparative History of Religion* (Maryknoll, N.Y.: Orbis Books, 1981), 4–5, 27–28.

55. Nance, "Mystery of the Moorish Science Temple," 138.

56. For more on metaphysical religions in American religious history, see Catherine L. Albanese, *A Republic of Mind and Spirit: A Cultural History of American Metaphysical Religion* (New Haven: Yale University Press, 2007).

57. Nance, "Respectability and Representation," 643.

58. Wilson, *Sacred Drift*, 30.

59. Nance, "Respectability and Representation," 633.

60. Ibid., 629.

61. Ibid., 630.

62. Fauset, *Black Gods*, 49.

63. Ibid., 50.

64. One source that takes seriously the role of women in the MST is Debra Washington Mubashshir, "A Fruitful Labor: African American Formulations of Islam, 1928–1942" (Ph.D. diss., Northwestern University, 2001). It is worth noting that the *Moorish Guide*, a bimonthly periodical, was edited in the late 1920s by a Moorish female poet, Juanita Mayo Richardson-Bey. See further Gomez, *Black Crescent*, 261–62.

FIVE · "The Consciousness of God's Presence Will Keep You Well, Healthy, Happy, and Singing": The Tradition of Innovation in the Music of Father Divine's Peace Mission Movement

LEONARD NORMAN PRIMIANO

I first read Arthur Huff Fauset's account of Father Divine in the 1980s, as a doctoral student at Fauset's alma mater, the University of Pennsylvania. Don Yoder, the dean of American folklife studies, liked to use *Black Gods of the Metropolis* in his classes, including "Sects and Cults in American Religion." The text spotlighted groups Yoder felt were extremely important for understanding the full picture of religion in America. Fauset's descriptions of the believers he encountered mirrored the ethnographic work that Yoder had done since the late 1940s with the Pennsylvania Germans, another group of understudied American sects. Yoder's admiration stemmed from Fauset's attempt to create a historical and contemporary picture of American religiosity based on fieldwork—direct contact with believing men and women. Furthermore, to his enormous credit, Fauset was one of the first scholars of American religion to take seriously the study of "sects" and "cults," and especially African American sects and their leaders, including Father Divine. Fauset did not write derisive exposes on Father Divine's sexuality, money, or possessions, but worked to achieve what he felt was a dignified analysis through ethnographically based research.[1] The fact that Fauset's research was primarily centered in the city of Philadelphia and that a Peace Mission hotel, the Divine Tracy, along with its public cafeteria, could be found only a few blocks from Yoder's Penn classroom in West

Philadelphia satisfied him even more because the students could experience at close range at least one of the communities that Fauset had studied.

Being trained in the folklife studies approach by Yoder, I recognized that attention to the nuances of everyday life is a singularly important contribution that ethnographic work can make to understanding religious culture, especially emphasizing aesthetic or artistic creation; historical process; the construction of mental, verbal, or material forms; and the relationship and balance of utility and creativity to such forms within a particular context.[2] As a budding folkloristic ethnographer, especially interested in the expressive culture of religious movements, I, therefore, was delighted that Fauset opened his discussion of Father Divine's Peace Mission Movement not with a portrait of Father Divine as so many other authors had done, but with the moving account of the conversion of a male follower named Sing Happy.[3] Fauset offered a portrait of this man, including Sing Happy's powerful testimony of how Father Divine helped him gain stability in his life and robustness in his health during seven years of committed belief in this religious leader, thought to be an incarnation of God on earth. Fauset also thoughtfully included an explanation of how this follower received his spiritual name. For Sing Happy made a public testimony with his name every day, conveying the importance of the tradition of singing in the lives and rituals of the Peace Mission membership. Fauset's approach to studying this man and his religious community can be viewed as folkloristic in nature, as he was mindful of this religion's rhythms of work, play, eating, and ritual, as well as the powerfully familiar musical and lyrical soundscapes that accompanied those occasions. Throughout his study, Fauset was particularly attentive to the music and songs of the Peace Mission, noting how the rhythm of life was best described through song in the case of one female follower.[4]

In paying attention to the beliefs and practices of such followers and by giving attention to how they expressed themselves—privately, publicly, ritually—Fauset both challenged and reassessed the scholarly and popular impression of the stiffness and rigidity of the members of so-called sects and cults.[5] Still, many questions appear to have been left unasked by Fauset. How, for example, did the variety of songs fit into the lives of followers and connect to Father Divine himself? What was it about the expressive culture of the Peace Mission that prompted this child of Father Divine to "Sing Happy" and be in such improved health?

Fauset, of course, was trained as a traditional sociocultural anthropologist of his time. Thus, while attentive to the worldview of members of African American sects, especially in such symbolic forms as their expressive arts of song, testimonial, and costume/dress, the chapters of *Black Gods* tend to emphasize these groups as social institutions relating to African American and non–African American society. After the opening sketch of Sing Happy, Fauset assumes a rather conventional anthropological stance of using the testimony of this man as a springboard for a discussion of the structure, social and hierarchical organization, finance, membership, history, and ritual of the Peace Mission. As sensitive as Fauset was to his fieldwork informants and their expressive culture, therefore, the beliefs and practices of everyday practitioners were added for illustrative purposes but were obviously not perceived as worthy of analysis as the activities and writings of the religious leaders or more public figures in the movement. Still, Fauset's text demonstrates his enormous sensitivity to the idea that one could ascertain significant data about an American religious group by interacting with its ordinary believers. In terms of an approach to data collection and analysis of material relevant to the study of American religion, then, Fauset's approach was revolutionary, was highly unusual for its day, and remains enormously useful.[6]

Undoubtedly, followers, such as "Father Divinites," presented unique fieldwork challenges to the young anthropologist because, quite simply, these members did not want to be observed and interviewed.[7] They resisted and were cautious about this fieldworker, both, I imagine, to see whether he wanted to become a follower (as they were responding to his questions about prayer and baptism and generally "enlightening him a bit") or whether he was another reporter or writer.[8] Given their theological perspective on self that deemphasized aggrandizement of the individual personality in public and even private ways, individual members did not seek to state their opinions in any public forums such as books, magazines, or dissertations. This reticence is evident in the notes Fauset provides on "Four women in a Father Divine Peace Mission dress shop" in appendix A, "Selected Case Materials."[9] Fauset notes here that his attempt to consult the women for information led to a discussion "among themselves [of] the worth-whileness of talking with the interviewer."[10] In addition, Fauset asks these sisters in the Peace Mission questions that appear to insult them, and he acknowledges this fact to his readers. What is wonderful in this account of the interview is how reflexive and frank Fauset is about the fieldwork experience and that he chose this example to inform and teach his readers about how wrong or inappropriate questions to believers in the field can prompt critical responses from them. While he does not specifically state it, the need for sensitivity between the researcher and informants/consultants is obviously of great concern to him. Fauset's approach, while attentive to some of the nuances of community religious life, missed details of their mercantile, artistic, and religious lives that would flesh out the culture of the Peace Mission Movement in the 1930s and 1940s: Where exactly was this dress shop? What were the women making? Who would wear these dresses? Who made decisions about their style and design and color? Did they make dresses for followers? It is into such gaps that the present chapter steps, simultaneously building on Fauset's initial insights while further contributing both to the process of working with religious groups and to contemporary readers' understanding of the Peace Mission's creative and adaptive worldview.

The Peace Mission: Contemporary Ethnographic Opportunity and Challenge

The challenges of ethnographic work with the followers of any religious community, especially within one's own society, are enormous. The demands of ethnographic work within the Peace Mission Movement, a community that wishes to be noticed and appreciated, but not necessarily studied or analyzed in publications by scholars, adds additional layers of complexity. According to Spickard, Landres, and McGuire, some relevant issues that need attention when considering contemporary religious ethnography are the following: "the problem of subjectivity; the insider/outside problem; the question of researcher identity; and issues of power."[11] I, of course, had none of these concerns in mind when I first encountered, over twenty years ago, the Peace Mission members that I had only read about in Fauset's work. I never decided to "study" the Peace Mission per se, but only gradually fell into a relationship of trust with the followers and Mother Divine that eventually allowed me to begin a research process that has included formal interviewing, photographing, videotaping, and much time dining, singing, and otherwise interacting with the members.[12] But, as my twenty-year relationship with them demonstrates, it is time that builds relationship—an element that ethnographers sometimes do not have in abundance—and often it takes much patience to abide and to absorb the culture.

My relationship with the Peace Mission thus began quite innocently about five decades after Fauset concluded his research and writing. It began quite easily and tastily—without any intention whatsoever by me of mounting such a study—over lunch. This inexpensive service was provided throughout the 1980s and 1990s at the mission's Keyflower Dining Room in the already-mentioned Divine Tracy Hotel adjacent to the university campus. Throughout many years of eating in the dining room, I naturally spoke with the staff, all "coworkers" in the Peace Mission, whom I saw several times a week. I read through, and sometimes took with me and filed, Peace Mission literature that was placed on an entrance table for the curious. One day, I was invited to a Holy Communion Banquet Service during the celebration of the wedding anniversary of Father and Mother Divine, an event still commemorated, even though Father Divine "voluntarily threw off his body" (that is, died) in 1965. It took me ten years of eating the wonderful food of the Peace Mission in the Divine Tracy Hotel cafeteria before I even contemplated a study of the members that I was encountering. My course on American religious movements prompted me to begin a relationship with Mother Divine and her followers, but it took fifteen years from the time I first brought students to the hotel before I felt comfortable even to appear at Holy Communion Banquet Services by myself, and then to bring guests of my own to special and weekly rituals. (Many members of the American Academy of Religion and the American Folklore Society have been my guests at these occasions.) The need for proper demeanor, daunting to outsiders in many Peace Mission contexts, was a trait that I developed going to Philadelphia parochial schools for twelve years and has been absolutely essential to carrying out my work with the community. Gradually, through persistence, and by showing knowledge of Father Divine's teachings, a willingness to learn more, and an appreciation for their community and years of service in Philadelphia, I was allowed to do ethnographic work within the Peace Mission. The followers knew I was a researcher—and a practicing Roman Catholic—but they also perceived that I had tremendous respect for this American religion.

I have been attentive over the years to the structure of their lives and organization, but, as a folklorist also trained in religious studies, I have also been most attracted to the artistry and aesthetics of their everyday lives, as well as the richness of these individual members' uses of architecture, foodways, testimonial, photography, and singing traditions. In addition, I have appreciated not only the community as a structure containing individuals, but also the community as a culture of individuals—men and women unified in belief, but not homogenous, monotoned drones of allegiance; men and women, sharing a code for living, but who, if one takes the time to know them, offer distinctive expressions and reflections of that religious system. Initially, this interest in the expressive culture of the Peace Mission led me to consider their "vernacular architecture of intention," that is, how they reused and restored buildings for their own theological, social, and economic purposes without the need to design and build new structures.[13] The present chapter works to illuminate one of those traditions that Fauset instinctually noticed as important but that he did not stop to consider in any detail: namely, song and music within the Peace Mission. As I explore here, a similar intentionality and creativity operates in this form of expression as well.

A Religious Culture of Music and Song

Speaking with authority about the musical culture of the Peace Mission would not be possible without the assistance of the followers themselves and their great generosity in sharing their personal and spiritual lives and thoughts with me. One such account was given to me by Miss G, a follower from Australia.[14]

It is 1931. In a house at 72 Macon Street, in Sayville, Long Island, a crowd of people are gathered in a dining room around a special T-shaped table. They are dining on a meal consisting of many courses, but this is not a dinner where conversation is the central activity. Instead, it is a religious service, the Holy Communion Banquet Service of the Reverend M. J. Divine, also known as "Father Divine." The assembled are serving themselves from large platters of food passed out by Father to the diners. Some people testify about Father Divine's positive influence on their lives; others occasionally shout ecstatic praise. Still others dance in the spirit. The expressive forms that dominate the service and carry it along for over three hours, however, are music and song: melodies played on a piano accompanying congregational singing. The crowd sings loudly and with confidence:

> Now isn't this a happy day
> We've reached the Promised Land.
> We will not be divided
> One holy, happy band.
> To Be with one another
> Forever More to Stay.
>
> Oh, Sing and Praise Him
> Sing and Praise Him,
> Sing and Praise Him
> For the Glorious Work He Has Done

On this day the Browns, an Australian couple, are present among the worshippers.

Introduced to the ideas of the Peace Mission in New Thought discussion groups in New York City, the Browns had decided to come to Sayville to experience Father Divine for themselves. And they were convinced, like many others present, that this diminutive, charismatic, African American preacher and healer and New Thought exponent was the incarnation of the Creator God. Though they wished to remain with Father, as foreign nationals they were forced to leave the United States during the Great Depression.

Back home in Australia, the Browns visited meetings influenced by the Unity

School of Christianity and Christian Science in Melbourne and elsewhere, and they recounted their personal experiences with Father Divine in Long Island. In Sydney, they influenced a recent university graduate, Miss G, a gifted modern dancer and student of Mrs. Brown, who herself had traveled to New York to study with Martha Graham. In recordings and films brought back by the Browns, Miss G heard Father Divine's voice as he preached and observed his movements serving the banquet table. For the first time, she also experienced Peace Mission songs sung by Mr. and Mrs. Brown. As Miss G explained to me, "They heard them from Father in Sayville. He sang them himself. Beautiful, simple songs. So metaphysical."[15]

Miss G would not actually meet Father Divine until she traveled to the church's headquarters in Philadelphia in 1953 as a Fulbright scholar. Now a forty-year resident of the city, Miss G, in an interview with me, emphasized the centrality of songs and the act of singing for followers—that "prayer and praise are synonymous." "We [in the Peace Mission] don't pray together, but . . . when we get together . . . we sing." Singing, she explains, allows you to "take your mind off of other things and place it on a focal point. It then remains in your subconscious and heart through repetition."

Miss G invokes a theology about song creation articulated by Father Divine himself, who composed some songs for his community back in the movement's formative years in Sayville.[16] In fact, during Holy Communion Banquet Services, it was singing and songs that often motivated his sermons, and always preceded them. Often referring to songs as "inspirations," he identified a spiritual center and focus of all such artistic expression—namely, himself. For example, on January 19, 1936, at an afternoon Banquet Service, he stated:

> Oh, it is a privilege to realize that the artistic stream from the mystery of God's Presence is in the undercurrents of your sub-consciousness waiting to be awakened by the spirit of My Presence, to inspire you with Wisdom, Knowledge, and Understanding, that you might be honest—scientifically honest from the art of singing, the art of playing, the art of drawing, and everything, for you have contacted this artistic stream. If you think on ME vividly and harmoniously, I will quicken that something within your sub-consciousness, and cause you to be inspired with an inspiration that will teach you wisdom, knowledge, and understanding, and you will come to be poetically inclined, as well as inspirationally inclined.[17]

Almost a decade later, in August 1942, at a Philadelphia service, again using the performance of a song as the foundation for his message, Father Divine reminded his followers about the creative meaning of their song and music traditions and how sincerity should be at the center of any such outward spiritual expression:

Peace, Everyone: That little inspiration as a composition just sung is well worth considering if you stop and consider what you sing and realize it is a prayer in itself. If you will make such a request, your prayer will be heard and answered speedily, for you will find a closer walk with God. We do not believe in merely singing to be singing—to make music, but we believe in singing with all sincerity and whatsoever your desires may be, when you sing or when you make a request, it be with all sincerity, even if you are speaking it in poetry; God knows the sincere desire of the heart; your prayers are heard and answered speedily and all will find that long-sought-for Something that will satisfy every desire.[18]

Today, such "inspirations" exist in abundance and are an example of a living tradition of American religious song located within the still-active remnant of the Peace Mission found in Philadelphia and New Jersey, under the leadership of an ever robust Mother Divine, Father Divine's Vancouver-born, "light-complected" (using their terminology) second wife.[19] The musical tradition of this indigenous American intentional community encompasses a repertoire of thousands of songs with hundreds in active use.

These songs, though internally created, are rarely identified with their composers. Employing a corporate sense of ownership, they are also never reproduced with personal identifications. Most songs are learned orally and remain alive only through repeated use, for followers eschew the use of a hymnal or printed text and most do not read music. Individual songs often contain repetitive lines or verses, which are typically sung by followers with increased gusto at every repetition, the musical expression deepening spiritual focus and impact. Some lyrics, and many melodies, moreover, were never written down and, thus, words and music of older (and now unused or forgotten) songs have been lost to memory: "Well, the music goes back where it came from, back into the infinitude," says Miss F, a longtime member.[20] Songs are understood as sacred inspirations reserved for community religious occasions. I was told that they are rarely discussed or recalled outside of contexts of creation, practice, or ritual use. As followers explained, the spirit inspires both their creation and performance; it follows that one, therefore, needs a spirit-filled context for the songs to emerge. I, however, have been present in more mundane contexts with members, for example, performing secretarial tasks or driving a car, when taped choral singing was played in the background to "contagionize," that is, fill, the atmosphere with Father and his words, which take the form of sung scriptures.

Similar to any religion that allows for both general and special ritual occasions, the Peace Mission follows a liturgical calendar, and there are songs to complement and lift the spirit in all contexts. There are patriotic songs sung to celebrate God having come to America, American independence, and the creation of the United States Constitution; love songs to express the devotion of members to Father and Mother Divine; marriage songs to celebrate the various wedding anniversaries of Father to his "spotless virgin bride"; Woodmont songs to mark September 10 as both the dedication of Father Divine's seventy-seven-acre Gladwyne, Pennsylvania, estate as "the Mount of the House of the Lord" and his "supreme sacrifice" of dying (that is, "giving up his life") in 1965. There are even Christmas songs that do not celebrate the birth of Jesus Christ—since no such holidays are celebrated in the Peace Mission—but rather the "American Christmas," noting the positive nature of the season and the birth of America, the New Eden, a country blessed by God's actual presence. In the words of Miss K, a pianist at Banquet Services: "We have a song for everything, we have a song for every occasion, for every calamity, we have a song for everything we do. . . . I think we just like to sing."[21] Indeed, the songs resonate personally to individual and spiritual experiences and also relate to communal experiences of racism, prejudice, and injustice, and to the efforts to achieve economic victory under Father Divine and the cooperative work of the Peace Mission.

Songs were composed both for congregational singing and for three choral groups that developed within the Peace Mission: the Rosebud Chorus of young virtuous women, the Lily-bud Chorus of previously married women, and the Crusader men's chorus. From the 1940s through the 1980s, these groups presented at a variety of weekly programs from Monday Righteous Government Meetings and Wednesday Devotional Hours to weekend Holy Communion Banquet Services. Today, the Rosebuds who gather around Mother Divine remain the only chorus that still sings on a regular basis at spiritually significant occasions.

The everyday lives of followers of Father Divine still balance two components of their communitarian and celibate tradition: the formality of structured living and the celebration of the freedom of the spirit. All coworkers, for example, adhere to a formal administrative structure of the various Peace Mission churches and carry out set duties, whether managing the Divine Tracy Hotel or cutting vegetables for the Banquet Service.

Their personal behavior is likewise ordered as in the case of set linguistic codes: No words with curses are spoken. Therefore, they do not say "hell-o" to one another; they say "peace." Proper etiquette is to be observed at Banquet Services: Food is abundant, but not to be wasted. Standards of dress are necessary. Women wear only skirts, never pants, and men wear coats and ties. Knowledge of proper handling of food platters and dinner plates is also seen as an asset. But in matters spiritual, freedom is perceived as a value, so followers read writers from macrobiotic thinker

Michio Kuchi to reincarnation exponent Edgar Cayce and allow the spirit to guide them "volitionally" when giving testimony or shouting praise during a Banquet Service. Peace Mission aesthetics also forge a creative space between structure and freedom; this negotiation is similarly represented in their performance of sacred song.

Indeed, in the actual performance of songs, musical precision is admired, but not required in congregational and choral activities. In the everyday musical life of the Peace Mission, the Movement's emphasis on structure and freedom has always meant and continues to mean leaderless choruses; extensive, spontaneous congregational singing; singers who in the majority of cases cannot read music; and choral singing without a great deal of structured practice. Reflections on the experience of being a member of the Rosebud Chorus are represented in Miss F's thoughtful account:

> We were never able to be together [to practice]. . . . We learned what we had to learn in New York . . . the Rosebud Choir Members in New Jersey learned what they were supposed to learn . . . then those in Philadelphia, they learned what they were supposed to about the song. Then we would get together intermittently to see how it all goes. There would be three pianists, in New York, New Jersey, and Philadelphia. And we didn't have a conductor, instructor, or director. The only one we had was God, Father Divine's Holy Spirit that instructed us. . . . The miracle is when you have fifty or one hundred voices together that do not know music, and they only learn through reiteration and memory—that is a miracle. I have seen outstanding choirs and they have their books and no doubt know how to read the notes. But ours were purely inspirational from Father Divine's Holy Spirit.

Such inspiration, coupled with an intentional creativity and adaptability, carries across all the ways that Peace Mission members live their religion.

Father Divine and his followers absorbed a diversity of musical styles to aid their philosophy of attaining perfection in this world. For example, they borrowed the melodies of spirituals, gospel song, jazz, Broadway show tunes, traditional church hymns, popular copyrighted compositions, and even classical music to create their song tradition. In this sense, their music shares a kinship with music in Holiness churches in the 1920s and 1930s where, according to Lawrence Levine, "musically, they reached back to the traditions of the slave past and out to the rhythms of the secular black musical world around them. They brought into the church . . . the sounds of ragtime, blues, and jazz . . . [and] also the instruments."[22] At the same time that these Holiness churches incorporated popular tunes into their services, they imbued the words with a new, religious meaning. Similarly, the Peace Mission worked to renew lyrics from secular consciousness to "God-consciousness." Jazz was a problematical musical form and culture for many African American ministers and congregations in the 1920s and 1930s. Father Divine himself associated jazz with "the underworld and the world of debauchery, of vice, and of crime," and he worked to "transform" such music into acceptable church songs. On January 14, 1934, he preached about this process in a noon sermon at 20 West 115th Street in New York City:

> The beautiful songs and praises that are put forth into expression here through the many different compositions, most of them have come through and from the world of jazz. They are expressions of the individuals and of the world of jazzism as it has been converted unto God, and it will glorify God in the fullness. It is indeed wonderful. . . . Then when you see these beautiful songs coming forth in praises to God, but in the same melodies and tones as the jazz songs, you can see that it is the spirit of the jazz world being converted unto God.[23]

During the mid-1930s when the Peace Mission sponsored radio broadcasts of its services, the songs of the Peace Mission sung congregationally with tunes borrowed from popular music of the era brought criticism and accusations of copyright law infringement, thereby forcing the members to stop singing certain compositions during services that were to be disseminated by radio. Father Divine addressed this issue of the "mortal version" of such songs by emphasizing the opportunity followers now had to compose their own original songs through his inspiration. In another sermon delivered at 115th Street in New York City on February 25, 1936, and then immediately published in the movement's newspaper, *The Spoken Word*, he proclaimed:

> Everybody happy? It is indeed wonderful! While listening at that little Song, I thought of our Radio Broadcast. Many of your numbers have been cut off because of them being songs that have been copyrighted. . . . GOD is Spirit. God is all Gifts and GOD is all Talents. God is all WISDOM. GOD is also all UNDERSTANDING. Because of this, we do not have to depend on another. Why should you lurk in the ideas and opinions, the compositions, the ways and doctrines of others, when MY Spirit within you is the great Composer? My Spirit in you is the Great Inspirator. MY Spirit in you will inspire you, will give you all you need to say, will give you all you need to sing, will give you all of the understanding necessary to get the issue through, therefore, when you see these seeming oppositions arise, they are for this purpose, even if it were to the extent that we would refrain to go on the air, after the manner of men. I did not reach the Twenty odd Million by going on the mechanical radio. It is indeed wonderful![24]

Father's words were heeded and additional original songs were composed in the United States and in other countries, including Australia, Panama, and Switzerland, where non-American followers gathered for Banquet Services and "praise meetings" of their own creation modeled on the rituals they read about in movement publications, *The Spoken Word* (1934–1937) or *The New Day* (1937–1992), and in letters or material sent from Father Divine or other members in New York City or Philadelphia.[25] Of course, the understanding of Father's words, that "the composer is within you," as one follower told me, did not preclude continued borrowing from other musical sources both to bring the secular world into the lives of the members and to transform the compositions themselves.

That words can effect positive change in everyday life is a part of New Thought and Peace Mission belief. The Peace Mission's approach to all songs has been that they potentially could aid human beings and be turned into something powerful, spiritual, self-referential, and positive. For this reason, melodies from the secular world could be used to complement new spiritualized words. Dr. LaVere Belstom, a composer of Crusader songs, a fact he reluctantly admitted to me, noted that "quite a few of our songs have been presented by substituting Peace Mission words for the words of the world."[26] He saw no problem, therefore, with writing new words to the tune of Irving Berlin's "White Christmas" (1940), and renaming the composition "True Christmas":

> We're living in a true Christmas
> In FATHER's Spirit and His Mind.
> Where we feel His presence
> with Peace and gladness
> And love in our hearts and souls.
> His Spirit is now within us
> When we are conscious of His love.
> May we know HIM ever and live
> In the Holy Consciousness of GOD.[27]

In another uncredited Crusader Christmas song, "Santa Claus Is Coming to Town" (J. Fred Coots and Haven Gillespie, 1934) was re-created "Divine style" as "Father Divine Is Everywhere":

> FATHER is here, FATHER is there.
> FATHER DIVINE is everywhere!
> I'm Talking About FATHER DIVINE!
>
> He makes us all so happy.
> He keeps us all so well.

And every time you see us
We have something new to tell. (Spoken) Well![28]

Finally, in a true representation of one American religious tradition negotiating the cultural traditions of another, the Crusaders took the "Notre Dame Victory March" (or Fight Song), retaining Michael J. Shea's tune from the first decade of the twentieth century but employing more relevant lyrics:

Cheer, cheer, For FATHER DIVINE
Wake up the echoes cheering His Name
Send the volleyed cheers on high
Shake down the thunder from the sky
Whether the odds be great or small
FATHER DIVINE will Reign over all.
While His loyal Crusaders go marching
Onward to Victory!
(Shouted) Cheer! Cheer! Cheer![29]

Such new lyrical compositions gain their integrity through "evangelizing," which in the worldview of the membership enables them to be salvaged like jazz for God's work. The art of the Peace Mission sometimes registers despair through a gloss of happiness, but always sees hope in the re-creation of the world, a practice observed even in their restoration and reuse of old buildings as mentioned earlier in relation to what I have termed the followers' "vernacular architecture of intention." Such architectural adaptations and reversals can be seen, for example, in the way the followers did not destroy an inappropriate object of Victorian ornamentation in one of their residences on North Broad Street in Philadelphia—a hand-carved mahogany mermaid with exposed breasts—but reimagined it with an appropriate cloth covering added.[30] The form's integrity was, therefore, preserved for appropriate reuse and display, while "converting" it to "our [Peace Mission] standard."[31] This standard prevails—and continues to transform—fifty years after the context in which Fauset observed this group.

The followers of Father Divine are now a remnant of perhaps 150 members, but their faith remains strong as they sing at Banquet Services in church buildings, including the Peace Mission Evangelical Home in West Philadelphia, a residence for those who are now too infirm to work. Mother Divine and the followers have become friendly with the Shaker community in Sabbathday Lake, Maine, who have even included a few Peace Mission songs about Father and Mother in their own current repertoire. In Mother Divine's era, there has been a shift to more songs on

"Americanism" and to less raucous but more genteel performances, but the sisters and the brothers of the Peace Mission still sing about prejudice, racial injustice, the need for better government, and always about Father.

Miss G, living at the Circle Mission Church (which lies on the same block on South Broad Street as black gospel songwriter Charles Albert Tindley's United Methodist "Temple"), is still physically active. Recently, a well-meaning friend took some of the residents of the Circle Mission Church, including Miss G, to a concert of the white gospel music of Bill and Gloria Gaither, where they sang about going to heaven. Miss G appreciated the rhythms and said they sang well, but "they kept singing about 'we're going to be on the other shore.' I don't want to be on the other shore," she explained, "I want to be on this one. We don't sing just to sing, we . . . know what we're singing."

As the membership grows older, the frailty of age has undoubtedly affected their music. Miss K was recently unable to play the piano at the Holy Communion Banquet Services where she has brilliantly searched for the proper key to hundreds of songs and guided the singing for years. Her absence meant that no one was available to provide piano accompaniment at services, but that did not stop the banquets, which run on their own spirited rhythm of over eighty years of song, accompanied or not; of spirit, quiet or enthusiastically expressed; and of food, always in abundance. In 2006, at the Holy Communion Banquet commemorating the sixtieth wedding anniversary of Father and Mother Divine, the Rosebud Choir, with their ranks severely depleted, used recordings of past singing to support their present performances in the set of five sacred songs used to open the service. By April 2007, this innovation of supplementing the traditional anniversary songs was abandoned, due, I speculate, to the spirited effect that live performance by even a dozen of the sisters has on the service.

In September 2005, I brought a former student of mine who is a jazz trumpeter to the Holy Communion Banquet Service to play a song that I had discovered was written in 1938 by Duke Ellington to honor Father Divine. As the "Crum Elbow Blues" made its soulful way through the crowd, one could feel how the sound of this instrument and this music took them back to the movement's days of spirited prominence in Harlem and, at the same time, situated them calmly with the spirit in West Philadelphia.[32] After the banquet was over, the followers noted to me how satisfying it was to know, in the words of Miss M, "that Father converted the blues!" In the Peace Mission, instruments such as the trumpet were never used for solo performances, which would exhibit too much self or personality to the detriment of the church as an impersonal body. Instruments, however, were negotiated by followers, such as Mr. Simon Peter and Johnny Porter, into congregational singing to exciting effect in such songs as "Do You Love That Body!" "You could feel the walls moving on the street, the vibration was so high," is how a childhood memory of those days was described by Mr. R, who was raised in the Peace Mission and now plays guitar at their services.[33] "You know, Dr. Primiano," recalled Mr. P about the music at those services, "we used to get down, way down."[34]

There is still much to learn about Father Divine's radio broadcasts of the 1930s and 1940s, the further role of breaking copyright in their musical creations and performances, and the influence of Father Divine on American popular music, as in the case of Johnny Mercer and Harold Arlen's song, "Accentuate the Positive, Elimi- nate the Negative," which owes its themes to a sermon by Father Divine.[35] This research is ongoing and begs for the consideration of such historical pathways in communications, popular music, even copyright law.

Men and especially women from sixty years ago, when Arthur Fauset did his field research, can still be interviewed if one secures Mother Divine's permission and their trust. One such follower was Miss Mary Justice, who taught me what I would classify as an "antispiritual." This song, "There's No Heaven in the Sky," does not look to the Christian heaven for a divine salve to earthly woes and oppression, but invokes the sentiment earlier expressed by Miss G of this-worldly hopes for divine integration. The song may sound bitter, but it is sung with great emotion and triumph, what I have come to understand as the group's triumphal contestation of the Christian soterio- logical tradition and the joy of Father Divine's gospel of powerful mindfulness of the present, still guiding the followers years after its first proclamation:

> There's no heaven in the sky
> Which has been some poor saint's cry.
> Longing for this happy day
> We now enjoy.
>
> We have heaven here on earth
> By our Father's transforming birth
> No more to die
> To meet our Savior in the sky.
>
> From the sky
> From the sky
> Thank you for taking
> Our minds and attentions from the sky.
> So for many, weary years

We toiled in sour, pain, and tears
Planning to die
To meet our Savior in the sky.[36]

Understood from their emic, insiders' perspective, members of the Peace Mission abandoned the promises of Christian denominations that failed to support their civil rights in favor of a sectarian religion that offered them security and specific positive support of their human rights in their present lives. They followed Father Divine even if that meant separating from their families and working many hours at traditional jobs and then for the church. Indeed, Father Divine's Peace Mission was a favorite example for Fauset in *Black Gods* of the economic, social, and spiritual power of indigenous African American religion: Followers could create, change, and assume control over their own lives in a difficult and abusive American society. Over sixty years later the followers are still exercising power over their own lives. While time has changed what they control and the amount of energy they retain to control it, they maintain an enthusiasm for the mission and Father Divine and a dominion over their own destiny that Fauset would admire. The Peace Mission followers may not have continued their economic power in American cities past the 1960s, but it is important to note that they maintained an economic presence, only closing their last hotel, the Divine Tracy, in July 2006.[37] This closing marked the end of their public enterprises. It is, however, in the edifice of their cultural creations, their ritual foods, their restored buildings, their spiritual narratives, and, significantly, their songs and music that the followers retain something very personal and powerful.

Fauset's ethnography of the Peace Mission from the 1930s and 1940s has become a useful source of historical information about this uniquely American religious community. It points to an informative early method in the study and appreciation of the contributions of urban intentional communities, large and small, and their expressive traditions of innovation that make them uniquely creative and religious. Fauset's reflexivity about the process of doing fieldwork with such a community—especially how to respect his informants—was decades ahead of its time.

A Space of Possibility

Throughout his life, Fauset evidently continued to think well of the accomplishments and vision of the Peace Mission Movement. In the author's note to the 1971 paperback edition of *Black Gods,* he refers to them directly when reiterating the point that "the American black church 'provided [the one] place where imaginative and dynamic blacks could experiment [without hindrance] in activities such as business, politics, social reform and social expression.' "[38] Barbara Savage comments in her foreword to the 2001 paperback edition of *Black Gods* that Fauset's original study "had focused on five small sects, none of which bore a direct role in the civil rights struggle as it came to be embodied by [Rosa] Parks and [Martin Luther] King. Fauset recognized this himself, as he spent the remainder of his author's note stretching to forge fragile links between Father Divine and the worldwide 'love not hate' movement of the 1960s and 1970s."[39] Savage's comments echo remarks among scholars and other intelligentsia of the African American religious experience tarnishing Father Divine's reputation; at stake is the question of how much Father Divine loved his race, for such assumptions underpin discussions of what constituted a leader of "civil rights" for African Americans. Yet much of this discussion might be seen to miss the point, as is noted, for example, in Jill Watts' 1992 study of Father Divine, which situates his position about race as rooted in his New Thought theological foundation:

> [I]t becomes apparent that Father Divine was initially a reluctant social leader who based his secular programs on his version of New Thought ideology. For instance, he believed that poverty resulted from negative thinking, and he did not offer welfare to the poor. Instead, he focused on job training and offered his disciples a spiritual reorientation toward positive thinking. His attitude toward racism was similar. Like some postmodernists today, Father Divine insisted that race did not exist but was a product of the mind. Negative thinking had created race, an artificial categorization that perpetuated oppression and inequality. Hence, Father Divine, who demanded that followers abandon negative language, extended that ban to racial labels. He also castigated those who identified themselves as black, contending that they were manifesting the derogatory qualities that society had assigned to African Americans.[40]

This deracialized perspective comes to light fully in the fascinating example of photographic representations of Father Divine and Mother Divine; these images flooded movement premises after his wedding to "Sweet Angel" in 1946 (and remain on the walls today). All prints of the couple were treated by specially trained followers to lighten the complexion of Father Divine and darken the complexion of his Canadian bride to unify their skin tones as much as possible. Even earlier than this balancing of skin tone in photographs of the newly married couple, Father Divine complained that newspapers, especially those papers owned by William Randolph Hearst, deliberately published the darkest photos of him available for the purpose of making him look criminal.

Fauset does not indicate whether he knew of this aspect of Father Divine's outlook on race after his many hours of participant observation at Banquet Services and even living with members, or was even conscious of it in the 1970s. If he knew or categorized such an ideology as black self-hatred, he certainly does not hold it against Father Divine. What Fauset did recognize, and shares, for example, with contemporary analysts of African American expressive culture, such as hip-hop music and song today, is the idea that the song culture of the Peace Mission "creates a space of possibility."[41] In the case of the Peace Mission, those possibilities have been spiritual, economic, musical, medical, and, yes, racial. When the congregation as a community and as a community of individuals sing a song such as "The Beautiful Body of God," they are praising the strength of the community of their church, but also highlighting the conviction that Father Divine is God, personified in the body of a short, dark-complected man who loved to sing, eat, and speak in the spirit like they do. For the members, the majority of whom were and are African American women, God is one of their own, with a special charisma that also attracted followers who were not dark-complected. The obvious appeal of the Peace Mission Movement was the space it created for a black God. No commemoration of Father Divine's passing on September 10, 1965, now known as the "Holy Days" within the movement's liturgical cycle, would be complete without singing the words, "I Know You are GOD," to the tune of the anthem of the Civil Rights movement in the United States, "We Shall Overcome." To this day, and throughout the year at services, followers sing with great enthusiasm a song about God in America:

> Here in America
> Is the Kingdom of Heaven
> Here in the land of the free
> We have the Body of GOD
> Here in America
> We have the new birth of freedom under God
> He brought us Peace
> He brought us Joy
> He brought us Hope, and Truth and Love
> Come on, Come on, join the Body of GOD!

The empowerment of the members through their songs highlights one of Cornel West's points that "the quest for black identity involves self-respect and self-regard, realms inseparable from, yet not identical to, political power and economic status."[42] Viewed through the lens of the followers' lyrics and songs, the frequent celebration of Father Divine's body conveys continually the message that the followers' bodies are of tremendous worth and, moreover, that political and economic power is in their hands, as well as in the hands of God. If, as West writes, "the fundamental crisis in black America is twofold: too much poverty and too little self-love," Father Divine's followers resolved those problems many years ago.[43]

Because of his agenda to challenge the Herskovits-Frazier debate about origins of African American culture, Fauset did not indicate or explicate Father Divine's erasure of racial identity agenda, but rather recognized his antidiscrimination activist stance. Put differently, Fauset did begin to formulate an emic interpretation of the community where he saw the empowerment that they gained from a life in the Peace Mission. It was not an easy life. Followers worked hard and long, but there was joy in their decision to work together and to believe a dark-complected man to be God.

Even today, if the followers read intricate theories of black self-hatred and racial and body politics, such as those included in the historical analyses offered by Beryl Satter and R. Marie Griffith, they would not see the relevance of that perspective in relation to themselves or the Peace Mission believers who have lived before them.[44] Nor would they share others' views of Father Divine's seemingly negative assessments of dark skin. In their worldview and, indeed, in their daily experiences, an enunciated intellectualized category of race has had nothing to do with their lives because, in their actual, practical lives, they have achieved many years of empowerment, freedom, equality, respect, sustenance, and even love in a community that, while not for everyone or their families, was positive for them. The members of the Peace Mission helped create and sustain a community space where for decades they have had responsibility for or controlled its money, property, economic decisions, businesses, aesthetics, and ritual display. It has been my experience that the women in the Peace Mission were especially influential. Their power was not circumscribed, but real, and felt both inside and outside their own religious community, whether they worked as domestics and contributed to the purchase of new Peace Mission properties; cafeteria cashiers who made certain that the restaurant business ran professionally and honestly; or one of Father Divine's secretaries who were careful that accounts were accurate, bills were paid, correspondence prepared, and records carefully kept.[45] Fauset, as a talented, innovative ethnographer—not afraid to study members of his own culture closely—recognized the power in the "church" headed by Father Divine. He saw it in their Banquet Services in New York City, their radical farming communities in Western New York State, their hotels in Philadelphia. He undoubtedly heard it in their songs.

Whether Father Divine deemphasized race or not, whether scholars "colonialize" them and their previous generation now with postmodern assessments about their lives and beliefs, members of the Peace Mission have been both empowered by their faith and by their own gentle negotiation and interpretation of that belief system for many years.[46] I have had the privilege to see that this living community—which most scholars think is now extinct, but which has actually existed longer without the physical presence of Father Divine than with him in their midst—is still alive, kicking, cooking, breathing, changing, and singing: "In the name of FATHER DIVINE, In the name of MOTHER DIVINE, we have the Victory." Their energy and control of their destinies has continued to exist beyond the withdrawal of Father Divine, beyond the departure or death of followers they knew well, and over the years of Mother Divine's personal jurisdiction. Mother Divine has introduced her own creative innovations of Father's ideas on appearance, health, eating, aging, spirituality, and the preservation of their heritage for the community's consideration, embrace, and negotiation. The Peace Mission followers today are and have been interpreting this belief system whether they still work to keep the community sustained or whether they now reside in the Peace Mission Evangelical Home.

Conclusion

Just when I think I understand the members of the Peace Mission, just when I feel smug that I appreciate their diversity of ideas and practices after many years of interacting with them, someone in the movement surprises me. On a recent summer Sunday afternoon (June 2007), I was kindly offered a ride by a Peace Mission member living at Woodmont—Father and Mother Divine's estate in Gladwyne, Pennsylvania—to a 2:00 PM Banquet Service. The follower arrived at my home on his Honda Goldwing fifteen-hundred-cubic-centimeter, six-cylinder motorcycle. As I rode on the backseat of this vehicle—something I have never done before—and we drove through Philadelphia's Mainline suburbs with Mr. R taking the turns slowly, due to my fear of flying off the backseat, I heard a familiar sound. Mr. R was playing a tape of his own guitar transcriptions of Peace Mission songs as we glided over the winding roads. The richness and unexpectedness of this occasion, I thought, was something that Arthur Huff Fauset would have loved: the tradition of innovation evident in the everyday life of an African American religious community. Public, private, ritual, mundane: The Peace Mission songs and music are everywhere reminding the followers of their lives in the church and Father Divine's admonition that the consciousness of God's presence will keep you well, healthy, happy, and singing.

Notes

This chapter was first presented as a part of panels at the 2004 meeting of the American Academy of Religion and the 2005 meeting of the American Folklore Society. I am especially thankful for the assistance of Mother Divine and various members of the Palace Mission and Circle Mission churches in Philadelphia; without their generous time and consideration, this research would not be possible. This work was supported by a faculty development grant from Cabrini College. I also wish to thank Deborah Ann Bailey, Lourdes Barretto, John Di Mucci, Shirley Dixon, Margaret Kruesi, Kathy McCrea, Kathleen Malone O'Connor, and Katie Reing, as well as Anne Schwelm and Corey Salazar of Cabrini College's Holy Spirit Library. My student Andrew M. Madonia was an invaluable research assistant. I am most grateful to Jeffrey Gingerich, Darryl Mace, Lisa Ratmansky, and my religious studies colleague Nicholas Rademacher, all from the Cabrini College's writer's group, for their comments and assistance during the draft stage. Fellow folklorists and Cabrini colleagues Charlie McCormick and Nancy Watterson, also members of the Cabrini writing group, kindly and diligently read final drafts of this chapter.

1. By contrast, see, for example, John Hoshor, *God in a Rolls-Royce: The Rise of Father Divine, Madman, Menace, or Messiah* (New York: Hillman-Curl, 1936); Jan Karel Van Baalen, *The Chaos of Cults*, 3rd ed. (Grand Rapids, Mich.: William B. Eerdmans, 1942); and Sara Harris, *Father Divine: Holy Husband* (Garden City, N.Y.: Doubleday, 1953).

2. For a discussion of folklife studies, see Leonard Norman Primiano, "Folklife," in *Folklore: An Encyclopedia of Beliefs, Customs, Tales, Music, and Art*, ed. Thomas A. Green (Santa Barbara, Calif.: ABc-CLIO, 1997), 1: 322–31.

3. Compare Robert Weisbrot, *Father Divine and the Struggle for Racial Equality* (Urbana: University of Illinois Press, 1983), and Jill Watts, *God, Harlem U.S.A.: The Father Divine Story* (Berkeley: University of California Press, 1992).

4. For example, Arthur Huff Fauset, *Black Gods of the Metropolis: Negro Religious Cults of the Urban North* (Philadelphia: University of Pennsylvania Press, 2002), 64–65, 83–85, 104–106, 118–19; "Life is a happy song," Fauset, *Black Gods*, 118.

5. Fauset, *Black Gods*, 117–19.

6. This approach to the leadership and structural elements of the Peace Mission is still taken in sociological, historical, and religious studies anthologies on the movement. See, for example, Joseph R. Washington, *Black Sects and Cults* (1972; Lanham, Md.: University Press of America, 1984); J. Gordon Melton, ed., *Encyclopedic Handbook of Cults in America* (New York: Garland, 1992); Robert Weisbrot, "Father Divine's Peace Mission Movement," in *America's Alternative Religions*, ed. Timothy Miller (Albany: State University of New York Press, 1995), 285–90; and Richard T. Schaefer and William W. Zellner, *Extraordinary Groups: An Examination of Unconventional Lifestyles*, 8th ed. (New York: Worth, 2008). For pedagogical purposes, the top-down approach to organized religions continues to take precedence among scholars.

7. "Divinites" is a designation employed in Fauset, *Black Gods*, 58, that I have never heard used within the conversation of members of the contemporary Peace Mission Move-

ment; the members refer to themselves as "sister" or "brother," Father and Mother Divine's "children," or as the "followers of Father Divine."

8. Fauset, *Black Gods*, 117. There was tremendous public curiosity about the movement starting in the 1930s with such articles as St. Clair McKelway and A. J. Liebling, "Who Is This King of Glory?," *New Yorker*, June 13, 1936, 21–34; June 20, 1936, 22–32; June 27, 1936, 22–36; and Edwin T. Buehrer, "Harlem's God," *Christian Century* 52 (December 11, 1935): 1590–93. The mission was also prominently on display in a 1936 report by the *March of Time*, a weekly newsreel series shown in movie theaters from 1935 to 1951, produced by the editors of *Time* magazine.

9. Fauset, *Black Gods*, 117–19. I have sought out other ethnographic notes from Fauset's work with the Peace Mission, but there is very little relevant material about his dissertation research included in the Arthur Huff Fauset Collection, Special Collections Department, Van Pelt Library, University of Pennsylvania, Philadelphia. I also asked Mother Divine in April 2007, during the preparation of this article, about any available and relevant correspondence between Father Divine, the movement, and Fauset. While Mother Divine remembers Fauset, she could not recall any specific correspondence or locate any at the time.

10. Fauset, *Black Gods*, 117. When the ethnographic study is of the Peace Mission, an additional consideration is that throughout its history, Father Divine and the movement have received considerable negative coverage from the print media, and have been offended at writers denigrating what they believe to be the deity of Father Divine. Most biographies of the Reverend M. J. Divine by scholars consider his past history as a man born in the United States, and the ahistorical consciousness of the movement sees such scholarship as inappropriate and "lowrating" Father. The movement also disapproves of being designated an *African American* religious "cult." They feel that the Peace Mission is neither a "cult" nor exclusively African American. While there is a large African American and female membership, they believe that the movement has appealed to both sexes and all races and is international in scope. Beyond disagreements about historical work, there remain scholars who simply publicly denigrate Father Divine, apparently not caring that there are individuals who still consider him their God. Henry Louis Gates Jr., for example, in a response to a letter to the editor of the *New York Times* about Divine, finished his point with: "Father Divine convinced thousands (he claimed millions) of his followers that he was God—and if that's not a con, then I'm sweet Daddy Grace." Reply to Letter to the Editor, *New York Times Book Review*, May 7, 1989, 41.

11. James V. Spickard, J. Shaun Landres, and Meredith McGuire, *Personal Knowledge and Beyond: Reshaping the Ethnography of Religion* (New York: New York University Press, 2002), 5.

12. I used my time over the years to develop questions that I could ask Mother Divine and the followers, based not on what popular writers or other scholars said about them but on what they said about themselves. Those questions formed the basis of filmed interviews in 1996–1997, which are the foundation of a current database website, "The Father Divine Project," produced by videographer Will Luers and myself. We have received Mother Divine's permission to post this material. I have continued asking questions and taking

notes since 1997, and my current research on the music of the Peace Mission is based on much of that fieldwork. As I began writing and contemplated publishing about the movement, I engaged in a reciprocal form of ethnographic experience in which I have presented material to the community or had Mother Divine or individual members read and then engage me about the material I had composed about them. A discussion of my reciprocal approach will be more fully elucidated in a future publication. For useful discussions of ethnography, religion, and reciprocal method, see Spickard et al., *Personal Knowledge;* for reflexive ethnography, see Charlotte Aull Davies, *Reflexive Ethnography: A Guide to Researching Selves and Others* (London: Routledge, 1999); and for reciprocal ethnography, see Luke Eric Lassiter, *The Chicago Guide to Collaborative Ethnography* (Chicago: University of Chicago Press, 2005).

13. See Leonard Norman Primiano, " 'Bringing Perfection in These Different Places': Father Divine's Vernacular Architecture of Intention," *Folklore* 115 (2004): 3–26.

14. Many followers of Father Divine receive spiritual names at some point in their time in the Peace Mission. Those names, such as Miss Holy Grace, Miss Sunshine Bright, Miss Stark Happiness, Mr. Loving Jeremiah, Mr. Equality Smart, or Mr. Radical Love, could come into their consciousness in a dream or a vision, through some other metaphysical contact with Father, or they could simply illustrate some characteristic of their personality. Followers, as previously noted, resist revealing any facts about their personal identities and lives before entering the Peace Mission. I have not revealed the name of any follower currently living, with the exception of Mother Divine, and use an initial instead. I also will not reveal the approximate ages of any individual member. For the sake of clarity for a reader, I feel it is necessary to state that generally the sisters and brothers in the first decade of the twenty-first century are between seventy and one hundred years old. I have retained the names of deceased members previously interviewed.

15. Miss G, interview with author, 2004. Two excellent recent introductions to the subject of sacred and religious song in America are Stephen A. Marini, *Sacred Song in America: Religion, Music, and Public Culture* (Urbana: University of Illinois Press, 2003) and Philip V. Bohlman, Edith L. Blumhofer, and Maria M. Chow, eds., *Music in American Religious Experience* (New York: Oxford University Press, 2006). The music and songs of the Peace Mission were noted even in the earliest articles written about the movement. See, for example, Buehrer, "Harlem's God," 1590–93; and the three-part report by McKelway and Liebling, "Who Is This King of Glory?" In the 1950s, Harris's *Father Divine,* 298, a text reviled by the movement, gave considerable attention to songs, even noting in a discussion of the Rosebuds' choral group: "Whether songs of praise to Father Divine or whether songs inspired by anger against the injustices Negroes have suffered in America, the Buds' songs are no orthodox hymns. They are original, colorful, completely alive outpourings. Often they attain the very heights of folk art." Beryl Satter, "Marcus Garvey, Father Divine and the Gender Politics of Race Difference and Race Neutrality," *American Quarterly* 48 (1996): 43–76, in her historical study of race and gender, states that it was Peace Mission women who "created a distinctive Divinite culture" (58), and this creativity included a culture of music and song (59).

16. Father Divine often mentioned how he was once offered a large sum of money for

one composition, presumably from a popular song publisher or the Victor Talking Machine Company, which he turned down because, "If I would sell an inspiration I would be worse than Judas who sold the Body of the Inspiration" (July 24–25, 1945, message; printed in the *New Day*, February 28, 1959, 3).

17. Printed in the *New Day*, July 11, 1970, 5.

18. *New Day*, August 27, 1942, 75.

19. See Leonard Norman Primiano, "Mother Divine," in *Encyclopedia of Women and World Religion*, ed. Serinity Young (New York: Macmillan, 1998), vol. 2.

20. Miss F, interview with author, 2004.

21. Miss K, interview with author, 2004.

22. Lawrence W. Levine, *Black Culture and Black Consciousness: Afro-American Folk Thought from Slavery to Freedom* (New York: Oxford University Press, 1977), 180.

23. Printed in the *New Day*, April 20, 1957, 4–5.

24. *Spoken Word*, February 29, 1936, 4.

25. Weisbrot, *Father Divine and the Struggle for Racial Equality*, 75–76, explains the development of each publication.

26. Dr. LaVere Belstom, interview with author, 2004.

27. *I Come to Light Your Candles*, n.d., 17.

28. Ibid., 5.

29. *Crusader Song Book*, n.d., 5. Crusaders' Day, which is celebrated on Father's Day in June, recalls the 1960 occasion when Father Divine donned a Crusader's powder blue jacket for the festivities at Woodmont. See Mother Divine, *The Peace Mission Movement* (Philadelphia: Imperial, 1982), 32, for a further explanation of this male group within the movement. Today, many crusader songs are sung on this occasion, and a small booklet of their lyrics has been created to promote congregational singing since the ranks of the Crusaders are so depleted. The two Christmas songs, which are quoted here, are taken from another small booklet also printed to assist congregational singing of songs by followers and visitors, especially during a celebration, developed by Mother Divine, known as the American Christmas.

30. Primiano, "Bringing Perfection," 10–11.

31. Mr. L, interview with author, 2004.

32. See Fauset, *Black Gods*, 93, on "Krum Elbow."

33. Mr. R, interview with author, 2005.

34. Mr. P, interview with author, 2005.

35. See Gene Lees, *Portrait of Johnny: The Life of John Herndon Mercer* (New York: Pantheon, 2004), 145.

36. See further "Heaven," Father Divine Project, www.taylorstreetstudio.com/divine/archives/heaven/.

37. Primiano, "Bringing Perfection," 13.

38. Fauset, *Black Gods*, xxiii.

39. Ibid., xv.

40. Watts, *God, Harlem U.S.A.*, xi–xii, and Satter, "Marcus Garvey, Father Divine," 43–76, problematize the race issue with relation to Father Divine and the followers even further.

To read of Father Divine's place within American metaphysical religion, see Catherine L. Albanese, *A Republic of Mind and Spirit: A Cultural History of American Metaphysical Religion* (New Haven: Yale University Press, 2007), 476–78.

41. Imani Perry, *Prophets of the Hood: Politics and Poetics in Hip Hop* (Durham, N.C.: Duke University Press, 2005), 25.

42. Cornel West, *Race Matters* (New York: Vintage, 2001), 97.

43. Ibid., 93.

44. Satter, "Marcus Garvey, Father Divine"; R. Marie Griffith, "Body Salvation: New Thought, Father Divine, and the Feast of Material Pleasures," *Religion and American Culture* 11 (2001): 119–53; and R. Marie Griffith, *Born Again Bodies: Flesh and Spirit in American Christianity* (Berkeley: University of California Press, 2004).

45. For a discussion of the female body within the Peace Mission, see Griffith, "Body Salvation," 119–53. Marla F. Frederick, *Between Sundays: Black Women and Everyday Struggles of Faith* (Berkeley: University of California Press, 2003), makes a strong argument about how social scientists have misunderstood the experience and practice of faith in the lives of African American women. Spirituality, she feels, should be observed not only in religious "signs, symbols, rituals, and structures" (ix), but also in relation to the cultures of work, tithing, education, personal behavior, sexuality, and activism that fill their lives. Although Frederick's analysis is based on a study of the African American women of Halifax County, North Carolina, the conclusion of this ethnography of spirituality is equally valid for the women of the Peace Mission Movement and the way they see the multitude of connections between their religious and so-called secular lives. Followers of Father Divine would see work of even the most menial or physical quality, for example, as an enactment of their faith in Father Divine, their belief in his divinity, and their dedication to promoting the unity and strength of their community.

46. By delving deeper than the religious group's founder, I have studied the vernacular religion of the members, that is, the religion of their everyday lives and the subtle and dramatic ways practitioners of this belief system creatively re-create their religion. Indeed, individual members of so-called sects have a vernacular religion, as much as Catholics, Buddhists, and Jews. For my definition of vernacular religion, see Leonard Norman Primiano, "Vernacular Religion and the Search for Method in Religious Folklife," *Western Folklore* 54 (1995): 37–56.

SIX · "A True Moslem Is a True Spiritualist": Black Orientalism and *Black Gods of the Metropolis*

JACOB S. DORMAN

Father George W. Hurley, who called himself "The Black God of the Aquarian Age" and who founded what would become the nation's largest black Spiritual church, the Universal Hagar's Spiritual Association (UHSA), published a remarkable pamphlet in 1930 called "Arabian Science." Using the pen name Aboonah Adam, Hurley announced the formation of an Arabic school with "Rev. Abraham of Aribia, speaking twenty-one different languages." His intent in promoting linguistic competence among his followers was to increase freedom for American "Ethiopians." "We, Ethiopians of the United States of America have been deplorably depressed by not speaking but one language and that is the English language," Hurley wrote in his opening sentence, noting that any "foreign brother or sister" of the Ethiopian race who speaks Spanish, "Arabian," Hebrew, or French "is given more privileges in the United States than we American born Ethiopians."

Hurley went on to relate how he met the "Moslem brethren" and how a missionary named Elias Mohammed Abraham stayed with him in his home during the fall of that year. The Detroit-based black Spiritual church leader was moved by "the Spirit" to open the Arabic school after "seeing the privileges that are extended to him [Abraham] by the American white man." Hurley, or Aboonah Adam, "decided to put the emergency Arabic language in English in order that we might understand it in case we need our Arabian brethren's help they would be willing to assist us."[1]

Edward Wilmot Blyden praised Arabic as a vehicle of black manhood in the nineteenth century, and many have noted that black Muslims of the contemporaneous Moorish Science Temple used their Moorish identities to demand their civil rights, but perhaps never before or since has the attraction of Arabic language and Muslim identity been expressed so succinctly and so powerfully.[2]

Moreover, Hurley's and Abraham's vision encompassed more than simply using the "emergency Arabic language" to expand black temporal freedoms. They also understood each other on a spiritual plane. Hurley wrote: "It is true that they treasure Mohammed as the only prophet, but After Rev. Abraham saw my gift and the way the spirit works with me and the expansion that our Association has made in the last seven years, he was perfectly willing to recognize me as a prophet of the new age."[3] Just as Elias Mohammed Abraham recognized Hurley's spiritual gifts, so too did Hurley recognize the compatibility of Abraham's teachings with his own. He wrote, "[W]e do acknowledge the doctrine, so far, of the Moslems because it is a Spiritual doctrine and the same doctrine that we are preaching if the explanation and interpretation has been given to me right."[4] That phrase "so far" is telling. This is the record of a religious collaboration, only two months after its initiation. Hurley admits the provisional nature of his assessment and his dependence on others for interpretation. His judgment of Islam, in effect, relies on a dual set of translations: the linguistic translations between English and Arabic, and the religious translations between Spiritualism and an African American version of Islam. Yet his provisional conclusion was that this black Muslim missionary was teaching a Spiritualist doctrine: Hurley's preface to the Arabic language primer and collection of stories about the life of the prophet Muhammad closed with a prayer that each of his followers, or "saints," acknowledge the fellowship of the "Moslem saints wherever you meet them for I find a true Moslem is a true Spiritualist."[5]

The argument of this chapter is that "black Orientalism" was generative of many African American new religious movements and must be recognized as an important part of the black cultural imagination in the late nineteenth and early twentieth centuries. Reexamining the content and the context of the "Black Gods of the Metropolis" that Arthur Huff Fauset chronicled sixty years ago demonstrates that black Jews, black Muslims, Rastafarians, and black Spiritual churches both generated and were generated by black Orientalisms that were contiguous with Euro-American Orientalisms.[6] Twentieth-century esoteric black sects primarily invented traditions not by retention of African pasts but through the invention of black Orientalist imaginaries constructed through performance, ritual, and commercial exchange. In ideological terms black Orientalism was a recalcitrant counterdiscourse that critiqued American racism and the discourse of civilization by exoticizing the self.[7]

Father Hurley's Islamic phase was brief. He seemed to absorb Islam and Arabic as he absorbed so many other belief systems into his heterogeneous Spiritualist practice, and the topic appears seldom in his voluminous writings between the time when he founded the UHSA in 1923 and his death in 1943. There is no mention of Islam or Arabic in the chapters on Hurley that form the majority of Hans Baer's *The Black Spiritual Movement*, and his present-day followers do not recall Islam becoming a very prominent part of their faith.[8] Nor is it possible to say with certainty who this missionary Elias Mohammed Abraham was, although his location in Detroit and his name are both reminiscent of those of Elijah Muhammad, the leader of the Nation of Islam. Hurley's descendants maintain that he knew Elijah Muhammad when he was still known as Elijah Poole and also knew many of the other black urban sect leaders, people such as Prophet Jones of Detroit, Sweet Daddy Grace, and Father Divine of Harlem. More likely, perhaps, is the supposition that Elias Mohammed Abraham was a member of one of the Muslim missionary organizations active among African Americans at this time, especially as there is a record of a "Mohammed Elias" associated with the Islamic Mission of America led by the Trinidadian-born Shaykh Daoud Ahmed Faisal.[9]

What is perhaps of greater importance than Mohammad Elias's precise affiliation is the fact that Hurley and this Muslim missionary were able to find a common spiritual language and come to an understanding that recognized Hurley's spiritual prophecy, Arabic's preeminence as both a spiritual and an efficacious language, and black Islam's kinship with Spiritualism. Hurley's statement that "a true Moslem is a true Spiritualist" is indicative of the fact that there was a great degree of overlap between the content and teaching of the various sects and gods of the black metropolis.

Thinking of African Americans as Orientalists upsets some of the categories that come most naturally to those familiar with either subject. In its simplest form, one could object that as Orientalism is associated with European high imperialism it is an ideology of oppressors; African Americans have historically been oppressed; therefore, African Americans cannot be Orientalists. However, such logic is at odds with understandings of discourse that suggest that even those who lack certain forms of power can effect change through claiming and manipulating the dominant discourse.[10] Seeing African Americans as definitionally powerless is also at odds with the last forty years of African American history. Time and again African Americans have resisted oppression and achieved some measure of control over their lives, even under the most dire circumstances imaginable.[11]

It is important that Hurley's initiation into Islam began with the acquisition of what he called the "emergency Arabian language" and that acquiring a language besides English was critical to his program for the betterment of "Ethiopian Americans." In his landmark 1978 work *Orientalism*, Edward Said described how the phenomena of the same name began with a scholarly phase, rooted in philology and the study of languages. According to Said, scholarly Orientalism led to a kind of utilitarian Orientalism as European empires learned to administer Eastern lands. This in turn led to the commercial exploitation of those empires, with their attendant commodification in the form of consumer products and commercial representations: Oriental finery, Oriental painting, Oriental-themed movies, and so forth.[12]

While Said gave a kind of "high church" version of Orientalism that fit European high imperialism, his successors have described how Orientalism was digested and translated in the vulgate. In the years since Edward Said's seminal work, anthropologist James Clifford has argued for the existence of nonreductive romantic forms of Orientalism, and Richard Fox has identified what he calls "affirmative Orientalism." Lisa Lowe has argued for "the nonequivalence of various orientalisms," calling instead for "the conception of orientalism as heterogeneous and contradictory."[13]

Since Said wrote, there has been an explosion of interest in the topic, fueled in part by unrest in the Middle East and America's two recent Iraq wars, as well as by new interest in "Occidentalism," or Eastern views of the West.[14] Whereas Said essentially dismissed the salience of Orientalism in this country, more recently Melani McAlister, Douglas Little, Susan Nance, Timothy Marr, and Michael Oren have produced a series of works examining America's interest in and representations of the Middle East, exploring the American dimensions of Orientalism in the process.[15] In addition, scholars of Asian American studies such as John Kwo Wei Tchen, Henry Yu, and Mari Yoshihara have produced studies of American Orientalism pertaining to the Far East and Asian Americans.[16] Studies of Orientalism in American film, American literature, African American literature, American Egyptology, Progressive Era consumerism, Gilded Age Freemasonry, and postwar American culture and foreign policy have also appeared.[17] Vijay Prashad, Robin Kelley, and Bill Mullen have explored how African Americans and "Orientals" have encountered and imagined each other, creating a literature of interracial experience between people of color that, interestingly, does not depend on Euro-Americans as a main referent.[18] There is now a related literature on the foreign policy views of African Americans toward Asia that notes the importance of Imperial Japan and Mao's China as refutations of white supremacy and beacons of hope for black Americans.[19] There is also work in progress on Orientalism as a motif in black theatrical performances around the turn of the twentieth century and as a signifier of modernity and urbanity in the Harlem Renaissance novels of Nella Larsen.[20]

In African American studies, some scholars have interpreted "black Oriental- ism" to be a term of opprobrium, while other scholars have begun to investigate the nuance and ambivalence within African American versions of Orientalism. Thus, in a path-breaking article, "The Asiatic Black Man," Nathaniel Deutsch considers whether Elijah Muhammad of the Nation of Islam could be considered an Oriental- ist, while Ali Mazrui castigates his friend Henry Louis Gates Jr. as a "Black Oriental- ist" for what he felt was the culturally insensitive manner in which he dealt with Africa in his much-discussed 1999 PBS series. Recently, Sherman Jackson termed African Americans with anti-Muslim prejudice "black Orientalists."[21]

Yet negative definitions of black Orientalism such as Jackson's do not consider the full range of Orientalist thought. Orientalism, in other words, means more than simply antihumanist essentialism that views the Oriental Other as hypersexual, violent, childish, and decadent. As Deustch and Mazrui well recognize, Orientalism also describes those who study the Orient, admire the Orient, commercialize the Orient, and seek to embody the Orient. Orientalism "expressed a whole range of voices, Islamophobics as well as lovers of Islam, hegemonic movements as well as counter-hegemonic endeavours," Ziauddin Sardar writes.[22] In this light, Scott Traf- ton has demonstrated how nineteenth-century black American travelers in Egypt such as Martin Delaney and Fredrick Douglass helped to create African American forms of Orientalism that overlapped with Euro-American Orientalisms. Reexam- ining the content and the context of the black urban new religious movements of the interwar period demonstrates that many of them were linked by a shared ideology of black Orientalism that had cultural, political, and commercial dimensions. Further- more, this black Orientalism has analogues to the three stages of classical Oriental- ism: the philological, the imperial, and the commercial.

Father Hurley's engagement with language study was characteristic of a number of black sect leaders. Bishop Cherry of Philadelphia's Black Jews studied Hebrew, and Hebrew schools were a central part of the educational practices of the contem- poraneous Black Israelites of Harlem in the movements led by Rabbis Arnold Josiah Ford and Wentworth Arthur Matthew. Ford taught both Hebrew and Arabic in his Beth B'nai Abraham congregation, and Matthew ran a Talmud Torah that taught Hebrew.[23] Matthew also used Hebrew as a magical language for his version of conjuring, which he called "cabbalistic science." In fact, in much the same way as Hurley's "emergency Arabian language" was a doorway into Islam and a valuable technology that afforded one physical protection, Hebrew for Black Israelites represented not just Judaic practice but the entire magical "science" of black Israelism.

Even Father Divine, the most famous of all the black gods of the metropolis and a man who never presented himself in Orientalist guise, was part of the wider network of black Orientalism. In Baltimore, John Hickerson, "The Bishop," had once lived and preached with George Baker, "The Messenger," and Samuel Morris, "Father Jehovia." Father Jehovia taught a version of the theology of the indwelling God, and together the triumvirate developed the theology of the indwelling God. When the trio split up, George Baker and John Hickerson headed for Harlem, where Baker became Father Divine and Hickerson took the name Bishop the Vine, or Bishop Eshof Ben Dovid.[24] Hickerson passed on esoteric teachings through the Garvey movement, claimed that he had taught Hebrew to Rabbi Ford and that Rabbi Ford had then taught Rabbi Matthew "everything he knows about Hebrew."[25] Interestingly, "Hebrew" among the Professors of Mystic Science was closely associated with the idea of the indwelling God: Contemporary anthropologist Ruth Landes reported Father Divine's "reputedly 'Jewish' doctrine was simply 'God is within man.' "[26]

Indeed, the philological as well as the imperial aspects of black Orientalism are on display in a 1931 letter that Rabbi Ford sent Rabbi Matthew from Ethiopia, where he had ventured with thirty followers to establish a "colony" for African Americans shortly after the coronation of Haile Selassie I in 1930. The letter accompanied a certificate of ordination for Matthew from the Ethiopian Coptic Church that Ford had managed to obtain with the help of his contacts in the Ethiopian government. In his missive, Ford translates the ordination document, which is written in Arabic, Amharic, and Hebrew, but notes of the Hebrew, "of course you can read this."

It was a short leap from translation to colonization: On the very next page, Ford recounts riding through the dusty streets of Addis Ababa on his donkey with his servant at his side when he was passed by the motorcar of Ras Hailu. Ford described his plans for a black "colony" in Ethiopia and related that the Ras's words were: "*Come, Build, Occupy!*" "This is our only hope, our only salvation as a race," Ford declared.[27] Rabbi Matthew resisted Ford's pleas to join him or send more settlers, but he and later black Israelites adopted the same language of emigration and colonization. After Ford's death, due to health problems, during the 1935 Italo-Ethiopian War, Matthew founded what he called his "colony," not in Ethiopia or Zion but in Babylon, Long Island, an interesting place-name for a colony of Israelites.[28]

The same spirit of colonization can be seen in the next generation of black Israelite movements emanating mostly from Chicago in the 1960s, groups that were trained in part by rabbis whom Rabbi Matthew had ordained. That wave produced the House of Judah Congregation of Black Hebrew Israelites, founded in 1960 by Prophet William A. Lewis. Lewis was originally from Alabama and created a rural settlement near Lacota, Michigan, that was bound together by strict discipline and corporal punishment. The most famous group of all was the Original African Hebrew Israelites, which moved from Chicago to Liberia in 1967 and then to Israel in 1969. They won few friends there with their colonization rhetoric by proclaiming that the land of Israel belonged to them and that they would push the imposter white Jews off the land.[29]

Of course, there is a significant difference between founding a colony with the consent of an African government and starting a colony at the expense of African self-governance. Neither Ford's ragtag group of settlers, decimated by poor planning and the invasion of Ethiopia by the Italian Fascists, nor the Black Hebrews, suffering through the muddy season in late sixties Liberia, can be equated with the British Raj. Black Orientalism is not synonymous with other Orientalisms, but the categories of thought are similar, even if their use and intent are counterhegemonic or, more properly, recalcitrant.[30]

The practice of literary Orientalism by black alternative religious figures can also be seen in the texts that they created and those they circulated. Rabbi Ford's texts employed exotic, sexual, Orientalist imagery in the hymns he wrote for Marcus Garvey's Universal Negro Improvement Association during his time in New York City. In his poetry, Africa is typically a woman whose people must be uplifted so that she might find union with a sexualized, Islamic godhead. His most famous composition, the Garvey anthem "One God, One Aim, One Destiny" includes the stanza:

> Arise, O Aethiop's daughter rise
> From thine Aionian sleep
> And to the Heaven's lift thine eyes.
> Thy tryst with Allah keep.
> "Not dead; but sleeping," Angels said
> "Those hands stretch'd forth shall be
> Afric shall once more raise her head
> Her children shall be free."[31]

In one verse, Ford depicts Africa as daughter, lover, and mother. Just as Africa is feminized and sexualized, Islam is sexualized in the long tradition of Western Orientalism.[32]

Returning to the example that opened this chapter, Spiritualist Father Hurley and Muslim missionary Elias Mohammed Abraham also could understand each other so well because they, like many black Orientalists, shared an investment in the same corpus of esoteric Orientalist religious texts, especially *The Aquarian Gospel of Jesus the Christ* by Levi Dowling and the collected publications of De Laurence, Scott & Co. As Susan Nance has explained, Moorish Science, although called Islam, "was only vaguely similar to any practices or beliefs among Muslims elsewhere and was in fact a form of black Spiritualism informed by the philosophies of American fraternal orders."[33] Noble Drew Ali borrowed half of his *Circle Seven Koran* from *The Aquarian Gospel* and added information from the Bible and *Unto Thee I Grant,* a 1925 Rosicrucian text.[34] Published in 1908, *The Aquarian Gospel* was a Theosophist text that filled in the missing years in Jesus's New Testament biography between adolescence and age thirty, claiming that he had traveled to India and learned the ancient secrets of the Vedic masters and the Egyptians before returning to Jerusalem and Calvary. That work was in turn inspired by *La Vie Inconnue de Jesus Christ,* published in 1894 by a converted Russian Jew named Nicolas Notovitch, who claimed to have discovered the story inscribed on an ancient manuscript in a Tibetan monastery.[35]

Spiritualist Father Hurley also revered the *The Aquarian Gospel,* and the Universal Hagar's Spiritual Association studies the text to the present day. The labels of the sects may have varied—black Muslim, black Jew, black Spiritualist—but they often revered the same holy texts and shared enough esoteric thought to recognize themselves in one another. Thus, studies of black sectarian movements that focus on a single group can obscure the origins of those movements by ignoring the commonality of their beliefs, commonalities that transcend sectarian labels. The new black religions of the urban North bred the most surprising and seemingly contradictory blends. Not only were Muslims sometimes Spiritualists, but Jews were sometimes Muslims: Rabbi Ford's Black Jews not only studied Arabic as well as Hebrew but they also observed Ramadan and sang hymns praising Allah.[36] Indeed, this Israelite-Muslim blend has continued in the Nation of Islam and the smaller Ansaru Allah sect.[37]

While *The Aquarian Gospel* was important, no set of esoteric texts had a bigger impact on the black sects and gods of the metropolis than the publications of the Chicago-based De Laurence, Scott & Co. Hurley's granddaughter, Reverend Cassandra Latimer-Knight, reports that Lauron William de Laurence was Father Hurley's "highest teacher."[38] De Laurence's publications have been widely used and absorbed in religions throughout Africa and the Diaspora, from vodou to Santeria, Obeah, candomblé, black Islam, black Israelism, and Rastafarianism.[39] De Laurence's basic strategy was to present what he represented to be translations of the mystical and magical systems of the Oriental world, especially India and Tibet, printed with his own extensive introductions and glosses containing strains of Theosophy and New Thought.[40]

The de Laurence publications were central to many of the black sects of the interwar period. Rabbi Matthew's aforementioned "cabbalistic science" used diagrams and Hebrew incantations drawn from de Laurence's edition of *The Sixth and Seventh Books of Moses*.[41] Leonard Howell, the founder of Rastafarianism, practiced root medicine in 1920s Harlem, operated a "tea room," and used de Laurence's *The Great Book of Magical Art, Hindu Magic and East Indian Occultism*, which claimed to be based on the "masters of *occult wisdom* on the high plateau of *Thibet*," who excel at "*telepathy, or mind-reading*," which "in *India* [is] a national characteristic."[42] The book included a chapter on dreams and visions complete with numerical translations of images for use in playing the numbers, a popular gambling pastime.

Rastafarian Howell's Orientalism can also be seen in the fact that he chose the Hindustani name Gangunguru Maragh or "Gong" when he first published *The Promise Key* in 1935, one of the foundational statements of the Rastafari faith.[43] Similarly, Howell's Rastafarian peer Joseph Hibbert told friends in 1918 that he was inspired by the idea that the Hindu gods of Jamaica's East Indian peasants could manifest themselves in human avatars. He felt that Ras Tafari, who became Ethiopian Emperor Haile Selassie I, could serve a similar function as a living godhead and so give strength and inspiration to people of African ancestry.[44] *Unto Thee I Grant*, the 1925 Rosicrucian text that formed the basis of another part of Noble Drew Ali's *Circle Seven Koran*, was itself copied from a 1923 de Laurence publication, *Infinite Wisdom*, which claimed to have been translated in 1749 from ancient Chinese manuscripts found in a Tibetan monastery, like the alleged source materials of *The Aquarian Gospel* and *The Great Book of Magical Art, Hindu Magic and East Indian Occultism*.[45] Esoteric Orientalist texts like these formed a crucial part of the teachings of many of the black sects of North America, as they did in the Afro-Atlantic world more broadly.

Textual traditions were not the only vectors of religious Orientalism among African Americans, and perhaps they were not even the most salient ones, compared to the transmission of Orientalism by popular culture, fraternal rituals, theatrical performance, religious missionaries, and the marketplace for religious services and exotic finery. Whether it was through prayer, healing practices, or fraternal rituals, people inscribed their Orientalist identities onto their very bodies, often rejecting the label of "Negro" in the process. Whether as "Moorish Americans," "Ethiopian Americans," or "Asiatic Black men," black religious Orientalists incorporated the East into their names, their bodies, and their souls.[46]

The story of black Orientalism and black Islam cannot be told without considering the impact of Timothy Drew or Noble Drew Ali (1886–1929), founder of the Moorish Science Temple. Michael Gomez writes that "in the final analysis, Noble Drew Ali is necessarily the bridge over which the Muslim legacies of the eighteenth and nineteenth centuries crossed over into the Muslim communities of the twentieth and twenty-first."[47] Drew Ali's centrality in twentieth-century black Islam is unquestionable, yet the only significant evidence of a historical connection to earlier forms of Islam that Gomez offers is what he admits is the "circumstantial observation" that Noble Drew Ali "grew up and achieved adolescence in a part of the South in close proximity to coastal South Carolina and Georgia, the gravitational center of the antebellum Muslim community in North America."[48] Even if Drew Ali had hailed from the seacoast rather than North Carolina, to make him Muslim by dint of geography alone is rather strained. Surveying the same territory, most scholars have concluded along with Richard Brent Turner that "by the eve of the Civil War, the old Islam of the original African Muslim slaves was, for all practical purposes, defunct" because Muslim individuals were not able to develop and perpetuate institutions and communities in nineteenth-century America.[49]

Before Noble Drew Ali founded the Canaanite Temple of America in 1913, the Associated Negro Press reports that Ali "was accompanying a Hindu fakir in circus shows when he decided to start a little order of his own."[50] Historians Vijay Prashad and Susan Nance have documented how images of Hindus and Muslims were commonly transmitted through traveling circuses in Progressive Era America.[51] Such Orientalist entertainments were also popular in African American urban communities in the era of the Great Migration. The culture of the stage and traditions of performance in American theater played major roles in the development of black Orientalist religions.

The circus was a fertile arena for such developments partly because of the tradition of comedic Orientalism of the Ancient Arabic Order of the Nobles of the Mystic Shrine for North America. The Shriners, as they are more commonly known, are known as the "playground" of Freemasonry. Only open to those who have achieved the highest levels in the other branches of Masonry, the Shriners sought to embody a spirit of Oriental decadence and frivolity, balanced by charitable works. The Shriners were founded in 1872 by the well-known New York thespian William J. (Billy) Florence and a prominent Masonic and "devoted Arabic" scholar, Dr. Walter M. Fleming.[52] The order took off in 1878 when they hired Albert Rawson, an Orientalist "expert" and friend of Theosophist Madame Blavatsky, and determined to "decorate it with all the mysticism of the Orient," and "a certain degree of mystery."[53] Mocking the solemnity of the Orientalist quest for authenticity in the East and the absurdities of fraternal regalia and hullabaloo, the Shriners created an intentionally fraudulent legend linking their secret order back to the nephew and son-in-law of the prophet Muhammad, allegedly founded in Mecca in 644.

Intent on having a good time, supporting charitable projects, and enjoying the fleshpots of Egypt as literally as possible, the Shriners seldom took their own legends too seriously. Even their own historians speak of the "fancies" and other liberties taken with their origin stories: "The placing of the origin of this Order at Mecca is a fancy of the imagination which historians in general have a license to claim use of," one Shriner historian wrote in 1906, referring to the rites of the order as a "compilation of facts and fancies which subsequently were handed out to a waiting and anxious constituency."[54] The Shriner's fancies had a distinctly Orientalist flavor, describing Muslim lands with exotica and erotica, as in the following passage: "Looking backward toward the home of the Order, we find the Brotherhood in Egypt flourishing and fruitful in good works, as beautiful as are the queenly palms which wave their feathery arms in the soft airs that crinkle the surface of the lordly Nile into rippling lines of loveliest corrugations, or cast their cooling shadows upon the star-eyed daughters of Egypt."[55]

The order's costumes also embodied Western Orientalist ideas of the East. The Nobles wore rich costumes "of Eastern character," made of silk and brocaded velvet "of oriental intensity of color," topped with a fez. According to the Shriners, the wearing of the fez originated from the time when the Crusaders interrupted the *hajj* to Mecca around 960 CE and "Mohammedans west of the Nile" journeyed to the city of Fez in Morocco instead.[56] As Susan Nance writes, the Shriners' rites were not a simple mockery of Islam but were part of a late nineteenth-century masculine burlesque of reverence and the feminizing influence of Theosophists and other Western admirers of Eastern spirituality. "Like many popular arts and amusements in the nineteenth century the Shrine ritual could be all things to all men," she writes. "Whether an initiate sought relief from the seriousness of Masonry, a humorous interpretation of exotic travel narratives, or just a lighthearted elite fraternal experience, whether they despised the Muslim Arabia, romanticized it, or were indifferent to it, they could all find their own meaning in the tricks and skits of the Muslim Shrine."[57] Orientalism was a protean and plastic phenomenon, not simply a derogatory one.

Meanwhile, African American Freemasonry originated with the induction of a Barbadian soldier named Prince Hall in 1755 and his subsequent founding of a black Masonic tradition in light of white American Masons' refusal to accept black brethren.[58] The World's Columbian Exposition held in Chicago in 1893 inspired African Americans to start their own version of the Shriners, substituting "Egyptian" for "Arabic" in their name: the Ancient *Egyptian* Order of Nobles of the Mystic Shrine.[59] Despite protests from some white Shriners, others supplied their black counterparts with regalia and sometimes meeting places. With the intensification of Jim Crow in the early twentieth century, such cooperation worked to the detriment of segregationists when the U.S. Supreme Court ruled against white Shriners in southern states who were attempting to bar African Americans from using the name and symbol of the order.[60]

It is worth considering how African Americans might have interpreted the Orientalist myth at the heart of Shrinerdom differently than their white peers, just as Joanna Brooks has argued that African Americans developed their own interpretations of Freemasonry in general.[61] American racism itself was a form of Orientalism, a Manichean othering that viewed people of African descent as irredeemably alien and savage. In the context of an explosion of Orientalism in fin-de-siècle America, the cotton fields of Dixie could be thought of as America's own internal Orient, the American Egypt. The association between African Americans and the Orient did not end with slavery or the South. Other authors described the residents of 1920s Harlem in similar terms, writing of "Negroes endlessly chewing pellets of pepsin, with eyes lost in far-away dream, in the grip of a mastication neurosis, mournful as Orientals fingering their beads."[62] The African American identification with the South as Egypt was echoed at times by white Americans' view of blacks in Orientalist terms.

Given the popularity and power of Orientalism in American culture, it is not surprising that African Americans developed their own variants of romantic Orientalism. Whether as soldiers, as travelers, as missionaries, or as religious practitioners, African Americans participated in empire and in Orientalism, and in so doing helped to recreate the identity of the black Diaspora. As Scott Trafton provocatively argues, "to construct the black Orient was to construct the black self" and to do so in ways "only possible within the context of a domestic American imperialism—an imperialism of the interior experienced by Africans in America every single day."[63]

In this context, it is worth considering not only the civic freedom to be gained by becoming a Moor or a Muslim, but also the psychic liberation to be won by extricating oneself from American racial logic by asserting one's identity as a non-Western person. For Timothy Drew, the Mystic Shrine was not just a comedic burlesque but was rather a repository of a powerful, oppositional counterhistory. Drew took the title "Noble" from the "Nobles of the Mystic Shrine" and adopted the fez, their regalia, and some of their mythology. He spent time as part of a Hindu circus sideshow act, interacted with an Indian Muslim Ahmadi missionary, and converted a Theosophist text into his own personal Qur'an. Finally, with the aid of esoteric texts by Lauron William de Laurence, Noble Drew Ali helped to establish the tradition that came to be known as twentieth-century African American Islam. The hypothesis that Timothy Drew, and hence twentieth-century black Islam, was linked to antebellum African Muslims is a "circumstantial observation" in the words of its strongest proponent, whereas Drew Ali's involvement in contemporaneous traditions of American Orientalism is immediate and verifiable.

We have seen the philological and the "colonial" aspects of black Orientalism, observed their debt to a corpus of esoteric Orientalist texts, and seen how traditions of Orientalist fraternal rituals and theatrical performances helped contribute to its rise. What follows is a discussion of the commercial aspects of black Orientalism, by which market practices formed networks of black urban practioners who created what they called "Oriental and African Mystic Science."

Orientalist images were common in black culture of the 1920s, as they were in American culture more generally. Orientalism flavored the entertainment of African Americans as well as other Americans; the Unique Colony Circle of America held an Oriental Costume Ball in 1926, like the Oriental balls that were common in New York white society.[64] Rudolph Valentino's *The Sheik* was a hit in Harlem's theaters, and Harlem slang transformed young male hipsters into slightly sinister "sheiks." The sheik's female equivalent was the "sheba," in honor of the biblical queen of Sheba, ruler of Ethiopia. Orientalism was a major theme of early films, with seventeen films with "sheik" in their titles and nine more featuring sheiks in their plots in the 1920s alone, along with such Orientalist fare as *Cleopatra* (1917), *Salome* (1918), *One Arabian Night* (1920), *Kismet* (1920), *The Morals of Marcus* (1915), *The Slim Princess* (1915), and three versions of the hit play *The Garden of Allah* (1916).[65]

Images of the Orient appeared from the funny pages to the editorial pages of black newspapers. In the mid-twenties, a black performer named Joe Downing went by the name Joveddah de Raja and dispensed "words of Oriental comfort and wisdom" on a New York radio station.[66] Many contemporary accounts of Harlem note the large number of mystics plying their trades: "Black art flourishes in Harlem —and elsewhere in New York," Winthrop D. Lane wrote in 1925, "Egyptian seers uncover hidden knowledge, Indian fortune-tellers reveal the future, sorcerers perform their mysteries. Feats of witchcraft are done daily. A towel for turban and a smart manner are enough to transform any Harlem colored man into a dispenser of magic to his profit."[67] There were storefront shops dedicated to selling candles, incense, powders, books, and other spiritual supplies, and every stationery store in Harlem carried a selection of dream and mystery books, many of which used Orientalist themes, such as the 1916 *Oriental Dream Book, with interpretations of all dreams as vouched for by the Orientals, Gypsies, witches, Egyptians, augors, astrologers, magi, fortune-tellers, sooth-sayers, prophets, seers and wise men of ancient and modern times.*[68]

Professors of Oriental and African Mystic Science constructed the black Orient and the black self in one motion by writing themselves into the romantic Orientalist imaginary. Harlem's Oriental scientists included the following: Professor Eatherin Monodu; Professor J. Du Jaja, "A Mohammedan Scientist" of the Asia and Africa Remedy Company; Professor S. Indoo of African Science, "Native of Nigeria"; Professor Alpha Roktabija, "Arabian Mystic Seer and Master of the Ancient Mysteries"; Oku Aba, "African scientist"; Amadu, "Mohammedan Scientist"; Professor Salin-dukee, "Native of Zulu"; Professor Thomas Ogunshola, "Native West African, Master of Science"; Professor Joseph Domingo, "Dealer in Root Medicine Direct from Kano, West Coast Africa"; Professor Eyo, "A Mohammedan scientist and Oriental Occultism [*sic*], Native of Africa just arrived"; and Professor R. S. Scarlett, "initiate magician of Eastern Order of Sacred Mysteries." The well-known Harlem magician Herman Rucker freely used Orientalist imagery in his self-authored biography, and the boycott leader and spiritualist Sufi Abdul Hamid claimed to be Sudanese and born in Egypt, although the FBI reported his given name was Brown.[69]

It is an open question as to how these men were received among the black population. Did most people view them as fakes and frauds, or did most view them credulously as representatives of Oriental faiths and dimly understood, faraway lands? Both views were well represented in the historical record, with the elite discourse of the newspapers and editorialists commonly ridiculing the street mystics, whom they depicted as sexual deviants and charlatans. Yet the omnipresent advertisements of the mystics testify to the fact that they had a large and loyal following.

In what sense were these professors of Oriental and African Science "scientists," and in what sense were they using the term "Oriental"? A scientist, in popular African American and West Indian parlance, was a religious magician, a person learned in secret magical religious practices.[70] They were also scientists because scientists held cultural, quasi-magical powers in the 1920s, when physics and chemistry were beginning to tear back the veil of the universe and expose its fundamental laws. As one advertisement put it, "Science and Oriental is great wonder."[71] But they also were scientists because they were pushing the frontiers of human knowledge, in the spiritual realm rather than the material realm. In the words of Aubrey Browser's *The Negro Times*, spiritualists "are groping after truth just as the most advanced scientists are doing, and they may uncover some aspects of the subject which the wisest have not as yet been able to reduce to understandable formulation."[72]

In marked contrast to the aversion to Africa in portions of respectable "colored" society, many of these men claimed to be from Africa, and it was common to advertise one's proximity to Africa—it was a bonus if either the scientist or his incense had "just arrived" from Africa. Indeed, in African American Hoodoo, Africa had long been considered a powerful place, home to particularly potent magic.[73] Yet these street scientists expanded Hoodoo's identification with Africa as the source of magic, adding another category called the "Orient," which often overlapped with "Africa." India, not the Middle East, was the key constituent of this Oriental imaginary, but African Islam also featured prominently in the advertisements, and China made a few appearances as well. Sometimes India and Africa were mixed promiscuously, as in the case of "S. Indoo [Hindu] of African Science," or "Professor Domingo, the Hindu Occulist [sic] and Healer from Kano West Africa." As Carolyn Morrow Long notes, the image of the Hindu swami appeared everywhere in African American spiritual advertisements and products as a symbol of occult knowledge. An investigator among southern blacks in the late thirties and early forties discovered the common belief that occult knowledge and spiritual products originated with Hindus.[74] Another motivation for embracing the Orient could be to distance oneself from Africa and the legacies of American slavery. Thus, emphasizing a "Moorish" or "Asiatic," "Oriental" or even Egyptian identity could be a way of distancing black Americans from the perceived savagery of sub-Saharan Africa.[75]

The newspaper advertisements of these healers, mystics, and self-proclaimed scientists show that they were deeply concerned with the discourse of civilization and reoriented its claims using Orientalism. One prominent example is the self-proclaimed magician and alchemist who went by the names Professor Akpan Aga, Prof. Akpandac, Dr. B. Grant, and Alla Gui Barn. His advertisements pictured him in either a fez or a turban and claimed he was a native of Africa and a "Professor of African and Oriental Occultism, Psychic Science, White and Black Magic, etc." Aga's many identities contradicted each other, yet that does not make his message any less interesting. In December 1922 his advertisements began appearing in Harlem newspapers as "Professor Akpan Aga, Wonderful Magician and Spiritualist by Alchemy and Fire."

By January he was calling himself "Professor Akpandac" and had a confederate named Dr. B. Grant. In his early advertisements, Akpandac wore a turban and preached about Jesus. By February he had moved to 129th Street and was calling himself "Alla Gui Barn, Professor Akpandac." To match his new Islamic identity, he pictured himself wearing a fez and ended his advertisement "Allah Be Praised!" The month of March saw a return of the turban, but the fez advertisements came back in April and May. Aga/Akpandac/Barn was not finished transforming himself, however. In August he began calling himself "Professor Edeteffiong, Professor of African and Oriental Occultism, Psychic Science, White and Black Magic, Etc. Native of Africa. Advice Given—Egyptian and African Formulae Used." Edeteffiong became "Professor Edet. Effiong" in September, October, and November, but he also used the old fez picture in an advertisement for the "Peamanda Co." selling "Oriental Incense." His advertisements disappeared from Harlem newspapers only to reappear in 1925 through 1929 as "Edet Effiong" or "Effiong Offiong, of the Nigeria Remedy Company, Dealer in Roots and Herbs." In this final incarnation, he dropped all references to Christianity. Now he wore a turban with Bedouin robes and claimed to be a "Mohammedan Master of Stricter African Science."[76] Perhaps he switched names to escape prosecution—it was not uncommon for healers to be sued for selling remedies that did not work as promised.

Aga/Akpandac/Barn/Effiong/Offiong's luck finally ran out when he was arrested for interstate mail fraud for selling an Indianapolis man a powder guaranteed to return anything that had been lost—from a lover to a cow. Another customer was a prisoner who had bought a powder that was said to be able to spring him free from jail. At the end of the day, Aga's "Oriental and African Science" and African science looked a lot like American Hoodoo remedies.[77] More than likely, the man going by the name Aga, Akpandac, and so forth was the same person as Professor Akpan Essien, "a mystery healer of the Mohammedan cult," who was arrested and jailed in Washington, D.C., in August 1923 on charges of practicing medicine without a license. If that was so, then his given name was not Aga or Akpandac or Effiong, but Thomas Williams.[78]

Yet the obvious fraudulence of Professor Akpandac's self-presentation does not mean that black Orientalists were not sincerely challenging the racist binaries of the discourse of civilization with the more complex claims of black Orientalism. It would be a mistake, in other words, to disregard the ideas of someone simply because he exchanged identities so freely. Like Noble Drew Ali, Akpandac preached a version of the teachings of Levi Dowling's *The Aquarian Gospel of Jesus the Christ*, which taught that Oriental mysteries were the source of Jesus's powers and that Christianity had cribbed its dogma from Eastern mythology: "When the statement is made that Christ was a Master, it means, literally speaking, that Christ was Master of Himself, educated and trod the path, receiving the instruction of the Masters in India and the Orient. This is a well-known fact and is also a matter of record that

Christ did belong to the ancient school of India."[79] According to Aga and other professors of mystic science, the Orient was the source of otherworldly powers, a reservoir of mysteries and magic that was superior to, and generative of, the religions of the West.

Aga and other mystic scientists depicted the Oriental East as the necessary counterpart to the materialistic West, a message that had particular resonance given the disheartening spectacle of World War I's mechanized warfare and the life experience of African American migrants who had left homes in mostly rural states and settled in cities in the industrialized North. Aga's ads argued that humans had learned to control the material world through Western technology but must turn to "the ancient occult mysteries of Africa and India" in order to gain spiritual wisdom. There were many variations on this theme of Western materialism versus "Oriental" spiritualism among the several dozen mystic healers who advertised in Harlem newspapers. A man who called himself Amadu, "the Mohammedan scientist dealing in religious incense," wrote that the modern materialist "commercializes everything and is blind to hidden Spiritual truths. . . . To Africa and the Orient, therefore, we must turn if we desire to benefit from these archaic truths."[80]

People who adopted Muslim, Israelite, Moorish, or other identities did not simply pretend to be from Oriental lands. Rather, they believed their ancestors to be from those places and did their best to embody a heterogeneous vision of the Orient, or, sometimes, "Africa and the Orient." To be sure there was some quotient of opportunism and fakery, but even if the Oriental images of black history presented by black Orientalists were self-conscious performances, those masks were no more implausible than the depictions of blackness in contemporary popular culture. The minstrel characters of "Zip Coon," "Uncle Tom," "Mammy," and "Jezebel" and the accompanying images of African savages and cannibals that dominated representations of black people for more than a hundred years were far more implausible and more grotesque than anything that black Orientalists presented.[81] The distastefulness of customary representations of blackness and black history is essential to understanding the appeal and the plausibility of black Orientalism to black Americans in the early twentieth century. As English professor Moustafa Bayoumi writes of Moorish Science, it is "revolutionary in its own way by providing a radical ontology of self. To reorient one's body towards the Orient means a refusal to engage with the first principles of white America's definitions of blackness."[82] Black Orientalism may not have always been confrontational, public, or typical of racially based identity politics, but it is not hard to see the recalcitrant defiance of antiblack racism in its "radical ontology of self."[83]

This chapter has discussed the distinctively black Orientalisms of black Muslims, black Jews, black Spiritualists, and the people who called themselves "professors of Oriental and African Mystic Science." Aside from Father Divine, it has not discussed Orientalism among black religious practitioners who did not represent themselves as being from Eastern lands. But religious Orientalism was such a common element of Christianity and Freemasonry of the day that we should be circumspect about assuming that any particular faith lacked some degree of Orientalism. Charles Parham, one of the originators of the doctrine of Pentecostalism, was fond of preaching in Palestinian robes and hoped to someday excavate the Ark of the Covenant in the Holy Land.[84] In the 1920s, black preachers took trips to Palestine and beauty product magnate Madame C. J. Walker sponsored a newspaper contest to send newspaper readers to the Holy Land.[85] The many similarities among the interwar black new religious movements illustrates that sectarian religious labels are too narrow to contain the black Muslims, black Israelites, Rastafarians, and professors of Oriental and African Mystic Science. Conceptualizing early twentieth-century black Islam or black Judaism as African American variants of established faiths misrepresents their contents and masks the many overlapping connections between different kinds of black Orientalism. If Father Hurley's statement "a good Muslim is a good Spiritualist" is correct, it was also correct that good Muslims believed themselves to be black Israelites, black Israelites observed Ramadan, and even Father Divine's doctrine of the indwelling god was connected to the "Hebrew" science of urban black Orientalist mystics. Black Israelites, like black Muslims, based their faith on elements of Spiritualism, Holiness Christianity, Kabbalah, and Freemasonry in addition to Judaism or Islam.

As we have seen, black Orientalism, like other Orientalisms, had philological, colonial, and commercial variations. It repackaged African American traditions of Hoodoo and Conjure and allowed working-class African Americans a means of criticizing and dismantling the discourse of civilization that hemmed them in on all sides. Surely some of the sellers of tonics, roots, and spirituality were hucksters. Yet it would be a mistake to disregard these black practitioners of Orientalism entirely, for their advertisements and activities engaged the modern age's concepts of science, technology, reason, and progress. The alternative religious practitioners of the black metropolis appropriated the discourse of Orientalism for their own purposes, discovering political critique, spiritual illumination, and a recalcitrant position within an imperialist intellectual tradition through a sustained engagement with the Oriental Other. Black urban alternative religious practitioners reunited the multiple personalities of the modern moment by bringing together magic, science, religion, and politics, and in so doing they challenged both modernity and the racism of the discourse of civilization.

Notes

The author is grateful for financial support from the Andrew W. Mellon Fellowship at the Center for the Humanities of Wesleyan University, which made the writing of this chapter possible. Thanks go also to the author's students, and to Elizabeth McAlister, Henry Goldschmidt, Mary-Jane Rubenstein, and the other members of the Wesleyan Religion Department for their valuable feedback and advice.

1. Aboonah Adam [George W. Hurley] and Elias Mohammed Abraham, "Arabian Science" (Detroit: Universal Hagar's Spiritual Association, 1930), 1–3, in the author's possession, and Father George W. Hurley Collection (in accession), Wayne State University, Detroit. Please note that Hurley's contemporary followers prefer the label "Spiritual" to "Spiritualist." However, because Hurley used the term "Spiritualist," I do as well, to avoid confusion. Hurley's church featured prominently in Hans A. Baer, *The Black Spiritual Movement: A Religious Response to Racism* (Knoxville: University of Tennessee Press, 1984).

2. On Blyden, see Edward E. Curtis IV, *Islam in Black America: Identity, Liberation, and Difference in African-American Islamic Thought* (Albany: State University of New York Press, 2002), 21–43, and Scott Trafton, *Race and Nineteenth-Century American Egyptomania* (Durham, N.C.: Duke University Press, 2004), 23–26. On the use of Moorish identity to assert civil rights, see the first of many examples: C. Eric Lincoln, *The Black Muslims in America*, 3rd ed. (Grand Rapids, Mich.: William B. Eerdmans, 1994), 49.

3. Adam and Abraham, "Arabian Science," 1–3.

4. Ibid.

5. Ibid., 3.

6. Arthur Huff Fauset, *Black Gods of the Metropolis: Negro Religious Cults of the Urban North* (1944; reprint: Philadelphia: University of Pennsylvania Press, 2002).

7. This self-estrangement or embrace of the exotic in one's self has been termed "self-exoticism," "autoexoticism," or, in French, "auto-exotisme." See Marta Savigliano, *Tango and the Political Economy of Passion* (Boulder, Colo.: Westview, 1995), 3; James Parakilas, "How Spain Got a Soul," in *The Exotic in Western Music,* ed. Jonathan Bellman (Boston: Northeastern University Press, 1998), 137–93; Anthony Shay and Barbara Sellers-Young, "Belly Dance: Orientalism-Exoticism-Self-Exoticism," *Dance Research Journal* 35, no. 1 (Summer 2003): 13–37; Nathalie Schon, *L'Auto-Exotisme dans Les Littératures des Antilles Françaises* (Paris: Karthala, 2003); and Soo Ah Kwon, "Autoexoticizing: Asian American Youth and the Import Car Scene," *Journal of Asian American Studies* 7, no. 1 (2004): 1–26.

8. Author's interviews with UHSA ministers, Detroit, Michigan, August 2006.

9. Ahmed I. Abu Shouk, J. O. Hunwick, and R. S. O'Fahey, "A Sudanese Missionary to the United States: Satti Majid, '*Shaykh al-Islam* in North America,' and His Encounter with Noble Drew Ali, Prophet of the Moorish Science Temple Movement," *Sudanese Africa* 8 (1997): 157–58.

10. Glenda Elizabeth Gilmore, *Gender and Jim Crow: Women and the Politics of White Supremacy in North Carolina, 1896–1920* (Chapel Hill: University of North Carolina Press, 1996); Sylvia R. Frey and Betty Wood, *Come Shouting to Zion: African American Protestantism in the American South and British Caribbean to 1830* (Chapel Hill: University of North Carolina Press, 1998).

11. Walter Johnson's investigation of the agency of enslaved people in the internal slave trade is but one example of a motif of agency that permeates most studies of African Americans published since World War II. Walter Johnson, *Soul by Soul: Life inside the Antebellum Slave Market* (Cambridge: Harvard University Press, 1999). Johnson has critiqued the concept of agency in "On Agency," *Journal of Social History* 37, no. 1 (2003): 113–24.

12. Edward Said, *Orientalism* (New York: Pantheon, 1978), 2–3.

13. James Clifford, "On Orientalism," in *The Predicament of Culture* (Cambridge, Mass.: Harvard University Press, 1988), 261; Richard Fox, "East of Said," in *Edward Said: A Critical Reader,* ed. M. Sprinker (Oxford: Oxford University Press, 1992), 146; and Lisa Lowe, *Critical Terrains: French and British Orientalisms* (Ithaca, N.Y.: Cornell University Press, 1991).

14. For new takes on Orientalism and "Occidentalism," see James G. Carrier, ed., *Occidentalism: Images of the West* (New York: Oxford University Press, 2003); and Chandreyee Niyogi, ed., *Reorienting Orientalism* (New Delhi: SAGE, 2006). A more polemical version is presented in Ian Buruma and Avisahi Margalit, *Occidentalism: The West in the Eyes of Its Enemies* (New York: Penguin, 2004). For an inventive recent account, see Maya Jasanoff, *Edge of Empire: Lives, Culture, and Conquest in the East, 1750–1850* (New York: Vintage Books, 2005).

15. Melani McAlister, *Epic Encounters: Culture, Media, and U.S. Interests in the Middle East since 1945,* updated ed. (Berkeley: University of California Press, 2005); Douglas Little, *American Orientalism: The United States and the Middle East since 1945* (Chapel Hill: University of North Carolina Press, 2002); Susan Nance, "Crossing Over: A Cultural History of American Engagement with the Muslim World, 1830–1940" (Ph.D. diss., University of California Berkeley, 2003); Timothy Marr, *The Cultural Roots of American Islamicism* (New York: Cambridge University Press, 2006); and Michael B. Oren, *Power, Faith, and Fantasy: America in the Middle East: 1776 to the Present* (New York: W. W. Norton, 2007).

16. Orientalism regarding the Far East is related to but different from Said's Orientalism, which focused on Muslim lands. See John Kuo Wei Tchen, *New York before Chinatown: Orientalism and the Shaping of American Culture 1776–1882* (Baltimore, Md.: Johns Hopkins University Press, 1999); Henry Yu, *Thinking Orientals: Migration, Contact, and Exoticism in Modern America* (New York: Oxford University Press, 2001); Mari Yoshihara, *Embracing the East: White Women and American Orientalism* (New York: Oxford University Press, 2002).

17. Matthew Bernstein and Gaylyn Studlar, *Visions of the East: Orientalism in Film* (New Brunswick, N.J.: Rutgers University Press, 1997); Malini Johar Schueller, *U.S. Orientalisms: Race, Nation, and Gender in Literature, 1790–1890* (Ann Arbor: University of Michigan Press, 1998); Crystal Anderson, "Orientalism and the Harlem Renaissance,"

paper presented at the annual meeting of the American Studies Association, Oakland, California, October 5, 2006; Scott Trafton, *Egypt Land: Race and Nineteenth-Century American Egyptomania* (Durham, N.C.: Duke University Press, 2004); William Leach, *Land of Desire: Merchants, Power, and the Rise of a New American Culture* (New York: Vintage, 1993), 104–11; Holly Edwards, "A Million and One Nights: Orientalism in America, 1870–1930," in *Noble Dreams, Wicked Pleasures: Orientalism in America, 1870–1930,* ed. Holly Edwards (Princeton, N.J.: Princeton University Press and the Sterling and Francine Clark Institute, 2000); McAlister, *Epic Encounters;* and Catherine A. Lutz and Jane L. Collins, *Reading National Geographic* (Chicago: University of Chicago Press, 1993).

18. Vijay Prashad, *Karma of Brown Folk* (Minneapolis: University of Minnesota Press, 2000); Vijay Prashad, *Everybody Was Kung Fu Fighting: Afro-Asian Connections and the Myth of Cultural Purity* (Boston: Beacon, 2001); Robin D. G. Kelley, *Freedom Dreams: The Black Radical Imagination* (Boston: Beacon, 2002); Bill Mullen, *Afro-Orientalism* (Minneapolis: University of Minnesota Press, 2004).

19. See, for example, Ernest Allen Jr., "When Japan Was 'Champion of the Darker Races': Satokata Takahashi and the Flowering of Black Messianic Nationalism," *Black Scholar* 24 (Winter 1994): 23–46; Ernest Allen Jr., "Waiting for Tojo: The Pro-Japan Vigil of Black Missourians, 1932–1943," *Gateway Heritage* 16 (Fall 1995): 38–55; Brenda Gayle Plummer, *Rising Wind: Black Americans and U.S. Foreign Affairs, 1935–1960* (Chapel Hill: University of North Carolina Press, 1996); Penny Von Eschen, *Race against Empire: Black Americans and Anticolonialism, 1937–1957* (Ithaca, N.Y.: Cornel University Press, 1997); Marc Gallicchio, *The African American Encounter with Japan and China: Black Internationalism in Asia, 1895–1935* (Chapel Hill: University of North Carolina Press, 2000); Kelley, *Freedom Dreams,* 60–109; and Gerald Horne, *Race War! White Supremacy and the Japanese Attack on the British Empire* (New York: New York University Press, 2003), 118–21.

20. Anderson, "Orientalism and the Harlem Renaissance."

21. For more on Orientalism and African Americans, see Ernest J. Wilson III, "Orientalism: A Black Perspective," *Journal of Palestinian Studies* 10, no. 2 (Winter 1981): 59–69; Allen, "When Japan Was 'Champion of the Darker Races'"; Allen, "Waiting for Tojo"; Ali A. Mazrui, "Black Orientalism? Further Reflections on 'Wonders of the African World,'" *West Africa Review* 1, no. 2 (2000); Biodun Jeyifo, "On Mazrui's 'Black Orientalism': A Cautionary Critique," *West Africa Review* 1, no. 2 (2000); Thomas E. R. Maguire, "The Islamic Simulacrum in Henry Louis Gates, Jr.'s *Into Africa*," *West Africa Review* 1, no. 2 (2000); Nathaniel Deutsch, "'The Asiatic Black Man': An African American Orientalism?" *Journal of Asian American Studies* 4, no. 3 (October 2001): 193–208; and Sherman A. Jackson, *Islam and the Blackamerican: Looking toward the Third Resurrection* (New York: Oxford University Press, 2005), 99–129.

22. Ziauddin Sardar, *Orientalism* (Philadelphia: Open University Press, 1999), 70.

23. Fauset, *Black Gods,* 34; Sidney Kobre, "Rabbi Ford," *Reflex* 4, no. 1 (January 1929): 28; Ira De Augustine Reid, "Let Us Prey!" *Opportunity* 4 (September 1926): 277.

24. Jill Watts, *God, Harlem U.S.A.: The Father Divine Story* (Berkeley: University of California Press, 1992), 21–30.

25. T. R. Poston, "'I Taught Father Divine' Says St. Bishop the Vine: 'And He Is

Not Doing Right by Theory,' Prophet Holds," *New York Amsterdam News*, November 23, 1932, 1.

26. Ruth Landes, "Negro Jews in Harlem," *Jewish Journal of Sociology* 9, no. 2 (December 1967): 187. On Father Divine, see Jill Watts, *God, Harlem U.S.A.*, and Robert Weisbrot, *Father Divine and the Struggle for Racial Equality* (Urbana: University of Illinois Press, 1983).

27. Correspondence, Rabbi Arnold Josiah Ford, Addis Ababa, Ethiopia, to Rabbi W. A. Matthew, New York, June 5, 1931, Wentworth A. Matthew Collection, Schomburg Center for Research in Black Culture, New York Public Library, Astor, Lenox, and Tilden Foundations. Ras Hailu was an Ethiopian noble with interests in the South where the Tsana Dam was planned and where the Ethiopian government hoped to bring African Americans with technical skills to aid in the completion of the dam and the development of the country. See George Shepperson, "Ethiopianism and African Nationalism," *Phylon* 14, no. 1 (1953): 9–18; William R. Scott, *Sons of Sheba's Race: African Americans and the Italo-Ethiopian War, 1935–1941* (Bloomington: Indiana University Press, 1993); Winston James, *Holding Aloft the Banner of Ethiopia: Caribbean Radicalism in Early Twentieth-Century America* (New York: Verso, 1998); and Robin D. G. Kelley, "This Ain't Ethiopia, But It'll Do," in *Race Rebels: Culture, Politics, and the Black Working Class* (New York: Free Press, 1994), 129.

28. Correspondence, Rabbi W. A. Matthew, New York, to Bishop C. H. Brown, Amity Hall, Jamaica, March 28, 1947, p. 2, Wentworth A. Matthew Collection, Schomburg Center.

29. Jacob Dorman, "Black Israelites aka Black Jews aka Black Hebrews: Black Israelism, Black Judaism, Judaic Christianity," in *Introduction to New and Alternative Religions in the United States*, ed. Eugene V. Gallagher and W. Michael Ashcraft (Westport, Conn.: Praeger, 2006), 5: 74–78; Israel J. Gerber, *The Heritage Seekers: American Blacks in Search of Jewish Identity* (Middle Village, N.Y.: Jonathan David, 1977); Morris Lounds Jr., *Israel's Black Hebrews: Black Americans in Search of Identity* (Washington, D.C.: University Press of America, 1981); James E. Landing, *Black Judaism: Story of an American Movement* (Durham, N.C.: Carolina Academic Press, 2001), 387–431; Wardell J. Payne, ed., *Directory of African American Religious Bodies: A Compendium by the Howard University School of Divinity* (Washington, D.C.: Howard University Press, 1991), 133; Jesse Nemerofsky, "The Black Hebrews," *Society* 32, no. 1 (November–December 1994): 72–77; and Merrill Singer, "Now I Know What the Songs Mean! Traditional Black Music in a Contemporary Black Sect," *Southern Quarterly* 23, no. 3 (Spring 1985): 125–40.

30. For a sample of the complex and many-faceted debates over hegemony, resistance, and recalcitrance, see T. J. Jackson Lears, "The Concept of Cultural Hegemony: Problems and Possibilities," *American Historical Review* 90, no. 3 (June 1985): 567–93; James Scott, *Weapons of the Weak: Everyday Forms of Peasant Resistance* (New Haven, Conn.: Yale University Press, 1985); Sherry B. Ortner, "Resistance and the Problem of Ethnographic Refusal," *Comparative Studies in Society and History* 37, no. 1 (January 1995): 173–93; and Jean and John Comaroff, eds., *Modernity and Its Malcontents: Ritual and Power in Postcolonial Africa* (Chicago: University of Chicago Press, 1993), xv–xxii.

31. Arnold J. Ford, "One God, One Aim, One Destiny," in *Universal Ethiopian Hymnal*, 1922, Manuscripts, Archives, and Rare Books Division, Schomburg Center for Research in Black Culture, New York Public Library, Astor, Lenox, and Tilden Foundations.

32. On the gendering and eroticization of the Orient, see Said, *Orientalism*, 167, 188, 190, 309; Reina Lewis, *Gendering Orientalism: Race, Femininity, and Representation* (London: Routledge, 1996), 16; and Derek Hopwood, *Sexual Encounters in the Middle East: The British, the French, and the Arabs* (Ithaca, N.Y.: Cornell University Press, 1996).

33. Levi H. Dowling, *The Aquarian Gospel of Jesus the Christ*, 6th ed. (1908; London: L. N. Fowler, 1920). The quote is from Susan Nance, "Respectability and Representation: The Moorish Science Temple, Morocco, and Black Public Culture in 1920s Chicago," *American Quarterly* 54, no. 4 (December 2002): 653. For more on the Moorish Science Temple, see Ernest Allen Jr., "Identity and Destiny: The Formative Views of the Moorish Science Temple and the Nation of Islam," in *Muslims on the Americanization Path?* ed. Yvonne Yazbeck Haddad and John L. Esposito (New York: Oxford University Press, 2000), 163–214; Curtis, *Islam in Black America*, 1–20, 45–62; and Susan Nance, "Mystery of the Moorish Science Temple: Southern Blacks and American Alternative Spirituality in 1920s Chicago," *Religion and American Culture* 12, no. 2 (Summer 2002): 123–66.

34. Levi H. Dowling, *The Aquarian Gospel of Jesus the Christ*, 6th ed. (1908: London: L. N. Fowler, 1920); Sri Ramatherio, ed., *Unto Thee I Grant*, rev. ed. (San Jose, Calif.: Supreme Grand Lodge of the AMORC, 1953). Although the Ahmadiyyah movement and a few others had introduced English versions of the Qur'an in these years, it is disputed whether Noble Drew Ali drew from the Qur'an in his own text. See Peter Lamborn Wilson, *Sacred Drift: Essays on the Margins of Islam* (San Francisco: City Lights Books, 1993), 19, and Richard Brent Turner, *Islam in the African American Experience*, 2nd ed. (Bloomington: Indiana University Press, 2003), 93, 259.

35. Nicolas Notovitch, *La Vie Inconnnue de Jesus Christ* (Paris: Paul Ollendorff, 1894). Fauset, *Black Gods*, 41, and Wilson, *Sacred Drift*, 19.

36. Landes, "Negro Jews in Harlem," 184; Arnold J. Ford, *Universal Ethiopian Hymnal*.

37. Kathleen Malone O'Connor, "The Nubian Islamic Hebrews, Ansaaru Allah Community: Jewish Teachings of an African American Muslim Community," in *Black Zion: African American Religious Encounters with Judaism*, ed. Yvonne Patricia Chireau and Nathaniel Deutsch (New York: Oxford University Press, 2000), 118–50; J. Gordon Melton and Christopher Partridge, *New Religions: A Guide: New Religious Movements, Sects, and Alternative Spiritualities* (New York: Oxford University Press, 2004), 142–43; and Karl Evanzz, *The Messenger: The Rise and Fall of Elijah Muhammad* (New York: Vintage Books, 1999), 147–48.

38. Reverend Cassandra Latimer-Knight, interview with author, Detroit, Michigan, July 19, 2006.

39. Patrick A. Polk, "Other Books, Other Powers: The 6th and 7th Books of Moses in Afro-Atlantic Folk Belief," *Southern Folklore* 56, no. 2 (1999): 128; W. F. Elkins, "William Lauron De Laurence and Jamaican Folk Religion," *Folklore* 97, no. 2 (1986): 215–18; and Scheible, *The Sixth and Seventh Books of Moses*. The use of de Laurence's works among contemporary healers in Jamaica is discussed in Edna Brodner, "Brief Notes on DeLaurence in Jamaica," *ACIJ Review* 4 (1999): 91–99.

40. On New Thought, see Charles S. Braden, *Spirits in Rebellion: The Rise and Development of New Thought* (Dallas: Southern Methodist University Press, 1963); Richard

Weiss, *The American Myth of Success: From Horatio Alger to Norman Vincent Peale* (New York: Basic Books, 1969), 144–45, 172–88; J. Gordon Melton, *New Thought: A Reader* (Santa Barbara, Calif.: Institute for the Study of American Religion, 1990); Watts, *God, Harlem U.S.A.*, 21–24; and Dell deChant, "The American New Thought Movement," in Gallagher and Ashcraft, *Introduction to New and Alternative Religions*, 3: 67–91. On theosophy, see Robert Ellwood, "The Theosophical Society," in Gallagher and Ashcraft, *Introduction to New and Alternative Religions*, 3: 48–66; Catherine Lowman Wessinger, *Annie Besant and Progressive Messianism 1847–1933* (Lewiston, N.Y.: Edwin Mellen Press, 1988); and W. Michael Ashcraft, *The Dawn of the New Cycle: Point Loma Theosophists and American Culture* (Knoxville: University of Tennessee Press, 2002).

41. Johann Scheible, *The Sixth and Seventh Books of Moses: The Mystery of All Mysteries . . .* (Chicago: De Laurence, Scott, 1914) and Jacob S. Dorman, " 'I Saw You Disappear with My Own Eyes': Hidden Transcripts of New York Black Israelite Bricolage," *Nova Religio: The Journal of Alternative and Emergent Religions* 11, no. 1 (August 2007).

42. Robert A. Hill, "Dread History: Leonard Howell and Millenarian Visions in Early Rastafari Religion in Jamaica," *Epoché: Journal of the History of Religions at UCLA* 9 (1981): 30–71; and Prashad, *Everybody Was Kung Fu Fighting*, 90–91. L. W. De Laurence, *The Great Book of Magical Art, Hindu Magic and East Indian Occultism, and the Book of the Secret Hindu, Ceremonial, and Talismanic Magic* (Chicago: De Laurence, 1915), 594–628, as cited in Prashad, *Everybody Was Kung Fu Fighting*, 91.

43. G. G. Maragh, *The Promise Key*, ed. E. S. P. McPherson (Clarendon, Jamaica: Black International Iyahbinghi Press, 1988).

44. Ajai Mansingh and Laxmi Mansingh, "Hindu Influences on Rastafarianism," in *Caribbean Quarterly Monographs: Rastafari*, ed. Rex Nettleford (Kingston: Caribbean Quarterly; Mona: University Press of the West Indies, 1985), 96–115; Prashad, *Everybody Was Kung Fu Fighting*, 90–91; and Hélène Lee, "The Hindu Influence," in *The First Rasta: Leonard Howell and the Rise of Rastafarianism* (Chicago: Lawrence Hill Books, 2003), 97–108.

45. Dr. Cao-Tsou, *Infinite Wisdom*, ed. Lauron William de Laurence (Chicago: de Laurence Co., 1923) and Wilson, *Sacred Drift*, 21.

46. Algernon Austin, "Rethinking Race and the Nation of Islam, 1930–1975," *Ethnic and Racial Studies* 26, no. 1 (January 2003): 52–69.

47. Michael A. Gomez, *Black Crescent: The Experience and Legacy of African Muslims in the Americas* (Cambridge: Cambridge University Press, 2005), 203.

48. Gomez, *Black Crescent*, 204. Indeed, the many caveats that Gomez employs throughout his text indicate the speculative nature of his hypothesis that antebellum African American Islam extended into the twentieth century, and did so on the slender back of Noble Drew Ali.

49. Turner, *Islam in the African American Experience*, 46. Gomez exposes many instances of individual Islamic practices in antebellum America but no examples of community ones, aside from Islamic naming customs that do not themselves indicate ritual practice or belief. He argues that the secretive nature of slave religion explains the absence of evidence and thus, the very lack of evidence supports the hypothesis that community prayer and Islamic practice must have existed. Gomez, *Black Crescent*, 171–72. Susan

Nance has criticized the tendency among many scholars to credit Islam for the recent, American, and polycultural faith of the Moorish Science Temple, an inclination that she combatively terms "retroactive Islamicization." Nance, "Mystery of the Moorish Science Temple," 125, 148–49.

50. Wilson, *Sacred Drift*, 17; Turner, *Islam in the African American Experience*, 92.

51. Prashad, *Karma of Brown Folk*, 27–34. See also Nance, "Crossing Over," 201–11.

52. Noble William Ross, Recorder and Historian, "Lu Lu" Temple, Philadelphia, "A History of the Ancient Arabic Order of the Nobles of the Mystic Shrine for North America," in *A Library of Freemasonry Volume V*, ed. Robert Gould (London: John C. Yorston, 1906), 1–2, Harry A. Williamson Masonic Collection, Schomburg Center for Research in Black Culture, New York Public Library, Astor, Lenox, and Tilden Foundations.

53. William B. Mclish, *The History of the Imperial Council, 1872–1921* (Cincinnati: Abingdon, 1921), 12, as cited in Nance, "Crossing Over," 158.

54. Ross, "A History of the Ancient Arabic Order," 1.

55. Ibid., 47.

56. Ibid.

57. Nance, "Crossing Over," 104–79; Marr, *The Cultural Roots of American Islamicism*, 178.

58. William A. Muraskin, *Middle-Class Blacks in a White Society: Prince Hall Freemasonry in America* (Berkeley: University of California Press, 1973); Joseph A. Walkes Jr., *Black Square and Compass: 200 Years of Prince Hall Freemasonry* (New York: Writer's Press, 1979); and Joanna Brooks, "Prince Hall, Freemasonry, and Genealogy," *African American Review* 34, no. 2 (Summer 2000): 197–216.

59. Turner, *Islam in the African American Experience*, 95; Nance, "Crossing Over," 227.

60. On at least two occasions in the early decades of the twentieth century, the Supreme Court of the United States took up the question of the legitimacy of black Masons and overturned the decisions of the high courts of the states of Georgia and Texas, ruling in *Creswill v. Grand Lodge Knights of Pythias of Georgia*, 225 U.S. 246 (1912) and in *Ancient Egyptian Arabic Order of Nobles of the Mystic Shrine, etc., et al. v. D.W. Michaux et al.*, 279 U.S. 737 (1929) that white Masons had abrogated their copyright and trademark rights by not defending them. No doubt motivated in part by racial liberalism, the Supreme Court justified its decision using the concept of *laches*, the principle that one is not allowed to entrap someone by not defending a certain property right—in this case, allowing African Americans to use the signs and symbols of Freemasonry for decades before bringing suit in southern states where Jim Crow was increasing. The rulings confirmed the viability of using the courts to seek redress for violations of black civil rights, a strategy that would become central to the black freedom struggle. See Nance, "Crossing Over," 227–35.

61. Brooks, "Prince Hall, Freemasonry, and Genealogy," 197–216.

62. Paul Morand, *New York* (Paris: E. Flammarion, 1930), 269.

63. Trafton, *Egypt Land*, 27.

64. "Oriental Costume Ball," Advertisement, *New York Amsterdam News*, February 10, 1926, 7; "Sheik of Harlem," Advertisement, *New York Amsterdam News*, August 1, 1923, 5.

65. Gaylyn Studlar, "'Out Salomeing Salome': Dance, the New Woman, and Fan

Magazine Orientalism," in Bernstein and Studlar, *Visions of the East*, 100; IMDB Internet Movie Database, www.imdb.com, accessed on May 1, 2007.

66. Prashad, *Karma of Brown Folk*, 39.

67. Winthrop D. Lane, "The Making of Harlem," *Survey Graphic*, March 1925, quoted in Jerome Dowd, *The Negro in American Life* (New York: Century Co., 1926), 27.

68. Ibid., 27; Vijay Prashad, *Everybody Was Kung Fu Fighting*, 90–91.

69. Various newspaper advertisements, *New York Amsterdam News*, 1920–1929; Black Herman [Herman Rucker], *Secrets of Magic-Mystery and Legerdemain: The Missing Key to Success, Health and Happiness*, 15th ed. (1925; reprint: New York: Empire, 1938); FBI Subject File 62–576, "Sufi Abdul Hamid," Washington, D.C., Federal Bureau of Investigation.

70. Polk, "Other Books, Other Powers."

71. "Use Pearse Health Builder," Advertisement, *New York Amsterdam News*, May 5, 1926, 3.

72. "Spiritualism," *Negro Times*, February 26, 1923, in Aubrey Browser Collection, Schomburg Center for Research in Black Culture, New York Public Library, Astor, Lenox, and Tilden Foundations, Box 2, Folder "The Negro Times." For an analysis of Spiritualism, Transcendentalism, and other forms of "antimodernism" in American culture, see T. J. Jackson Lears, *No Place of Grace: Antimodernism and the Transformation of American Culture, 1880–1920* (Chicago: University of Chicago Press, 1981), xv–xx, 3–58, and Caryn Cossé Bell, "Spiritualism's Dissident Visionaries," in *Revolution, Romanticism, and the Afro-Creole Protest Tradition in Louisiana 1718–1868* (Baton Rouge: Louisiana State University Press, 1997), 187–221.

73. Yvonne Chireau, *Black Magic: Religion and the African American Conjuring Tradition* (Berkeley: University of California Press, 2003), 35–57.

74. Carolyn Morrow Long, *Spiritual Merchants: Religion, Magic, and Commerce* (Knoxville: University of Tennessee Press, 2001), 117–18.

75. See, for example, Austin, "Rethinking Race and the Nation of Islam."

76. Akpan Aga et al., Advertisements, *New York Amsterdam News*, December 13, 1922, 2; January 24, 1923; January 31, 1923, 3, 8; February 7, 1923, 8; February 14, 1923, 3; February 28, 1923, 3; March 7, 1923, 3; March 21, 1923, 3; March 28, 1923, 2; May 30, 1923, 3; April 18, 1923, 2; April 25, 1923, 2; May 2, 1923, 2; May 9, 1923, 2; May 23, 1923, 2; June 6, 1923, 6; August 15, 1923, 3; September 5, 1923, 3; October 13, 1923, 14; October 24, 1923, 3; October 31, 1923, 3; November 7, 1923, 3; and "Effiong in Toils; Waits U.S. Action," February 6, 1929, 1.

77. On hoodoo and a discussion of conjure men and women in northern cities in this period, see Chireau, *Black Magic*, 138–49.

78. "Divine Healer Jailed," *New York Amsterdam News*, August 29, 1923, 2.

79. Akpan Aga, Advertisement, *New York Amsterdam News*, January 24, 1923, 3.

80. Prof. Akpandac, "Prof. Akpandac," Advertisement, *New York Amsterdam News*, April 11, 1923, 2; Amadu, "The Mohammedan Scientist Dealing in Religious Incense," *New York Amsterdam News*, March 9, 1927, 13.

81. Among the numerous works on minstrelsy, see Eric Lott, *Love and Theft: Blackface Minstrelsy and the American Working Class* (New York: Oxford University Press, 1993)

and Louis Chude-Sokei, *The Last "Darky": Bert Williams, Black-on-Black Minstrelsy, and the African Diaspora* (Durham, N.C.: Duke University Press, 2005).

82. Moustafa Bayoumi, "East of the Sun (West of the Moon): Islam, the Ahmadis, and African America," *Journal of Asian American Studies* 4, no. 3 (2001): 257.

83. As such, black Orientalist traditions should not be excluded from the protest-based category of "black religion." Rather, their heterogeneity destabilizes the concept altogether and challenges attempts to build exclusionary categories of religious experience, such as those found in Hans A. Baer and Merrill Singer, *African-American Religion in the Twentieth Century: Varieties of Protest and Accommodation* (Knoxville: University of Tennessee Press, 1992). On "black religion," see Jackson, *Islam and the Blackamerican*, 25, 28–48.

84. While Parham's student William Seymour rejected the Anglo-Israelite theory, Bishop Charles Mason, cofounder of the Church of God in Christ (COGIC), one of the largest black Pentecostal denominations, was sympathetic to Israelite ideas, according to scholar Sherry Sherrod DuPree. It is also interesting to note that some of the leaders of black Israelite movements in the 1960s came from COGIC backgrounds. See Sherry Sherrod DuPree, *Biographical Dictionary of African-American Holiness-Pentecostals, 1880–1990* (Washington, D.C.: Middle Atlantic Regional Press, 1989); Sherry Sherrod DuPree, *African-American Holiness Pentecostal Movement: An Annotated Bibliography* (New York: Garland, 1996); Sherry Sherrod DuPree, conversation with author, 1999; and Cecil M. Robeck, *The Azusa Street Mission and Revival: The Birth of the Global Pentecostal Movement* (Nashville, Tenn.: Thomas Nelson, 2006).

85. Madame C. J. Walker Papers, "Around the World and Holy Land contests, 1920s," William Henry Smith Memorial Library, Indiana Historical Society, Indianapolis, Box 12, Folder 22; and Hilton Obenzinger, *American Palestine: Melville, Twain, and the Holy Land Mania* (Princeton, N.J.: Princeton University Press, 1999).

PART 2

❦

Resurrecting Fauset's Vision for
African American Religious Studies

SEVEN · Religion Proper and Proper Religion: Arthur Fauset and the Study of African American Religions

SYLVESTER A. JOHNSON

When Arthur Fauset set out to examine African American religions in the northern urban centers of the twentieth century, he was necessarily entering upon the site of multiple contestations. Fauset's objective was not to map what was characterized as "normative" religion; so, for instance, he was not studying the "Black Church." His primary interest, in fact, lay in making visible the patently unusual and novel manifestations of African American religion that were not reducible to normative Christianity or conventional church-based religion. These religious communities were the "cults," the new religious movements among primarily urban African Americans of the increasingly populous metropolitan North.

Arthur Fauset's work was distinctive for several reasons. First, given that the ethnographic study of religion among modern Westerners is still establishing itself in the twenty-first century, it is remarkable that Fauset was employing this method of study in the 1940s. Second, Fauset was directing his attention to religious communities that were not normatively Christian. These religions were not only outside of the realm of expressive normativity, but they were also performed by a marginal demographic—African Americans, largely from the South, who were viewed as unsophisticated misfits in a cosmopolitan world. These persons were also marked as racially inferior—unintelligent, naturally backward, and prone to criminality. Third, Fauset was keenly interested in examining ideas about the relationship between

African religious culture and the new religious movements among these African American religionists.

I identify these three points as especially noteworthy and most helpful for parsing the methodological implications of Arthur Fauset's work for those concerned with studying African American religions today. I am especially interested in what these points reveal about a central question that informs the title of this chapter: What counts for religious data in the study of African American religions? How does one recognize "real" religion when one sees it? Arthur Fauset, for instance, was not attempting to ridicule feeble attempts by blacks who claimed Jewish descent (such as Rabbi Wentworth Matthew) or even divine status (such as Father Divine). Instead, he interpreted these instances of expression as authentic religious data to be taken seriously in the intellectual study of black religious life.

Fauset's Intellectual Context: Twentieth-Century Studies of African American Religion

The major context for Fauset's work lies in the disciplined history of imagining religion among African Americans through the category of the Black Church, an entity whose historical reality is not nearly equal to the exaggerated proportions that emerge in the majority of scholarly histories of black religion. The earliest scholarly study of African American religion is perhaps best recognized as W. E. B. Du Bois's *The Negro Church.*[1] Phil Zuckerman has rightly emphasized the tremendous debt that current scholars in sociology, religious studies, and history owe to Du Bois's pioneering application of sociological methods to examining religion in America.[2] As the nation's first sociologist, Du Bois was centrally concerned with moving beyond armchair theories of society and grounding social analysis in ethnographic research. The result was his rich volume that incorporated an impressive level of data to make sense of how African American churches actually functioned. Despite the title of the book, however, Du Bois was clearly aware that African religion was a vital and central aspect of religion among African Americans. In fact, in both *The Negro Church* and in his classic *Souls of Black Folk,* Du Bois would clearly indicate his view of the importance of African religion in black American life: "The first Negro church was not at first by any means Christian nor definitely organized; rather it was an adaptation and mingling of heathen rites among the members of each plantation, and roughly designated as Voodooism. . . . After the lapse of many generations the Negro church became Christian."[3]

Carter G. Woodson's study of African American churches, on the other hand, departed quite forcefully from Du Bois's view of black religion, rendering African religion invisible and primarily employing a Christian denominationalist view of African American religion.[4] Woodson's study fits well within the trajectory of white scholarship on church history, which was also in essence a history of denominations and notable parish ministers. Woodson, in other words, was merely employing common strategies of historical representation. Unfortunately, this actually hampered the development of the more nuanced approach that Du Bois had instigated. By the 1930s, several scholars of African American religion had taken notice of the new developments in urban religion. Benjamin Mays published a study of black religion in 1938 that employed a literary approach.[5] And five year later, Mays would co-author with Joseph Nicholson *The Negro's Church*.[6]

The studies that most succinctly captured African religions in this era were produced by African American women in anthropology.[7] Katherine Dunham's *Dances of Haiti* appeared in 1938 and examined religion in Haiti as derived from Africa.[8] Zora Neale Hurston's *Mules and Men,* which appeared in 1935, examined folk expressions of African religion in the American South.[9] St. Clair Drake and Horace Cayton's *Black Metropolis* was a major study of African American churches in the urban North and was published in 1945.[10] Like Fauset, Dunham, and Hurston, Drake was also trained as an anthropologist. And his view of African American religion was attentive to the novel conditions being created by rapid urbanization and attending demographic shifts. Such studies surely indicate that at least a few scholars of African American religion were taking seriously the emergence of non-Christian religious movements and urbanization as an important development that conditioned the sites of black religious formation.

Method and Critique in Fauset's *Black Gods of the Metropolis*

It was in this context that Fauset's study of African American urban cults burst onto the scene. Arthur Fauset's *Black Gods of the Metropolis* applied discrete, ethnographic methods of study to (1) the Mt. Sinai Holy Church of America; (2) Bishop Grace's United House of Prayer for All People; (3) Prophet Cherry's Church of God, a community of African American Jews; (4) Noble Drew Ali's Moorish Science Temple movement; and (5) the Peace Mission Movement, led by Father Divine (a.k.a. George Baker). Fauset, a trained anthropologist, interviewed members of these religious communities with a primary interest in elucidating the impetus behind their decision to affiliate with the respective bodies. Fauset quoted extensively from his field notes, and he also included in an appendix to the book a representative sample of excerpts from these interviews. In addition to these interviews, Fauset spent considerable time as an embedded observer in the religious meetings of the religious bodies he studied.

The result was an intriguing narrative of each religious movement that explained in a serious way why the theologies, experiences of community, and promises of deliverance these groups offered made sense to their respective adherents. In fact, one easily perceives that Fauset is especially anxious to present his readers with a view of these groups that will locate them conceptually within the rubric of proper religion and thus religion proper. In other words, Fauset's subjects appear not as pathologically gullible, intellectually inept sheep following some herd instinct toward cultic affiliation due to deprivation or racial backwardness. Fauset paints a portrait, rather, of human beings whose desire to affiliate with particular religious communities is an intelligent response to very real social imperatives that are not unlike the needs experienced by the vast majority of white Americans, who were granted a normative status as a matter of course. Indeed, I would suggest that the primary concern of Fauset's analysis is ultimately to render a portrait of these new religious movements as sites of authentic religious data (religion proper) and as religious communities whose manifestations of cultic behavior are normative not pathological, modern not primitive (proper religion).

A vivid example of Fauset's strategies of portrayal occurs, for instance, when he explains the efforts of the cults to generate revenues through selling cultic objects or through urging followers to start their own business. Skeptics often described the cults as "nothing but a racket," always talking about money instead of focusing on the spiritual realm. But Fauset proposes a very different view of this emphasis on making money. In his chapter "The Cult as a Functional Institution," Fauset identifies economic empowerment as a social need that becomes transformed into a cultural imperative in the theology of the cults. By this he means that economic empowerment becomes a symbol of authentic black expression, of existential rectitude and fulfillment, or of race mission when articulated by the various religions. His emphasis on functionalism leads him to emphasize the utterly bitter and racially hostile climate of the urban North for African Americans. He points out, for instance, that African Americans in the South were as a rule more financially successful than northern blacks because the South, ironically, provided greater access to financial activities than the North, although African Americans in the North were better educated.[11]

Because of the fundamentally apartheid nature of American society, blacks were barred from participating in the traditional secular realm of financial activity. So investment banking, for instance, was off-limits to blacks. New York City, literally the financial capital of the world, is a clear demonstration of Fauset's critique. On one end of the island of Manhattan, to the south, was the financial district, strictly off-limits to blacks, except perhaps as janitors or street cleaners. Uptown, in Harlem, blacks were peddling wares and preaching a gospel of prosperity in the churches and cults, but doing so as a racial group largely excluded from the heart of Western capitalism.

In this vein, Fauset explains, the religious concern with entrepreneurship, viewed as "racketeering" by critics, is simply a means of countering the eviscerating effects of American apartheid. This is why Fauset compares Prophet Cherry's entrepreneurship with that of the "magnates" in the secular realm.[12] The independent religious establishments were the one place African Americans could develop an agenda for economic empowerment. In their religious houses, they were not barred due to white privilege. By implying that religion is no less religious because of this business activity, therefore, Fauset depathologizes these urban forms of African American religion.

Fauset, furthermore, concedes that most of these entrepreneurial ventures by blacks failed for myriad reasons. But he maintains as paramount, nevertheless, that the potential for success was dormant in all of these movements. As evidence of this, he pointed to Father Divine's Peace Mission Movement, whose national network of hotels was a response to historical conditions of antiblack racism. As Fauset writes, "White Americans look forward to travel as one of life's richest boons; but the American Negro contemplates travel in the United States with a degree of misgiving amounting to dread."[13] Fauset indicates that the movement's hotels were providing African Americans with their first experience of the ability to travel and to have reliable accommodations instead of encountering the white terrorism, harassment, and hunger they usually met with as a regular part of distant travel.[14] The financial gains that those affiliated with the Peace Mission were making by investing in real estate, Fauset urged, were no less than impressive. And the antiracist imperatives of the movement meant that profit was not the sole impetus. Room and board were had cheaply by travelers with very limited funds. The movement even prohibited tipping.

This historiographical interest that Fauset exhibits is tied to yet another strategy of metarepresentation; his study of the cults culminates in a critique of social-scientific claims about African American religion. These scientific claims identified a religious essence within blacks that caused them to be naturally more religious than whites. Insofar as religion in the secular age was expected to take a backseat to rational thought, blacks were viewed as primitives, trapped in an earlier, prerational ontology vis-à-vis their more rational, logic-oriented white counterparts. Fauset rejected this mythological system of ranking racial capacities. Fauset, on this point, specifically responds to the work of Robert Park and Melville Herskovits. He praises Herskovits, on the one hand, for proposing creative solutions to questions of African influences on both blacks and whites in the Americas.[15] On the other hand, he soundly criticizes Herskovits's attempts to naturalize religious practices of African Americans.[16] Fauset insisted that any historical practices among blacks were historical and sociological in origin, not natural.

By rejecting this naturalization of racial differences, Fauset also pointed out that black men were far less likely to attend than either white women or white men.[17] There was simply no empirical basis for claiming that blacks were naturally more religious than whites. Any differences that existed between blacks and whites were due to social-historical factors, not some mystical racial essence. And it was specifically racial apartheid, he argued, that was the reason institutions of religion were more central to the lives of blacks than to the lives of whites.

This leads to the third and arguably most problematic aspect of Fauset's work: his concern with the relationship between African culture and religion among African Americans. Although Fauset, on the one hand, foregrounds the common-sense imperative that Africans could not have forgotten literally every meaningful cultural disposition of African religion during the Ma'afa, he nevertheless concludes that by far and away the substance of African American religion, particularly in the new urban cults, was due not to African influences but to "American culture."[18] In fact, Fauset provides two anecdotal narratives of white cultic members performing worship in a stereotypically black liturgical style (e.g., dancing with rapid body motions as if under spirit possession and singing in a charismatic fashion) to suggest to the reader that these liturgical forms were not at all unique to blacks and were simply a part of American culture.

I will deal below with the reasons Fauset's rejection of substantial African influences in African American religion is an inadequate response, but for now I would like to suggest, at the risk of giving him too much credit, that Fauset's intention is primarily an effort to read African American religions as *American*, and no less so than any of the religious practices of white Americans. His concern, again, is to inscribe urban black religion solidly within the bounds of normative American cultural expression. And in this sense, Fauset is technically correct when he attributes any distinctive aspects of African American religion to "American culture." In sum, the constructive implications of Fauset's study of the cults emerge from rendering visible his efforts to map new religious movements onto the narrative of African American religious history and to do so in order to portray African American religion as the expression of normative and authentically American ideas and ideals.

Fauset was not alone in this endeavor. Several years before the appearance of Fauset's work, Miles Mark Fisher, interestingly enough, exhibited a remarkably progressive scholarly stance toward new religious movements among African Americans. Fauset never mentions the work of Fisher in his notes or bibliography, yet it is difficult to believe he knew nothing of Fisher's articles on the new religious movements among African Americans. Whether or not this was the case, it would aid our endeavor to consider the major concerns of Fisher because his work approaches the contours of Fauset more closely than that of any other writer in Fauset's milieu.

(Ac)counting for Religious Data

Miles Fisher (1899–1970), who taught church history at Shaw University in Raleigh, North Carolina, had observed and had written about the emergence of "the cults," new religious movements among urban African Americans, as early as the 1930s. Fisher believed these religious movements not only marked important shifts in the historical trajectory of African American religion but also constituted, in a serious way, valid data for the study of religion proper. Fisher's sensitivity to religious formations such as the Peace Mission Movement of Father Divine or the radio ministry of Harlem's Mother Rosa Horne indicates a methodological openness and sophistication all too rare in religious historiography of the time.

Most telling in this regard is Fisher's response to the 1926 U.S. Census of Religious Bodies, which he critiqued in hopes that the 1936 census would be more inclusive. The U.S. Census of Religious Bodies began with federal legislation in 1902 that transformed the census office from an occasional to a permanent establishment; this allowed census personnel to avoid starting from scratch each time the population was counted. This also enabled the office to collect various data over a period of years instead of simultaneously tackling all metrics at the end of each decade. The office decided to identify U.S. religious bodies during the sixth year of each decade. The result was an official count of organizations (not a direct count of individuals) for the years 1906, 1916, 1926, and 1936.[19]

Fisher was concerned that the census of 1936, which had yet to be published when he wrote his article, should include the new religious movements that were emerging among African Americans, typically in urban regions of the United States. The years since the last census of 1926 had witnessed a continuing influx of migrants from the South seeking better economic opportunities in the industrial North. And as these migrants increased in number, typically settling in concentrated areas of the myriad urban centers, their religious lives increasingly captured the interest of social scientists and historians.

In response to these developments, he published "Organized Religion and the Cults" in 1937. Fisher began his article, "I nominate the religious movements which are led by Bishop Grace, Elder Michaux, Father Divine, et al. for inclusion in the Census of Religious Bodies: 1936." He ended by reminding his readers that "Christianity itself and all evangelical denominations were once cults."[20]

Despite Fisher's optimism, however, the 1936 census would be the most poorly funded and disorganized of all. It included the fewest religious bodies—only 74—of all counts; the 1916 census had included 109. Furthermore, from the start, the census identified primarily Christian and white Jewish institutions. Minor exceptions included a count of Buddhist temples in 1916. This pattern was to remain consistent throughout the counts. As it turned out, the 1936 census recorded only African American religious bodies that were among the independent Baptist, Methodist, and Pentecostal denominations. The "cults" were simply ignored once more. This may have been impacted by underfunding, but it was more likely due to the inertia of rigid ideas about what constituted religion proper.[21]

One can also glean a fair sense of Fisher's historiographical sensibilities from his ideas about the historical narrative of African American religions.[22] He summarized the emergence of African American Christianity largely as a result of white missionaries active on slave plantations. Fisher adumbrates the many factors that would complicate and characterize this history, such as the role of deep-seated dissent over African colonization, a movement that dominated the nineteenth century and that viewed the African continent—not the United States—as the rightful home of blacks who were not enslaved, or the tension created by the institutionalization of white surveillance over black religion in the wake of Nathaniel Turner's rebellion against slavery. Fisher viewed these developments in the history of African American churches as culminating in the approximate bifurcation of black parishioners into white-controlled denominations, on the one hand, and into independent churches that constituted denominations controlled by African Americans, on the other hand.

Fisher, however, clearly writes in service to an overriding agenda: adding an important "chapter" to this history of African American churches—the rise of the urban cults during the twentieth century.[23] The religious communities of Islam, Baha'i, Unity, and Christian Science are just a few of those he names in order to map their presence onto the cartography of black religious history. Although his critique of standard narratives of black religious history is in the main historically interested, he is partial to these cults for partly theological reasons. Because many were multira-cial, he viewed such religious communities as neither "black" churches nor "white" churches per se, but rather as more "pristinely" Christian churches.[24] Fisher also lauded the notable degree of leadership by women in these new religious move-ments, in contrast to the overwhelmingly male leadership of more historical de-nominations.[25] In addition, Fisher was intrigued by religious bodies such as Father Divine's Peace Mission Movement or the Moorish Science Temple movement be-cause they explicitly organized their efforts around social transformation—increas-ing employment and financial empowerment among their members, emphasizing physical well-being, and instilling race pride as a progressive response to the all-too-common self-hatred that haunted blacks in a white supremacist society. Fisher intimated that the mainline denominations were not committed to the same degree of social reform and were less relevant to the social lives of their adherents. The cults, however, responded to the quotidian needs of those who had grown disillusioned with traditional churches.

What Fisher shared with Fauset was an interest in modifying the story of religion among African Americans; it is not merely the story of Christianity and black churches. It is also the story of new religious movements that are beyond the domain of Christian identity and that must be taken seriously as religious data for understanding the trajectories and content of African American religion.

Proper Religion and the Colonial State

It is imperative to understand this issue of religious data in relationship to govern-mentality. One should not be misled into thinking that the "cults" simply went unnoticed by the U.S. government. To the contrary, federal authorities were inti-mately familiar with the Moorish Science Temple, with Garveyites, and with the emerging African American Muslims. All were identified as subversive threats, as enemies of the state. They were subjected to suppressive strategies of surveillance, detainment, torture, infiltration, harassment, and disruption. The Federal Bureau of Investigation, which was first organized in 1908, took seriously its role in safeguard-ing the interests and longevity of the United States as a white supremacist, apartheid nation-state. Insofar as that government was, in the words of the United Nations General Assembly, a "racist regime"[26] intent upon squashing activities related to the liberation of blacks and other subjugated nonwhite peoples,[27] the U.S. government had no truck with those religious groups that recognized God in black flesh or that propagated anticolonial theologies as did the Moorish Science Temple.

Fisher wrote only a few years before the development of COINTELPRO, the government's secretive program against freedom movements such as the black liberationist movement.[28] COINTELPRO had its predecessors in the 1920s and 1930s, however, for it was then that the United States was developing its first wave of government operatives to suppress black organizations under the direction of J. Edgar Hoover, who was continually appointed and reappointed as FBI director from 1924 to 1972. In these early years of the twentieth century, for instance, the United States would arrest and detain blacks as political prisoners for promoting moral criticism of white supremacy and colonial domination over nonwhites in the context of global colonial oppression.

More than a decade before Fauset would publish his *Black Gods,* the Philadelphia office of the FBI first communicated to J. Edgar Hoover its findings from the covert investigation of the Moorish Science Temple of America (MSTA). In 1931, during the early phase of its covert surveillance, the FBI quickly assessed MSTA's teaching of "equality for all races" to be fanatical and a threat to the state. The FBI's vilifying inscription of antiracist theology as fanaticism merely demonstrates how deeply committed the U.S. Department of Justice (an ironic nomenclature) was devoted to white supremacy and its attending imperatives. However, insofar as the MSTA did oppose white supremacy and resisted the apartheid nature of American society, the FBI was correct in identifying it as antithetical to American whiteness. In this sense, the movement was subversive; there was no way to reconcile the theology of the MSTA with American apartheid and antiblack racism.[29] The FBI was even confounded by MSTA's refusal to comply with American racial taxonomy: Religious communicants insisted on being Moorish and not Negroes. One undercover agent was careful to note that his subject possessed "the appearance and characteristics of a full blooded negro," clearly indicating in his report that the self-designation of "Moorish" should not deter authorities from recognizing that they were dealing with plain, nonethnic black people.[30]

When the FBI infiltrated the MSTA in Springfield, Illinois, in 1941, the Department of Justice was especially interested in the alleged claims by Robert Washington, who led a local religious body, that African Americans would be freed from racism once the Japanese conquered America. The logic of such a sentiment stemmed from the anticolonial theology of the MSTA that urged all peoples of color throughout the world to unite against European colonialism and racial subjugation. After ascertaining that Washington depended on income from selling badges and robes to new converts in the MSTA, the Illinois State Attorney General's Office, in coordination with the FBI, then informed Washington in no uncertain terms that they would prosecute him for "obtaining money under false pretenses," whereupon Washington agreed to cease proselytizing.[31]

The exercise of state power against these new religious movements was by no means limited to incarceration, intimidation, and general tactics of suppression. The FBI was acutely interested in creating and asserting a working definition of proper religion as a means of undermining these African American religious movements. Among the most elaborate examples of this taxonomic strategy is the FBI's activity against the Nation of Islam (NOI). The Central Research Section of the bureau prepared a classified monograph in the 1950s that marshaled an array of evidence to construct an "orthodox" Islam that existed in radical contrast to the Nation of Islam, which the FBI specifically designated the "Muslim Cult of Islam" or "MCI."[32] Unlike "real" Islam, the FBI asserted to its field agents, this MCI was an "especially anti-American and violent Cult." This training manual for FBI agents trolled through the categories of doctrines, political ideas, rituals, taboos—all in an effort to "illustrate the chasm existing between the orthodox religion of Islam and the unorthodox MCI."[33] The NOI appeared as one of the "most deformed branches" of "real" Islam in this construction of proper religion and its antithesis; the FBI portrayed African American Islam as marked by "extreme fanaticism" and lacking any "doctrinal core," except perhaps its teaching of "racial hatred."[34]

The federal government's official position, however, was to deny the existence of such suppression. Neither Miles Fisher nor Arthur Fauset would have known enough to grasp the full context of government suppression operating in their own time. FBI surveillance records from the early twentieth century would become available only long after anything could be done to address the plight of the victims.[35]

In this context, it is vital to understand that counting the cults as religious bodies would have rendered legitimacy upon their theologies and ideological resistance to colonialism and white supremacy. It would seem, to understate the case, unlikely that the Bureau of the Census would have done such a thing. In this context, Fisher's optimism, though admirable and well placed, appears as political naïveté in hindsight. The issue of accounting for religious data, in other words, is instantiated within the networks of colonial power, antiblackness, and American nationalism. To say this differently, the matter of observing religion has never been separate from the strategic practices and imperatives of colonial authority. Other factors, of course, were operative in rendering categories of "legitimate" religion for the census, especially notions of orthodoxy by observers; in this way, new religious movements are frequently deemed something other than "real" Islam or "real" Christianity or "real" Judaism. But let the reader understand that insofar as these black cults were concerned, the FBI was collecting *massive* amounts of data by observing these religious communities. These data, however, were not for publication in census reports but were instead for informing and coordinating persecution and suppression of those identified as implicated in subverting white supremacy. U.S. state power to define proper religion emerges as a sophisticated and disturbingly consequential strategy that clearly located numerous black religions, whose theologies explicitly critiqued colonialism and white supremacy, beyond the boundaries of normative religious expression.[36]

Constructive Implications of Fauset's Study for Contemporary Scholarship

Arthur Fauset's approach to examining these new religious movements is instructive for contemporary scholarship in several ways and implies key directions for future research. First, the study of African American religion will benefit tremendously from the growth of ethnographic approaches (typically modeled by scholars trained in anthropology but increasingly employed by religionists), largely because this method allows us to map the existence and influence of religious communities or movements that are not mainstream and that are typically absent from standard narratives of American religious history. It is no accident that the majority of early studies of non-Christian religious communities were conducted by persons trained in anthropology. In this sense, Fauset's work is certainly pioneering and instructive.

Second, I have attempted to examine Fauset's work in a way that highlights his criticism of scholarly tendencies to pathologize religion among African Americans. I interpret Fauset's critical disposition as an important part of a decolonizing imperative because what he rejects are the claims about ontology and essence that inhere to colonial dilemmas. Essentially, I want to suggest that the fundamental problem to which Fauset responds is best understood as the problem of representing conquered peoples, a demographic situated by colonial conquest. But colonial conquest in the modern era involves a great deal more than the use of brute force. In the modern era, both foreign and domestic colonialism emphasizes the use of politics and ideology to assert power over the vanquished. Fauset rejects that colonial posture, and rewrites the story of African Americans religions from a postcolonial perspective.[37]

In the twenty-first century, I am persuaded that our methods of examining

African American religion must take more seriously than ever before the insights of postcolonial theory. As early as the 1960s, Charles Long identified the methodological challenges of studying African American religions as proceeding from colonialism. Long argued that those who wished to understand the situation of studying religion must take more seriously than ever the relationship between European Enlightenment theories about religion proper, on the one hand, and the physical and cultural genocidal destruction experienced by colonized peoples, on the other hand. The production of colonizing "knowledge" about conquered peoples has meant, for instance, that blacks have been regularly overdetermined as racial subjects. Anything they might do—from musical expression to speaking to playing sports—is reduced to a pathological result of "being black." Lewis Gordon, whose critical philosophy of colonial existence has been far-reaching, makes the same point in different language when he poignantly surmises that the dilemma of racial overdetermination for conquered blacks is to experience blackness as being "too Black."[38] This problem of racial overdetermination, Long urges, has led to numerous problems and constraints at the methodological level. It literally obscures the humanity of the overdetermined subject. Long linked this to the problem of the very practice of studying religion.[39]

This early analysis by Long has been followed by numerous studies that confirmed his conclusions regarding the problematic relationship between the noetics and concepts of studying religion and the administration of colonial authority over conquered subjects. As a result, scholars of religious studies today readily acknowledge that the very category of religion has proceeded from imperial practices of observing indigenous peoples in an effort to understand what white authorities believed was their radical exoticism and inferiority. Such practices of power emerged through gathering information about their habits of dress and their rituals, assessing their suitability for depopulation (i.e., genocide), eradicating their cultures in missionary efforts to destroy their non-Christian religions so as to elevate them to civility, and creating knowledge about them in order to represent their status as human subjects—or not.[40] The recent critical assessments of the academic study of religion by Jonathan Z. Smith, Russell McCutcheon, and Robert Segal ably evidence the degree to which religious studies today is marked by a cautious—even skeptical— disposition toward the semiotic, representative pitfalls of studying religion, pitfalls that derive in large part from the colonial origins of the discipline.[41]

Histories of African American religions have, with few exceptions, avoided analyzing African American religions explicitly within the context of colonialism per se. Racial slavery and color prejudice, instead, have been the domain objects of concern, and with good cause. Chattel slavery was, after all, the means whereby

Africans were transported as human property to the New World. Abolitionism, moreover, became the most explosive political movement of the nineteenth century, interfacing with suffragist, moral reform, and feminist activisms to imbue within mainstream religions new, forceful dimensions of activism and consciousness. The perduring strategies of racism in the twentieth century, moreover, provoked the civil rights movement, which dramatically and indelibly altered the relationship between organized religion and politics in America while banishing explicit forms of white supremacy to the shadowy terrain of shameful discourse and political incorrectness.

The overwhelming and fundamental relationship between colonialism and African American religions, unfortunately, has been largely ignored. Several issues have contributed to this analytical reticence, not least of which is the practice of treating colonialism as a Third World phenomenon. Because African Americans are located in the United States, in the heart of the First World's most powerful nation-state, it is not readily evident even to trained observers that the United States is home to colonized peoples. After all, the canonical stance from which to write about the experiences of African Americans renders them as agents in nation-building, major contributors to the nation's history.

Recent research into colonialism and religion, however, has pressed the need for examining African American religions within this context. The rise of subaltern studies, for instance, prompted scholars of religion to revisit religions in India in light of the recognition that religion itself was an analytical category generated among colonial intelligentsia.[42] Of special importance has been the recent attention to religion and colonialism in Latin America. Irene Silverblatt's *Modern Inquisitions*, for instance, persuasively demonstrated the urgency of studying the religious-bureaucratic technologies of modernity from their inception with *Spanish* colonialism. From the disturbing insights of Hannah Arendt, who identified the violent structures that have actualized Western civilization, to the postcolonial analysis of Joel Martin, whose study of Native American religions has moved the condition of colonialism to the foreground—it should be apparent to the field of African American religious scholarship that the moment of postcolonial analysis is well upon us, a point that Joel Martin has made explicitly.[43]

It was common during the 1990s for social theorists to speak of a "postmodern turn"; at this juncture, what is required is an epistemological shift in the field of African American religions that might effect a "postcolonial turn," a serious application of recent theoretical insights from postcolonial theory toward understanding the study and content of religions among blacks in the Americas. One pressing implication of this colonial condition of African Americans as conquered, colonized peoples and of religion itself as a colonial category is evident in the need for intellectual attention to the religious hatred, specifically anti-African, that has overwhelmingly shaped the religious history of African Americans. This sentiment is so deeply instantiated in American culture that for generations even black Americans have loved to hate—to viscerally despise—African religions as the epitome of all that is evil and decadent. Despite all of this, the *American* history of religious hatred against African religion has yet to be written. Students in an undergraduate course on American religious history will commonly study the problems of anti-Catholicism in the United States; American histories of anti-Semitism are regularly examined as well. It is profoundly exceptional, however, to encounter a discussion of African American religious history that takes seriously the strategies that effected cultural genocide in order to create the suppression and hatred of African religion as a normative disposition. Jon Butler's *Awash in a Sea of Faith* is a notable exception. Butler actually employs the term "spiritual holocaust" to frame the seminal context of African American religious history. And he relates in no uncertain terms that the Christianization of African Americans was neither natural nor beatific but strategic and decimating, effecting a genocidal erasure of African religions.[44]

Colonialism has been contingent in a very basic, foundational way upon physical and cultural genocide. The Christianization of African peoples in the Americas was a violent, genocidal process. From this foundation of antiblackness and genocidal violence have stemmed the myriad problems of existence, representation, and domination that indelibly mark the history of African American religion. But one might hardly tell, based on the standard narratives of African American religious history dominant throughout the twentieth century that celebrate this process as a triumphant story for the birth of the "Black Church." It will be up to the present generation of scholars studying African American religion to determine whether this historiographical pattern remains in place.

This methodological attention toward colonialism, furthermore, necessitates a move beyond examining only racism to mapping the gamut of issues that colonialism comprises—genocide in its physical and cultural manifestations, the experience of diaspora and transnationalism, forced displacement, missionary religion, taxonomies of religion and race, the modern construction of history as a canonical phenomenon into which conquered peoples are driven to seek entry, and the perduring problem of racially overdetermining historically dominated peoples.

Finally, it is imperative that contemporary scholars of African American religion take seriously how religion in the Americas, particularly in the United States, is related to African cultural influences. Arthur Fauset, as I have indicated earlier, was technically correct when he identified the varieties of African American religions, whether Christian or not, as authentically American. The historical uses of this term "American," however, have characteristically functioned as metalanguage for "white." Americanness, in this way, has been constructed around a core of white subjectivity. It is not at all clear that Fauset was critical of such connotations when he insisted that the sources of black religion were essentially "American." To find whites and blacks demonstrating the same cultic behavior was proof enough for him that such behavior was not black in origin but (white) American. In his well-intentioned effort to map African American religion as authentically American, I would proffer that he wrongly ignored the veritable influences of African culture among not only black Americans but also white Americans.

This oversight had serious consequences for Fauset's methodology. Religious phenomena that should have otherwise been represented as veritable exempla of African religion in America were simply ignored, invisible to Fauset and other scholars. This invisibility of African religion in American religious studies hampered not only scholarly and popular understanding of American religion but also the capacity of people who came to be known as African Americans to be recognized as human in the same ways that their conquerors were so recognized. In the American context, black people, a people without a history, were not understood to be agents who created and transmitted culture.

I will cite one historical instance of this problem. What has been termed the "Herskovits-Frazier debate" is familiar to students of African American religion. This refers to the competing claims by E. Franklin Frazier, on the one hand, who denied that any meaningful retention of African culture was operative in African American religion, and by Melville Herskovits, on the other, who argued for the presence of multiple forms of African retention among African Americans. It is telling that both of these writers were primarily interested in the degree of retention among African American Christians. Frazier especially focused on churches. Now, consider that as early as the 1800s, the local press of New Orleans regularly reported the influence of Vodun among not only African Americans but also Euro-Americans. The famous New Orleans "Voodoo queens"—influential initiated priests, the overwhelming number of whom were women—frequently described their religion as "African" religion.[45] The *loas* they invoked are unquestionably African in origin. And one would be hard pressed to claim that the rituals and cosmology they performed were not African. New Orleans continued to be the "capital" of Vodun in the United States well into the twentieth century. This was a very visible and public cultus in the United States.

So, why is it that Vodun never counted in a serious way as religious data—as religion proper—for the vast majority of scholars examining African American religion? In this sense, the fundamental question of whether African religion was present in the United States, whether among African Americans or Euro-Americans or any other racial group, should never have been a legitimate starting point. The debate, rather, should have focused perhaps on the *nature and extent* of this African religious presence—for instance, how numerous were the adherents or clients of African religion—or on some other aspect of the subject.

Eventually, of course, scholars of African American religion would take seriously the presence of Vodun as well as Santeria, Yoruba, and more "diffuse" or noninstitutionalized practices of "Conjure" as patent evidence of African religions in the United States.[46] But this would not occur until the end of the twentieth century. And the work that has been done on African religions in the United States has barely disturbed either popular or scholarly narratives of African American religious history. In other words, black religion in America is still largely equated with the "Black Church." Even the considerable progress toward serious scholarly engagement with African American Islam, Darnise Martin reminds us, has not extended to other traditions or types of religious communities in African American religion. African American involvement in the roles of spiritual guides and readers and in the traditions of metaphysics, Judaism, and Buddhism, among others, deserves greater intellectual attention that will result from changes at the level of method.[47]

Implications for Arthur Fauset's Context

It is helpful to surmise what the theoretical concerns raised in this essay might imply for Arthur Fauset's world. This is not to ignore what was progressive and critically insightful about Fauset's scholarship. As I have indicated above, he pioneered an impressive array of decolonizing strategies in his study and his theoretical rendering of African American religions that remains instructive for us today. But we can also learn something from the complex problems that emerge between the claims of some religious bodies he studied and Fauset's consternation over the Americanness of black religions. I have in mind here particularly the black Jewish community established by Prophet Cherry and the black Muslim community established by Noble Drew Ali.

Succinctly, these two religious communities claimed to be derived from historical religions that predated the American experience of slavery and colonialism. These Jewish and Muslim identities directly implied what Richard Brent Turner has described as a distinctive signification of identity that carried distinctive expressions of dress, language, diet, and history.[48] Practicing these signs marked off the identities of these black Jews and Muslims from those of other Americans. In other words, these significations constituted an experience of *ethnicity*. And it is precisely this assertion of ethnicity—the notion of black ethnics—that viscerally marks the colonial matrix of a tenacious problem that not even Fauset managed to navigate successfully.

We can pose this problem as a heuristic question: Can blacks in America be ethnic? Are they ever more than racial subjects? I pose the question in this way to illuminate what lies beneath the history of scholarly debates over African retention and the contention represented by the Herskovits-Frazier debate. In his *Wings of Ethiopia,* the historian Wilson Jeremiah Moses poignantly posed this very question of black ethnicity in a critical reflection upon his childhood in Detroit, Michigan, living in a largely German and Italian Catholic neighborhood. Moses notes that while the white ethnics in his neighborhood were at once members of a common racial group and comfortably situated within specific ethnic identities, he himself, a practicing Catholic in his youth, was merely a Negro—a black person who attended a Catholic church. Blacks were not allowed to be ethnic; they were simply reduced to a homogenous racial taxon with no implications for cultural specificity or heritage.[49]

White colonialism has produced a double-layered violation against black subjects. In the first instance, European colonizers effected a literal cultural genocide against Africans in the Americas through the legal and extralegal suppression of African cultural forms (particularly religious forms). In the second instance, the colonial postures embedded in the structures of meanings about black subjects deny their capacity to be ethnic, authentic bearers of signifying practices that differentiate them from being merely dark-skinned people in America, that permit them to be represented through categories of identity that cohere beyond the category of race. Wilson Moses demonstrated the cruel dehumanization and raw dishonesty (substantiated through strategies that derive from antiblackness) inherent in denying the conceptual possibility of "black ethnics." According to the semiotics of colonialism, African Americans cannot be ethnic. They are not allowed this possibility of identity.

Assata Shakur vividly portrayed this same problem by relating how her grandmother faked being Hispanic to gain entry into a theme park during the legal era of American apartheid. After years of Assata's begging to go to the park—her grandmother never explained to her the rules of apartheid but only feigned excuses for why they could not venture to the park—her grandmother one day makes Assata promise not to utter a word to the park officials and then tromps to the entrance with fare in hand, wildly gesticulating and speaking in Spanish. The attendant at the entrance gate becomes confused immediately and calls for assistance. A small group of white officials gather around Assata's grandmother, attempting to understand her increasingly vociferous gesticulations and (to them) strange speech, reluctant to grant her entry. The more they resist, the louder she becomes. The frustrated park attendants finally conclude that she speaks no English and, being a foreigner, should not be denied entrance the way blacks were. Assata and her grandmother enjoyed the thrill of a lifetime on the exhilarating rides that day.[50]

The point here is that people from outside the United States, even if initially perceived as being Negroid based on phenotype, are not reduced to the status of being "mere" black Americans because they are allowed to signify ethnicity—Jamaican, Hispanic, Nigerian, Brazilian, and the like. It is typically the case that they are perceived to be smarter and more sophisticated than black Americans, even if they look just like African Americans. This was the baseline issue that lay behind Noble Drew Ali's emphasis on Moorish identity and W. D. Fard's emphasis on being Asiatic. Drew Ali's strategy of discarding "Negro" identity and asserting that of "Moorish American," with the attending accoutrements of ethnic religion, dress, names, and history, was predicated on the observation that whites accorded more humane treatment to ethnic blacks than to "ordinary Negroes."

What is remarkable about Fauset's era and the religions he examined in *Black Gods* is the turn toward "religions of Blackness," their largely shared interest in representing distinctive history, religion, philosophy, foods, and dress that might constitute the identity of "Negro."[51] W. E. B. Du Bois's sociological studies of American society led him to an astute assessment of the relationship toward black and American identities—they were experienced as immiscible "warring forces." Du Bois was aware of (and had, in fact, contributed to) the shifting views of culture.[52] Culture, by nineteenth-century Victorian standards, was spelled with a capital *C*; one either had culture (cultivating a refined sense of appreciation for high-brow art, literature, poise, and manners, etc.) or did not. According to this view, blacks, as uncivilized social dregs, were in need of religious and civilizational uplift. By the early twentieth century, however, the roots of ideological multiculturalism were producing visible fruits as a more pluralistic view of culture emerged, emphasizing differences not as inherent deficiencies necessarily but as putative evidence of cultural specificity. It was no longer the case that one simply had culture or not. There were many cultures, and these were constituted not by an array of high-brow sensibilities but rather by a complex of signifying practices achieved through distinct language, dress, and especially religion. In this way, the Victorian notion of racial contributions was transformed into the emergent discourse of ethnicity.[53]

Fauset grappled with this issue under the rubric of culture, but his angst over the Americanness of black religions seems to have motivated him to mishandle the implications of the significations of identity that marked the new religions among black urbanites. Had he recognized that the discourse of ethnicity was emerging as an outgrowth of multiculturalism, he might have been better able to parse the conundrum of the relationship between the black urban "cults" and Americanness, recognizing that what he viewed as an unproblematic American identity was ephemeral and historically constituted through metalanguage that signified white racial subjectivity. And he might have appreciated that the assertions of black Jews and Muslims, when they claimed to possess distinctive histories, religion, language, or scriptures and as they rejected generic, nonethnic Christianities (that did not afford them cultural specificity), were preeminently responses to conundrums of race and imperialism.

Resistance to the conceptual possibility of black ethnicity continues to plague perceptions of African Americans, as indexed by the fact that scholars and laity alike dismiss such signifying practices of African American religion as dilettantism or fakery. As a recent example, Colin Kidd's otherwise brilliant, watershed study of the relationship between race and scripture in the modern world stubbornly relegates African American Islam and black Judaism to being heretical forms of Protestantism.[54] Kidd represents these religions as creative concoctions—hodgepodge, hybrid religions. This category of syncretic religion of course depends on the wildly fictitious notion of pure religions that are not concocted or imagined. Historically, there is no such thing. Any honest historian of Christianity, Islam, Judaism, or Buddhism (or any other religion) would have to recognize that hybridity, mythmaking, and concoction are the essential, enabling means whereby religions—all of them—emerge and develop.[55] This is precisely what historians such as Burton Mack, Daniel Brown, Ziony Zevit, and John Wansbrough have emphasized.[56] In fact, what is ironic is how those who attempt to delegitimize African American religions by reading them as artificial concoctions in this way become blind to the immense commonalities among the originary matrices of religious movements—Paul's imaginative and intellectually indefensible exegesis of Jewish scripture to legitimate his new religion of Jesus; early Judaism's exilic mythmaking that denied all but one of ancient Israel's *many* gods and that introduced biological purity as a standard of the new religion; early Islam's denial of Allah's affiliation with the many other gods of Arabia (these suddenly became idols).[57]

Edward Curtis has taken the lead in producing a compelling and overwhelming case for why strategies of denying authenticity to African American Muslims are indefensible on intellectual and methodological grounds. For years, critics of African American Islam have relied on an arbitrary selection of formal creeds and practices (such as the Five Pillars and reading Arabic scriptures) to construct an orthodox Islam vis-à-vis African American Islams. Curtis has promoted a very different approach, however, that examines phenomenological aspects, particularly the very act of identifying as Muslim. The profundity of identifying is no less serious or consequential than following the Five Pillars or reading Arabic. Curtis recognizes the implications of self-definition to be far-reaching and thus an imperative for historians to resituate their approach to understanding the locus or constitution of being Islamic.[58]

It is precisely this level of sophistication and methodological acuity that must mark the future of African American religious studies. Fauset's efforts placed him among the avant-garde in his own time. His pioneering efforts, though not without flaws, should nevertheless serve as incitement to more critical analysis. Insofar as his scholarship served decolonizing imperatives, Fauset's interpretation of African American religions rightfully becomes a legacy that should inspire further study of linkages between colonialism, the state, and African American religions. Parsing the problem of black ethnicity must certainly become part of the array of concerns that occupies the attention of those historians who want to understand the central transformations that characterized the new religious movements of twentieth-century African America.

Notes

1. W. E. B. Du Bois, *The Negro Church* (Walnut Creek, Calif.: AltaMira, 2003).

2. Phil Zuckerman, *The Social Theory of W. E. B. Du Bois* (Thousand Oaks, Calif.: Pine Forge, 2004).

3. W. E. B. Du Bois, *The Souls of Black Folk* (1903; New York: Signet Classic, 1995), 216.

4. Carter G. Woodson, *The History of the Negro Church,* 2nd ed. (Washington, D.C.: Associated Publishers, 1945).

5. Benjamin Mays, *The Negro's God as Reflected in His Literature* (Westport, Conn.: Greenwood, 1969).

6. Benjamin E. Mays and Joseph William Nicholson, *The Negro's Church* (1933; New York: Arno, 1969).

7. The critical historiographical assessment of Tracey Hucks and Dianne Stewart is especially relevant here. See their "African American Religions: History of Study," in *The Encyclopedia of Religion,* vol. 1, 2nd ed., ed. Lindsay Jones (Detroit: Macmillan Reference USA, 2005). Hucks and Stewart highlight the fact that serious attention to African religions

as such was pioneered by African American female scholars. Unfortunately, the male-dominated scholarship would not surrender a historiographical shift that followed their lead until the end of the twentieth century.

8. Katherine Dunham, *The Dances of Haiti: A Study of Their Material Aspect, Organization, Form, and Function* (n.p., 1938).

9. Zora Neale Hurston, *Mules and Men* (Philadelphia: J. B. Lippincott, 1935).

10. St. Clair Drake and Horace Cayton, *Black Metropolis: A Study of Negro Life in a Northern City* (New York: Harcourt, Brace and Co., 1945).

11. Arthur Huff Fauset, *Black Gods of the Metropolis: Negro Religious Cults of the Urban North* (1944; Philadelphia: University of Pennsylvania Press, 2002), 87n2.

12. Ibid., 89.

13. Ibid., 92–93.

14. Ibid., 93.

15. Ibid., 103.

16. Ibid., 96–98; Fauset examines several works by Herskovits. See especially Melville Herskovits, *The Myth of the Negro Past* (New York: Harper and Bros., 1941); and Robert E. Park, "The Conflict and Fusion of Cultures with Special Reference to the Negro," *Journal of Negro History* 4, no. 2 (April 1919): 111–33.

17. Fauset, *Black Gods*, 97.

18. Ibid., 101, 108.

19. See Kevin J. Christiano, *Religious Diversity and Social Change: American Cities, 1890–1906* (Cambridge: Cambridge University Press, 1987), 29–31.

20. Miles Mark Fisher, "Organized Religion and the Cults," *Crisis* 44, no. 1 (1937): 30.

21. Association of Religion Data Archives, www.TheARDA.com, accessed February 28, 2007.

22. Miles Mark Fisher, "The Negro Churches," *Crisis* 45, no. 7 (1938): 220, 239, 245–46.

23. Ibid., 246.

24. Fisher, "Organized Religion and the Cults," 8.

25. Ibid., 10.

26. United Nations General Assembly, "Basic Principles of the Legal Status of the Combatants Struggling Against Colonial and Alien Domination and Racist Regimes," *American Journal of International Law* 68, no. 2 (April 1974): 379–81.

27. The hostile suppression by the U.S. federal government and state governments was not directed against only black religious organizations. Native American and Chicano movements were also regarded as anti-American because they challenged white supremacy and colonialism. See Edward J. Escobar, "The Dialectics of Repression: The Los Angeles Police Department and the Chicano Movement, 1968–1971," *Journal of American History* 79, no. 4 (1993): 1483–1514, and Ward Churchill and Jim Vander Wall, *Agents of Repression: The F.B.I.'s Secret Wars against the Black Panther Party and the American Indian Movement,* 2nd ed. (Cambridge: South End Press Classics, 2002).

28. The organized strategies of persecution by the U.S. government in this era were tied to its ascent as an imperial superpower. It had acquired its first colonies—Guam, the Philippines, Hawaii, Puerto Rico, and Samoa—at the turn of the century and was expanding

its foreign control over six million historically dominated nonwhite peoples. See Cornel West's examination of the relationship between America's system of democracy and its practice of colonialism in his *Democracy Matters: Winning the Fight against Imperialism* (New York: Penguin, 2004), 50–51. Black intellectuals, religious leaders, and activists were connecting the plight of African Americans to that of other Third World peoples. This is one reason why, despite his explicit, robust (literally) flag-waving support for American nationalism, Noble Drew Ali and other Moorish Americans were arrested and detained by the United States. Colonial conquest over nonwhite peoples was not new, but the acquisition of U.S. colonies and the subsequent dominance as a military superpower was. Throughout the twentieth century, the United States would both suppress anticolonial struggles abroad while persecuting domestic activities by blacks.

29. U.S. Department of Justice, FBI file 62–25889, "Moorish Science Temple of America," part 1 of 8, Rhea Whitley to Director of FBI [J. Edgar Hoover], memorandum, September 12, 1931, 3, http://foia.fbi.gov/foiaindex/moortemp.htm, part 1a, accessed June 1, 2007.

30. Ibid.

31. U.S. Department of Justice, FBI file 62-25889, "Moorish Science Temple of America," part 1 of 8, report made at Springfield, Illinois, January 28, 1942, file no. 100-3095, unnumbered page, http://foia.fbi.gov/foiaindex/moortemp.htm, part 1a, accessed June 1, 2007.

32. U.S. Department of Justice, FBI, SAC letter no. 55–43, June 28, 1955, unnumbered page, http://foia.fbi.gov/foiaindex/nation_of_islam.htm, part 1, accessed June 1, 2007.

33. U.S. Department of Justice, FBI, preface to report on "Muslim Cult of Islam," p. i, http://foia.fbi.gov/foiaindex/nation_of_islam.htm, part 1, accessed June 1, 2007.

34. U.S. Department of Justice, FBI, preface to report on "Muslim Cult of Islam," pp. i–ii, http://foia.fbi.gov/foiaindex/nation_of_islam.htm, part 1, accessed June 1, 2007.

35. For instance, only in 1980 did the FBI make public its files on the Moorish Science Temple Movement, which first came under surveillance in September 1931. Relevant here are the several studies of the relationship between colonialism, surveillance, and governmentality. Among those I have found most helpful are Lennox S. Hinds, *Illusions of Justice: Human Rights Violations in the United States* (Iowa City: School of Social Work, University of Iowa, 1979); Hannah Arendt, *The Origins of Totalitarianism* (New York: Harcourt Brace Jovanovich, 1973); Michael Taussig, *The Magic of the State* (New York: Routledge, 1997); Michel Foucault, *Discipline and Punish: The Birth of the Prison* (New York: Pantheon Books, 1977); Graham Burchell et al., eds., *The Foucault Effect: Studies in Governmentality* (Chicago: University of Chicago Press, 1991); Irene Silverblatt, *Modern Inquisitions: Peru and the Colonial Origins of the Civilized World* (Durham, N.C.: Duke University Press, 2004).

36. The relationship between early modern practices of observing and classifying religions and the twentieth-century activities of the U.S. state in doing the same are not unrelated. Common to both eras is the reality of colonial authority and domination over nonwhite subject people. For an engaging and historically rich study that examines FBI surveillance of African Americans, see Mark Ellis, *Race, War, and Surveillance: African Americans and the United States* (Bloomington: Indiana University Press, 2001).

37. I refer here to the fields or domains of social power outlined by Michael Mann; he proffers the following categories for theorizing the sources of social power—ideological, economic, military, and political. Mann's assessment of the history of power on a global scale achieves comparative breadth while avoiding the pitfalls of the old Victorian anthropological school. See his *Sources of Social Power*, 2 vols. (Cambridge: Cambridge University Press, 1986–1993).

38. Lewis Gordon, "African-American Philosophy: Theory, Politics, and Pedagogy," *Philosophy of Education* (1998), www.ed.uiuc.edu/EPS/PES-Yearbook/1998/gordon.html, accessed June 1, 2007. See especially his *Existentia Africana: Understanding Africana Existential Thought* (New York: Routledge, 2000), 62–80.

39. Charles H. Long, *Significations: Signs, Symbols, and Images in the Interpretation of Religion* (Philadelphia: Fortress, 1986), 1–7; and "Perspectives for a Study of Afro-American Religion in the United States," *History of Religions* 11, no. 1 (1971): 54–66.

40. David Chidester, *Savage Systems: Colonialism and Comparative Religion in Southern Africa* (Charlottesville: University Press of Virginia, 1996).

41. Russell T. McCutcheon, *Manufacturing Religion: The Discourse on Sui Generis Religion and the Politics of Nostalgia* (New York: Oxford University Press, 2003); Robert A. Segal, "Classification and Comparison in the Study of Religion: The Work of Jonathan Z. Smith," *Journal of the American Academy of Religion* 73, no. 4 (2005): 1175–88; Robert A. Segal, "The Function of 'Religion' and 'Myth': A Response to Russell McCutcheon," *Journal of the American Academy of Religion* 73, no. 1 (2005): 209–13; Jonathan Z. Smith, "Religion, Religions, Religious," in *Critical Terms for Religious Studies*, ed. Mark C. Taylor (Chicago: University of Chicago Press, 1998), 269–84; Jonathan Z. Smith, *Imagining Religion: From Babylon to Jonestown* (Chicago: University of Chicago Press, 1988).

42. Richard King, *Orientalism and Religion: Postcolonial Theory, India and "the Mystic East"* (London: Routledge, 1999).

43. Arendt, *Origins of Totalitarianism;* Silverblatt, *Modern Inquisitions;* Joel Martin, "Indians, Contact, and Colonialism in the Deep South: Themes for a Postcolonial History of American Religion," in *Retelling U.S. Religious History*, ed. Thomas Tweed (Berkeley: University of California Press, 1997).

44. Jon Butler, *Awash in a Sea of Faith: Christianizing the American People* (Cambridge, Mass.: Harvard University Press, 1990).

45. Ina Johanna Fandrich, "Defiant African Sisterhoods: The Voodoo Arrests of the 1850s and 1860s in New Orleans," in *Fragments of Bone: Neo-African Religions in a New World*, ed. Patrick Bellegarde-Smith (Urbana: University of Illinois, 2005).

46. Yvonne Chireau, *Black Magic: Religion and the African American Conjuring Tradition* (Berkeley: University of California Press, 2003); Karen McCarthy Brown, *Mama Lola: A Vodou Priestess in Brooklyn* (Berkeley: University of California Press, 1991); Anthony B. Pinn, *Varieties of African American Religious Experience* (Minneapolis: Fortress, 1998).

47. Darnise Martin, *Beyond Christianity: African Americans in a New Thought Church* (New York: New York University Press, 2005).

48. Richard Brent Turner, *Islam in the African-American Experience* (Bloomington: Indiana University Press, 1997).

49. Wilson Jeremiah Moses, *The Wings of Ethiopia: Studies in African-American Life and Letters* (Ames: Iowa State University Press, 1990), 3–14, 27ff.

50. Assata Shakur, *Assata: An Autobiography* (Chicago: L. Hill Brooks, 2001), 53–55.

51. Catherine L. Albanese uses this term in her discussion of African American urban religions during the early twentieth century. See her *America: Religions and Religion*, 4th ed. (Belmont, Calif.: Wadsworth, 2007), 147–51.

52. Du Bois, *Souls of Black Folk*, 43–47. Du Bois applied this latter understanding of culture to explain why African Americans were not just like whites. The usual response was to point to slavery as an experience that had rendered them uncultured, barbaric, and in need of reform. Du Bois proffered a different explanation, however, by representing many of these differences as a result of African cultural retention. This was the first sociological effort to explain African American "idiosyncrasies" as the result of something other than pathology. Such an approach has by now, of course, become standard fare in the social sciences.

53. Werner Sollors, *Beyond Ethnicity: Consent and Descent in American Culture* (New York: Oxford University Press, 1986), 25–36. I have relied here on Werner Sollors's conception of ethnicity. Sollors's theoretical framework for understanding ethnicity is rightly grounded in recognizing that the category is historically constituted through *ideas* about identity; it is not a natural condition of "social content." Ethnicity, in other words, is an empty symbol. Sollors emphasizes the semiotic nature of ethnicity not to trivialize it as a "merely" imagined entity but to highlight the power of this concept since the twentieth century.

54. Colin Kidd, *The Forging of Races: Race and Scripture in the Protestant Atlantic World, 1600–2000* (Cambridge: Cambridge University Press, 2006), 52–53, 263–67, 270. Kidd's is a pioneering cultural history of race-making through recourse to biblical interpretation. Kidd examines this issue across four centuries and devotes robust attention to the international nature of this discourse. Kidd's is destined to be a watershed text, yet it is beleaguered by the all-too-common distortion of African American Islam, Judaism, and Christian heresies. This is, ironically, precisely how Westerners categorized early Islam in Arabia. In fairness, I would emphasize that this interpretive weakness of the book is by no means unique to Kidd. What distinguishes Kidd's text, rather, is its astute attention to internationalism and his thorough, comprehensive mapping of how scripture functioned in the discourse of race theory and related social sciences.

55. I do not intend here to single out religion-as-concoction in a unique sense; secular formations like race, the nation-state, and legal discourse operate in the same fashion. A brilliant demonstration of this is Taussig, *The Magic of the State;* see also Talal Asad, *Formations of the Secular: Christianity, Islam, Modernity* (Stanford, Calif.: Stanford University Press, 2003).

56. See Burton L. Mack, *The Christian Myth: Origins, Logic, and Legacy* (New York: Continuum, 2001); Daniel Brown, *A New Introduction to Islam* (Malden, Mass.: Blackwell, 2003); Ziony Zevit, *The Religions of Ancient Israel: A Synthesis of Parallactic Approaches* (London: Continuum, 2001); and John Wansbrough, *The Sectarian Milieu: Content and Composition of Islamic Salvation History* (Oxford: Oxford University Press, 1978).

57. The fundamental function and articulation of early Islam, in fact, was ethnocentric; it was preeminently a religion of the Arabs, God's revelation to them, vis-à-vis the people of the Book (Jews and Christians). From that point on, Arabs would also have written scriptures. It is analytically fruitful (though not at all necessary for any purpose of authenticity) to recognize the same nature of concern in the emergence of African American Islam.

58. Edward E. Curtis IV, "African American Islamization Reconsidered: Black History Narratives and Muslim Identity," *Journal of the American Academy of Religion* 73, no. 3 (2005): 659–84; see especially 679–80.

EIGHT · The Perpetual Primitive in African American Religious Historiography

KATHRYN LOFTON

"Singing, dancing, shouting, clapping the hands, etc., while generally characteristic of American Negro cult worship, are not essential features," declared Arthur Huff Fauset in the "Summary of Findings" to his *Black Gods of the Metropolis* (1944).[1] Among the many accomplishments of Fauset's ethnography was his constant emphasis on the intellectual, political, and economic facets of black religious belief. Unlike his social-scientific forebears, Fauset believed African American religious behavior was more than a jig and a song. However, despite this landmark rebuttal, scholars of religious studies continue to contend with such romantic reductions of the African American religious subject, positing it as the attendant opposite to the modernist, the contemplative, the cosmopolite. Historiography of the civil rights movement in particular dawdles in the consolidating patronage of scholars uneducated to denominational difference or theological discord. Despite the alacrity of Arthur Fauset's mid-twentieth-century exemplum, narratives of black spiritual life continue to simmer with primitive suppositions, as political resistance is maintained by a generic spiritual resilience, and organizational similitude explained by mass cohesion to the Black Church. Even if Fauset intended to designate other "essential" worship features to "American Negro cult worship," his intention hardly disseminated to the subsequent historical record. The African American believer remains the body in motion, the voice in song, with eyes affixed, unblinking, to God.

Consider the recent *Routledge Historical Atlas of Religion in America*, published in 2000 and authored by Bret E. Carroll.[2] This atlas is a part of a larger series that includes volumes mapping the history of American railroads, women, African Americans, and presidential elections. Slender and beautifully illustrated, these volumes offer a charming and affordable accessory to an introductory course, integrating transhistorical geographic scope to the documentary readers or textbooks normally assigned in order to translate processes of history to neophyte students. The contents of Carroll's particular contribution are admirable, including plots of revival barnstorming and Vedanta temples, Southern Baptist percentages and black Catholic migrations. Bracketing the details of the scholarly labors of this text, a turn to the cover of the volume reveals a staggering summation of its contents. Recall that the purpose of this 140-page book is to map the history of religion in the United States, the missionary successes and indigenous displacements, the immigrant occupations and charismatic trends. The summary surface icon of these presumed summary contents? A black woman, arms outstretched, mouth agape, apparently singing. Her plump form is encased in a housedress of quilted print fabric, her singing head capped with a white bonnet reminiscent of plantation labor. Behind her are about fifteen skinny white youth, assembled in some sort of protest, all of their gazes, including hers, faced toward an unseen center. She dominates the tableau and translates the greatest protest enthusiasm—she is not merely protesting, she is the protestation, the spiritual bracket on a nation's geographic past and political possibility. The background of this black-and-white photograph is a map borrowed from the volume, the one demarcating "northern hunting traditions" of precontact indigenous Americans. Bannered above her bonneted head, then, are labels reading "vision quests," "buffalo rites and dances," "earth diver tales," and "cannibal spirits." If this cover is to be believed, the entirety of U.S. religious history might be aptly outlined by primal experience, from cannibal phantoms to black protest wails, each offering the beginning and end of essential faith, real faith, and earnest experience.[3] Religion in America is not pulpits or creeds, doctrinal squabbles or ethnic differentiation; religion in America is the suffering of the oppressed, the displaced, the enslaved, captured in an open-mouthed melody and a nostalgic memory for a time when visions and dances and song comprised faithful action. Religion in America is a celebration of the signifying primitive.

For any scholar of African America, such a cover, such a summary reduction, is hardly surprising. We know that the African American religious subject lingers still in abstraction. We know that the sale of books is best served not by a complex, differentiated, denominated believer, but by a shiny face singing songs of universal wisdom. Where does this primitive subject come from? Why is it so tempting to our religious redactions? Why is it so hard to relinquish "singing, dancing, and shouting" in the historiography of African American religion? To answer this question, a return to the past is inevitable: a return to the problem of the primitive, its emergence as a critical analytic category in the early twentieth century, and its propagation in theories of religion, history, anthropology, and art. Arthur Fauset's anthropological labors seem to have limited trickle-down effect within the broader historiography of religious studies; it seems the black subject is still a singularly reduced one, embodying the primitive essentials that all other religious (and racial) forms subsequently complicate. In order to encourage a shifted position for the primitive subject, then, it seems necessary to recollect the sources of this primitive character. Through an examination of the primitive compulsion in early twentieth-century scholarly literatures, we will find that the primitive has a primal hold on our disciplinary origins. Rereading the history of the "primitive" within religious studies points to the way religious studies itself has been knit with a racial particularity. This essay offers a preface to Carroll's wailing cover, to the ways in which the primitive prescription has dominated research into African American religiosity.

The Primitive and the Modern

Describing something as "primitive" implies originality, purity, and simplicity. Such inferences presume a comparative subject. If there is an original, it means something else is deemed not to be; if something is pure, it implies an impurity. The primitive thus functions as an ideal space for the construction of otherness. It can refer to a stage of time (the earliest era), an inhabitant of a certain land (the native), or the comparative quality of an object. At the turn from the nineteenth to the twentieth century, several different genres of the primitive were at play among American intellectuals. First, within several disciplines, the study of primitive cultures dominated.[4] Religious studies, for example, can conceivably source its intellectual inception in this cauldron of primitive talk. "The origins of the discipline," reflected historian of religions Charles Long, "took place in the milieu of E. B. Tylor's researches into primitive cultures, of Charles Darwin's evolutionary theories, and of the popularity of James Frazer's *Golden Bough*." The conjunction of scientific and anthropological evolutionary schema is a productive perpendicular, with each goading the other to more accurate renderings of how we became this way, in this modern world. According to Long, if religious studies was a disciplinary product of modernity, then the history of religious studies is intractably bound to the concept of the primitive: "The problematic character of western modernity created the language of the primitives and primitivism through their own explorations, exploitations, and disciplinary orientations."[5] For many contemporary theorists, Long's connection between religious studies and modernity poses disciplinary problems, and fails to account for pre-Enlightenment traditions of religious comparison and analysis. Despite this chronological impediment, the historically overlapping writings of E. B. Tylor, R. R. Marett, and Lucien Lévy-Bruhl—all formative figures within the incipient history of religions—focus on a definition of the primitive as a version of the modern self. Through their descriptions of "primitive culture," these social scientists established a primitive paradigm in order to adequately grasp the essence of the modern subject.

In this particular description of the primitive as an ideal type of modern subject, anthropologists ruled the day.[6] Franz Boas's landmark descriptions of the "primitive" repeatedly pointed to the universal attributes of this subject. "It would seem that, in different races, the organization of the mind is on the whole alike, and that the varieties of mind found in different races do not exceed, perhaps do not even reach, the amount of normal variation in each race," Boas announced in 1901.[7] Boas was a headlining figure within a broad spectrum of anthropological analysis. Historians have marked this spectrum with two poles. On the one end, anthropologists evoked Enlightenment principles and figures to construct "the black as a noble savage, in a state out of which whites had long ago evolved and which could be addressed by assimilation into a superior culture." On the other end of the discursive spectrum, there were anthropologists using racial theory to evoke "an image of the black as unregenerate and barbaric savage, which subhuman condition could be mitigated through control of a superior culture but could not be altogether suppressed."[8] Most historians of religion fell nearer to the former category than the latter in their explorations, promoting the essential spiritual sagacity of the "noble savage." However, before running too quickly in the direction of those deductions, it is important to note that a linguistic exchange just took place: In an effort to define the range of anthropological thinking on the "primitive," I have cited material that deploys "primitive" and "black" interchangeably (the *black* as noble savage and the *black* as barbaric savage). In the imperial epoch of anthropological production, the primitive was inevitably equated with the main colonial possession: Africa.

Anthropologists emphasizing religious behavior returned again and again to data from Africa and Aboriginal Australia, data determined by definitions of the "primitive" as a black subject. These treatments of the dark primitive were as varied as the scholars themselves, posing the black savage as noble and barbaric, as controlled and desired by their "civilized" counterparts.[9] Connections among the many genres of primitive talk—anthropological, religious, and artistic—were abundant.

Consider, for example, the weighty influence of Franz Boas, founding anthropologist at Columbia University. Boas's expansive views of racial similarity had a huge impact on his student Zora Neale Hurston, and on W. E. B. Du Bois, who would later use Boas's heroic rendition of the primitive in his descriptions of African America. However, just as anthropology influenced formative figures in black religious studies, so was anthropology a production of a religious impulse. As George Stocking has documented, nineteenth-century anthropology began as a frankly theological enterprise and continued, for many, as "substitutionary atonement," with scientific revelations taking the place of religious ones. E. B. Tylor, the first labeled professor of anthropology, wrote anonymously, "Theologians all to expose, / 'Tis the *mission* of Primitive Man."[10] The quest for the primitive is thus a quest for the primal religious subject, the human before history, pure in belief and unconscious in practice. Meanwhile, as anthropologists trailed primitive religiosity and W. E. B. Du Bois reified the noble black American, texts summarizing the evolutionary progress of homo sapiens (from primitive to modern) had an immense impact on the literary culture of the day. Asserting that no book had a greater effect on modern literature than Sir James Frazer's *The Golden Bough*, Lionel Trilling argued famously that the "primitive imagination" is at the center of the modernist tradition. Thirty years later, Daniel J. Singal's essay, "Towards a Definition of American Modernism," underscored the same emphasis, noting that the "modernist embrace of natural instinct and primitivism" was necessary to understanding modernism.[11] Just as anthropologists and religionists sought the authentic primitive subject, so did painters and writers relentlessly seek authentic representations on the page and canvas.

This "primitivism" then refers to modern art that alludes to specific stylistic elements of tribal objects and other non-Western art forms.[12] According to historian Sieglinde Lemke, primitivism has to be understood as one of four modernist aesthetic lines: the formally experimental or avant-garde (with which she associates the poets Ezra Pound and Wallace Stevens); the minimalist (where she places Ernest Hemingway and Gertrude Stein); the politicized realist aesthetic, which "speaks on behalf of the proletariat"; and the primitivist aesthetic. Lemke further delineates the latter category into four subsets describing the aesthetic and anthropological manifestations of primitivism:

"Chronological primitivism" denotes the belief that ancient or prehistoric times were superior to modern times. "Cultural primitivism" is the romanticization of non-Western peoples, usually idealizing their instincts, sexuality, and their proclivity to the natural. "Spiritual primitivism" appeals to the dark-irrational mystical powers and to

Dionysian ecstasy. The fourth term we might think of as "aesthetic primitivism." It is based on the assimilation of non-European art forms.[13]

Thus, Lemke has categorized four treatments of the primitive with four forms of primitivism. Each category incorporates a privileged subject: chronological primitivism prefers ancient to modern times; spiritual primitivism suggests the virtues of mysticism outside those of rationalism, and so forth. In each version of primitivism, something is included and another excluded, something preferred and another denied. "That the modern covets the primitive—perhaps even created it—is another frequently acknowledged fact," noted Michael North in his study *The Dialect of Modernism*, "[b]ut to view this attraction merely as a return to nature, a recoil from modernity, is to focus myopically on a rather vapid message while missing its far more intriguing medium."[14] For every mention of the primitive, for every citation of its affirming (or degrading) powers, the civilized ensure the persistence of the inverse category.

Nowhere is this irony more pronounced than in the concurrent construction of Christian primitivism. During the same age when artists cultivated an aesthetic primitivism based on their encounters with primitive crafts and continents, American Christians pursued a "primitive" church based on their imagined portrait of third- and fourth-century Christianity. Within the academy, this quest was largely hypothetical. As biblical criticism crossed the Atlantic from Germany, U.S. scholars of Christianity became intrigued by the possibility that they could describe vividly the apostolic church through adequate research. Such a reclamation was not merely an intellectual exercise; many hoped this reconstructed "primitive church" would find its way into local churches, that the original redaction would form the basis for a contemporary revision.[15] However, the most activist versions of this ambition were not based in scholarly research. Rather, this second move toward the "primitive church" was sourced in a diverse set of prophecies and American religious contexts that emerged from the nineteenth century. Although the terms "primitivism" and "restorationism" have been used interchangeably to describe this impulse, "restorationism" is a term primarily applied to the nineteenth-century movement that produced the Christian Church (Disciples of Christ). Primitivism, on the other hand, is a broad tradition linked to a number of denominational families.

Historians of religious primitivism argue that the one central theme that connects primitivist movements is their common rejection of history. In the quest to return to a pure time, an epoch prior to moral defilement or sectarian diversity, primitivists cultivate a historical amnesia.[16] In the beginning, according to primitivist narratives, religion was simple and man was unified in his religious practice. In the end, Christians must reclaim that clean slate, that original church, if they are to bring about the kingdom of God. For most historians, American Pentecostalism is the first exhibit in any discussion of primitivism.[17] Pentecostalism is a twentieth-century movement distinguished by its emphasis on the experience of the Holy Spirit. "Baptism" in the Holy Spirit is characterized by ecstatic speech in unknown languages, also known as glossolalia.[18] Using the book of Acts, Pentecostals argued that the centrality of such "signs," the preeminence of sanctification, made their churches closest to the original designations of Jesus Christ. Thus, they formed "primitive" or "apostolic" parishes that iterated signs abandoned by other denominations and incarnations. With Pentecostalism, the interceding churches were lost to history; the apostolic church had been reestablished.[19]

It seems that this was a landscape strewn with such primitive practice and original pursuits. It would be easy to decide that these assessments were the harbingers of their epoch, intellectual signposts of post-Reconstruction racism and antimodern anxiety.[20] However, what links these threads is a possession with the "Negro" subject. Naming this subject was no mere primitive prescription: For many anthropologists, artists, and scholars of religion, African Americans were not just primitive, they were modern because they were primitive. Black primal "savagery" served as the composite object for evolutionary narratives, social-scientific explications of human psychology, and aesthetic revolutions. "The Negro, assigned the role of infantilized and brutalized child in the family romance of Victorian America, has become the father, even a Founding Father, of modern American culture," explained historian Ann Douglas.[21] For anthropologists, definitions of the "primitive" served to both deconstruct and reify evolutionary plots for human development. Among artists, images and texts by "native" Africans (and, to some extent, African Americans) informed a growing interest in abstract forms and realist dissimilation. Historians of religion conceived of the "primitive" as an ambition (to re-create the apostolic church) and archetype (the essence of religious belief and practice). The black primitive was a mobile object, under intense scrutiny and in great demand. The only consistency within all these manipulations and managements was the very modernity of these primitive constructs. To define the primitive subject was to enter tactics and methods adjudicated by nascent universities, emergent scholarly disciplines, and evidence gathered under imperial auspices. The primitive was the product of modern making; the religious primitive would therefore be the epicenter analytical agency in an era of debunking and declaiming.

The Primitive and the Negro Religious

Within this Negrophilia, the black believer formed an obsessive subcategory of intellectual interest. In 1917, a young Columbia University graduate named Frederick Morgan Davenport reissued his doctoral dissertation, *Primitive Traits in Religious Revivals: A Study in Mental and Social Evolution* (1905), which had enjoyed a popular run through Macmillan Publishing House. The title adequately anticipated its contents: Davenport's study sought to identify the "primitive traits" in religious revivals that "need elimination or modification in the interest of religious and social progress." Echoing the liberal academic impulse of the era, Davenport did not want to "beat back" the tide of faith; rather, he wanted to contribute to "the better ordering of religious method," to suggest a smarter rendition of tabernacle touring. Including chapters on the Ghost Dance, Scotch-Irish revivals of 1800 and 1859, and the tactics of Jonathan Edwards, John Wesley, and Charles Finney, *Primitive Traits in Religious Revivals* documents the growing sociological interest in religious behavior and the increasing social-scientific awareness of the powerful role religion, and religious revivals, played in American history. In his study, Davenport spoke in the familiar cadences of the modern skeptic. "The mind of the crowd is strangely like that of primitive man," he wrote. "Most of the people in it may be far from primitive in emotion, in thought, in character; nevertheless the result tends always to be the same. Stimulation immediately begets action. Reason is in abeyance." As a persuasive and self-described "scientific" writer, Davenport believed that sourcing revival behavior in primitive man might motivate participants to rethink their actions. Who, after all, would want to look primitive? To discourage the triumph of primitive traits, Davenport recommended pacing revivals to include long breaks, so that "rational inhibition" could "intervene and do its work." Davenport diagnosed the primitive in the religious so as to encourage what he determined to be its opposite: "religious gatherings controlled by sound sense and rational though deep feeling." The primitive revival was thus transformed into a modern meditation session, bracketed by thoughtful conversation and meaningful collegiality.[22]

In their 1996 definition of "primitive," art historians Mark Antliff and Patricia Leighton explain that it is a term that does not constitute an essentialist category but "exemplifies a relationship." Like the word "modern" (with which it is often paired), "primitive" infers a contrasting subject. "The term 'primitive' cannot exist without its attendant opposite," Antliff and Leighton conclude, "and in fact the two terms act to constitute each other."[23] In *Primitive Traits in Religious Revivals*, Davenport established the modern as a carefully demarcated, collaborative rationality. However, most of the book is devoted to sharpening the definition of its attendant opposite, the "primitive." His fifth chapter, "The Religion of the American Negro," offers a prime definitional landscape, using the African American as an archive of primitive traits. In 1930, Carl Jung would specify the allure of African America to whites this way: "Since the Negro lives within your cities and even within your houses, he also lives within your skin, subconsciously."[24] In the rhetorical landscape of early twentieth-century America, the black man functioned as the "attendant opposite" to almost any postulation of rationality. He simmered beneath the skin, constantly provoking analysts to scratch.

"No one doubts, I suppose, that in the Negro people, whether in Africa or America, we have another child race," Davenport began. "The old slave system of the Southland snatched the ancestors of this race from savagery only one or two hundred years ago." Davenport expressed grief for the evils of slavery, particularly as it inhibited blacks from genuine progress. The chapter continues, rapidly outlining the resultant features of the race ("dense ignorance and superstition, a vivid imagination, volatile emotion, a weak will to power, and a small sense of morality") and its distinguishing religious characteristics ("the rhythm, the shout, the 'falling out'"). Through Davenport's description, the Negro emerged as the perfect primitive, the perfect opposite to his ideal religious prescriptions. Describing the "Negro preacher" and his sermonic style, Davenport wrote that the minister appealed "to the instinctive emotions of fear and hate as well as love, the mourner, the shouter, the visioner, rioting in word picture, his preaching an incoherent, irrational rhythmic ecstasy." This Negro preacher was, in Davenport's estimation, "a primitive man with primitive traits in a modern environment." Despite this caustic assessment of black religiosity, *Primitive Traits in Religious Revivals* fairly vibrated with the allure of his subject. Davenport described in vivid detail black revival meetings in Florida and Tennessee, lingering over the dialect and "muscular discharges" of those events. He even concluded the chapter on an admiring note: "There is something intrinsically noble in a race which has manifested such an original genius for beautiful music."[25] Echoing Jean-Jacques Rousseau's eighteenth-century profile of the "noble savage," Davenport temporarily relinquished his disgust with black primitivism to savor black musicality.[26] The very thing he most distrusted—unfettered emotionalism—also endorsed his central admiration. In the songs of black folk, Davenport found temporary refuge from his rationalism.

Also writing at the opening of the twentieth century, William Hannibal Thomas took no pleasure from this song or the dance. Davenport, a white anthropologist, might not be able to resist the songs he heard at black revival meetings, but for

Thomas, a black educator and reporter for the *Christian Recorder*, opposition to these same songs centered his studies of African America. "No sane person doubts that a sensuous faith and practice will always lead men away from God to unbelief, impiety, and physical degradation," Thomas wrote in *The American Negro* (1901). Although Thomas had experienced racial prejudice firsthand (he was denied entrance to the Union army), he translated these experiences into a stunning racial reproach. "In his native home, the Negro was a fetish worshipper, devoid of reverence, but possessed of superabundant awe of unseen gods," explained Thomas in his profile of the black American. "He was brought here with a savage religion ingrained in every fiber of his being." Despite missionary efforts and a high conversion rate, African Americans remained, in Thomas's opinion, fundamentally primitive: "Seriously speaking, what is the Negro other than the unassimilated ward of Western civilization, and our chief exemplification of imitative conformity to its external models?" Little could be done to save the black man from his uncivilized essence. "A savage at heart," Thomas wrote, "he is our most consummate representative of illiterate stolidity, a type whose habits and customs have been transmitted by ancestors through interminable ages of sameness, and whose history, whether in savagery or civilized submergement, is a record of lawless existence, led by every impulse and every passion." Frederick Morgan Davenport may have found some pleasure in Negro singing, but he and Thomas agreed on the problematic physicality of black religious belief. For both, the black was a savage, and a primitive, despite his immersion in American civilization. He was, to recall Davenport, a "primitive man with primitive traits in a modern environment."[27]

Writers in the nascent *Journal of Negro History* offered more judicious yet not less disappointed descriptions of their poorer, more primitive relations. "The religion of the Negroes on the plantation was then as it is today, of a much more primitive sort," commented historian Robert E. Park in a 1919 assessment of black culture. Park found a great deal of charm and metaphorical meaning in the musical productions of blacks. Speaking of the "plantation hymns," Park wrote, "These folksongs represent, at any rate, the naïve and spontaneous utterance of hopes and aspirations for which the Negro slave had no other adequate means of expression." Park emphasized that any wisdom of the songs was "naïve and spontaneous," not produced due to any intellectual clarity or purpose. But as a historian, he had the capability to reclaim these songs as archival documents and to celebrate their allegorical weight in literary terms: "In the imagery of these songs, in the visions which they conjure up, in the themes which they again and again renew, we may discern the reflection of dawning racial consciousness, a common racial ideal."[28] In a 1926 article for the *Journal of Negro History*, L. W. Kyles would arrive at the same conclusion: "The Negro made the long night of his enslavement vibrant with his songs— songs of hope and faith born of sorrow and suffering."[29] This emphasis on song and musicality was followed by some of the leading black intellectuals of the era. In their writings on black culture and, more specifically, the critical role of the "Negro church," W. E. B. Du Bois, Carter G. Woodson, and Benjamin Mays would highlight the genius of black spirituals.[30] While there were diverse representations of these songs and their meanings, the interpretive conclusion repeatedly reduced them to something similar to Robert E. Park's awkward summation:

> Everywhere and always the Negro has been interested rather in expression than in action; in life itself rather than in its reconstruction or reformation. The Negro is, by natural disposition, neither an intellectual nor an idealist like the Jew, nor a brooding introspective like the East Indian, nor a pioneer and frontiersman like the Anglo-Saxon. He is primarily an artist, loving life for its own sake. His métier is expression rather than action. The Negro is, so to speak, the lady among the races.[31]

Clogged with caricature, Park's assessment was intended as affirmation. Acknowledging black creativity—in song, in movement, and in sermon—was meant to underline his contributions to humanity. Nevertheless, in order to achieve such a backhanded compliment, Park needed to reduce the black man to his simplistic expression, to his bodily representation. Lacking reformations or reconstructions, the black man was merely a body, posed and singing, the lady among the races, diva standing open-mouthed for the divine.

Primitive Queen of the Black Church

Recall, then, the cover image to Bret E. Carroll's *Routledge Historical Atlas of Religion in America* (2000). Now, the singing female figure seems not merely an incidental signifier but an intellectual redaction, an inheritance of anthropological and historical scholarship that offered up the black believer as the sacrificial totem of U.S. religious creativity. This anonymous singer is, of course, just one in an army of such servants. As Nell Painter adroitly assessed in her 1996 biography of Sojourner Truth, black women have always served at the visual leisure of an American spiritual public. In that volume, Painter dissects Sojourner Truth as a commodity, an image sold for political profit (abolition, feminism) and for capitalist gain (posters and mugs bearing the slogan, "Ain't I a woman?").[32]

Carroll's cover does not spotlight Sojourner Truth, but an anonymous black figure, ostensibly representing the spiritual component of the 1960s political counterculture. Her dress and postulated context recall the representative iconography of Fannie Lou Hamer, African American grassroots activist and eloquent spokesperson for the American civil rights movement. Scholars have lavished considerable interpretive consequence on Hamer's body and voice in terms not altogether different from the primitivist praise of their early twentieth-century counterparts. According to contemporary historian Janice Hamlet, Fannie Lou Hamer became a "national symbol of the [civil rights] movement" when she sang "Go Tell It on the Mountain" at the 1964 Democratic Convention.[33] What, exactly, did Hamer symbolize through her public act of song? "Her faith, like that of most extremely religious people, was not separable from her practical conception of action in the day-to-day world," wrote David Chappell of Hamer. "In that sense, she was premodern or antimodern."[34] Despite the acumen of Chappell's research in prophetic religion and the civil rights movement, he still finds himself reaching for primitivist constructions to explicate the depths of Fannie Lou Hamer's faith. She cannot be so powerful and still modern; her faith comes from a place before civilized time.

This primitive profile of Hamer is replicated again and again the biographical renderings of Hamer's religious beliefs. Of the three existent biographical surveys, only one, Kay Mills' *This Little Light of Mine: The Life of Fannie Lou Hamer* (1993), makes specific reference to Hamer's religious genealogy: "Her faith also contributed to Fannie Lou Hamer's strength. She joined the Strangers Home Baptist Church at age twelve and was baptized in the Quiver River. Many of her religious principles she learned at home, from her mother. One of the most important lessons she was taught was that hating made one as weak as those filled with hatred."[35] The last sentence is a telling one. The rubrics of denomination are here countered by the proud matriarch whose lessons were expansive and positively generic. Throughout *This Little Light of Mine,* Mills repeats the same trio of attributes: Hamer is large, she is feisty, and she is spiritually wise. Mills quotes Harry Belafonte remarking that in every one of Hamer's songs he could hear "the struggle of all black America. . . . I thought that when she sang, there was indeed a voice raised that was without compromise of all of us." Under Mills' narrative construction, Hamer is a body, a symbol, and a voice; she is not derived from a specific sect or a cultural context. Hamer is *sui generis.* "Her greatest power," writes Mills, "was spiritual, a trait shared by many of her background." For Mills, it is enough to cite Hamer's universal appeal and suggestive metaphysical depth in order to explicate her religiosity. Denomination is left at age twelve, theology is consigned to her physical features; Hamer is a spiritual symbol, *not* a complex, intellectual religious actor.[36]

In her thesis, "Fannie Lou Hamer: From Sharecropper to Freedom Fighter" (1990), Kay Griffin-Juechter promisingly states that "Mrs. Hamer could sing in such a way that people forgot their fears, and as a speaker she was gifted with the awesome combination of focused intelligence and vision. Her religion was the source of her vision and strength."[37] Griffin-Juechter here echoes Janice Knight, who wrote, "Hamer's greatest source of inspiration was her unquenchable spirituality and honesty."[38] Readers may be excited to learn of the specific social contours of this sourcing spirituality and religion; sadly, they will be disappointed. Griffin-Juechter's (and Knight's) analysis is limited to admiring glances at Hamer's "practical Christianity" and review of Hamer's renowned rewrites of famous "Negro spirituals." No discussions of religious precedent, theological positions, or religious conflict with other African Americans are noted. Like Mills, Griffin-Juechter emphasizes Hamer's universal, earthly spirituality, which is evidenced publicly for these scholars by her musicality. Commenting on Hamer's skill as a public speaker, Griffin-Juechter writes, "Though unlettered, [Hamer] had the special gift of articulation, and when she spoke everyone knew and understood what she was saying."[39] Her Christianity is practical not intellectual, spoken not thought, understood though never excavated. Arthur Fauset's dream of a complex African American religious sociology is defeated in the celebration of Hamer's primitive, melodic Christianity.

In Chana Kai Lee's *For Freedom's Sake: The Life of Fannie Lou Hamer* (2000), we again find the deep religiosity of Hamer's mother. We learn that her father was a minister, but not for what church. All we know is that Hamer came from a "deeply religious" Christian family, that "her thinking and living, like that of her parents, were guided by a moral economy that blended a Christian worldview with southern realism."[40] Like Mills, Lee emphasizes how feisty Hamer was, particularly when it came to church authority. "She was widely respected for her knowledge of the Bible and her outspokenness," Lee writes. "She often challenged pastors in their own churches, calling on them to address the immediate obstacles hampering black life and to embrace the movement in whatever way possible."[41] Such confrontations receive only sidelong glances from Lee, however. Nowhere does Lee interrogate these moments as incidents of religious dissent, iconoclastic antiauthoritarian moments, or as potential fissures within the larger civil rights movement. Instead, she portrays Hamer as the parachurch operator, equally acceptable in one congregation as another, singing the same song, again and again.

For some, the pursuit of Hamer's specific denominational affiliation may seem an anachronistic quibble. Why force a particular Protestant profile on someone whose self-presentation encouraged unity over difference, spiritual solidarity over denominational discord? Moreover, the pursuit of a *religious* explication of heroic historic figures is frequently indicted by historians outside of religious history as the secret attempt to insert the "moral" in the secular methods of historical practice. So perhaps we should drop the query and just listen to Fannie Lou Hamer sing.

The problem is, of course, that our failure to know Hamer's religious genealogies betrays a more systemic racism: the subliminal understanding that we all already *know* just who Hamer was when it comes to religion. As her biographies demonstrate, there is a troublesome ease to our language about African Americans and religion. Rooted in the obscuring image of the Black Church, countless historical examinations of black figures rely on a generalized sense of black faithfulness, without taking the time to pursue the particularities of individuated African American faith commitments. The primitive presumption prevails, with a universal corporeality standing in for any clarified religious positioning or difference.

Thus, Hamer's religious commitment and critique—the supposed foundation of her charm and fortitude—are ambiguous, reduced to sanctimonious quotations. Even a study as erudite as Charles Marsh's *God's Long Summer: Stories of Faith and Civil Rights* (1997), which devotes an entire chapter to Hamer's "theological sources," fails to penetrate this caricature. According to Marsh, the "black church" fostered Hamer's "complicated" theological conceptions of God and suffering. This theological exegesis, however, exists in a vacuum; never does he use religious history or cultural differences to enunciate his claims about Hamer's theology. Again, this is made particularly irritating in the face of comments from Hamer herself. For example, she is quoted (by Marsh) as saying: "Sometimes I get so disgusted I feel like getting my gun after some of these chicken eatin' preachers. . . . I know these Baptist ministers."[42] Her gun? These *Baptist* ministers? This is tough talk for a woman born into the hierarchies of black male church authority, and subversive talk in the context of the Baptist-led southern civil rights movement. Yet every time this comment is quoted—and it is quoted in every biography—there is never an interrogation of its consequences, religious or political.

These biographers of Hamer are perhaps not to blame for the religious lacuna she occupies in the historiography. Historians of U.S. religion contribute to this ignorance by affirming descriptions of the "Black Church," a category which still seems to summarize some unified spiritual entity that imbues its members with certain spiritual credentials, a certain shared history of suffering, feeding a shared rhetoric of trial, endurance, and triumph. Indeed, the "Black Church" is that rare academic phrase that has been fed into the common lexicon, a cultural referent with which few would be unfamiliar of the essential assumed contours. This is on our shoulders: This is a category constructed and celebrated by historians of African American religion.[43] C. Eric Lincoln and Lawrence H. Mamiya's groundbreaking survey, *The Black Church in the African American Experience* (1990), canonized the Black Church as a useful paradigm for understanding the African American religious experience.[44] The works of Andrew Billingsley, Kelly Brown Douglas, Anthony Pinn, Milton Sernett, R. Drew Smith, Clarence Taylor, and Cornel West further endorse this category as a presumptive summary of black religion. For these scholars, the Black Church functions as *the* black institution, that rare thing that has been defined by and sustained by African Americans. Liberationist black scholarship reinforced the historical importance of the Black Church, casting it as the critical bridge away from slavery, from economic depravity, and from a state of victimization. The Black Church was, therefore, intended to resist the primitivist consignments of white culture; it constructed a sophisticated, institutionalized alternative to the folk and the primitive. It was external structure for a people denied the ability to mold external freedom; it was, at the very least, a trap of their own making. In some ways, it hurts to deconstruct a term carrying such revolutionary virtue. But when attempting to complicate black history, the Black Church acts as a beached whale on the highway. The "Black Church" is not an offensive term simply because it is monolithic and irritatingly vague to the scrupulous archival historian but because it obscures individual intellectual agency for African Americans. Such analytic vagary encourages a view of African Americans as static, universal, and essentially corporeal, while whites are allowed the possibility of historical change and intellectual agency. Concepts like the Black Church are inherently resistant to individuation. While individual whites develop, regress, complicate, and contemplate over time, African Americans possess certain eternal categories of description as easily read in any individual member as in the Black Church. Such a broadly prescriptive term becomes particularly unwieldy when one begins to study figures of political or religious dissent. Whereas in "white" culture, individuals who contradict institutional authority are lionized, those in the black community who dare to contradict established patterns of the Black Church are deemed traitors by liberal whites and by moderate blacks who demand institutional success over and above racial reconciliation. The subjects of Arthur Fauset's groundbreaking research—the subjects resuscitated in this volume—have long been exiled at the margins of historiography and African American intellectual life precisely because they fail to fit neatly the patterns of respectability mapped onto the bureaucratized contours of the Black Church.

No matter how tendentious she became, Hamer could not escape the shadow of this primitive historiography. She was predisposed by the narrative of her moment to be a product of the Black Church as well as the symbolic descendant of a long line of earthy, sagacious black women. She *had* to be; the narrative of American manifest destiny could tolerate no more from her. And the public, hungry for fetish, could tolerate no less. Could, then, a black symbolic figure ever be a person of intellectual contradiction and complexity? Could a black heroine be allowed to criticize black male authority? Hamer's dissent was muffled by a public willing to tune out her voice for the sake of a song and bosomed embrace. Hamer sang songs of absolution and unity, her body reached out to encompass, not exclude. Whatever critiques she offered were forgotten the minute she closed her eyes and started to sing. To the world, her body was the Black Church. Safe, comforting, and confined to a context whites could understand and, if need be, control. The debunking of this perpetual primitive may be the primary labor of contemporary scholarship in African American religion.

Notes

1. Arthur Huff Fauset, *Black Gods of the Metropolis: Negro Religious Cults of the Urban North* (1944; Philadelphia: University of Pennsylvania Press, 2002).

2. Bret E. Carroll, *The Routledge Historical Atlas of Religion in America* (New York: Routledge, 2000).

3. The composition of this photograph is no constructive accident; photographic practice in the twentieth century included the framing of religious life in particular ritual poses. For more on the framing of the religious subject by photographers, see Colleen McDannell, *Picturing Faith: Photography and the Great Depression* (New Haven, Conn.: Yale University Press, 2004).

4. Representative texts include Frank Baker, "Primitive Man," *American Anthropologist* 11, no. 12 (December 1898): 357–66; Daniel G. Brinton, *Religions of Primitive Peoples* (New York: G. P. Putnam's Sons, 1896); Moriz Hoernes, *Primitive Man* (London: J. M. Dent, 1900); Robert H. Lowie, *Primitive Society* (New York: Boni and Liveright, 1920); and John R. Swanton, "Three Factors in Primitive Religion," *American Anthropologist* 26, no. 3 (July–September 1924): 358–65.

5. Charles H. Long, "Primitive/Civilized: The Locus of a Problem," *History of Religion* 20, nos. 1–2 (August–November 1980): 43 and 60. For more on the "primitive" problem, see Richard Lee, "The Primitive as Problematic," *Anthropology Today* 9, no. 6 (December 1993): 1–3.

6. See also Max Weber, "The Social Psychology of the Worlds Religions," in *From Max Weber*, ed. and trans. H. H. Gerth and C. Wright Mills (New York: Oxford University Press, 1958).

7. Franz Boas, "The Mind of Primitive Man," *Journal of American Folklore* 14, no. 52 (January–March 1901): 11. Boas also contributed to conversations about primitive art:

Franz Boas, *Primitive Art* (1927; New York: Dover, 1955). Tomoko Mazusawa provides a review of the role of Boas and Tylor in religious studies. See her essay "Culture," in *Critical Terms for Religious Studies*, ed. Mark C. Taylor (Chicago: University of Chicago Press, 1998), 70–93, specifically 78–80.

    8. Mark Antliff and Patricia Leighton, "Primitive," *Critical Terms for Art History* (Chicago: University of Chicago Press, 1996), 179.

    9. There were "two alternating and yet complementary pulsations in our century's involvement with primitive societies and with the idea of the primitive: a rhetoric of control, in which demeaning colonialist tropes get modified only slightly over time; and a rhetoric of desire, ultimately more interesting, which implicates 'us' in the 'them' we try to conceive as the Other." Marianna Torgovnick, *Gone Primitive: Savage Intellects, Modern Lives* (Chicago: University of Chicago Press, 1990), 245.

    10. See George Stocking Jr., *Victorian Anthropology* (New York: Free Press, 1987), chapters 1–3. Tylor is quoted in Stocking, *Victorian Anthropology*, 191. "Primitive Man in Modern Beliefs," a poem by folklorist Henry Phillips, provided another pithy summation of the anthropological quest:

> Beliefs that ruled man long ago
> Within our actions ofttimes show;
> The habits of primeval days
> Still beset our modern ways;
> And thoughts we scorn, with boastful pride,
> Our steps, unconscious, often guide.

Henry Phillips, "Primitive Man in Modern Beliefs," *Journal of American Folklore* 3, no. 8 (January–March 1890): 60. Read on November 29, 1889, at the annual meeting of the American Folk-Lore Society in Philadelphia.

    11. James George Frazer, *The Golden Bough*, was first published in 1890. Lionel Trilling, *Beyond Culture: Essays on Literature and Learning* (New York: Harcourt Brace Jovanovich, 1965), 19; and Daniel J. Singal, "Towards a Definition of American Modernism," in *Modernist Culture in America* (Belmont, Calif.: Wadsworth, 1991).

    12. For more on the primitivism of artistic modernism, see *Antimodernism and Artistic Experience: Policing the Boundaries of Modernity*, ed. Lynda Jessup (Toronto: University of Toronto Press, 2001); Frances S. Connelly, *The Sleep of Reason: Primitivism in Modern European Art and Aesthetics, 1725–1907* (University Park: Pennsylvania State University Press, 1995); Shelly Errington, "What Became Authentic Primitive Art?" *Cultural Anthropology* 9, no. 2 (May 1994): 201–26; John Jervis, *Transgressing the Modern: Explorations in the Western Experience of Otherness* (Malden, Mass.: Blackwell, 1999); Jill Lloyd, *German Expressionism: Primitivism and Modernity* (New Haven, Conn.: Yale University Press, 1991); Susan Hill, ed. and comp., *The Myth of Primitivism: Perspectives on Art* (New York: Routledge, 1991); Elazar Barkan and Ronald Bush, eds., *Prehistories of the Future: The Primitivist Project and the Culture of Modernism* (Stanford, Calif.: Stanford University Press, 1995); Sally Price, *Primitive Art in Civilized Places* (Chicago: University of Chicago Press, 2001); and William Rubin, "Modernist Primitivism: An Introduction," in *"Primitiv-*

ism" in Twentieth-Century Art, ed. Kirk Varnedoe and William Rubin (New York: Museum of Modern Art, 1984).

13. Sieglinde Lemke, *Primitivist Modernism: Black Culture and the Origins of Transatlantic Modernism* (New York: Oxford University Press, 1998), 145 and 26. For more on black modernism, see Houston A. Baker Jr., *Modernism and the Harlem Renaissance* (Chicago: University of Chicago Press, 1987); and Edward M. Pavli, *Crossroads Modernism: Descent and Emergence in African American Literary Culture* (Minneapolis: University of Minnesota Press, 2002).

14. Michael North, *The Dialect of Modernism: Race, Language, and Twentieth-Century Literature* (New York: Oxford University Press, 1994), preface.

15. Two early scholarly attempts to reconstruct the "primitive church" were Moses M. Henkle, *Primitive Episcopacy* (Nashville, Tenn.: Stevenson and Owen, 1857) and Peter King, *Inquiry into the Constitution, Unity, and Worship of the Primitive Church* (New York: Lane and Sandford, 1841). Later exemplars of this efforts include Shirley Jackson Case, "The Nature of Primitive Christianity," *American Journal of Theology* 17, no. 1 (January 1913): 63–79; Ernst von Dobschütz, *Christian Life in the Primitive Church*, trans. George Bremner and ed. W. D. Morrison (New York: G. P. Putnam's Sons, 1904); Burnett H. Streeter, *Primitive Church* (New York: Macmillan, 1929); William H. Withrow, *The Catacombs of Rome, and Their Testimony Relative to Primitive Christianity* (New York: Nelson and Phillips, 1874). Shirley Jackson Case was probably the most prominent proponent of this intellectual work in America. See Paul Schubert, "Shirley Jackson Case, Historian of Early Christianity: An Appraisal," *Journal of Religion* 29 (1949): 30–46; Mark A. Noll, "Shirley Jackson Case and the Chicago School," *Journal of Biblical Literature* 106 (September 1987): 493–509; Jay D. Green, "A Creed for Modernism: Shirley Jackson Case and the Irony of Modern Approaches to 'Faith and History,'" *Fides et historia* 29 (Fall 1997): 38–49.

16. Grant Wacker argues that primitivists possess "a yearning somehow to return to a time before time, to a space outside of space." See Grant Wacker, "Searching for Eden with a Satellite Dish: Primitivism, Pragmatism, and the Pentecostal Character," in *The Primitive Church in the Modern World*, ed. Richard T. Hughes (Urbana: University of Illinois Press, 1995), 143. For more on the difference between "restorationism" and "primitivism," see Richard T. Hughes, "Preface: The Meaning of the Restoration Vision," in *The Primitive Church in the Modern World*, ix–xviii. Also in this collection is Martin E. Marty's "Primitivism and Modernization: Assessing the Relationship," 1–13, a very satisfying discussion of the complex relationship between the modern and the primitive in American religious history. See also Richard T. Hughes and C. Leonard Allen, *Illusions of Innocence: Protestant Primitivism in America, 1630–1875* (Chicago: University of Chicago Press, 1988).

17. Grant Wacker, "Playing for Keeps: The Primitivist Impulse in Early Pentecostalism," in *The American Quest for the Primitive Church*, ed. Richard T. Hughes (Urbana: University of Illinois Press, 1988), 196–219. Wacker complicated his portrayal of Pentecostalism in his essay "Searching for Eden with a Satellite Dish," in *The Primitive Church in the Modern World*, 139–66. In this essay, and in his subsequent history of early Pentecostalism, *Heaven Below* (2001), Wacker defined Pentecostalism as the productive tension between a "primitivist" and "pragmatic" impulse. "The genius of the Pentecostal movement," Wacker

writes, "lay in its ability to hold to seemingly incompatible impulses in productive tension."
It is this tension that also fed Wacker's ultimate description of Pentecostals as "modern
Americans." See the introduction to *Heaven Below: Early Pentecostals and American Culture*
(Cambridge, Mass.: Harvard University Press, 2001), particularly 11–14.

18. For a summary bibliography of scholarly literature analyzing glossolalia, see Watson E. Mills, *Speaking in Tongues: A Guide to Research on Glossolalia* (Grand Rapids, Mich.:
William B. Eerdmans, 1986).

19. Here I rely heavily on Wacker, *Heaven Below.* In addition, see Robert M. Anderson,
Vision of the Disinherited: The Making of American Pentecostalism (Peabody, Mass.: Hendrickson, 1979); Nils Bloch-Hoell, *The Pentecostal Movement: Its Origin, Development and
Distinctive Character* (New York: Humanities Press, 1964); Edith Blumhofer, *Restoring the
Faith: The Assemblies of God, Pentecostalism, and American Culture* (Urbana: University of
Illinois Press, 1993); Harvey Cox, *Fire from Heaven: The Rise of Pentecostal Spirituality and
the Reshaping of Religion in the 21st Century* (Reading, Mass.: Addison-Wesley, 1995);
James R. Goff, *Fields White unto Harvest: Charles F. Parham and the Missionary Origins of
Pentecostalism* (Fayetteville: University of Arkansas Press, 1988); David Edwin Harrell, *All
Things Are Possible: The Healing and Charismatic Revivals in Modern America* (Bloomington: Indiana University Press, 1975); Donald Miller, *Reinventing American Protestantism: Christianity in the New Millennium* (Berkeley: University of California Press, 1997);
and Vinson Synan, *The Holiness-Pentecostal Tradition: Charismatic Movements in the Twentieth Century* (Grand Rapids, Mich.: William B. Eerdmans, 1997).

20. Black rhetoric occasionally mirrored these primitive manipulations, indicting
white mobs for their bestial postures in the lynching ritual. However, as Mia Bay points
out, there is no white analogy to the "black beast," and the majority of scourges by blacks
against white behavior were posited ironically to mock purportedly "civilized" men and
did not indict whites as "primitive." The "primitive" was reserved for a blackened actor;
"uncivilized" was the worst epithet Ida Wells-Barnett or Walter White could conjure to
swipe the opposite. Nevertheless, this confluence of primitive talk is indicative of a particularly chauvinistic moment of civilizational self-promotion, when the desire to distinguish self from other emerged from individual psychology and into newspaper headlines, political arguments, and newly constructed social sciences. See Mia Bay, *The White
Image in the Black Mind: African-American Ideas about White People, 1830–1925* (New
York: Oxford University Press, 2000).

21. Ann Douglas, *Terrible Honesty: Mongrel Manhattan in the 1920s* (New York:
Farrar, Strauss and Giroux, 1995), 272.

22. Frederick Morgan Davenport, *Primitive Traits in Religious Revivals: A Study in
Mental and Social Evolution* (New York: Macmillan, 1917), viii, ix, 27, and 31.

23. Antliff and Leighton, "Primitive," 170.

24. Carl G. Jung, "Your Negroid and Indian Behavior," *Forum* 83, no. 4 (April 1930): 196.

25. Davenport, *Primitive Traits*, 45, 54, 50, and 59.

26. See Jean-Jacques Rousseau, *Discourse on the Inequalities of Men* (1754) and
Maurice Cranston, *The Noble Savage: Jean-Jacques Rousseau, 1754–1762* (Chicago: University of Chicago Press, 1999).

27. William Hannibal Thomas, *The American Negro: What He Was, What He Is, and What He May Become* (New York: Macmillan, 1901), 137, 149, and 129. Charles T. Walker published *A Sequel to "The American Negro"; A Reply to William Hannibal Thomas, Author of a Book Recently Published by the McMillan Company Called "The American Negro"* (New York, 1901?). See also William Hannibal Thomas, "Characteristics of Negro Christianity," *Quarterly Review of the United Brethren* 8, no. 3 (July 1897): 217–30. *The American Negro* was understandably not well received by blacks. Thomas's racial reductions drew the ire of such black intellectuals as Booker T. Washington, W. E. B. Du Bois, and Charles W. Chesnutt. Following the publication of *The American Negro*, Thomas spent the rest of his life in relative obscurity; he worked as a janitor in Columbus, Ohio, until his death in 1935. For more on Thomas, see John David Smith, *Black Judas: William Hannibal Thomas and The American Negro* (Athens: University of Georgia Press, 2000).

28. Robert E. Park, "The Conflict and Fusion of Cultures with Special Reference to the Negro," *Journal of Negro History* 4, no. 2 (April 1919): 120, 123, and 126. For more commentaries on religion within the first twenty years of the journal, see also R. A. Carter, "What the Negro Church Has Done," *Journal of Negro History* 11, no. 1 (January 1926): 1–7; Rufus E. Clement, "The Church School as a Social Factor in Negro Life," *Journal of Negro History* 12, no. 1 (January 1927): 5–12; Luther P. Jackson, "Evaluation and Conclusions," *Journal of Negro History* 16, no. 2 (April 1931): 234–39; and G. Cecil Weimer, "Christianity and the Negro Problem," *Journal of Negro History* 16, no. 1 (January 1931): 67–78. Note also Newbell N. Puckett, "Religious Folk-Beliefs of Whites and Negroes," *Journal of Negro History* 16, no. 1 (January 1931): 35; this was a redaction of Puckett's *Folk Beliefs of the Southern Negro* (Chapel Hill: University of North Carolina Press, 1926).

29. L. W. Kyles, "The Contribution of the Negro to the Religious Life of America," *Journal of Negro History* 11, no. 1 (January 1926): 14.

30. W. E. B. Du Bois, *The Souls of Black Folk: Essays and Sketches* (Chicago: A.C. McClurg & Co., 1903); Carter Godwin Woodson, *The History of the Negro Church* (Washington, D.C.: Associated Publishers, 1921); Benjamin E. Mays and Joseph William Nicholson, *The Negro's Church* (New York: Institute of Social and Religious Research, 1933). Recent scholarship on W. E. B. Du Bois has attempted to complicate his position on the study of black religion, suggesting that he sought not to unify the experience of African Americans but to encourage more local congregational scholarship. See Edward Blum, "The Soul of W. E. B. Du Bois," *Philosophia Africana* 7, no. 2 (August 2004): 1–15; Ibid., "Religion and the Sociological Imagination of W. E. B. Du Bois," *Sociation Today* 3, no. 1 (Spring 2005), www.ncsociology.org/sociationtoday/v31/blum.htm; and Curtis Evans, "W. E. B. Du Bois: Interpreting Religion and the Problem of the Negro Church," *Journal of the American Academy of Religion* 75, no. 2 (June 2007): 268–97.

31. Park, "Conflict and Fusion of Cultures," 129.

32. Nell Irwin Painter, *Sojourner Truth, A Life, A Symbol* (New York: W. W. Norton, 1996).

33. Janice Hamlet, "Fannie Lou Hamer: The Unquenchable Spirit of the Civil Rights Movement," *Journal of Black Studies* 26 (May 1996): 571.

34. David L. Chappell, *A Stone of Hope: Prophetic Religion and the Death of Jim Crow* (Chapel Hill: University of North Carolina Press, 2004), 73.

35. Kay Mills, *This Little Light of Mine: The Life of Fannie Lou Hamer* (New York: Dutton Books, 1993), 17.

36. Mills, *This Little Light of Mine*, 21 and 22.

37. Kay Griffin-Juechter, "Fannie Lou Hamer: From Sharecropper to Freedom Fighter" (M.A. thesis, Sarah Lawrence College, 1990), 77.

38. Janice Knight, "Fannie Lou Hamer: The Unquenchable Spirit of the Civil Rights Movement," *Journal of Black Studies* 26 (May 1996): 566.

39. Griffin-Juechter, "Fannie Lou Hamer," 80.

40. Chana Kai Lee, *For Freedom's Sake: The Life of Fannie Lou Hamer* (Urbana: University of Illinois Press, 2000), 2.

41. Lee, *For Freedom's Sake*, 43.

42. Charles Marsh, *God's Long Summer: Stories of Faith and Civil Rights* (Princeton, N.J.: Princeton University Press, 1997), 25.

43. For contemporary attempts to historcize the "Black Church," see Curtis Evans, "The Burden of Black Religion: Representing the Race and Enlisting the Black Churches in the Nation's Racial Struggle" (Ph.D. diss., Harvard University, 2005); Laurie Maffly-Kipp, "Mapping the World, Mapping the Race: The Negro Race History, 1874–1915," *Church History* 64, no. 4 (December 1995): 610–26.

44. C. Eric Lincoln and Lawrence H. Mamiya, *The Black Church in the African American Experience* (Durham, N.C.: Duke University Press, 1990).

NINE · Turning African Americans into Rational Actors: The Important Legacy of Fauset's Functionalism

CAROLYN ROUSE

Because the American Negro's experience in other institutional or "secular" forms is limited, the one institution with which he is closely identified tends to act as a channel for various kinds of expression. Thus the Negro leader finds in the church a mechanism preeminently suited to the needs of leadership along numerous lines. It seems reasonable to suppose that many of these leadership expressions would not develop within the framework of the religious experience of the Negro if the outlets for expression in other institutionalized life in our culture were more normal.

—ARTHUR HUFF FAUSET

Most scholars are aware that *Black Gods of the Metropolis: Negro Religious Cults of the Urban North* challenged anthropologist Melville Herskovits's cultural continuity thesis, but few consider the merits of Fauset's functionalist counterargument. In this quote from his summary of findings, Fauset claims that there are innate and necessary forms of leadership expression that blacks are only allowed to perform in the "church" (representing African American beliefs and practices broadly). Later in his summary he depicts the leadership and social networking encouraged within the church as a "normal urge" that can contribute to the "advancement of the group."[1] Put simply, the black church promotes group and individual survival through the cultivation of leadership and networking.

Functionalism was developed in the 1920s by one of the founders of British anthropology, Bronislaw Malinowski. As a theoretical approach to cultural interpretation, functionalism attempts to uncover how cultural beliefs and practices promote individual survival.[2] In the 1940s sociologists and anthropologists began shifting the theoretical focus away from how cultural institutions increase individual survival and began to consider instead the contributions of culture to social reproduction. This theoretical paradigm is known as structural-functionalism. Until the 1970s structural-functionalism competed with structuralism and neo-Marxism as a dominant theoretical approach in anthropology. Since the 1970s, interpretivism, which relies on what Clifford Geertz describes as "thick description," has eclipsed other paradigms within anthropology but not to the exclusion of earlier theoretical approaches, including structural-functionalism.[3]

My point is not to expound on each paradigm, but to note how far anthropology has come since it embraced functionalism in the 1920s and 1930s. The strict functionalism employed by Malinowski in which he connects Trobriand Islander practices to physical survival has been critiqued for reducing culture to digestion. Our physical survival and the reproduction of our social institutions simply validate what we already know about the world and turn explanations for why we do things into tautologies. Functionalism is not missing from anthropology; only now we do not view cultures as rational articulations of a will to live. Only a small fraction of cultural practices and beliefs support physical survival; the rest is superfluous.[4] Far more important to anthropologists today is an understanding of how the things we *think* we need have more to do with making sense of our world than with physical reproduction.

Fauset argues that cult affiliation functioned as an adaptive strategy for African American migrants in the North. In the South there existed structurally mediated methods, problematic or not, for social advancement that allowed blacks to endure segregation. In contrast, northern urban centers lacked the white paternalism and economic opportunities that blacks were adept at exploiting in the South. Fauset claims that the South offered relatively more economic opportunities but fewer opportunities for the acquisition of other forms of capital—namely educational—than the North. Fauset cleverly casts conditions in the North as "all head and no body."[5]

Even though today it is easy to dismiss functionalism as reductionistic, functionalism served three very important purposes within Fauset's text. First, functionalism stands in direct opposition to race essentialism. Functionalism locates social and cultural practices in material culture and therefore rejects the idea that cultural practices are the residue of some afunctional historical essence. As Sylvester Johnson notes, by locating racial identity as a response to present circumstances Fauset repositions race as ethnicity. Second, functionalism asserts that cultural practices support basic human needs, an argument that necessarily turns Trobriand Islanders or African American cult followers into rational actors. Like utilitarianism, functionalism presumes that people act rationally. Third, Fauset does not differentiate the secular from the religious—an assumption that shapes his methodological and theoretical approach to his field. At the time he wrote *Black Gods of the Metropolis*, "cult" members were often depicted as brainwashed sociopaths who lacked intelligence. By refusing to delineate the secular from the religious and by utilizing the anthropological disciplinary approach known as cultural relativity, Fauset recovered the humanity of the other.

Fauset's functionalist framing of black religious practice was radical and disrupted conversations taking place on what we might now call the Right and Left. Fauset described five "cults" in Philadelphia in the mid-twentieth century. He listed origin, organization, membership, finance, sacred text, beliefs, ritual, and finally practices. The consistency of Fauset's survey approach to each cult allows the reader to compare the sects. It also makes his anthropological research seem more objective and removed from race politics. Described as testimonies, the conversion narratives that open each chapter are enticing ethnographic snapshots of a world of suffering made better by faith. The converts interviewed include a man whose wife's pregnancies and subsequent miscarriages made her so sick she almost died several times. Other testimonies come from a woman who lost her baby to "teething" and a syphilitic man who lived most of his seventy years in physical pain. These well-chosen vignettes reveal such suffering, mundane and tragic, that the reader does not question why these people converted. For Fauset, religious conversion is a functional response to suffering.

But why one faith over another? And why are women overrepresented in church membership and attendance in Fauset's study? In this chapter I want to address the aspects of African American conversion that are not captured using a functionalist approach. There is something to be gained by a more detailed look at the messy data not easily accounted for in survey methods or functionalist theory. Particularly for my work on gender and religion, interpretivism (an analysis of symbols and meaning) and discourse analysis (a social constructivist approach to language and culture) are far more useful than functionalism or structural-functionalism for explaining why women convert. Writing about African American converts to Islam, I have had to find ways to explain why co-wives stayed with an unemployed and extremely abusive husband. These women were not poorly educated, and they had extensive knowledge of the Qur'an and Sunnah, or the traditions of the prophet Muhammad. I have had to try to make sense of a woman's decision to continue to frequent a *masjid*, or mosque, where men publicly sanctioned and ridiculed her for being outspoken.[6] From a functionalist perspective, in the United States women gain very little materially from converting to Islam, and some even lose the support of their families and friends. So why do African American women and men convert to Islam?

In addressing this question, I want to explore Fauset's findings from the vantage of late twentieth-century converts to Sunni Islam in Los Angeles. Many African Americans in South Central Los Angeles migrated from the South and Midwest. Much like Philadelphia in the 1940s, economic opportunities for blacks in South Central are few and educational opportunities are shrinking. In this respect, my interlocutors are similar, although admittedly not the same, as Fauset's interlocutors. For Fauset the conversion stories provide a rationale for why people convert. But conversion narratives are more than just rationales. Within them one gets a sense of religious interpretation, gender roles, social suffering, individual suffering, the borders of the faith community, and the philosophy of the everyday, otherwise known as phenomenology.

In the ethnography that follows, I describe an interaction between an African American male and female convert. This interaction demonstrates that men and women often convert to Islam for very different reasons and that we cannot take residence, social economic level, or race for granted as researchers. The interaction between this man and woman demonstrate that people who fit into the same demographic profile may have very different conceptual universes. Conversion is not really about functionalism in the sense of physical survival, but about how people choose to function given the circumstances of their lives.

South Central Los Angeles

After much debate, in February 2007, Mayor Antonio Villaraigosa and Police Chief William Bratton named the eleven most violent gangs in Los Angeles. Five of these gangs are identified as African American and six as Latino. Currently there are anywhere from 720 to 1,200 gangs, and anywhere from 20,000 to 80,000 members.[7]

In 2006, there were 478 murders in Los Angeles; 56 percent were gang related. Without exception, the most violent African American gangs control areas within and adjacent to South Central Los Angeles, which is just south of downtown and east of the 405 freeway.[8] About 70 percent of blacks in South Central are poor or lower-middle class. The average family income hovers about 50 percent above the poverty level, and the majority of children live with single parents.

Polemic explanations for why these gangs exist usually focus on the family (single-headed households), personal responsibility, or structure (poverty, poor schools, etc.). All these explanations have some merit and scholars often take sides, favoring one argument over another. But for an ethnographer, these connections always seem too neat in light of the fact that the experiences that form us are varied, often contradictory, and most importantly messy. One must remember that for anthropologists, when it comes to creating conceptual categories, gangs and college fraternities belong in the same conceptual universe: tribal affiliation, rites of initiation, occasional violence, and gender exclusivity.

The stale polemics that assert a causal link between gangs and family, personal responsibility, or structure are often unrecognizable by the people they claim to be speaking about. People decry, for example, teenage childbearing, but the data often contradict easy assertions of causation. In 2004 Arline Geronimus described how teenage childbearing in high-poverty urban areas in the United States does not correlate with greater infant mortality, poorer academic performance in their children, or even reduced lifetime earnings.[9] Poor African American women are presumed to have, in the words of cultural critic John McWhorter, "open-ended" numbers of children in order to collect more welfare benefits.[10] In fact, since the War on Poverty began in the middle 1960s, the fertility rate among all native-born American women has decreased from about 3.1 to about 1.8 children per woman. Is the causal link welfare, or is it feminism, education, more employment opportunities for women, or simply the increasing expense of raising children?

In addition to the conservative explanations that focus on individual responsibility and family values, structural explanations often ring hollow for the inner-city folks they claim to speak for. The structures are cast as inanimate obstacles obstructing the path to a better life. They fail to acknowledge that the inner-city poor have a relationship to these obstacles, often fraught, but nevertheless a relationship with individual police officers, social workers, and school teachers. For the poor, the idea that structures are simply immobile, inanimate obstacles blocking social empowerment is a quaint theory.

The spiritual, intellectual, and emotional lacunae filled by affiliation with violent and nonviolent gangs are perhaps best understood by attending the 11,493 churches and about eight *masjids* in South Central. It is in these spaces that men and women come to find new ways to understand and adapt to the struggles and opportunities that frame their lives. Rather than focus on a single narrative of religious conversion, reconversion, or inspiration, I have chosen to focus on an interaction that took place between a male and a female convert to Islam around the question of gangs.

Finding Sister Yusra

In the fall of 2002, I went to Los Angeles in search of Sister Yusra. Sister Yusra's daughter, Hind, had taken my video production class during the summer of 1991. After filming around South Central, I would drop Hind off with her mother. Talkative and full of energy, Yusra and I would often manage to spend the next several hours visiting different African fabric stores, talking in her small shop where she made West African–style clothing appropriately modest for devout Muslim women, or eating in a local black-owned vegetarian mom-and-pop diner where we talked about her plans to start an import/export business that she would run from Guinea, West Africa. These experiential tangents I documented on video and in photographs with the vague understanding that perhaps Hind could use them for the video course.

I realized the value of these visual documents after deciding that a photograph I took at an outdoor event at a *masjid* would make a terrific cover photo for my book. Dark-skinned, Yusra dressed in beautiful, flowing clothing that complimented her angular and quite stunning face. She never smiled or posed for the camera. Instead, the images and footage I captured of her showed an unguarded, unapologetic Afrocentric Muslima. Her characteristic self-confidence made her seem African rather than African American. There was only one problem with my desire to use her photograph—I needed Yusra's permission.

The last time Yusra and I had spoken she was on her way to run an import/export business out of Guinea. After the *masjid* we both frequented for very different reasons was torn down following the 1993 earthquake, I did not see Yusra. I imagined she was in Guinea living the life of an American expat in a country full of Muslims, thankfully not burdened by the crime and violence that punctuated life in South Central Los Angeles.

I decided to go to Los Angeles and visit African fabric stores in hopes that perhaps a store owner imported Yusra's wares. After talking with several shopkeepers I had accumulated a number of vague assurances that "so-and-so knows her." I was sent on several wild-goose chases that should have made me wonder why I flew three thousand miles with no assurances of success. But I did not have much time to worry about the frivolousness of my pursuit because it was Friday, which meant I had a chance to visit the *masjid*.

It did not take long to locate Yusra at the *masjid*. Nour, dressed in conservative *hijab*, or head scarf, told me, "We run a school together just down the street." How could she be so close and yet for ten years I didn't see her? What happened to Yusra's dreams? Was she disappointed? These were just some of the questions I had.

After the Friday *khutbah*, or lecture, I camped out in my car in the parking lot of the church just across the street from Yusra and Nour's school. I finally spotted her. She looked as though not a year had passed since we last spoke. She was still beautiful, petite, and dressed in a dark blue West African caftan. She recognized me immediately, although I cannot say I had aged as well. With the students ranging in age from two to eleven gathered around her, Yusra unlocked the gate protecting the front door of the school.

The school was a small, dark, cheap apartment rental converted into a classroom. The classroom space measured only ten by ten feet. There was a small bathroom, and a five-by-five-foot room where she kept supplies. The dumpiness of the space was masked in part by the order of the objects filling the space: the desks, shelves, and wall posters. The classroom was crammed with desks for ten girls. Two of the students were her own children and one was Hind's two-year-old daughter. Hind was now a bank manager, and she drove a white Ford Expedition while her mother drove a van with rusted-out holes in the bottom. The children enjoyed observing the road through these holes when Yusra drove them home every day.

Soon after meeting Yusra I learned that she did not attend the *masjid* just down the street because it concerned itself too much with the social issues of the day rather than Qur'anic readings and other activities she associated with orthodoxy. Yusra, who had grown up in Little Rock, Arkansas, was initially drawn into the faith by members of the Nation of Islam. At fourteen she began talking to the bean-pie salesmen on the streets of Little Rock. A self-described wild girl, Yusra began replacing her partying with Qur'anic study groups.

When I met Yusra at the age of thirty-five, she did not draw a sharp distinction between Islam and the Nation of Islam, and therefore did not mark a time when she transitioned to Sunni Islam. Nevertheless, she sought orthopraxy and measured her beliefs and practices against those of the *ummah*, or worldwide Muslim community. Most notably, she did not celebrate Kwanzaa or Martin Luther King Jr.'s birthday.

At thirty-five, Yusra had four children ranging in age from seven to fifteen. She was married to a postal worker, and they seemed to be roommates rather than partners. When I met up with her again she had already been married and divorced with three more children ages five to eleven, and she was on her third marriage to a man ten years her junior. She was pregnant again, but within a month she had had a miscarriage.

In 1991 I interviewed Yusra on video, asking her to respond to a comment her daughter Hind made during one of our video production classes. In my class the students described how they believed it was harder for girls to be Muslim than boys. I asked Yusra to help me understand what Hind meant by this. Defensively, Yusra dismissed the comment saying, "Hind hasn't been married. Hind has never had children. Hind has never suffered discrimination. How does she know what is and is not difficult?" For Yusra, Islam is pragmatic and informs her about how to cope with her marginal economic status, the violence in her community, racism, marriage, and raising children.

What strikes me when reviewing my old videos is how profoundly her faith informs her daily practice. Like her daughter Hind who skipped two grades, Yusra is smart, and she makes a direct connection between her exegesis and her agency. When I met up with her again, these qualities were consistent. Most notably, her faith gave her the strength to hold up the sky. More than half of the students were not paying her school's minuscule tuition, and yet as poor as she was she was donating food on a regular basis to two of her students from Fiji. Her purpose in life was to help make the lives of the people around her a bit better. She did not discriminate, and she connected her actions to her understanding of her faith.

What do these life details have to do with issues related to gender and Islam in the inner city? I paint a picture of Yusra not because she is representative of all African American women converts, but because she embodies a somewhat common ethos. In particular, she tries to divorce Islam from race or tribe, and she uses Islam to confront everyday struggles particularly related to family, career, and community.

Gangs and Male Conversion

My initial request to use Yusra's photo was met with tremendous ambivalence and in true entrepreneurial spirit Yusra asserted, "What can you do for me in return?" I withdrew my request and asked instead if I could spend time observing her school. It was during these observations that the disconnect between African American male and female converts became most striking to me.

During my second day of observations, an extraordinary exchange took place between Yusra and her guest Hashim, who was invited to speak to the children.

Hashim was a former gangbanger, ex-convict, and convert to Islam. While the majority of male converts to Islam are not ex-gangbangers or ex-convicts, there are a substantial number who find their way to Sunni Islam while in prison. For Elijah Muhammad, black people were prisoners of white supremacy, and this perspective shaped his understanding of Islam. The discourses that inspired Malcolm Little while in prison in the 1940s echo today in the religious interpretations of many African American Sunni Muslim men.

The speaker, Hashim, was handsome and came dressed in loose dress pants with a nice long-sleeved rayon button-up, which he kept untucked. He seemed comfortable and relaxed before he began a speech that he had undoubtedly repeated numerous times.

Yusra introduced him as someone who could help the children learn to read the graffiti and other gang symbols in order to become more aware of their surroundings. Hashim started, "The topic is gangs. How many y'all know about Unity T.W.O? Unity T.W.O is a gang prevention and intervention organization." The children remain silent. "Remember the riots," he said, trying to jostle the memories of a class full of children all but one of whom was born after 1992. "Remember the riots behind Rodney King? But before that I'm going to go a little farther than that because a lot of people that didn't affiliate with the Crips and Bloods, they wanted to see if the Crips and Bloods would come together to stop killing each other, right." African American Muslims have a small but significant presence in various gang prevention programs in Los Angeles.

"So, Crips and Bloods . . . at first it was the Nation of Islam, then it was the Black Panthers, then it was called the Baby Cribs. It was . . . instead of a *P*, it was a *B*. What that meant was California Revolution Independent People. So, the Crip and Blood thing was a thing to keep the youngsters like myself from understanding what's going on as far as our history. As far as our destination, as far as our future."

Yusra looks puzzled and impatient. Then she interrupts him saying, "Okay, now, why did you become a blue?"

Hashim corrects her, "Why did I become a Blood? That's the area my mother lived in."

Yusra responds, "So what do you have to do to be a Blood?"

Surprisingly Hashim says, "By being yourself."

Needing clarification, Yusra probes deeper. "OK, say for instance, I live over in the area of West Los Angeles in the area where the Playboys are. So, now because my son lives in the area, he has to be a Playboy? Is that what you're saying? Because your mother lived in . . ."

Hashim interrupts, "You don't have to be. You can be from a tribe across town, but it depend on if he hang right there. If he hang with the dudes in that area, and one of the older guys like his style, like his profile, like his get down, then he's the next soldier to be recruited."

Once Yusra establishes that membership is based upon matrilocal tribal identification, she asks what gang members do. "Hang out" is his answer.

Frustrated, Yusra asks him why Unity One and T.W.O. were necessary if all they do is hang out. "So, what do you do? I mean, what do Crips and Bloods do?"

Hashim responds, "What do you mean? As far as what?"

Yusra: "I mean, we want to know their lifestyle."

Hashim: "The lifestyle is we do everything you do. Have picnics, BBQs, go to parties, you go to clubs, dance, eat, you know, make babies, pay rent."

Pushing Hashim, Yusra says, "OK, but what I'm saying is are they good, are they bad?"

Hashim finally understands that he has not been invited to paint gangs as dynamic social organizations, "It's both. It's both. To me, it's a misguidance of energy. Because see, a lot of people don't understand it's like a war. Like, for instance, you go in a party, or you go in a store, and you got two tribes in a store. They don't have that understanding or the knowledge to really communicate because they pride is on the line. So, the shooting take place. And, there ain't no talking, there ain't no rationalization."

More relaxed, Yusra asks, "But, why do they want to kill each other?"

"Because that was part of the plan, that was part of the . . . uh . . . the power system plot, to keep us from becoming men. We young men, and we want to identify what our strength that's within us. The history that we been taught, it wasn't relating to us. It wasn't relating to the environment."

With a furrowed brow Yusra replies, "I'm forty-five years old, and when I see Crip and Blood the only thing that I know is that they kill each other. They have no love for each other, and they kill innocent people in the communities. So, when you say it's good and bad, I'm confused."

Hashim responds: "It's both because they are the protector of the community too. It's just like a Muslim when they say, 'Well, Muslims blowing up buildings, killing innocent people. How are they good and bad?' Well, the good is that when they first started, it was unity. They wasn't attacking just everybody. You was getting attacked because you were messing with somebody's mamma, or you're doing something negative to this community. But as the drugs came and the guns came in the community, then it became negative. It became disloyalty because everybody wanted some money, everybody wanted the power. Now, you hear a lot of innocent people got killed. It goes back to lack of knowledge because, remember, you got the leaders in jail, or all the leaders killed. Who's there to teach the youngsters? Who is there to teach the young men on how to be a man? The reason Unity T.W.O. and Unity One came, is because we've been rehabilitated. We've been educated to come back to talk to our people. Like in the Qu'ran it said, 'Allah will raise up somebody amongst themselves to go back and teach their people.' Like, I ain't no prophet or none of that, but Allah raised me up to come back and teach my own. See, that's what changed me, Islam. Islam prepared me to come back out here to the streets." Hashim then spends about ten minutes discussing the signs used by gangs, from the clothing to tattoos to graffiti signs to the use of bling to attract girls.

Hashim eventually shows a picture of himself at twelve just before he went to prison for ten years for homicide. Then he shows a picture of his mom. He warns the children: "Respect your mother because you only get one and she only live one time. My mother was killed. She got shot in the back of the head, and that's her right here [points to picture]. Really, you young ladies should really respect your mother. Don't talk back to her, listen to her because she got a lot to tell you and she got a lot to teach you. And, if you listen to her you'll be successful, you'll have a good life if you listen to her. But, you be hardheaded, and you be disobedient, you wind up in jail, or hurt, or you wind up in these superficial tribes. Your mother and father is there to teach you how to be a real tribal member. Now that my mother passed, I hear her words ring through my ears. And that's what make me be successful, and that's what made me change. Since I've changed my life, Allah blessed me to go a lot of places and to meet . . . how many y'all know Russell Simmons?"

After passing around pictures of himself with Russell Simmons in New York City he says, "We need the young black men. That's the only way our future will manifest itself. How many of you know what 'manifestation' means? Manifestation means coming to . . . like, Martin Luther King. How many y'all heard Martin Luther King say, 'I might not get to the promised land, but we shall get to the promised land'?"

Hashim converted in prison. Three weeks after being released, his mother was shot. He could have retaliated, but, as he put it, all of his homies had already been buried and he knew that if he kept going that would be his destiny.

Yusra, checking his sincerity, asks, "Are you married?"

"Yeah."

"You got children?"

"Yeah."

"How many?"

"Actually, biologically, I've got one. But, since I've been married, I've been raising her three kids since I've been home. That's my decision. When I was doing time, I saw that there's a lot of sisters out here raising kids by themselves. So, I said it don't matter if I meet a sister that got kids. I'm going to handle my business. So, I stepped up to the plate."

Now trusting Hashim, Yusra's pointed questioning becomes clearer as she opens up. She explains that her son is a wannabe gangster and she does not understand his need to be cool. "One time recently my son was coming home and it was late. And, I was telling him, don't walk. Of course, you know, he's hardheaded and he's going to walk. Right. And he got shot, in the hand, right. So, I'm thinking now does that mean he's in a gang, or does that mean somebody was trying to . . ."

Hashim reassures her, "No, you can get shot and be innocent. Civilians get shot. That don't mean he was in a gang. That just means they was popping at him."

"Where I live in Culver City, when I first moved there, it looked like a nice area. Still, nobody ever bothered me or anything. Then, when I moved away, I found out that there was a gang."

"Yeah, some communities keep it under control. Like I said, when the Crips and Bloods first started they had it under control. After a while it just got ruined. It's just like, 'Well, why our community don't look clean like Beverly Hills?' That's because your people is not keeping your community clean. The people not telling, 'Hey, we watching you with all that gang writing and all that trash you're throwing down on the ground and all that stuff.' Like Beverly Hills, they are watching their community."

A girl asks about girl gang members and Hashim describes them as supporters of the tribe. He said, "They act normal just like you. They just do things that you don't do. They probably drink, smoke weed, and party, you know. Then, you got some of them changing their lives too, where they don't drink, smoke, they don't party. They just do the motherly thing. They just support their man. Or maybe support the tribe like, cook or whatever their husband ask them to do. I think that everybody in this whole world is part of a tribe, even Muslims."

Yusra reacts strongly, "I don't agree with that because when I die, I'm not going to be identified with a tribe. That's like a question Allah won't ask me. Our foundation is Islam. Allah ain't going to ask me about no color, no tribe, none of that."

Hashim abstracts to the global level, "But, Muslims and Christians are killing each other right now today. That's gangbanging."

Yusra counters with religious exegesis, "Well, in Islam you can't fight. You fight with those who fight with you. Now, Islam, it tells you, 'Do not kill women and children and innocent people.' Now, if you do that, then that's on your soul. War is permissible, I believe in that. Islam is not against that."

Hashim challenges Yusra's definition of war: "Well, if that's the case, then you can't be against Crips and Bloods then. Just because you don't understand it, but they at war. You got Muslims killing a lot of innocent people."

Very disturbed about the direction Hashim has taken the conversation, Yusra states emphatically, "We're talking about Crips and Bloods, we're not talking about Muslims right now. It's not the same thing. You can't mix that. We're trying to learn about Crips and Bloods, OK. We have discussions in our class about Muslims killing and all that at different times. So, to tie it in is irrelevant."

Defending his statement, Hashim says, "I study Islam too, but I hear other people fake Islam. They try to twist Islam." Then Hashim argues that Muslims who justify killing others are not different from gangbangers. "You just doing it on some religious things. But, these dudes is doing . . . this is their religion. Like all these tattoos. This was my God. Allah wasn't my God. I didn't even know nothing about him. This was my God. This was my wife, this was my gun, this was my God, this was my money." After describing how he grew to love everything about his gang, then Hashim says that when people stray from the path of worshipping God, violence and negativity happen.

Condemning both South Central and his religious community, Hashim laments, "I don't see no business. I see the same brothers talking the same talk. I don't see no community across the world, or in South Central. I see everybody talk that crazy talk, and then they go back to Islam." Then he repeats that he hears a lot of Muslim brothers justifying violence in the same way his gang brothers justified violence.

Fauset argues that the Black Church, broadly defined, is functional because it provides an outlet for various expressions of leadership not otherwise available in "secular" institutions. Through the enactment of this "basic urge" the group advances itself in politics, business, and social reform.[11] Hashim would agree. Hashim believes that tribal affiliation exists in secular and religious life, and that tribes are a source for good. They can mobilize people to improve communities and can lead to community sustainability and growth, as in the case of Beverly Hills or Culver City. What leadership requires is the correct consciousness, or truth (*haq*), which Hashim finds in Islam but not necessarily in Muslims.

Hashim identifies with the instrumental or functional aspects of his faith.

Throughout his life Hashim has identified closely with a group of men: the Bloods, Unity T.W.O., and his Muslim brothers. The last two affiliations, which are themselves linked, have brought him speaking engagements, income, and valuable connections. Equating his religious practices with his secular practices does not strike him as taboo or problematic. Instead, the wisdom of the Qur'an is reflected in the fact that it acknowledges and articulates ways of ethically channeling the hearts of men, or what social scientists might call human nature.

Yusra, in contrast, identifies as an individual. Yusra frames Islam as a faith disconnected from location and tribe. As a system of symbols and meanings, Islam provides Yusra with, among other things, rationales for choosing poverty and generosity over material comfort, for leaving her husbands, for embracing a new race consciousness, and for dressing and eating the way she does. Having been disappointed by the leadership in the African American Sunni Muslim community and by her husbands, she identifies with the expressive rather than the instrumental aspects of her faith. She refuses to connect herself to people whom she believes fail to uphold the tenets of Islam, and she makes personal choices regardless of how the community might respond.

For a number of reasons, African American women tend to identify with Islam in ways that men do not. This is reflected in patterns of attendance. While female converts often use the mosque solely as a place of worship, the men use it as a place to worship and network. Whether or not women actually want a more pronounced leadership role remains a question. I know women who would like to use their business skills to manage mosques that are poorly run but know that their leadership would not be taken seriously. On the other hand, I know many women who are overwhelmed with jobs and children and prefer not to be involved. For reasons ranging from the pragmatic (maintaining a household) to the biological (gender roles), most African American female converts to Islam approach Islam differently than most men. Similar to Yusra, women often treat their faith as a personal journey, one of developing disciplinary practices that bring one closer to God. In the pages of *Azizah*, a magazine touted as the "voice for Muslim Women," the women featured seem to embrace independence and prefer to define their own spiritual trajectory.

Thinking as a functionalist, one could argue that the social mobility of black Muslim men in South Central Los Angeles is hampered by their limited education; for some, by their ex-convict status; and by racism against black men that differs from racism against black women. Black men are seen as threatening in ways that black women are not. As a result, black men often rely on social networks organized through institutions, such as the mosque, in order to increase their social and economic opportunities. Black women, on the other hand, do not have nearly the incarceration rates of men, their educational attainment is greater, and networks grow naturally out of a need for community support raising children. Therefore, women often do not rely on institutions to help them reach out to other women for support. And they do not need networks of Muslim men to help them find and retain a job. Women are often compelled by a need to put food on the table, educate their children, and secure housing. Within the inner city, women are generally not able to depend on men, and the fact that the faith does not constrain women by demanding their involvement in the community mirrors their personal lives.

The functional explanations offered by Fauset about conversion work better for explaining why men convert than why women convert and stay in the faith. But even in the case of male conversion, questions remain. For example, is it functional for a male convert to treat Islam as a patriarchal religion?[12] The divorce rate within the African American Muslim community is high and possibly higher than the African American community as a whole, and one reason women leave their husbands is that men try to assert their authority. In addition, there are a number of Christian churches in Los Angeles with connections to powerful individuals. Of what value is affiliation to a relatively small organization with very few power brokers?

Discourse analysis helps explain what Islam offers in addition to the functional benefits of group leadership. Racial disparities in wealth, income, education, incarceration, and health coupled with housing segregation in the inner city demand redress. Many poor and lower-income blacks who have experienced urban deindustrialization, racial discrimination, and all the attending ills associated with them would like to see real change. The religious organizations described by Fauset all attempted to address entrenched racism, poverty, and exclusion through faith. But many of the programs proposed by Marcus Garvey, Elijah Muhammad, and Father Divine failed to reduce racial disparities. So the organizations are not functional, but through conversion people develop new approaches to dealing with entrenched power. Conversion creates a community of people with similar political, social, and economic goals. It is through discourse that they redefine their goals, their dispositions, and their relationships to one another. The emergent discourse is not necessarily functional, but it is expressive of a group identity and shared beliefs. Religious debates often focus on how best to interpret the faith in order to empower blacks—integration versus segregation, tribalism versus greater individualism, socialism versus capitalism, and the like.

The conversation between Yusra and Hashim was not just about gangs, but about what sorts of religious dispositions are legitimate within Islam and which will further the cause of black empowerment. Yusra finds justification for her fierce independence in Islam but does not understand why her approach to Islam does not give her son the strength to ignore the gangs. Yusra's understanding and approach to Islam are essentially useless to her son, given the pressures to join a gang and the attractiveness of membership. Hashim explains to Yusra that membership in the *ummah* is another form of tribalism and that a positive Muslim tribalism can displace a negative gang tribalism.

Using very informal religious interpretation, or *ijtihad,* Yusra and Hashim develop a new appreciation for their faith. Hashim in particular broadens Yusra's exegetical borders. Until that conversation, Yusra had never recognized the benefits of tribal identity in Islam. It is through discourse that Yusra was able to see the benefits of making an effort to connect her son to Muslim boys his age. From our conversation following Hashim's presentation and departure, I realized that Yusra's change was not dramatic, but she asked me a series of questions trying to make sense of Hashim's message.

There are a number of things Yusra and Hashim share simply by converting to Islam. They share a belief in the five pillars of Islam, and they both see Islam as a counterdiscourse to mainstream discourses that they believe reproduce racial hierarchies in the United States. But, Yusra's and Hashim's knowledge of Islam is gendered. Yusra understands Islam through the lenses of womanhood, sisterhood, and motherhood, while Hashim understands it through the lenses of manhood, brotherhood, and fatherhood. Sisterhood within the Muslim community is extremely strong. Women are typically involved in extensive exchange relationships and close friendships. The worlds of Muslim women and men often orbit one another rather than intersect. It is when these worlds come together through marriage or during a school presentation that one sees how gendered the knowledge and practice of faith is.

It would be unwise to dismiss Fauset's functionalism as a theoretical relic. By repositioning race as ethnicity, showing that his subjects are rational actors, and revealing the humanity of "cult" followers, Fauset changed scholarly discussions about black religions. We could use Fauset's functionalism similarly to disrupt racist notions about black gang affiliation. That said, Fauset's conclusions are more reflective of the slightly more instrumental approach to Islam often employed by male converts as opposed to the more expressive approach to Islam often employed by female converts. In the case of both men and women, functionalism fails to explain why they continue to participate in a faith that offers very few material benefits. What interpretivism provides is a way of understanding the meaning and value African American converts assign to symbols and how that meaning system informs their everyday performances and social interactions. What discourse theory provides is a way of seeing how the community develops a shared understanding of their faith and moral universe in response to the world outside. What Fauset's functionalism does is ground those meaning systems and related social practices in a material reality.

Notes

The epigraph is from Arthur Huff Fauset, *Black Gods of the Metropolis: Negro Religious Cults of the Urban North* (1944; Philadelphia: University of Pennsylvania Press, 2002), 88.

1. Ibid., 107–108.

2. Bronislaw Malinowski, "The Group and the Individual in Functional Analysis: Personality, Organization, and Culture," in *High Points in Anthropology,* ed. Paul Bohannan and Mark Glazer (New York: Alfred Knopf, 1973), 275–93.

3. Clifford Geertz, *The Interpretation of Cultures* (New York: Basic Books, 1973).

4. J. Baudrillard, *For a Critique of the Political Economy of the Sign* (St. Louis, Mo.: Telos, 1981), 26–87.

5. Fauset, *Black Gods,* 88.

6. Carolyn Rouse, *Engaged Surrender: African-American Women and Islam* (Berkeley: University of California Press, 2004).

7. See Luke Y. Thompson, "Ganging Up on City Hall," *LA Weekly News,* March 7, 2007; Perry Crowe, "Gangland Colonoscopy," *LA City Beat,* April 13, 2006, 3; and "Los Angeles names most violent gangs despite risk of raising their profiles," February 9, 2007, www.policeone.com/gangs/articles/1211654/, accessed June 1, 2007.

8. Patrick McGreevy and Richard Winton, "200 LAPD officers target 11 violent gangs," *Los Angeles Times,* February 9, 2007, www.latimes.com/news/local/la-me-gangs9fe b09,1,624268.story, accessed June 1, 2007, and compare www.policeone.com/gangs/arti cles/1211713/.

9. Arline T. Geronimus, "Teenage Childbearing as Cultural Prism," *British Medical Bulletin* 69 (2004): 155–66.

10. NPR, "Rave, Poverty and Katrina," *Talk of the Nation,* September 22, 2005.

11. Fauset, *Black Gods,* 108–109.

12. Robert Dannin, *Black Pilgrimage to Islam* (Oxford: Oxford University Press, 2002), 189–213.

TEN · Defining the "Negro Problem" in Brazil: The Shifting Significance of Brazil's African Heritage from the 1890s to the 1940s

KELLY E. HAYES

Arthur Huff Fauset's *Black Gods of the Metropolis* was part of an extraordinary florescence of creative, intellectual, literary, and anthropological interest in the "New World Negro" in the first four decades of the twentieth century. Researchers in the United States, Brazil, and the Caribbean in this period turned their attention to various aspects of black culture in the Americas, building on the work of pioneering forebears like W. E. B. Du Bois and Carter Woodson in the United States and Nina Rodrigues in Brazil. While most analysts of *Black Gods of the Metropolis* situate the book within the social and historical context of the United States, its truly groundbreaking aspects can best be appreciated when seen against the larger backdrop of Afro-diasporan studies of the 1930s and 1940s.

As Fauset himself noted, much of the literature on New World black religions in this period focused on the presence of African cultural survivals, a framework that Fauset found inadequate for his own research. Although this approach was attractive for a number of reasons, its focus on a dehistoricized and romantic African past shifted scholarly attention away from issues of class and race particular to the American context in which these religions developed. These issues were central to Fauset's analysis in *Black Gods of the Metropolis* and for his understanding of the success of the five cult groups that were the book's subject. Further, by calling attention to the breathtaking eclecticism of Afro-American religious expression, *Black Gods of the*

Metropolis suggested that Africa was not the only alternative heritage or source of identity available to blacks in the 1930s and 1940s. Despite these important contributions, Fauset's work has languished, unknown to many students of black religions, while work that focused on the African dimensions of Afro-American religions achieved international recognition and authoritative status. An examination of the scholarly literature on black religions in Brazil helps illuminate the persuasive appeal of Africanity in transnational debates about the "New World Negro" that marked this period.

Race and the African Heritage in Brazil

As the largest importer of African slaves to the New World and the last country to finally abolish the trade, Brazil was one of the most important sites for debates about race and the significance of the New World's African heritage. In the course of the 1930s and 1940s it quickly became a "locus classicus" in the social science literature, attracting scholars from both hemispheres of the Americas and Europe, including Melville Herskovits, E. Franklin Frazier, Ruth Landes, Roger Bastide, Alfred Métraux, Jean-Paul Sartre, and Simone de Beauvoir.[1]

For many of these scholars, what was appealing about Brazil was the extent to which blacks had been able to preserve their African heritage in the context of a multiracial culture whose members seemed to live together in harmony. Most often, the comparison was to the United States, whose segregation and intolerance was invoked, explicitly or implicitly, to underscore Brazil's "racial democracy." Describing her research trip to Bahia in the late 1930s, Ruth Landes wrote: "We had heard that the large Negro population lived with ease and freedom among the general population and we wanted to know the details. We also wanted to know how that interracial situation differed from our own in the United States."[2]

Despite the absence of Jim Crow, Landes discovered that a variety of formal and informal mechanisms buttressed prejudicial attitudes about Afro-Brazilians and that race relations in Brazil were far more complex than she had thought. Although blacks "were at liberty to cultivate their African heritage" in the Afro-Brazilian religion of candomblé, Landes wrote, they were also "sick, undernourished, illiterate, and uninformed, just like poor people among them of other racial origins." She concluded that the reason was not racism per se, but "political and economic tyrannies." With little access to education or other avenues to upward social mobility, blacks had created an alternative universe in candomblé, whose "vigor and pageantry . . . were a matter of excitement and pride to the rest of Brazil too."[3]

In associating candomblé with an alternative African heritage, and the sufferings of blacks with socioeconomic rather than racial discrimination, Landes's analysis was characteristic of the work on Afro-Brazilian religions produced in the 1930s and 1940s. Since then, the idea has become commonplace that candomblé represents, as Roger Bastide put it, "a piece of Africa" in the New World, a "harmonious and coherent system of collective representations and ritual gestures" that transplanted the ancestral world of Africa to Brazilian soil.[4] When seen in its historical context, one of the most remarkable aspects of this scholarship was the striking transformation in the meanings and symbolic significance of Brazil's African heritage, once considered a fount of primitive savagery that threatened the nation's prospects for the future. By the time of Landes's fieldwork in the late 1930s, this heritage increasingly was seen as a vital contributor to Brazil's unique culture and a source of national "excitement and pride."

This transformation was prompted by a series of factors both internal and external to Brazil, including political, social, and economic changes; a growing nationalist sentiment; literary and artistic movements inspired by Brazilian folklore and popular culture; and the development of new scholarly paradigms that shifted the intellectual focus from race to culture. In this chapter, I address the latter, contrasting the scholarship on Afro-Brazilian religions produced in the 1930s and 1940s with its late nineteenth-century predecessors. Fin-de-siècle scholars understood Brazil's African heritage in protogenetic terms as an inferior and polluting menace and often referred to the degeneracy of "Negro blood," which many hoped eventually to breed out. Reversing this evaluation almost entirely, their successors of the 1930s and 1940s saw Brazil's African heritage as a cultural inheritance that had contributed positively to the nation. In both cases, the religious traditions of Afro-Brazilians were seen as privileged sites in which this African heritage was most fully preserved. As a result, the study of these religions was central to elite efforts to address the "Negro problem," that is, to evaluate the relationship of the nation's African heritage to its future.

In the next section I provide a brief overview of racial thinking in fin-de-siècle Brazil before considering in more detail the work of Nina Rodrigues, whose treatment of Afro-Brazilian religions established many of the main themes that would characterize later scholarship. A typical representative of late nineteenth-century racial thought, Rodrigues considered Afro-Brazilian religions to be an inferior form of fetishism that reflected the innate primitivity of the black race, which he considered to be incapable of civilization. For Rodrigues and his colleagues, the "Negro problem" was the threat that the nation's black blood posed for Brazil's ability to modernize.

Arthur Ramos, one of the most prominent scholars of the 1930s and 1940s, later employed much of Rodrigues's data in his own studies of Afro-Brazilian religions. Ramos's work in particular demonstrates how the key interpretative concept for understanding Brazil's African heritage shifted from race to culture in this era. Ramos's *O Negro Brasileiro* (1934) echoed many of Rodrigues's notions about the inferiority of black religions and their consequences for the nation. As his relationship with the American anthropologist Melville Herskovits developed, however, Ramos began to abandon the evolutionary hierarchy that had suffused his earlier writings on Afro-Brazilian religions, replacing it with concepts drawn from cultural anthropology.

This transformation is evident in *A Acculturação Negra no Brasil* (Black Acculturation in Brazil), a volume of collected essays published in 1942 after Ramos had returned from a series of extended visits to the United States. As its title suggests, Ramos's main concern was to reinterpret his earlier research as evidence of the acculturative process in Brazil. His introduction to the book is a striking indication of how the conceptualization of the "Negro problem" had shifted from the social Darwinist view represented by Nina Rodrigues to one based on Herskovits's theory of acculturation. In it, Ramos dedicated himself to reframing Nina Rodrigues's discourse about race as a discourse about culture: It was Rodrigues, argued Ramos, who in fact had originated the study of acculturation in Brazil. This claim required Ramos to minimize or misconstrue Rodrigues's own understanding of the "Negro problem," a strategy that obscured the racial thinking that had undergirded late nineteenth-century understandings of Brazil's African heritage.

Race, Nation, and Religion in Fin-de-Siècle Brazil

Unlike their counterparts in the United States, nineteenth-century Brazilian elites seldom justified the sociopolitical order that had been built on slavery in terms of the absolute racial inferiority of Africans. This was a comparison that was not lost on Brazilian abolitionists themselves, who, in the course of heated legislative debates over abolition, frequently defended their own assertions of Brazil's ostensible "racial harmony" through contrast with their North American counterpart. As the great abolitionist Joaquim Nabuco wrote: "[C]olor in Brazil is not, as in the United States, a social prejudice against whose persistence no character, talent, or merit can prevail."[5]

Notwithstanding Nabuco's assertion, Brazilian society throughout the slave period rested on implicitly racist assumptions of white superiority encoded within a hierarchical system in which social classification correlated highly with color: Landowners were overwhelmingly white, while slaves, laborers, tradesmen, and skilled workers were overwhelmingly black or mulatto. Indeed, the very same abolitionists who so passionately asserted Brazil's racial harmony also frequently conceived of Brazil's future as one in which the superior white element would gradually triumph through the purifying effects of miscegenation.[6]

While white and black, slave and free could coexist in relatively peaceful proximity when their interactions were regulated within a hierarchically structured system in which the superiority of the white elite was encoded in the very social order, the final abolition of slavery in 1888 altered the legal basis upon which this putative racial harmony had rested. The transformation of the black Brazilian from slave to citizen made it necessary to redefine these regulating structures, to create new markers of social distance by which relations among former slaves, former masters, and a growing mulatto class could be governed.[7]

According to Thomas Skidmore, it was precisely this transformation that marked the emergence of race as a prominent category of historical and sociological analysis—and social concern—in Brazil.[8] As the nineteenth century gave way to the twentieth, the implicit racial hierarchies that had undergirded the social order prior to abolition were increasingly expressed as concerns about the degenerate and polluting nature of the nation's "black blood" and the threat it posed to the country's future, and more particularly its ability to modernize. Especially perturbing to elites were the spiritual practices of the blacks and lower classes, felt to reflect their primitive mental state and credulity, but also the potential—in the form of black magic, or *feitiçaria*—to wreak social havoc.

In an effort to address this perceived degeneracy, intellectuals and the ruling class adopted various strategies in the late nineteenth and early twentieth centuries. Some, drawing on European theories of social Darwinism and race evolution, had the explicit aim of whitening (*branqueamento*) the population and thus assuring the nation's progress. These strategies ranged from treatises glorifying miscegenation as a way to breed out the nation's degenerate African blood, to political incentives that encouraged European immigration.[9] The latter policy eventually brought thousands of white Europeans (especially Italians and Germans) to the hinterlands of Brazil, where, it was hoped, they would both increase Brazil's economic production and mate with the natives, gradually producing a whiter—and thus more evolved—population.[10]

Other tactics, also animated by racial fears, took shape as a discourse of public health and order, focusing on Afro-Brazilians as vectors of illness, criminality, and contagion that warranted containment. For instance, various campaigns to eradicate disease and to clean up urban centers in the course of the nineteenth century had as a consequence the forced removal of Afro-Brazilian communities to the urban margins.[11] Yet other strategies sought to discipline the cultural practices of Afro-Brazilians, particularly their religious traditions. In 1890, three new provisions concerned with the "illicit" practices of medicine, magic, and curing were appended to the penal code.[12] In effect, this gave the state jurisdiction and punitive power over Afro-Brazilian religions and their practitioners, who were subject to various forms of police persecution until late in the twentieth century.[13]

It was within the context of these late nineteenth-century efforts to grapple with the Negro problem that Nina Rodrigues undertook the first scientifically respectable ethnographic study of Afro-Brazilian religions. He attempted to identify the tribal origins of the slaves brought to Brazil and the provenance of the "religious survivals" that he observed. This research was part of a larger effort to systematically measure the cultural and mental level of Brazil's black populations and to assess their consequences for national development. Through the efforts of Arthur Ramos and other members of the "Nina Rodrigues school," Rodrigues's work was disseminated to a wider audience and became a fundamental reference point for students of Brazil's African heritage, for whom it established the major themes and organizing questions that guided research into Afro-Brazilians' religions in the late 1930s and 1940s.

Nina Rodrigues: Hierarchies of Race and Religion

A chaired professor in the College of Medicine at the University of Bahia, Rodrigues held the popular late nineteenth-century view that Afro-Brazilians were less evolved than their white neighbors, more prone to superstition, psychologically immature, and incapable of "civilized behavior." And like many of his compatriots, Rodrigues was convinced that these factors contributed to the inferiority of Brazilians as a people and impeded the nation's prospects for social and economic advancement.[14]

Drawing on contemporary European theories of cultural evolution, Rodrigues sought to assess the mental and cultural state of Afro-Brazilians through an examination of their religious traditions, which he felt served as the best indicator of the mentality of a particular population. He set about the task with methodical precision, producing a detailed account of religious beliefs and practices based on the reports of informants as well as his own observations. Although he ultimately dismissed these religions as an inferior category of fetishism and considered the central ritual practice of spirit possession a form of group hysteria, Rodrigues was the first scholar to take Afro-Brazilian religious practices as worthy of "scientific" consideration and to study the African influence on Afro-Brazilian cults systematically.

Fitting his observations within a framework of cultural development grounded in the social Darwinist thought of the time, Rodrigues arrayed Afro-Brazilian religions along an evolutionary continuum. Of the Africans brought to Brazil, Rodrigues felt that the "Sudanese," particularly the Nagô (Yoruba), were the most advanced because of the complex mythology and organizational structure of their religion.[15] He argued that this, together with their numerical superiority and the wide diffusion of their language, had made Nagô culture hegemonic in Bahia and, as a result, other ethnic groups had adopted the Nagô beliefs and religious practices as well.[16] According to Rodrigues, only the Nagô possessed a "true mythology" and, more importantly, a conception of the divinized celestial firmament—an idea that "at its highest level reveals the capacity of religious abstraction."[17] Inferior to the Nagô were a variety of "less advanced" tribal groups whose religions lacked a developed pantheon and a graded structure of ritual authority.[18] Of course, for Rodrigues even the "superior African animism" of the Nagô was inferior to Catholicism, since blacks possessed only a rudimentary intelligence and were incapable of completely assimilating the abstract and superior monotheism of the whites.[19]

Just as white religion expressed the superiority of the whites, black religion thus expressed the inferior mental state of the blacks, a hypothesis that led Rodrigues to argue against the police persecution of Afro-Brazilian religions that had been legislated in the penal code of 1890. Because it treated whites and blacks equally, without taking into account the inferiority of nonwhite races, Rodrigues considered the penal code anachronistic and unscientific. The law, in attempting to equalize what science had clearly demonstrated to be unequal by nature, unfairly judged blacks by the same criteria as whites.[20]

For Rodrigues the regulation of these religions properly came under the jurisdiction of psychiatry, not the law or the police. Since the central ritual experience of Afro-Brazilian religions, spirit possession, constituted a pathological state, the penal code treated as a crime what was in actuality a consequence of pathology. Therefore, control of the Afro-Brazilian was a medical-psychiatric—not a legal—issue. In this way, Rodrigues linked Afro-Brazilian religions with abnormality rather than criminality.[21] When seen against the larger backdrop of concerns about the impact of Afro-Brazilians on the progress of the nation, it is perhaps no coincidence that, in the words of Beatriz Dantas, Rodrigues "developed in Brazil, just at the moment in which the Negro became free, a 'scientific' discourse that attempted to institute for him a new status of inferiority—this one in the name of science."[22]

Rodrigues's work made its greatest impact on Brazilian social scientists when it was edited and republished under the direction of Arthur Ramos, who considered himself heir to Rodrigues's legacy. Like his intellectual forebear, Ramos initially sought to assess the mental and cultural level of Afro-Brazilians by studying their religious traditions and identifying their precise African origins. Following the framework that Rodrigues had established, he linked these traditions to culturo-linguistic groups like the Nagô or Bantu, and ranked them along an evolutionary continuum from most advanced (Nagô) to least (Bantu). As we will see, once scholars and their informants began to organize politically for the legalization of Afro-Brazilian religions in the 1930s and 1940s, claims about the purity of a particular community's tradition as indexed by fidelity to an ostensibly African tradition drew on and enhanced this idea of Nagô exceptionalism.

Arthur Ramos: Substituting Culture for Race

A medical doctor trained in psychiatry and forensic medicine, Arthur Ramos was a prolific contributor to the literature on the "Negro question" in the 1930s and 1940s. In addition to his tireless efforts to revive scholarly interest in Rodrigues's work, Ramos published a series of influential studies drawing on Rodrigues's material. Like Rodrigues, he was drawn to ethnography in his efforts to assess the psychological and cultural level of Brazil's black populations. And, like Rodrigues, Ramos's early studies of Afro-Brazilian religions were part of a larger effort to assess the consequences of Brazil's African heritage for national development.

However, unlike Rodrigues, Ramos linked the inferiority of Afro-Brazilians to class rather than race. In his 1934 classic *O Negro Brasileiro,* Ramos argued that Afro-Brazilians constituted a "backward class" (*classe atrasada*), whose cultural and religious representations were consequences of a "pre-logical" mentality. This mentality was independent of race because it occurred in all ethnic groups and under a variety of conditions, manifesting itself in "the poor, children, and neurotics, as well as in dreams, art and determined conditions of psychic regression."[23]

Through "a profound educational revolution, a 'vertical' and 'interstitial' revolution that reaches into the remote depths of the collective unconscious," these prelogical modes of thought could be corrected and raised to "higher stages."[24] It was therefore important to recognize this prelogical mentality in its various cultural forms, and Ramos devoted himself to charting the various cultural productions of Afro-Brazilians.[25] Much of his ethnographic research was conducted when he worked as a government functionary, first for the medical service of the state of Bahia, and later for the federal secretary of education, where he ran a government service of mental hygiene in the schools of Rio de Janeiro. Thanks to the latter position, Ramos wrote in *O Negro Brasileiro* that he was able to "progressively penetrate" the cults and "centers of black magic" of Rio's shantytowns.[26]

Following Rodrigues, Ramos believed that the most direct way to "penetrate the psychology of a people" was "the study of the religious sentiment" because it alone "leads directly to the profound levels of the collective unconscious, revealing to us this common emotional base which is the true source of social forms."[27] Thus, the magical and prelogical thought of the backwards classes was reflected particularly in their religious traditions, just as the higher mentality of the more advanced classes was reflected in the abstractions of more advanced religions like Christianity.

Ramos argued that following "the law of evolutionary transformation," inferior religions evolved when in contact with a more advanced religion. Thus, Nagô candomblé, with its highly developed mythology and complex organizational structure, had absorbed the less highly developed religious forms of other African groups such as the Jeje and Bantu.[28] Contact with the superior religion of Catholicism had in its turn transformed the fetishism of the Nagô into a polytheistic system centered on the veneration of African deities called *orixás*.

Reciprocally, "a superior religion degenerated under the influence of primitive religions," and thus Christianity had suffered the incorporation of superstitious elements.[29] Nonetheless, Ramos expressed confidence that the tendency over time was a constant state of progressive evolution. However, due to the extremely slow nature of the process, he argued that it had to be aided by an educational program of substituting reason and rationality for the mysticism and prelogical mentality of the backwards classes.

This hierarchical schema was reflected in the chapter arrangement of *O Negro Brasileiro*. After a detailed discussion of Nagô candomblé, which Ramos considered the most advanced of the backwards classes, he examined a variety of less-advanced "cults," which had absorbed a great deal of admixture, eventually degenerating into the magical practices found in urban centers of Bahia and Rio de Janeiro.[30] Compared to Nagô candomblé, which had preserved a high level of African purity and thus an integrated, collective system of belief and ritual, these degenerate forms retained "only a remote connection to the primitive religious forms transplanted from Africa" and thus, Ramos concluded, were of little interest to the scholar.[31]

At the recommendation of Gilberto Freyre, Ramos sent a copy of *O Negro Brasileiro* to Melville Herskovits in 1935, along with two other volumes from a series that he was editing. The latter's enthusiasm may be judged by the promptness of his response: a letter written the day after he received the books, accompanied by a set of his own articles and books. This was followed by a collegial exchange of ideas, resources, expertise, and visits between the two men. In 1940 Ramos traveled to the United States where he taught a class at Louisiana State University, presented his work at various conferences, and attended a workshop led by Herskovits. He returned in 1941 to lead a seminar at Northwestern that had been organized for him by Herskovits. That same year, Herskovits traveled to Brazil where he conducted fieldwork in Bahia, Porto Alegre, and Recife.[32]

In his 1958 preface to *The Myth of the Negro Past*, Herskovits acknowledged that Ramos's description of syncretism in *O Negro Brasileiro* had provided a key conceptual tool for his understanding and analysis of cultural contact and change among New World blacks.[33] Syncretism, he wrote, captured the processes through which, in a situation of cultural contact, certain traits of a group's original culture were retained or reinterpreted, resulting in new cultural forms. The characteristic example of this process was Ramos's discussion of Nagô candomblé, a religion in which "cult members who are at the same time faithful Catholics identify their African deities with the saints of the Church."[34] Although Ramos had not explored syncretism's "implications for cultural theory," Herskovits himself "recognized that this process of identification represented a pattern of first importance in understanding the religious life on New World Negro societies."[35]

Ramos's failure to explore the implications of his research for cultural theory seems to have been rectified as his relationship with Herskovits developed. This was apparent in *A Aculturação Negra no Brasil*. In several of these essays, Ramos devoted himself to reinterpreting material initially presented in *O Negro Brasileiro* (and other publications) as evidence of the acculturative process. Gone were the psychoanalytic precepts and evolutionary language of *O Negro Brasileiro*, replaced by an emphasis on the "harmonious fusions" and "cultural mosaics" that syncretism had produced in Brazil. What he had previously described as more advanced and less advanced religious forms were now understood as consequences of different phases of the acculturation process. Nevertheless, a notion of hierarchy persisted in Ramos's insistence on the relative "purity" of Nagô candomblé when compared to cults of other ethnic provenances that had degenerated through the absorption of diverse cultural influences.

Ramos's introduction to the volume, an extended panegyric to Nina Rodrigues, proffered a similar reframing of Rodrigues's work. Most strikingly, Ramos extolled the older man as a pioneer in the study of acculturation: "The nomenclature and the methodological orientation may vary," he wrote, but the "methodological essence of the study of acculturation is there in the work of the Bahian master."[36] Elsewhere Ramos explained how, by reading Rodrigues's discussion of race and racial differences as a discussion of culture and cultural differences, his theories were in perfect consonance with contemporary anthropological theories of acculturation.[37] Ramos then concluded that it was Nina Rodrigues who had established the organizing principles for the study of the New World Negro, namely, (1) the need to systematically study his African origins and (2) the analysis of the basic mechanisms of cultural contact and change.[38]

As the Brazilian historian of anthropology Mariza Corrêa observed, this claim required Ramos to ignore the theoretical basis of Rodrigues's work, which rested on a notion of racial hierarchy and the degenerating effects of Brazil's inferior black blood.[39] Although Ramos briefly mentioned these racist ideas, they were, he argued, part and parcel of the academic discourse of his day and thus superfluous to Rodrigues's real contribution: the methodology of acculturation. By transforming one of the foremost proponents of social Darwinist thought into the father of acculturation studies in Brazil, Ramos simultaneously gave this conceptual framework a Brazilian pedigree and obscured the racial hierarchy of nineteenth-century social thought. The answer to the "Negro question" was to be found not in the language of race and eugenics, but in the language of culture and syncretism. No longer a threat to the nation, Afro-Brazilian religions had become the model for a universal theory of culture contact and change. This shift in intellectual assumptions had important consequences for the scholarly literature on Afro-Brazilian religions.

African Purity and Religious Authenticity

Personal and institutional connections among researchers interested in Afro-Brazilian religions ensured that a relatively small number of candomblé communities in Bahia served as field sites. Primary among these was the Gantois community, which Nina Rodrigues first studied at the close of the nineteenth century and which was mentioned by nearly every student of candomblé afterward. As a result of this community's prominence in the literature on candomblé and the political savvy of its head priestesses, Gantois today enjoys a reputation as one of the oldest and most venerable candomblés in Brazil. This position has granted the community innumerable benefits, not the least of which is international attention and quasi-official patronage by state officials interested in promoting tourism among Afro-diasporan roots seekers.

Another result of these networks of patronage and power was to ensure that the accounts of privileged informants were disproportionately represented in the literature.[40] And because the scholarly preoccupation with African cultural survivals in this period reinforced the claims of a small number of practitioner-informants who themselves had a vested interest in asserting the "purity" of their community's religious traditions, an implicit model of religious authenticity was created.[41] Indexed by fidelity to an African, and more particularly Nagô or Yoruba heritage, this model excluded more heterogeneous Afro-Brazilian forms, whose eclecticism was seen as a mark of pollution or degradation.[42]

Moreover, scholarship that questioned or could not be accommodated within this framework was dismissed as inadequate or erroneous, as Ruth Landes's case demonstrates. No less an international authority than Melville Herskovits accused Landes of being "ill-prepared" to conduct research on Afro-Brazilian religions because "she knew so little of the African background of the material she was to study that she had no perspective."[43] As Herskovits's objection suggests, Landes was not concerned with African retentions and her focus on gender discomfited many of her well-connected peers.[44] Arthur Ramos devoted an entire chapter of *A Acculturação Negra no Brasil* to an emphatic denunciation of Landes's research methods, comportment in the field, and conclusions. Pierre Verger later echoed these charges, accusing Landes of grossly misunderstanding what she had observed during her fieldwork because of her lack of knowledge about Africa.[45]

Not coincidentally, the claim that candomblé represented an ancient African tradition faithfully preserved on Brazilian soil proved politically useful in the 1930s and 1940s, helping to unite various constituencies in projects advocating its legalization. Organizers and participants of the second Afro-Brazilian Congress, held in Bahia in 1937, drafted a petition to the state governor in which they demanded that candomblé, as the religious heritage of the African slaves, be legally recognized as a true religion and its practitioners freed from police repression.[46] On the heels of this congress, the Union of Afro-Brazilian Sects of Bahia was established with the goal of rigorously maintaining the "purity" of the African traditions, becoming, in the words of Beatriz Dantas, "the first formally organized attempt to claim and defend a measure of legitimacy."[47] The link between African purity and religious authenticity meant that those elements of Afro-Brazilian religions that deviated from a putatively African model often were minimized, ignored, or dismissed as aberrant.

In spite of these political efforts, practitioners of Afro-Brazilian religions continued to be subject to varying levels of police harassment until the late 1970s, periodically accused of harboring communists and other "subversive" elements, or of offending the public morality. Ruth Landes reported that during the time of her research in Bahia in 1938, government officials frequently accused candomblés of being centers of communist propaganda.[48] Landes herself was eventually forced to leave the country as a result of her fraternization with candomblé practitioners and their supporters. Even the well-respected sociologist Gilberto Freyre was briefly imprisoned in 1934 for the crime of organizing the first Afro-Brazilian Congress.[49]

Although political efforts to legalize Afro-Brazilian religions were unsuccessful at the time, scholars like Freyre and Ramos helped lay the groundwork in the 1930s and 1940s for a radically different analysis of Brazil's "Negro problem." By shifting the explanatory paradigm from race to culture, their work enabled a new understanding of the nation's African heritage and contributed to a burgeoning socio-anthropological literature in which the Afro-Brazilian contribution to Brazil's civilization, history, and national development figured prominently. In books, articles, conference proceedings, and collections of folklore and myth, Freyre, Ramos, and others documented various aspects of Brazil's African heritage as expressed in popular culture, music, art, and religion.

It was this work to which Herskovits referred when he observed in *The Myth of the Negro Past* that "more concentrated research has been done on the African forms of religious life of the Negro in Brazil during the past decade than in any other part of the New World."[50] Herskovits drew extensively on this research to support his own argument about the extent and coherence of African survivals in the Americas, helping make Brazil a privileged site in transnational debates about the nature of the African contribution to New World cultures and candomblé an ideal example of the process of acculturation.

In emphasizing the integrity and adaptability of the African heritage in the New World, Herskovits's thesis about African cultural survivals shifted the explanatory framework from race to culture and offered a compelling counterargument to those who would claim the inferiority of the Negro. Although controversial at the time, his thesis was supported by a vast amount of cross-cultural data documenting striking similarities in forms of black cultural expression among blacks in Brazil, the United States, and the Caribbean. Its persuasive power is attested to by the prominent place Herskovits continues to hold among students of the African diaspora.

However, while it illuminated much about Afro-diasporan religions and remains an invaluable contribution, Herskovits's work left other aspects in the shadows, unexplored and unelaborated. By framing their research as a search for African survivals, scholars working in this vein tended to exclude, minimize, or ignore the non-African elements of these religions. This is particularly true of the literature on Afro-Brazilian religions, but it also helps account for the obscurity into which Arthur Huff Fauset's work has fallen. Given this history, it is all the more important that we revisit Fauset's *Black Gods of the Metropolis,* for it reminds us not only of the incredible vitality and diversity of black religions but of the inadequacies of scholarly models to fully account for their ever-evolving heterogeneity.

Notes

1. The phrase "locus classicus" is from J. Lorand Matory, *Black Atlantic Religion: Tradition, Transnationalism, and Matriarchy in the Afro-Brazilian Candomblé* (Princeton, N.J.: Princeton University Press, 2005), 11.

2. Ruth Landes, *The City of Women* (1947; Albuquerque: New Mexico Press, 1994), 1.

3. Ibid., 248.

4. Roger Bastide, *O Candomblé da Bahia: Rito Nagô*, trans. Maria Isaura Pereira de Queiroz, technical revision by Reginaldo Prandi (1958; São Paulo: Companhia das Letras, 2001), 73; 23–24. I address this at greater length in Kelly Hayes, "Black Magic and the Academy: Macumba and Afro-Brazilian 'Orthodoxies,' " *History of Religions* 46, no. 4 (May 2007): 283–315.

5. Joaquim Nabuco as quoted in Thomas E. Skidmore, *Black into White: Race and Nationality in Brazilian Thought* (Durham, N.C.: Duke University Press, 1993), 23.

6. On this point, see Skidmore, *Black into White*.

7. Paul C. Johnson, *Secrets, Gossip and Gods: The Transformation of Brazilian Candomblé* (Oxford: Oxford University Press, 2002), chapter 4.

8. See Skidmore, *Black into White*, chapters 1 and 2.

9. An 1890 decree prohibited the immigration of Asians and Africans, except by special congressional approval, lest these populations impede the whitening process. After 1907 the ethnic provision was dropped and Japanese settlers were granted entry, although as a columnist for the Rio daily wrote, "We are not very sympathetic to yellow immigration." See Skidmore, *Black into White*, 130. The Federal 1808 *Lei de Terras* (Law of the Lands) granted free land to European settlers, and in São Paulo the provincial government mounted a program to recruit and subsidize immigrant, primarily Italian, labor for commercial agriculture (ibid., 138–39).

10. Skidmore estimated that as of 1890, three million Europeans had settled in Brazil. See *Black into White*, 45.

11. The history of the city of Rio de Janeiro is instructive in this regard. Over the course of the late nineteenth and early twentieth centuries, the city was reconstructed in the shape of a "tropical Paris," a simulacrum of European refinement meant to announce to the world the civilizing potential of the tropics. In social terms, this reconstruction meant not only the creation of spacious boulevards and central parks, but the destruction of the tenement housing and *cortiços* (slave quarters) inhabited by the lowest classes, and their removal to the outskirts of the city center. However, among elites of the capital, the sentiment expressed by Afrânio Peixoto (1876–1947), a leading figure of the educational establishment, professor of medicine and law, and later dean of the University of the Federal District, well captured the critical importance of these transformations: "Before we can lay claim to a place in the world, we must prepare for such a role, exhibiting the decency and confidence of the

civilized. Any sacrifice is small in pursuit of such an inspiration" (Afrânio Peixoto, *Poeira da Estrada*, 86, as quoted in Skidmore, *Black into White*, 132). Paul C. Johnson also analyzed the reconstruction of Rio de Janeiro in terms of contemporary concerns about race, hygiene, and social progress in Johnson, *Secrets*, 85–88.

12. Article 156 prohibited "the practice of any medicine, dentistry or pharmacology, homeopathy, hypnotism or animal magnetism without necessary legal certification." Article 157 prohibited "the practice of spiritism, magic and its sorceries, the use of talismans and cartomancy to arouse sentiments of love or hate, the promise to remedy curable or incurable illnesses; in sum to fascinate and subjugate public credulity." Article 158 prohibited "administering or prescribing any natural or prepared substance as a curative for internal or external use, thus performing or exercising the office denominated as *curandeiro* [religious healer]." See Yvonne Maggie, *Medo do Feitiço: Relações entre Magia e Poder no Brasil* (Rio de Janeiro: Arquivo Nacional, 1992), 21–22.

13. Johnson, *Secrets*, 83.

14. As Rodrigues wrote, "What is important for Brazil is to determine the level of inferiority it will encounter owing to the difficulty of civilizing the black populations that it possesses and if, on the whole, this inferiority will be compensated for by the miscegenation, a natural process by which the blacks are becoming integrated into the Brazilian nation, of the great mass of its colored population." See Nina Rodrigues, *Os Africanos no Brasil*, 5th ed., with a preface by Homero Pires (1906; São Paulo: Campanhia Editora Nacional, 1977), 264. Skidmore asserted that Rodrigues, unlike the majority of his colleagues, felt that miscegenation was not the answer to this dilemma but had in fact merely slowed down the elimination of superior white blood by producing a class of mixed bloods marked by mental degeneracy and a penchant for criminal behavior. But although Rodrigues garnered great distinction and his work was widely read by those interested in race, his ideas about miscegenation had little impact on the mainstream of Brazilian thought, which continued to consider miscegenation the key to Brazil's social progress. Skidmore provides a succinct overview of Rodrigues's theories on race in *Black into White*, 57–62.

15. The term "Nagô" is used in Brazil to refer to Yoruba-speaking peoples. It was used by slave traders to refer to slave cargo that departed for the New World from the Bight of Benin on the west coast of Africa. It appears to be derived from *anago*, a Fon (Dahomey) term for Yoruba speakers. For this derivation, see Mikelle Smith Omari, "Candomblé: A Socio-Political Examination of African Religion and Art in Brazil," in *Religion in Africa*, ed. Thomas D. Blakely, Walter E. A. van Beek, and Dennis L. Thompson (Portsmouth, N.H.: Heinemann, 1994), 137; and Pierre Verger, *Orixás: Deuses Iorubás na Africa e no Novo Mundo* (São Paulo: Editora Corrupio, 1981), 14.

16. In a series of articles that appeared in 1896 in the *Revista Brasileira*, later republished as *O Animismo Fetichista dos Negros Bahianos*, Rodrigues singled out factors external to the Nagô religion as determinative—the numerical superiority of the Nagôs or the fact they had maintained commercial relations with Lagos. See *O Animismo Fetichista dos Negros Bahianos*, with a preface by Arthur Ramos (1900; Rio de Janeiro: Civilização Brasiliera, 1935), 25. In a later work, he revised this original hypothesis to emphasize the superior organizational structure of the Nagô cults. See *Os Africanos*, 215.

17. Rodrigues, *Os Africanos*, 216–17.

18. Ibid., 215.

19. See, for example, Rodrigues, *Animismo*, 26, and *Os Africanos*, 215.

20. See Skidmore, *Black into White*, 59, and Beatriz Dantas, *Vovó Nagô e Papai Branco: Usos e Abusos da África no Brasil* (Rio de Janeiro: Graal, 1988), 166–67.

21. In subsequent generations the "treatment" for the problem posed to the social progress of the nation by these religions would oscillate between the poles of criminality and pathology, although ultimately neither would entirely displace the other. For more on this point, see Dantas, *Vovó Nagô*.

22. Ibid., 167.

23. Arthur Ramos, *O Negro Brasileiro*, 5th ed. (Rio de Janeiro: Graphia, 2001 [1934]), 30–32.

24. Ibid., 32.

25. As a survey of representative titles indicates: *O Folclore Negro do Brasil* (Black Folklore of Brazil), *As Culturas Negras do Novo Mundo* (The Black Cultures of the New World), and *Negros Escravos* (Black Slaves).

26. Ramos, *Negro Brasileiro*, 31.

27. Ibid., 28–29.

28. Ramos, following Rodrigues, argued that Bantu religion was oriented toward the ancestors rather than elemental deities and thus resembled a cult of the dead. For this reason, it had easily absorbed spiritist beliefs, also oriented toward cultivating the spirits of the dead, degenerating in this way into a form of "low spiritism." See Ramos, *Negro Brasileiro*, chapter 4 and passim.

29. Ibid., 123.

30. Ramos referred to Nagô religion as Jeje-Nagô because it had absorbed Jeje elements from slaves brought to Brazil from the region of Dahomey.

31. Ramos, *Negro Brasileiro*, 144.

32. Antonio Sérgio Alfredo Guimarães, "Comentários à correspondência entre Melville Herskovits e Arthur Ramos (1935–1941)," www.fflch.usp.br/sociologia/acag, accessed June 10, 2007.

33. Melville Herskovits, *The Myth of the Negro Past* (1941; Boston: Beacon Press, 1990), xxxvi.

34. Ibid.

35. Ibid.

36. Arthur Ramos, *A Acculturação Negra no Brasil* (São Paulo: Companhia Editora Brasileira, 1942), 28.

37. Mariza Corrêa, *As Ilusões Da Liberdade: A Escola Nina Rodrigues e a Antropologia no Brasil* (São Francisco: EDUSF, 1998), 285, quoting Arthur Ramos, preface to the *Collectividades Anormaes* by Nina Rodrigues, ed. Ramos (Rio de Janeiro: Civilização Brasiliera, 1939), 12.

38. Ramos, *Acculturação*, 29.

39. Mariza Corrêa, *As Ilusões*, 285–88.

40. For a more detailed account of these interrelationships, see Stefania Capone, *La*

Quête de l'Afrique dans le Candomblé: Pouvoir et Tradition au Brésil (Paris: Éditions Karthala, 1999) and Matory, *Black Atlantic Religion*. For example, Martiniano do Bonfim served as a key informant for, and was cited by, Nina Rodrigues, Arthur Ramos, Ruth Landes, and E. Franklin Frazier.

41. Matory argued that the emphasis on Yoruba purity as the criterion for candomblé authenticity was primarily a product of the West African "Lagosian Cultural Renaissance" brought to Bahia with Afro-Brazilian travelers and merchants in the late nineteenth century. Among other things, the value placed on Africanity helped these Afro-Brazilian merchants sell the religious goods they purchased in Africa to their Brazilian clientele. Because many of these merchants and travelers, such as Martiniano do Bonfim, served as key informants for scholars, their interested claims about Yoruba purity influenced several generations of scholarly work. See further Matory, *Black Atlantic Religion*.

42. I address this in more detail in Hayes, "Black Magic."

43. Melville Herskovits, review of *The City of Women, American Anthropologist* 50, no. 1 (January–March 1948): 124.

44. There is a significant literature exploring various ramifications of Ruth Landes's experiences in Brazil, her work, and its significance for gender studies and the history of anthropology. See, for example, Sally Cole, *Ruth Landes: A Life in Anthropology* (Lincoln: University of Nebraska Press, 2003); Cole, "Ruth Landes in Brazil: Writing, Race, and Gender in 1930s American Anthropology," in Landes, *The City of Women*, vii–xxxiv; Cole, "Ruth Landes and the Early Ethnography of Race and Gender," in *Women Writing Culture*, ed. R. Behar and D. Gordon (Berkeley: University of California Press, 1995), 166–85; Mariza Corrêa, "O Mistério dos Orixás e das Bonecas: Raça e Gênero na Antropologia Brasileira," *Etnográfica* 2 (2000): 233–65; Mark Healey, "Os Desencontros da Tradição em A Cidade das Mulheres: Raça e Gênero na Etnografia de Ruth Landes," *Cadernos Pagu* 6–7 (1996): 153–200; Healey, " 'The Sweet Matriarchy of Bahia': Ruth Landes' Ethnography of Race and Gender," *Dispositio/n* 23 (1998 [2000]): 87–116; Olívia Maria Gomes da Cunha, "Imperfect Tense: An Ethnography of the Archive," *Mana* 10, no. 2 (October 2000): 287–322; Ruth Landes, "A Woman Anthropologist in Brazil," in *Women in the Field: Anthropological Experiences*, ed. P. Golde (Berkeley: University of California Press, 1986), 119–39; and Edison Carneiro, "Uma Falseta de Artur Ramos," in *Ladinos e Criolos: Estudos Sobre o Negro no Brasil*, ed. E. Carneiro (Rio de Janeiro: Civilização Brasileira, 1964), 223–27.

45. Pierre Verger, "A Contribuição Especial das Mulheres ao Candomblé do Brasil," in *Culturas Africanas* (São Luiz: UNESCO, 1985), 110.

46. For the text of the petition, see Dantas, *Vovó Nagô*, 190–91.

47. See ibid., 190–92.

48. On just such charges of communist involvement the ethnologist Edison Carneiro had been forced to take refuge from the police in a Bahian cult center shortly before Landes's arrival. See Landes, *City of Women* and "A Woman Anthropologist."

49. Landes referred to this incident, without specifically naming Freyre, in *City of Women*, 5.

50. Herskovits, *Myth of the Negro*, 16.

ELEVEN · Fauset and His *Black Gods:*
Intersections with the Herskovits-Frazier Debate

STEPHEN W. ANGELL

An enduring, far-reaching controversy erupted in the 1930s between Melville J. Herskovits and E. Franklin Frazier over the question of the degree of cultural continuity (or, as Frazier would emphasize, discontinuity) between contemporary African Americans and the African heritage of their ancestors who had been stolen away from their mother continent. Arthur Huff Fauset engaged this controversy robustly in his seminal work, *Black Gods of the Metropolis: Negro Religious Cults of the Urban North*. In this book, Fauset had sincere words of appreciation for both men, describing Frazier as a "profound student of the origins of Negro institutions in America" and praising Herskovits for his "bold spirit of scientific inquiry and his careful statement and elucidation of the facts."[1]

Fauset, Frazier, and Herskovits each participated in the cultural reawakening of the Harlem Renaissance in the 1920s, and each also propounded a strongly critical view of religious orthodoxies of earlier generations, at least partly on the ground of social justice. Each also was attracted to radical, socialist, or extreme liberal political views from the 1920s to the 1940s. Since their sociopolitical worldviews were similar, I argue that their scholarly disagreements arose mostly from varying interpretations of historical data, and will examine briefly how the work of University of Chicago sociologist Robert Park influenced all three men.

Following that is a closer examination of how Fauset analyzed the arguments of Herskovits, Park, and Frazier in his *Black Gods of the Metropolis*. Like Frazier (although in a clearer and more emphatic fashion), Fauset opposed Park and Herskovits and anticipated the work of later scholars such as J. Lorand Matory in his argument that instinctual impulses embedded in collective memory (or what Herskovits called "a deep religious bent") have not played an especially large role in African Americans' religious formation, as compared to that of other people.[2] Against both Herskovits and Frazier, Fauset was also one of the first scholars to posit a strong and positive connection between politics and varieties of prophetic religion in regard to early twentieth-century African American religious communities.

Comparative Lives

Arthur Huff Fauset lived a life that skirted the edge of the canon, if the canon is to be defined by the newest incarnation of collective biography for the United States, the *American National Biography*.[3] Other protagonists in this chapter—Edward Franklin Frazier, Melville Jean Herskovits, and Robert Ezra Park—were included in this twenty-four-volume work, as was the woman to whom Arthur was briefly married, activist for human rights and social justice, state legislator, and internationalist Crystal Bird Fauset, and his older half sister, novelist and Harlem Renaissance pillar Jessie Redmon Fauset. However, while he is mentioned in the entry for Crystal, there is no entry for Arthur himself. Perhaps the main reason for this is that Arthur devoted his life to several worthy ends, and his kind of eclecticism has not always been well served by such canons. He produced first-rate writing and scholarship, dabbling in a number of different genres and fields. He happily left it all behind when he had more pressing work in other areas. (In addition to being an anthropologist and sociologist of religion, he was renowned as a folklorist, a short-story writer, and a political columnist.)[4] He was a teacher and school administrator, not in a prestigious university setting, but mostly at the more humble elementary school level. He was a union organizer and a social and political activist on a mission to eliminate racial injustice, certainly the work closest to his heart, but he was an activist at a time when scholars were often supposed to guard their objectivity by remaining aloof from taking public stances on social and political issues.[5]

This essay honors Fauset for his seminal contribution to the study of religion, especially of African American religions, but the main collector thus far of his biographical data—and a person who conducted retrospective interviews with him prior to his death in 1983—was a Canadian folklorist, Carole H. Carpenter. She appropriately called him "a Renaissance humanist" and "a pioneer of black cultural studies," but his favored designation for himself was "campaigner for social justice." His "marginality," she observed, was "conditioned by chance and by choice. He was to the end as he was born—a mélange, between worlds, uniquely himself." David Levering Lewis, who also interviewed Fauset, calls him "an extraordinary person, matchlessly cosmopolitan."[6]

Arthur Huff Fauset was born in 1899, the son of sixty-two-year-old Redmon Fauset, a minister in the African Methodist Episcopal Church who had acquired the reputation of a radical, and his second wife, Bella Huff Fauset, a white woman who had two children from a previous marriage to an African American. She was a Jew who had converted to Christianity. Arthur Fauset was only four years younger than Melville Herskovits and five years younger than E. Franklin Frazier. Although scholarship on religious matters was an important part of each man's life, none of the three can properly be termed a theist, and none maintained a connection with organized religion. Redmon Fauset died when his son was four, and Arthur was subsequently raised as a Presbyterian, but, in his later years, he regarded himself as a "freethinker." Herskovits's collegiate education included, at his father's urging, a year at the Hebrew Union College in Cincinnati, with the prospect of preparing for the rabbinate, but he withdrew from Hebrew Union College when he had a crisis of faith and ceased to believe in God. Frazier was renowned as an outspoken atheist from his adolescence onward.[7]

Fauset's views on religion are illuminated helpfully in his short stories "Symphonesque"[8] and "Safe in the Arms of Jesus," written in the 1920s.[9] In these works, he clearly displayed a disdain for the workings of organized religion, which, in his young adult years, should be understood to comprise mainly the long-established religions in the black community, the Baptists and the Methodists. With an insider's eye, he characterized the staleness, superficiality, and deception that seemed inherent in much well-established ritual and the venality of those who administered that ritual. In the area of doctrine, Fauset's skepticism toward any form of theism is clearly manifested in these short stories. In "Symphonesque," his main character Cudjo asks,

> What was all this talk about God? These niggers and their God! Fools, that's all they were, they and their God.
>
> Did they think that God gave a tinker's damn for them, they in their dirty shacks that bred scorpions, bedbugs and rats, and gave forth a stench that would knock down a polecat! Where was their God when White Man came along at the end of the harvest season and told the niggers they hadn't made enough cotton to pay for their grub, to say nothing of their shelter, their clothing, their very liberty.
>
> And what was He doing on that hot afternoon when White Man took Zack Jones and riddled his body with bullets after he had been strung up to a big tree for being in

the neighborhood when little "Miss" Dora suddenly took a notion it would be funny to pretend that some nigger had said naughty things to her?

In these stories, Fauset did not stake out the position of a doctrinaire atheist. When Cudjo disrupts an outdoor baptism ceremony, pulling a young woman about to be baptized out of the water, Fauset hinted that Cudjo was assuming a messianic role and possibly substituting a baptism of the Spirit for the inferior ceremony of water baptism.[10] However, Fauset also problematized Cudjo, suggesting that he may have been possessed by either a divine or a demonic source, or both; thus Cudjo's friend Amber Lee suggests that sometimes it can be only "some fierce demon . . . with frightful eyes like Satan's" that is watching her through his eyes.

While Fauset entertained a skeptical outlook toward theism, he was greatly disturbed by the spiritual and material corruption that pervaded many established black churches of the early twentieth century. It was the latter revulsion that provided the emotional power for his unsettling portrait of the Reverend De Witt Coleman in his short story "Safe in the Arms of Jesus." Coleman's church was the poster child for personality cult (the reverend's own name adorned the tabernacle), but the church was anything but a manifestation of spiritual vitality. Fauset makes clear that the pastor's apparent spiritual absorption was actually a cover for the fact that "he was bored to distraction," and goes on to detail other financial or spiritual deceptions in the De Witt Coleman Tabernacle. This combination—a devastating, visceral attack on established black churches for their political, financial, and spiritual shortcomings, with pointed questions about the underlying theology lurking in the background—was fairly common for black intellectuals in the Harlem Renaissance. The ultimate meaning of this sort of ecclesiastical discourse is less clear. Michael Lackey portrays Langston Hughes in a way similar to the way he portrays Fauset and designates Hughes's worldview as atheist, while Jon Michael Spencer renders a similar portrait of James Weldon Johnson and argues that it would be better to describe Johnson as holding an uncompromising version of the social gospel than to describe him as an atheist. Spencer makes the same case for Hughes in passing. Both kinds of assessment of Harlem Renaissance figures have analytical strength, and both judgments could be made of Fauset as well.[11]

How does *Black Gods of the Metropolis* look against this theological backdrop from the Harlem Renaissance era? Possibly Fauset undertook this work because of the possible contrasts that these new religious movements posed to established black churches. For example, the Fauset on display in Carole Carpenter's interview harbored a fondness for the Father Divine movement.[12] The freethinking Fauset may have been hoping to find some spiritual vitality—a re-enchantment, if you will—among new religious movements, rather than the spiritual dullness that he described in his short stories on the established churches. (On the other hand, he certainly could insert acerbic comments on the religions that he studied, for example, finding Father Divine's followers "surpassing in intensity" the fanaticism of Nazis under Hitler's rule.)[13] *Black Gods* is certainly more evenhanded and less dismissive of new religious movements than an oft-cited article on the subject by another contemporary African American intellectual—Ira de A. Reid's "Let Us Prey," written a decade and a half before Fauset's slim volume.[14]

Fauset, Frazier, and Herskovits completed university degrees in the late 1910s or early 1920s, Frazier with a bachelor's degree from Howard University in 1916 and a master's degree from Clark University in 1920; Fauset with an A.B. from the University of Pennsylvania in 1921; and Herskovits with a bachelor's degree from the University of Chicago in 1920, and master's and doctoral degrees from Columbia in 1921 and 1923 respectively. Fauset, unlike the other two men, largely viewed his education as a means of avocational personal improvement and "intellectual exercise," certainly not as a means to attaining career goals of engaging in scholarship and teaching at a college or university level. In the 1920s, the only teaching jobs that were open to Fauset and Frazier were at black universities; Herskovits, as a Jew, also experienced prejudice that undoubtedly helped to account for the fact that his first offer of a university teaching appointment (at Northwestern University, an offer that he accepted) came four years after he completed his doctorate.

While Fauset noted the severe constraints that racial prejudice would have placed upon his career had he pursued a university teaching career, his primary reason for not pursuing such a career was a desire to remain rooted in his home community of Philadelphia. In fact, when he received his degree from the University of Pennsylvania in 1921, he was already an elementary school teacher in Philadelphia, and within five years he became the principal of an all-black elementary school in Philadelphia, Joseph Singerly School, where he remained for the next two decades. As Philadelphia had no black high schools at the time, elementary school principal was the most highly ranked position available to him. While Fauset began his elementary school teaching and Frazier his university teaching without doctorates, both subsequently earned terminal degrees, Frazier in 1932 from the University of Chicago and Fauset a decade later from the University of Pennsylvania.[15]

Philadelphia was transformed in the 1910s, 1920s, and 1930s by the influx of a large number of mostly impoverished African Americans from the South (as, of course, were many other northern cities at the same time). Fauset was renowned as one of the few Philadelphians from the old established black families to overcome prejudices relating to social class and color in order to actually welcome these southern migrants. While conceding that "old Philadelphians" often objected to their crude language, Fauset admired the pluck and shrewdness of many of the southern migrants. Indicative of the love-hate relationship that many Philadelphians have with the group claiming religious descent from their founding fathers, Fauset referred to the black establishment Philadelphians as "'black Quakers' because they dressed so plainly, pretending that nothing mattered to them while all the time their noses were up in the air and they wouldn't do anything with the masses of the people." He observed that with their drive and willingness to challenge the existing power structure, the migrants tended to accomplish more than the older African American families of Philadelphia, as the latter accommodated themselves more readily to the status quo.[16]

In his 1939 book, *The Negro Family in the United States,* E. Franklin Frazier's assessment of the effects of the African American migration from the South was less sanguine. His primary emphasis was on the disorganization, poverty, and demoralization of the migrants. Only secondarily did he commend their positive influence upon the community life of African American neighborhoods in the northern cities.[17] Given the fact that the new religions profiled in *Black Gods of the Metropolis* drew most of their strength from these migrants, Fauset's ability to see the positive attributes of the migrants must surely have been an important factor in his ability to portray their religious organizations fairly.

One cultural movement that drew strength from this migration of African Americans to the North was the Harlem Renaissance. Fauset, Frazier, and Herskovits all contributed in some way to this movement. While it would be outside the scope of this essay to detail all of their contributions, it is appropriate to notice that each was friend to the African American philosopher Alain Locke. Significantly, each of these three men contributed to the seminal 1925 work edited by Locke, *The New Negro.* Locke wrote:

> This volume aims . . . to register the transformations of the inner and outer life of the Negro in America that have so significantly taken place in the last few years. . . . [W]ithout ignoring the fact that . . . the attitude of America toward the Negro is as important a factor as the attitude of the Negro toward America, we have nevertheless concentrated upon self-expression and the forces and motives of self-determination.[18]

At that time, Fauset was known primarily as a folklorist, so Locke asked him to contribute a chapter on "American Negro Folk Literature," as well as to compile the bibliography for "Negro Folk Lore." Fauset wrote that African American folktales were "borrowed . . . most certainly . . . from Africa," and he strongly urged that there be "a scientific collecting of Negro folk lore before the original sources of this material altogether lapse." Fauset stated that the "nearness to nature" and the "lack of the self-conscious element" were among the factors demonstrating the African character of the Br'er Rabbit folktales.[19] With none of the sharp critique featured in his later work *Black Bourgeoisie*, E. Franklin Frazier celebrated the success of the burgeoning black middle class in his essay "Durham: Capital of the Black Middle Class."[20] Melville Herskovits contributed an essay, "The Negro's Americanism," commenting that among the black people in Harlem there was "not a trace" of African culture.[21] Obviously, each of these youthful contributions to Locke's collection was somewhat provisional in character, subject to revision in the scholars' later work.

David Levering Lewis credits Fauset with an early obituary of the Harlem Renaissance. By 1933, Fauset saw the Harlem Renaissance as an unrealistically elitist movement. With the economy and African Americans in such deep trouble, the arts simply did not seem very pressing. While "the argument for cultural education must always be answered in the affirmative," arts education in itself was not adequate for the times. Instead, "the immediate task of Negro education is to develop in the boys and girls of the race an individual and racial psychology that will fashion them into eager, self-assured and self-contained, positive individuals who even in this most hostile milieu cannot be denied because they *will* not know the meaning of defeat."[22]

In 1931, the thirty-two-year-old Fauset married thirty-eight-year-old Crystal Bird, an African American teacher, politician, and community activist. Bird had begun her activism in 1918 as a field secretary for the Young Women's Christian Association. Starting in 1927, she served as a staff person for the interracial section of the American Friends Service Committee. Later she helped to found the Institute of Race Relations at Swarthmore College. As a Democrat, she ran for the state legislature on a platform that advocated affordable housing and fair employment practice, and won a seat in 1938. Her marriage to Arthur Fauset was childless and relatively short in duration. In 1944, Crystal changed her registration to the Republican Party, in part because of a personality clash with a Democratic National Committee chairman. Two days later, Arthur filed for divorce; they had already been separated for some years.[23] Arthur Fauset never remarried.

While Crystal moved to the right, Arthur remained on the left politically—indeed, to the left of Franklin Delano Roosevelt and the "New Deal." In the late 1930s, he worked intensely with the National Negro Congress, an organization working on behalf of labor unions and African American civil rights, with an emphasis on nonviolent direct action. When the congress fell under the control of the U.S. Communist Party in about 1940, Fauset departed, although, as Carpenter notes, he "was not opposed so much to the ideology as to its application: for him, the group no longer represented and worked for black people."[24] A partial list of Fauset's many activities on behalf of human rights and social justice includes the following: in the 1920s, the Anti-Lynching Committee; he was a longtime member of the National Urban League; in the 1930s, the Philadelphia Committee for the Defense of Ethiopia; also in the 1930s, he was an organizer of the Philadelphia branch of the Scottsboro Defense League; in the mid-1940s, he was chairman of the United Peoples' Action Committee, a radical civil rights group that he proudly noted served as "a spur to the NAACP."[25]

Recent examinations of Fauset, Frazier, and Herskovits all remark upon the relevance of the politics of the 1930s to the scholarship they produced. Jonathan Holloway attributes E. Franklin Frazier's relentless focus on social class questions in his scholarship to his fervent conviction that "racial antagonism was a manifestation of economic forces," a conviction that he combined with active, unrelenting opposition to racial segregation. Frazier's view was similar to that embraced in the 1920s by the Communist Party (U.S.A.), but in the 1930s he often came into conflict with others who saw politics primarily through a racial lens. Indeed, in the 1930s, the Communist Party embraced the "Black Belt" theory, leading to a more primary role for race in its political analysis, and such major figures as W. E. B. Du Bois also moved away somewhat from an integrationist stance to a position more focused on strengthening African American communities.[26] Frazier did not move with them.

Carpenter remarked, without elaboration, that Fauset had a "personal and intellectual connection" with Frazier, and surely his friendship with Frazier would have been strengthened by their common views on such controverted political questions. The activist Fauset combined his integrationist commitment with a pan-Africanist worldview, but he never endorsed the kind of African emigrationism promoted by Marcus Garvey and Henry McNeal Turner. Carpenter observed that Fauset was philosophically opposed to "oppression of any sort."[27] None of these three men ever belonged to the Communist Party. Fauset professed no major objections to Communist thought, but he averred that he could never have worked under the dictation of party leadership.[28] There were, however, in the 1940s several occasions when Fauset became a target for repression because of his radical viewpoints.[29] Frazier also engaged in political activism, especially in his youth, but certainly not to the extent of Fauset.[30]

In his youth, Melville Herskovits was a critic of capitalism, and he briefly joined the Industrial Workers of the World (IWW). During the 1930s, like Frazier, he had an interest in supporting alliances between African Americans and whites in the working class. In later years he maintained membership in such organizations as the Progressive Citizens of America and the Evanston Council for Democratic Action. Herskovits was an opponent of anti-Communist policies in the post–World War II years, believing that the Communist threat worldwide had been overhyped. While he was generally an opponent of racism, he was apparently less consistent than either Fauset or Frazier in his opposition to racial segregation. In 1943, he wrote a letter asking for assistance to gain admission into a whites-only club.[31]

The nascent fields of African and African American scholarship had their share of turf struggles and infighting in the 1930s and 1940s, and Herskovits and Frazier participated in some of these battles (but Fauset, with his other interests, stayed away). Herskovits's biographer Jerry Gershenhorn has analyzed the battles over the Encyclopedia Africana proposed by W. E. B. Du Bois. Herskovits was a determined opponent, although most of his opposition was conducted quietly behind the scenes. His motives for this seem to have been quite complex; they included a distrust of Du Bois's objectivity and a wish to have anthropological perspectives better represented in the project. But Gershenhorn also shows that Herskovits wished for white scholars to play a controlling role in African and African American studies.[32] Herskovits often seemed to distrust black scholarship; one black anthropologist, Hubert Ross, recalled that "Herskovits appeared unsupportive of African Americans" because he believed them "to be too emotional and to lack objectivity in studying themselves or people of color."[33]

Du Bois, of course, would not change course to suit Herskovits or anyone else, and thus Herskovits unfortunately decided to undermine his efforts. Frazier, too, was a critic of the project, although the grounds of his criticism were focused on the quality of the scholarship proposed. Frazier wrote: "The planning and execution of the Encyclopedia should devolve upon scholars," and asked for a conference of "competent scholars" to rework the plan. Gershenhorn interprets these developments as part of "a generational rift," in which younger scholars like Herskovits and Frazier showed solidarity in opposing ill-considered plans by the older Du Bois. The opponents were successful in preventing the completion or publication of any more than one preliminary volume of this encyclopedia.[34]

With the contrasting stances that Fauset, Frazier, and Herskovits adopted on the question of the origins and continuing nature of African American religion and culture, one might expect to find significant differences in worldview when examining their biographies, differences that might have helped to shape their views on the origins question. This seems largely not to be the case. The attitudes of these three men in the area of socioeconomic matters, politics, and faith; their friends and social connections; and even their positioning in academic turf battles are fairly similar. Their variant stances on the origins question then ought to rest primarily on differences in interpretation of the historical data and of the literature on these questions already accumulating by 1942.

A description of the Herskovits-Frazier debate as it currently has an impact upon the thinking of twenty-first-century scholars would be anachronistic (as well as superfluous).[35] Many significant works by Frazier on the topic of African survivals in African American religion and culture had not yet been written when Fauset wrote his book, much less published. Of great interest to religion scholars was his *Negro Church in America,* based on lectures he delivered at the University of Liverpool in 1953 and published posthumously a decade later.[36] Inasmuch as the latter work figures into this essay, it must be seen as an effect of Fauset's scholarship, not a cause.

Most relevant here are works cited by Fauset in his text, including Frazier's *The Negro Family in the United States,* first published in 1939, and what remains Herskovits's most enduring contribution to the debate, *The Myth of the Negro Past,* published in 1941, in the midst of Fauset's writing of his dissertation. Also relevant are book reviews, including the reviews that Frazier and Herskovits published on each other's work (both of their reviews were published in the *Nation,* in 1940 and 1942). While the Frazier-Herskovits controversy may seem an old chestnut to those of us who have lived with it all of our scholarly lives, to Fauset it was anything but old and stale. It was a new controversy and, judging by his intense engagement of it, immensely exciting and invigorating.

The Influence of Robert E. Park

Robert Ezra Park (1864–1944), a towering figure in American sociology early in the twentieth century, was a journalist turned Harvard- and Heidelberg-trained sociologist who anchored the sociology department at the University of Chicago from the 1910s until his retirement in 1933. His teaching career was preceded by eight years in the employ of Booker T. Washington, whom he served as a professional writer. According to Park's entry in the *American National Biography,* "His solid, candid personality, his broad experience and theoretical reflection, his enthusiasm and persistence all made him a classic doctor-father figure."[37] Of the scholars under consideration here, Park was closest to Frazier. He supervised Frazier's Ph.D. dissertation, but while Frazier appropriated much of his sociological framework from

Park, he was not uncritical of Park by any means.[38] However, all three—Fauset, Frazier, and Herskovits—quoted Park, in appreciation or critique or both, very near to the beginning of their major works under consideration here.

In his review of *The Myth of the Negro Past*, one of Frazier's strongest indictments of Herskovits's work was that Park had been ill-served in Herskovits's portrayal of him: Herskovits "lumps together the conclusions of competent scholars and the opinions of obviously prejudiced writers on the cultural background and racial characteristics of the Negro. The conclusions of such scholars as Robert E. Park, Edward B. Reuter, and Guy Johnson may be wrong, but they are not the result of race prejudice and should not be classed with the opinions of men who think that 'Negroes are naturally of a childlike character.'"[39] Frazier's critique seems mistaken. Herskovits clearly intended to engage in greatest depth the scholars with the most credibility, that is, those who pursued their studies with the wholehearted intention of having their work free from racial prejudice. Herskovits likely agreed with Frazier that Park met this criterion. Thus, in *The Myth of the Negro Past*, after outlining the myths that he intended to disprove, the first two scholars that Herskovits quoted, as he began to fashion his critique, were Robert E. Park and E. Franklin Frazier.[40] If, in fact, no highly credible scholar believed that "Negroes are naturally of a childlike character," that is, the first of the myths that Herskovits intended to refute, then he should certainly have omitted it and shortened his list of myths. But, in "The Conflict and Fusion of Cultures" (see below), Park did offer his characterization of the American Negro as "representatives of a primitive race."[41] While that may not be precisely equivalent to stating that "Negroes are naturally of a childlike character," it comes pretty close, and thus we may conclude, over and against Frazier's protestations, that Herskovits was justified in preserving his list of myths at full strength.

We have not examined Frazier's statement that Park's scholarship was "not the result of race prejudice." Anthony Platt has shown that Frazier had ample grounds for this assertion, if his judgment rested on the quality of his personal relationship with his mentor. Park strenuously encouraged Frazier to apply to the University of Chicago. When Frazier accepted the offer, Park found ways to make it easier for him to concentrate on his research in a friendly atmosphere. Park's encouragement included facilitation of a substantial three-year grant from the Social Science Research Council to Frazier. Frazier and Park often differed sharply. Park told Frazier at one point, "Whenever I want a damn good fight, I know where to come." Charles Johnson, an African American student who preceded Frazier as a student of Park, wrote that Park took him "seriously and without the usual condescension or oily paternalism of which I had already seen too much." St. Clair Drake's assessment seems apt: "In a generation when nobody was opening doors for blacks who wanted to be scholars, Park opened doors for Frazier."[42]

Park's critics have noted his belief in racial hierarchies. Along these lines, Oliver Cox, writing in the 1960s, observed of Park and certain others of his colleagues at the University of Chicago that

> [t]hey were profound liberals in the sense in which that term is currently defined by direct action leaders. They were men possessed of praiseworthy attitudes towards Negroes, but still opposed to any definition of them as fully equal to whites; they were willing to do many things *for* Negroes but sternly opposed Negroes taking such initiative as would move them along faster than a *proper pace;* and they would rather turn conservative than tolerate independent thinking or acting Negroes.[43]

Park's mentorship of African American graduate students showed him to be an ally in the battle for racial justice, but, as we shall see below, his scholarship did not provide convincing evidence of racial egalitarianism. Cox's charge that the Chicagoans would not tolerate independent thinking among African Americans, however, seems inapplicable to Park.

How Fauset, Frazier, and Herskovits Read Park

In his later years, Arthur Huff Fauset was not always the most reliable guide to his own previously published thoughts. The author's note to the paperback edition of his *Black Gods of the Metropolis,* written in 1970, contained these two sentences: "Many still assume that dependence on religion is a natural function of a black man's African heritage. E. Franklin Frazier and Robert E. Park dissented, and the present author concurs with them."[44] If this had indeed been all of what Fauset had been up to when writing his dissertation (which was later published as *Black Gods of the Metropolis*) in the early 1940s, it would have been a standard assessment of the debate between Herskovits and Frazier, with Park arrayed solely on Frazier's side. In fact, the youthful Fauset perceived a more complex web of relationships, sometimes agreeing and sometimes disagreeing with the positions that Herskovits, Park, and Frazier had taken.

Judging by their frequent and prominent citation of it, Herskovits, Frazier, and Fauset agreed that Park's most important publication in their area of common interest was his essay "The Conflict and Fusion of Cultures with Special Reference to the Negro," an address that Park delivered to the American Sociological Society at its 1918 annual meeting, which was subsequently published in the *Journal of Negro*

History.[45] The fact that the *Journal of Negro History* was the venue for the publication of this address is significant. When his article appeared in print, the *Journal of Negro History* was a fledgling publication, only in its fourth year of precarious existence. Park actively supported this publication during its early years. Working amicably with the founder of the journal, Carter G. Woodson, Park was president of the journal's Executive Council from 1917 until 1921. He provided substantial financial assistance for the first issue in 1916 and worked diligently, although it seems unsuccessfully, to obtain foundation support for subsequent years of publication.[46]

Park's impressionistic article was suffused with a sort of romantic racialism that was common in social science and humanities scholarship at the beginning of the twentieth century. Park operated from a framework that emphasized assimilation (or the "melting pot") as the ultimate goal for the United States. What Park believed to be especially African about American "Negroes" was their "temperament," although he presented his "thesis merely as a hypothesis."[47] Frazier's disagreements with Park over this issue were reflected by a request to readers of *The Negro Family in the United States* that they disregard Park's sentiments on this issue, though Frazier otherwise commended the passage in which the comments were embedded. Commenting on Park's work, Herskovits believed the issue of distinctions in racial temperaments to be an "important" one, but attempts to substantiate it would raise insuperable "methodological difficulties."[48] Thus, Herskovits did not disagree so much with the substance of Park's argument as with the difficulty of documenting it with any persuasiveness.

Herskovits chose the following general statement from Park as an example of the myths against which he was arguing: "My own impression is that the amount of African tradition which the Negro brought to the United States was very small. In fact, there is every reason to believe, it seems to me, that the Negro, when he landed in the United States, left behind him almost everything but his dark complexion and his tropical temperament. It is very difficult to find in the South today anything that can be traced directly back to Africa."[49]

Frazier preferred detailed sections of Park's article that began to set up a narrative as to how African customs and tradition could have been lost in the massive sale and dispersion of human beings to the New World. These would include the scattering of African nationalities in the various transactions that took place between the African interior and the New World plantation; the small average size of slaveholdings in the United States, giving scant opportunity for socializing among slaves based on African customs; the extensive use of English and ridicule of African languages, something that Park believed to have taken place among white and black Americans alike; the implicitly European, non-African background of the "free and evangelistic types of Christianity, the Baptists and Methodists," which was the form of Christian piety that first reached the black masses; and the appeal of apocalypticism to human beings who were suffering the extreme stresses associated with slavery.[50]

In its opening chapter, Fauset's *Black Gods of the Metropolis* reviewed some of this argumentation by Park, Herskovits, and Frazier. Fauset agreed with Frazier and Park on their detailed narrative regarding the loss of African culture, but he had little to add to this part of the debate. In passing, we might note that Fauset sided with Frazier's judgment that "only with the coming of the Methodists and Baptists that the masses of slaves found a form of Christianity that they could make their own," characterizing this as a matter of "general agreement" among scholars. Moreover, Fauset doubted Herskovits's assertion that African American worship was influenced by African spirit possession; by way of contrast, Fauset observed that the sanctificationist theology of Holiness churches had an internal integrity all of its own, and he further implied that Herskovits's external explanations related to spirit possession were superfluous.[51]

A Natural Religious Temperament?

In his final two chapters, Fauset did make his own contribution to the debate, on the matter of whether American Negroes have a natural religious temperament, or, to use Herskovits's phrasing, "a deep religious bent."[52] Here Fauset agreed with Frazier and built upon his work, but disagreed with both Herskovits and Park.

In their dueling book reviews in the *Nation*, both Herskovits and Frazier touched on these matters in their concluding paragraphs. Reviewing *The Negro Family*, Herskovits complimented Frazier on taking such a clear position (against African survivals) on "the African background of American Negro life," even though it was a stand with which he disagreed. Herskovits concluded by reflecting on why this issue mattered. "For this is one of the most vital elements in the psychological foundation of race prejudice in the United States, just as it is the most important single factor in the spiritual demoralization that comes to many Negroes from their deep-seated conviction, which I believe is a false one, that they have no past except in slavery."[53]

Frazier's review of *The Myth of the Negro Past* conceded nothing on the issue of racial psychology. His concluding sentence asked, "[W]hen Professor Herskovits says that the Negro problem is psychological—the African patterns of thought prevent the complete acculturation of the Negro—as well as economic and sociological, is he not saying that even more fundamental barriers exist between blacks and whites than are generally recognized?"[54]

Fauset distilled from the writings of Park and Herskovits their conviction "that there is something in the Negro amounting almost to an inner compulsion which drives him into religious channels."[55] Then he sought to bring some hard data to the task of determining whether Park and Herskovits were right. He cited the analysis of 1926 census data by Mays and Nicholson that showed that 73 percent of Negro women were church members, as compared to 62 percent of white women, but that only 46 percent of Negro men were church members, as compared to 49 percent of white men. His subsequent discussion focused on the figures relating to male attendance:

> Thus it becomes apparent that more than 40 per cent of Negroes never attend church at all; and this compares with the total non-church going population of America which according to Mays and Nicholson is 42 per cent; but what is more significant, considerably less than half the Negro men attend, and this is below the proportion for white men. Nevertheless the opinion of the universality of religious attitudes among Negroes, as contrasted to whites, persists.

It would seem that Herskovits's observation that "in an age of skepticism, the Negro has held fast to belief" requires some modification.[56]

The most obvious shortcoming of Fauset's analysis was that he failed to examine the other side of the gender divide. Several years after Fauset's death, sociologists from a later generation, C. Eric Lincoln and Lawrence Mamiya, would ask in relation to the "Black Church," "where have all the men gone?" and would inquire into reasons for the large majority of female members in black churches.[57] But Fauset himself did not explore the reasons for gender disparity in church involvement.

Fauset, however, was making a very cogent stipulation that his previous examination of five colorful but relatively small new religious movements should not be generalized in an unwarranted fashion in order to constitute a statement about the religious psychology of all Americans who would be construed to belong to a Negro race. He did not deny the importance of a healthy racial psychology (in fact, he had previously urged inculcating a "spiritual and psychological readiness" for coming struggles), but he did dispute assertions that healthy African American psychological outlooks necessarily contain a specifically religious component.[58]

Thus his hardheaded analysis poked holes in similarly breezy analyses of two white scholars, Herskovits and Park, who were at odds with each other on most other issues in the discipline of African American studies. Recall our examination of comparative lives. Fauset, Frazier, and Herskovits all disclaimed any vital theistic belief system. (I exclude Park from the discussion because his religious belief system is unknown to me.) Of the three, it might be said that only Herskovits could claim a "religious bent" for American Negroes without thereby holding in some tension his own orientation toward religious questions (and this, only if he had not overcome his own racial preconceptions sufficiently to have as his dominant mental construct a humanism positing a universal capability for sharing experience). In other words, the only nontheist who could readily project a prevalence of religious belief and practice onto an Other in this particular debate was Herskovits. While difficulty in projecting unwanted thoughts on the Other surely did not preclude them from clearly thinking through their subject matter, it is without a doubt that Frazier and Fauset justifiably subjected any claims of the inherent religiosity of the Negro to the most severe scrutiny.

New Religious Movements and Politics

Fauset, however, was interested in the psychological aspects of religion not solely for their own sake, but also as a springboard into an exploration of an area of life that had great vitality for him, that is, the connection between religion and politics. Here again, his point of departure was an argument with Herskovits. Fauset quoted this passage from Herskovits:

> Religion is vital, meaningful, and understandable to the Negro of this country because . . . it is not removed from life, but has been deeply integrated into the daily round. It is because of this, indeed that everywhere compensation in terms of the supernatural is so immediately acceptable to this underprivileged folk, and causes them, in contrast to other underprivileged groups elsewhere in the world, *to turn to religion rather than to political action or other outlets for their frustration.*[59]

The italicized phrase is the one that Fauset was most interested in critiquing. For Herskovits, the italicized assertion was offered as an aside; there is no sustained argument anywhere in *The Myth of the Negro Past* that addresses the supposed turning away from political action by African Americans.

Fauset's observation was that three of the five religious movements under consideration in his study fostered political action of various sorts. While Fauset understood that such evidence could not be taken to be conclusive, he also correctly intimated that, at the very least, this empirical evidence that seemed to contradict Herskovits's thesis required an explanation.

Fauset made some rather subtle and important observations in pointing out those places where religion and politics intersect. He observed that although black religious organizations often engage in the political process, they do not all engage in the same way. He drew a distinction between black nationalist politics and integrationist or assimilationist politics, explicitly identifying the Church of God and the Moorish Science Temple with the former (although in slightly different ways) and implicitly associating Father Divine's Peace Mission Movement with the latter. Of course, these different emphases long precede the 1940s when Fauset was writing.[60] Furthermore, such diversified emphases persist to the present.[61]

Fauset also called attention to the irrepressibly prophetic role played by many black church leaders and congregations. In doing so, he oversimplified the dance between prophecy and accommodation that has often been played out in black church settings. In the political involvement of the new religious movements of African Americans, what Fauset witnessed "would seem to be a continuation of the very kind of an adaptation of an institution to a given need against which the slaveholders hoped to safeguard themselves by forbidding Negroes to congregate even for purposes of religious worship."[62] What he ignored with this sentence were black churches that sometimes bolstered the slave order by helping to enforce slave discipline, perhaps because the risks of defiance were too great.[63] Nor did he provide any acknowledgment of the more mundane aspect of church involvement in patronage or clientage politics.

Vaguely, Fauset observed, "There is an increase in the proportion of Negroes who are entering the trade unions, organizing by means of consumer cooperatives, economic boycotts, protest groups of various kinds, and those who are otherwise girding for political action."[64] While this may have reflected his own pro-union activism, which included organizing a Philadelphia chapter of the American Federation of Teachers,[65] any connection between growing trade unionism and the activities of any black church, whether a new or old religious movement, was problematic.[66] Churches and church leaders influenced by the social gospel constituted an exception; generally black churches have stayed aloof from pro-union organizing. Indeed, Fauset never explicitly claimed a tie between black churches and unionism, but the relevance of his observation is rather doubtful if he did not implicitly believe that there was one.

According to Fauset, the most innovative religious movements were the ones most likely to adopt a political stance:

> There is an indication that as American Negro cults become more intent upon social, economic, and political problems, the literal adherence to the Bible as a book of reference diminishes. The most rigid adherence to the Bible is by the cults which have

the least political or economic programs, and conversely, those cults with original economic, social, and political programs tend to develop their own sets of rules, even going so far as to discard the Bible almost entirely.[67]

Father Divine's Peace Mission Movement, the Moorish Science Temple, and the Church of God met the latter portion of Fauset's description most closely, so presumably this description was meant to apply to them.[68] This description of the connection between religion and politics tended to discount substantially the social gospel movement, the African Americans who were influenced by it, and the links that it had drawn between the teachings of the Hebrew prophets on social justice matters and the teachings of Jesus on the kingdom of God.

Possibly, with emphasis on such political angles as trade unionism and the de-emphasis of such religious angles as the Bible, his vague prose was more autobiographical than descriptive of larger trends among African American religious movements. But there is much that Fauset got right in his portrayal of the intersections between politics and the Black Church, including the diversified politics within black churches that embraced both black nationalist and integrationist approaches, and his emphasis on the prevalence and importance of a prophetic religious faith.

On this matter, Frazier and Fauset seem to have different analyses of the data. Frazier's analysis of "Negro Religion in the City," written in the 1950s, was heavily dependent on the findings of *Black Gods of the Metropolis* for his descriptions of all five cults chronicled by Fauset.[69] Nevertheless, Frazier did not appear to share Fauset's conclusion that his data demonstrated political involvement among any of the five new religious movements therein chronicled. Instead, Frazier's analysis of the cults fits neatly into his generalization that black churches generally provided a refuge or an escape from a hostile white world: "They based their appeal on the Negro's desire to find salvation in the next world and to escape from sickness and insecurities of this world."[70] Fauset's insistence on asserting the importance of the connection between politics and black religious movements, then, was one that he developed in opposition to an aside from Herskovits and was an issue on which he differed with Frazier. Fauset's scholarship has fared well in this area where he differed from both of his eminent colleagues, as subsequent scholarship on African American new religious movements has strengthened Fauset's contention that some African American new religious movements have a political angle.[71]

Arthur Huff Fauset was a more significant contributor to the Herskovits-Frazier debate than one would expect from the slim volume of his publications. The politically radical, nontheist worldview that the three men generally shared and their sense of genuine (if perhaps also fleeting) excitement for such cultural movements as the Harlem Renaissance undoubtedly nurtured the venturesome quality of their scholarship and lives. They cut loose decisively from ancestral spiritual moorings and were content to traverse unknown seas assisted mainly by a compass of emerging sociological and anthropological scholarship.

We should not undervalue Fauset's scholarly contributions simply because, for Fauset himself, the academic arena was not very important and the political arena, in terms of working for social justice, was more important. His striking contributions, especially his challenge to Herskovits on religious psychology and to both Frazier and Herskovits on the importance of a diverse and robust politics intersecting with religion for many African Americans, followed with great integrity from close observation of African American religious life, as well as from his exemplary life witness. Fauset's ethnographic abilities are a very impressive part of his book, but his theoretical vision and ability, and his mastery and critique of scholarly literature in the field of African American religion and culture, were quite substantial, if more subtle. Here also he has helped to provide solid foundations for continuing, illuminating, and multidimensional research into the many facets of African American religions.

Notes

I would like to thank my Earlham colleague James Logan for his comments on this essay.

1. Arthur Huff Fauset, *Black Gods of the Metropolis: Negro Religious Cults of the Urban North* (Philadelphia: University of Pennsylvania Press, 1970), 3 (Frazier), 101 (Herskovits).

2. J. Lorand Matory, *Black Atlantic Religion: Tradition, Transnationalism, and Matriarchy in the Afro-Brazilian Candomblé* (Princeton, N.J.: Princeton University Press, 2005), 11, 278–79.

3. John A. Garraty, Mark C. Carnes, and American Council of Learned Societies, *American National Biography* (New York: Oxford University Press, 1999).

4. *Black Gods of the Metropolis* has been variously characterized as both an anthropological and a sociological treatment of religion. Barbara Dianne Savage complains that most reviewers missed Fauset's extensive use of ethnography, an anthropological methodology. Both characterizations of this book have merit. Savage, foreword to Arthur Huff Fauset, *Black Gods of the Metropolis: Negro Religious Cults of the Urban North* (Philadelphia: University of Pennsylvania Press, 2002), xii–xiii.

5. Robert L. Hall, "E. Franklin Frazier and the Chicago School of Sociology: A Study in the Sociology of Knowledge," in *E. Franklin Frazier and the Black Bourgeoisie*, ed. James E. Teele (Columbia: University of Missouri Press, 2002), 53–54; and Jerry Gershenhorn,

Melville J. Herskovits and the Racial Politics of Knowledge (Lincoln: University of Nebraska Press, 2004), 127–30, 204ff.

6. Carole H. Carpenter, "Arthur Huff Fauset, Campaigner for Social Justice: A Symphony of Diversity," in *African-American Pioneers in Anthropology*, ed. Ira E. Harrison and Faye V. Harrison (Urbana: University of Illinois Press, 1999), 215; David Levering Lewis, personal communication, May 18, 2007.

7. Carpenter, "Fauset," 219; Anthony M. Platt, *E. Franklin Frazier Reconsidered* (New Brunswick, N.J.: Rutgers University Press, 1991), 18; Gershenhorn, *Melville J. Herskovits*, 13.

8. A. H. Fauset, "Symphonesque," *Opportunity* 4 (June 1926): 178–80, 198–200.

9. A. H. Fauset, "Safe in the Arms of Jesus," *Opportunity* 7 (April 1929): 124–28, 133.

10. Carole Carpenter writes (233–34) that "Symphonesque" was based on a real event, an Alabama baptism that Fauset witnessed.

11. Michael Lackey, *African American Atheists and Political Liberation: A Study of the Sociocultural Dynamics of Faith* (Gainesville: University of Florida Press, 2007), 96–116; Jon Michael Spencer, "The Black Church and the Harlem Renaissance," *African American Review* 30, no. 3 (Autumn 1996): 452–60; James O. Young, *Black Writers of the Thirties* (Baton Rouge: Louisiana State University Press, 1973), 175–78.

12. Carpenter, "Fauset," 229, 240n18.

13. Fauset, *Black Gods*, 67.

14. Ira De Augustine Reid, "Let Us Prey!," *Opportunity* 4 (September 1926): 274–78.

15. *American National Biography*, s.v. "E. Franklin Frazier," by Eric R. Jackson; *American National Biography*, s.v. "Melville J. Herskovits," by John P. Jackson; Carpenter, "Fauset," 220.

16. Allen B. Ballard, *One More Day's Journey: The Story of a Family and a People* (New York: McGraw-Hill, 1984), 201. While this is the first time I have seen this construction of Quakerism applied to African Americans in Philadelphia, this critique of social class diffidence among Philadelphia Quakers is far from uncommon in the literature on the majority white Quakers, especially from a few who have lived in close proximity with Philadelphia Quakers. See, for instance, Frederick B. Tolles, *Meeting House and Counting House: The Quaker Merchants of Colonial Philadelphia, 1682–1763* (New York: W. W. Norton, 1948); and E. Digby Baltzell, *Puritan Boston and Quaker Philadelphia: Two Protestant Ethics and the Spirit of Class Authority and Leadership* (New York: Free Press, 1979). On issues of Quakers and race, see Henry Cadbury, "Negro Membership in the Society of Friends," *Journal of Negro History* 21 (1936): 151–213. Fauset's apparent distaste for Quakers did not extend widely among his African American peers; some of his Harlem Renaissance contemporaries became Quakers later in life, for example, Jean Toomer (see Cynthia Earl Kerman and Richard Eldridge, *The Lives of Jean Toomer: A Hunger for Wholeness* [Baton Rouge: Louisiana State University Press, 1987], 255–56) and Ira De Augustine Reid (see Kenneth Ives, *Black Quakers: Brief Biographies* [Chicago: Progresiv Publishr, 1991], 82).

17. E. Franklin Frazier, *The Negro Family in the United States*, rev. and abridged ed. (Chicago: University of Chicago Press, 1966), 209–44.

18. Alain Locke, *The New Negro: An Interpretation* (New York: Arno Press and the New York Times, 1968 [1925]), ix.

19. Ibid., 240–42.

20. E. Franklin Frazier, *Black Bourgeoisie* (Glencoe, Ill.: Free Press, 1957); E. Franklin Frazier, "Durham: Capital of the Black Middle Class," in Locke, *The New Negro*, 333–40.

21. Melville Herskovits, "The Negro's Americanism," in Locke, *The New Negro*, 353–61.

22. Arthur Huff Fauset, "Educational Procedures for an Emergency," *Opportunity* 11 (January 1933): 20–22. I wish to thank David Levering Lewis (personal communication, May 18, 2007) for supplying this information; his introduction to *The Portable Harlem Renaissance Reader*, ed. David Levering Lewis (New York: Penguin Books, 1994), xxxix, had incorrectly placed Fauset's contribution "at the beginning of 1934."

23. *American National Biography*, s.v. "Crystal Bird Fauset," by Steven J. Niven.

24. Carpenter, "Fauset," 234. Also see Lawrence S. Wittner, "The National Negro Congress: A Reassessment," *American Quarterly* 22 (Winter 1970): 883–901.

25. Carpenter, "Fauset," 234–35; Ballard, *One More Day's Journey*, 60–61.

26. Jonathan Scott Holloway, *Confronting the Veil: Abram Harris, Jr., E. Franklin Frazier, and Ralph Bunche, 1919–1941* (Chapel Hill: University of North Carolina Press, 2002), 4, 126.

27. Carpenter, "Fauset," 224, 232–33.

28. Ibid., 234–35.

29. During World War II, despite successful completion of officer candidate school, he was denied an officer's commission because of investigation into his past activities. The FBI unsuccessfully attempted to persuade the University of Pennsylvania Press not to publish *Black Gods of the Metropolis*, probably because of alleged ties to subversive groups. He resigned from the Philadelphia school system because he perceived that he was held "in disgrace for his alleged affiliation with the communist movement. Fauset was simply humiliated." Savage, foreword to Fauset, *Black Gods of the Metropolis*, viii–ix; and Carpenter, "Fauset," 235 (quotation from Carpenter).

30. Hall, "E. Franklin Frazier," 58–59; Holloway, *Confronting the Veil*, 137–41.

31. Gershenhorn, *Melville J. Herskovits*, 15, 131, 152, 219.

32. Ibid., 148–57.

33. Ira E. Harrison, "Hubert B. Ross, the Anthropologist Who Was," in Harrison and Harrison, eds., *African-American Pioneers in Anthropology*, 269, 272–73n1.

34. Gershenhorn, *Melville J. Herskovits*, 151–52. The encyclopedia volume is *Africana: The Encyclopedia of the African and African American Experience*, ed. Anthony Appiah and Henry Louis Gates, Jr. (New York: Oxford University Press, 2005).

35. This task has been accomplished well elsewhere. See Matory, *Black Atlantic Religion*, 10–17; Joseph E. Holloway, *Africanisms in American Culture* (Bloomington: Indiana University Press, 1991), ix–xvii; and Albert Raboteau, *Slave Religion: The "Invisible Institution" in the Antebellum South* (Oxford: Oxford University Press, 1978), 46–60.

36. E. Franklin Frazier, *The Negro Church in America*, and C. Eric Lincoln, *The Black Church since Frazier* (New York: Schocken Books, 1974); Frazier's volume was originally published in 1963 by the University of Liverpool. Also see E. Franklin Frazier, *The Negro in the United States*, rev. ed. (New York: Macmillan, 1957); the revised edition contains a fuller

response by Frazier to the Herskovits thesis than did the first edition published in 1949, also by Macmillan.

37. *American National Biography,* s.v. "Robert Ezra Park," by Jane S. Knowles.

38. Platt, *E. Franklin Frazier Reconsidered,* 89–90; Hall, "E. Franklin Frazier," 65–66.

39. E. Franklin Frazier, "The Negro's 'Cultural Past'" (review of *The Myth of the Negro Past*), *Nation* 154 (February 14, 1942): 195–96.

40. Melville Herskovits, *The Myth of the Negro Past* (1941; Boston: Beacon, 1990), 3–4.

41. Robert E. Park, "The Conflict and Fusion of Cultures with Special Reference to the Negro," *Journal of Negro History* 4, no. 2 (April 1919): 115.

42. Platt, *E. Franklin Frazier Reconsidered,* 78–79, 88, 90 (Park quotation), 94 (Drake quotation), 136; Winifred Raushenbush, *Robert E. Park: Biography of a Sociologist* (Durham, N.C.: Duke University Press, 1979), 101 (Johnson quotation), 156; Martin Bulmer, *The Chicago School of Sociology: Institutionalization, Diversity, and the Rise of Sociological Research* (Chicago: University of Chicago Press, 1984), 215.

43. Oliver C. Cox, introduction to *The Black Anglo-Saxons,* by Nathan Hare (1965; New York: Collier Books, 1970), 28, quoted in Hall, "E. Franklin Frazier," 65.

44. Fauset, *Black Gods,* xi.

45. Park, "Conflict and Fusion of Cultures," 111–33.

46. Jacqueline Goggin, *Carter G. Woodson: A Life in Black History* (Baton Rouge: Louisiana State University Press, 1993), 35–36, 41, 56–57.

47. Park, "Conflict and Fusion of Cultures," 130.

48. Ibid., 128, quoted in Frazier, *Negro Family in the United States,* 23; Park, "Conflict and Fusion of Cultures," 129, quoted in Herskovits, *Myth of the Negro Past,* 13.

49. Park, "Conflict and Fusion of Cultures," 116, quoted in Herskovits, *Myth of the Negro Past,* 3.

50. Park, "Conflict and Fusion of Cultures," 117, 119, 128, quoted in Frazier, *Negro Family in the United States,* 6, 23, 24.

51. Fauset, *Black Gods,* 3–4, 10–11, 82; Frazier, *Negro Family in the United States,* 24; Herskovits, chap. 7 (esp. 211).

52. Herskovits, *Myth of the Negro Past,* 207, quoted in Fauset, *Black Gods,* 4, 96–97.

53. Melville Herskovits, "The American Negro Family" (review of *The Negro Family in the United States*), *Nation* 150 (January 27, 1940): 105.

54. Frazier, "The Negro's 'Cultural Past'," 196.

55. Fauset, *Black Gods,* 96.

56. Ibid., 97.

57. C. Eric Lincoln and Lawrence H. Mamiya, *The Black Church in the African-American Experience* (Durham, N.C.: Duke University Press, 1991), 304–306.

58. Fauset, "Educational Procedures for an Emergency," 22.

59. Emphasis mine. Herskovits, *Myth of the Negro Past,* 207. The whole passage is quoted at Fauset, *Black Gods,* 4. Fauset quoted the italicized phrase three more times in *Black Gods,* at 96, 98, and 108–109.

60. Fauset, *Black Gods*, 98–100. I have written on a black nationalist precursor, Henry M. Turner. See Stephen Ward Angell, *Bishop Henry McNeal Turner and African American Religion in the South* (Knoxville: University of Tennessee Press, 1992).

61. See, for example, R. Drew Smith, *New Day Begun: African American Churches and Civic Culture in Post-Civil Rights America* (Durham, N.C.: Duke University Press, 2003).

62. Fauset, *Black Gods*, 100.

63. John W. Blassingame, *The Slave Community: Plantation Life in the Antebellum South* (New York: Oxford University Press, 1979), vii, 132–33; Mechal Sobel, *Trabelin' On: The Slave Journey to an Afro-Baptist Faith* (Princeton, N.J.: Princeton University Press, 1988), 150–52, 154–55.

64. Fauset, *Black Gods*, 100.

65. Savage, foreword to Fauset, *Black Gods of the Metropolis*, viii.

66. See, for example, Milton Sernett, *Bound for the Promised Land: African American Religion and the Great Migration* (Durham, N.C.: Duke University Press, 1997), 176–77.

67. Fauset, *Black Gods*, 108.

68. "Father Divine discourages reading the Bible. . . . Some members say Father Divine *is* the Bible, so why read it?" Fauset, *Black Gods*, 60–61, 73.

69. E. Franklin Frazier, *The Negro Church in America* (1963; New York: Schocken Books, 1974), 52–71; in his footnotes, on pages 96 to 98, Frazier cites *Black Gods of the Metropolis* fourteen times.

70. Frazier, *Negro Church in America*, 59.

71. Robert Weisbrot, *Father Divine and the Struggle for Racial Equality* (Urbana: University of Illinois Press, 1983); Hans Baer and Merrill Singer, *African-American Religion in the Twentieth Century: Varieties of Protest and Accommodation* (Knoxville: University of Tennessee Press, 1992), 111–46, 215–19.

CONTRIBUTORS

Stephen W. Angell is the Geraldine C. Leatherock Professor of Quaker Studies at the Earlham School of Religion and author of *Bishop Henry McNeal Turner and African-American Religion in the South*. He has also served as academic advisor and on-air expert for *This Far by Faith*, a six-part documentary of African American religious history that aired nationwide on PBS stations.

Edward E. Curtis IV is Millennium Scholar of the Liberal Arts and Associate Professor of Religious Studies and American Studies at Indiana University–Purdue University Indianapolis. He is author of *Black Muslim Religion in the Nation of Islam, 1960–1975* and editor of the *Columbia Sourcebook of Muslims in the United States*.

Jacob S. Dorman is Assistant Professor of History and American Studies at the University of Kansas. He is author of the forthcoming *Mystic Science: Black Israelites and Black Orientalism*.

Clarence E. Hardy III is Assistant Professor of Religion at Dartmouth College. He is author of *James Baldwin's God: Sex, Hope and Crisis in Black Holiness Culture*.

Kelly E. Hayes is Assistant Professor of Religious Studies at Indiana University–Purdue University Indianapolis. She is completing a book-length ethnographic study of the Afro-Brazilian spirit entity known throughout Brazil as Pomba Gira.

Sylvester A. Johnson is Assistant Professor of Religious Studies at Indiana University Bloomington. He is author of *The Myth of Ham in Nineteenth-Century American Christianity: Race, Heathens, and the People of God*, winner of the American Academy of Religion's Best First Book Award in the History of Religions.

Kathryn Lofton is Assistant Professor of American Studies and Religious Studies at Yale University. She is the 2006–2007 recipient of the LGBT Religious History Award, given by the Lesbian, Gay, Bisexual and Transgender Religious Archives Network, for her work on John Balcolm Shaw (1860–1935).

Leonard Norman Primiano is Associate Professor and Chair of Religious Studies at Cabrini College. He is co-producer of *The Father Divine Project*, a multimedia documentary and video podcast about Father Divine, Mother Divine, and the Peace Mission Movement.

Carolyn Rouse is Associate Professor of Anthropology at Princeton University. She is author of *Engaged Surrender: African American Women and Islam* and is completing a book on racial healthcare disparities and sickle cell disease in the United States.

Nora L. Rubel is Assistant Professor of Religion at the University of Rochester. She is author of "Chicken Soup for the Souls of Black Folk: African American Converts to Judaism and the Negotiation of Identity."

Danielle Brune Sigler is Curator of Academic Affairs at the Harry Ransom Center at the University of Texas at Austin. She is co-founder of the Religion and American Culture Caucus of the American Studies Association and author of "Beyond the Binary" and "Daddy Grace: An Immigrant's Story."

INDEX

Aba, Oku, 129

Abeta Hebrew Cultural Center, 60

abolitionism, 158, 212, 213

Aboriginal Australia, 174

Abraham, Elias Mohammed, 116, 117, 118, 122, 123

aesthetic primitivism, 175–76

affirmative Orientalism, 119

Africa: and black Orientalism, 130, 132; as Holy Land, 61; North Africa, 51; the primitive associated with, 174; racist attitudes toward, 57, 64, 159; repatriation to, 60, 152. *See also* African religious culture

African American Christian theology: and Ali, 73–74; and Carter, 62; and Cherry, 55, 57; and Grace, 9, 32–33, 35–39, 41, 45; Pinn on, 6; West and Glaude on, 7

African American religions: African American women anthropologists' study of, 147; and African religious culture, 10–11, 146, 147, 150, 159–60, 209–10, 235; American culture in, 150, 159, 160, 161, 164; and anti-African bias, 57, 67n38; authenticity of religious data, 146, 148, 151–53, 159–60; and Black Church as cultural referent, 184–85; and black man as God, 55, 154; and black Orientalism, 120, 133–34, 142n83; and colonialism, 157, 158–59; commonalities transcending sectarian labels, 123, 133; and control over lives, 106; Arthur Huff Fauset's contributions to study of, 1, 5, 6, 7, 11, 156–61; Arthur Huff Fauset's critique of social-scientific claims about, 149–50; and Arthur Huff Fauset's intellectual context, 7, 146–47, 148, 171; Fisher on, 151–53; origins of, 234–35; and postcolonial theory, 157, 158; scholarship on, 64–65, 111n6, 145, 146–47, 156–61, 186; secondary literature of, 4–5; and transnational con-

Islam (*continued*)
churches, 4; textbook Islam, 78, 79, 83, 84, 88n25; and transnationalism, 25; and Western Orientalism, 122; and worldly deliverance, 53, 77. *See also* black Muslims; Nation of Islam
Islamic Mission of America, 118
Islamic *salat*, 79, 82
Israel, Asiel Ben, 61
Israel, Hebrew Israelites in, 61–62, 122
Israelites: Africa or Ethiopia as origin of, 57; and black Spiritualism, 133; blacks as original Israelites, 50, 51, 52, 53, 54, 65–66n9; and Church of God in Christ, 142n84; and emigration and colonization, 121–22; and esoteric texts, 123; Hebrew Israelites, 60–62, 122; and Hebrew language, 120–21; and Judaism, 60, 64, 133; and Matthew, 58–59; and Palestine, 51–52, 55, 57; as South African sect, 67–68n44
Italo-Ethiopian War, 121, 122

Jackson, Sherman, 120
James, C. L. R., 25
Japan, attack on Pearl Harbor, 27, 46n19
Jefferson, Blind Lemon, 40
Jehovah's Witness, 54, 56
Jehovia, Father, 121
Jeje people, 217, 224n30
Jesus litmus test, 68n66
Jet (magazine), 40
Jewish identity, 65, 69n77, 161–62
Jim Crow America, 23, 127, 140n60, 210. *See also* racial apartheid; racial segregation
Johnson, Charles, 236
Johnson, Guy, 236
Johnson, James Weldon, 229
Johnson, P. Nathaniel, 81
Johnson, Paul C., 223n11
Johnson, Sylvester A., 10, 194
Johnson, Walter, 135n11

Jones, C. L., 42–43
Jones, Prophet, 40, 118
Journal of Negro History, 5, 180, 181, 237–38
Judaism: and Black Church/black cult dichotomy, 6; and Church of God, 52, 54–55, 63; and Commandment Keepers of Harlem, 58–59, 60; definition of Jewish identity, 65, 69n77; exilic mythmaking of, 164; and Israelites, 60, 64, 133; and legitimacy questions, 63–65; and scholarship on African American religions, 65; and storefront churches, 4; and white Jews, 51, 58, 60, 62, 63, 64, 122, 152
Jung, Carl, 179
Justice, Mary, 105

Kelley, Robin, 119
Kidd, Colin, 164, 169n54
King, Martin Luther, Jr., 107
King, Rodney, 200
Kismet (film), 128
Knight, Janice, 183
Kuchi, Michio, 100
Kyles, L. W., 181

laches concept, 140n60
Lackey, Michael, 229
Landes, Ruth: on Afro-Brazilian religions, 211; on black Jews, 63; on Brazil, 210; on candomblé, 220–21; on Divine's Jewish doctrine, 121; ramifications of experiences in Brazil, 225n44
Landing, James E., 52, 63, 65n8
Landres, J. Shaun, 94
Lane, Winthrop D., 128
Larsen, Nella, 120
Latimer-Knight, Cassandra, 123
Latin America, 158
Law of Return, 61
Lee, Chana Kai, 183
Leighton, Patricia, 178

Lemke, Sieglinde, 175–76
Levine, Lawrence, 100
Lévy-Bruhl, Lucien, 174
Lewis, David Levering, 228, 232, 246n22
Lewis, Sinclair, 3
Lewis, William A., 122
Liberia, 61, 122
Lincoln, C. Eric, 185, 240
Little, Douglas, 119
Little, Malcolm, 200
Locke, Alain, 2, 231–32
Lofton, Kathryn, 10
Long, Carolyn Morrow, 130
Long, Charles, 157, 173–74
Lowe, Lisa, 119
Luers, Will, 112n12
lynchings, black rhetoric on, 189n20

Mack, Burton, 164
Madison, Daddy, 45
Malinowski, Bronislaw, 193
Mamiya, Lawrence H., 185, 240
Mann, Michael, 168n37
Mann Act, 44
Marett, R. R., 174
Marr, Timothy, 119
Marsh, Charles, 184
Martin, Darnise, 161
Martin, Joel, 158
Marty, Martin E., 188n16
Mason, Charles, 20, 142n84
Matory, J. Lorand, 225n41, 227
Matthew, Wentworth Arthur: and cab-
    balistic science, 60, 124; and coloniza-
    tion, 121, 122; and Ford, 58, 59; and
    Hebrew schools, 120; Jewish descent
    claimed by, 146; and lack of separatism,
    60, 62. See also Commandment Keepers
    of Harlem
Mays, Benjamin, 147, 181, 240
Mazrui, Ali, 120
Mazusawa, Tomoko, 187n7
McAlister, Melani, 119

McCullough, Daddy, 45
McCutcheon, Russell, 157
McGuire, Meredith, 94
McKay, Claude, 25
McPherson, Aimee Semple, 33
McWhorter, John, 196
men: black Muslim practice among, 10;
    church attendance of, 240; and conver-
    sion to Islam, 195, 199–207; limitations
    on women, 20; and Moorish Science
    Temple, 77. See also women
Mercer, Johnny, 105
Messianic Jewish Congregations, 68n66
messianic-nationalist sects, 53
Methodist Church: in black community,
    228, 239; and Great Migration, 16;
    Holiness culture differentiated from, 23;
    relationship to Pentecostal religious cul-
    ture, 17; and U.S. Census of Religious
    Bodies, 152
Métraux, Alfred, 210
Michaux, Elder, 152
millennialism, 55
Mills, Kay, 182, 183
miscegenation, 213, 223n14
missionaries: and Ahmadiyya movement,
    81; and black Orientalism, 117, 124;
    and cultural eradication, 157, 159; and
    Islam, 80; on slave plantations, 152
missionary tongues, 36
Moabites, 54–55, 73
modernity: in Brazil, 211; and the primi-
    tive, 173–77, 178, 188n16
Monodu, Eatherin, 129
Moorish Guide (periodical), 90n64
Moorish identity: and Ali, 54, 71, 73, 74,
    77, 154, 163; and black Orientalism,
    117, 124, 130, 132
Moorish Science Temple: anticolonial the-
    ology of, 154–55; attitude toward
    United States, 54; authenticity as Mus-
    lim group, 78, 123; and black identity,
    51, 72, 73; and black nationalism, 53,

Reid, Ira, 16, 230
religions, hybridity of, 164, 169n55
religious communities: and black identity,
    26; church mothers' expansive view of,
    21–24, 27; and evangelism, 21–22, 24;
    exchange among marginal/mainstream
    religious groups, 8, 17, 18; flow of per-
    sons and ideas among, 8; reconception
    of, 18, 23, 24, 27. *See also* black Jewish
    communities
respectability, 18, 22, 23, 24, 27
restorationism, 176
Reuter, Edward B., 236
Richardson-Bey, Juanita Mayo, 90n64
Rio de Janeiro, Brazil, 216–17, 222–23n11
Robinson, Bishop Ida: on *Black Gods of the
    Metropolis,* 5; Grace compared to, 32;
    and individuality, 24; as "Mother," 20;
    and preservation of women's right to
    ordination, 17, 19; role of, 7–8, 17; and
    role of leader, 17–18; and transnational-
    ism, 27; vision of, 21. *See also* Mt. Sinai
    Holy Church of America
Rodrigues, Nina: on Afro-Brazilian reli-
    gions, 209, 211, 214–16, 217; on Bantu
    religion, 224n28; and black inferiority,
    212, 214, 215, 223n14; and Gantois
    community, 219; on Nagô cults, 215,
    223n16; and pathology, 215; and racial
    hierarchy, 214–16, 219; and Ramos,
    212, 215–16, 217, 218–19
Roktabija, Alpha, 129
Roosevelt, Franklin D., 232
Rosebud Chorus, 99, 100, 104, 113n15
Rosicrucianism, 72, 76–77, 123, 124
Ross, Hubert, 234
Rouse, Carolyn, 10
Rousseau, Jean-Jacques, 179
*Routledge Historical Atlas of Religion in
    America* (Carroll), 171–72, 181–82
Royal Order of Ethiopian Hebrews, 60
Rubel, Nora L., 9
Rucker, Herman, 129

Sadiq, Muhammad, 81
Said, Edward, 119
Salome (film), 128
Santeria, 123, 161
Sardar, Ziauddin, 120
Sartre, Jean-Paul, 210
Satchel, Charles, 19
Satter, Beryl, 109, 113n15, 114n40
Savage, Barbara Dianne, 17, 28n7, 107,
    244n4
Scarlett, R. S., 129
Schneerson, Rebbe, 66n21
Second Congress of Black Artists and
    Writers (1959), 25
Segal, Robert, 157
self-exoticism, and black Orientalism, 118,
    134n7
separatism: and black Jewish commu-
    nities, 63; Hebrew Israelites move from,
    62; and Moorish Science Temple, 74, 77;
    reconception of, 26
Sernett, Milton, 6, 16, 185
Seven Keys, 57–58
Sevitch, Benjamin, 32
Seymour, William, 142n84
Shakur, Assata, 162–63
Shaw, George Bernard, 3
Shea, Michael J., 103
The Sheik (film), 128
Shi'a Muslims, 78, 84
Sigler, Danielle Brune, 9
Silverblatt, Irene, 158
Simmons, Russell, 202
Singal, Daniel J., 175
Singer, Merrill, 53, 56
Skidmore, Thomas, 213, 223n14
slave trade, 5, 210
slavery: Africa associated with, 130; and
    African retentions, 238–39; Ali on, 74;
    and biblical Hamitic myth, 51; and
    black identity, 169n52; and black Orien-
    talism, 127; in Brazil, 210, 212, 213; and
    characterizations of Black Church, 185;